PAPERS IN
LANGUAGE VARIATION

For
Woodford A. Heflin
James B. McMillan
I. Willis Russell

PAPERS IN
LANGUAGE VARIATION

SAMLA-ADS COLLECTION

Edited and with Preface by
David L. Shores and Carole P. Hines

and an Introductory Essay by
Paul A. Eschholz

THE UNIVERSITY OF ALABAMA PRESS
University, Alabama

Library of Congress Cataloging in Publication Data

Main entry under title:
Papers in language variation.

  Papers originally presented at annual meetings of the
South Atlantic Modern Language Association and the South
Atlantic Section of the American Dialect Society.
  Bibliography: p.
  Includes index.
  1. English language in the United States — Addresses,
essays, lectures. 2. English language — Variation —
Addresses, essays, lectures. I. Shores, David L.
II. Hines, Carol P. III. South Atlantic Modern Lan-
guage Association. IV. American Dialect Society. South
Atlantic Section. V. Series.
PE2841.P3 1977   427   76-23162
ISBN 0-8173-0504-1

CONTENTS

CONTENTS

CONTENTS

PREFACE

For well over twenty years now the South Atlantic Section of the American Dialect Society (SA-ADS) has held its annual meetings in conjunction with the South Atlantic Modern Language Association (SAMLA). Though an independent organization, the SA-ADS has been accepted by SAMLA as one of its sections and has been furnished with meeting rooms; program listing and promotion; hotel reservations, privileges, and rates; abstract publication; and with the opportunity to publish in the South Atlantic Bulletin and to attend many other sections and special events. The SA-ADS group from the very beginning has functioned as a SAMLA section, and the relationship since then has been a cordial and valued one. In fact, the group has more often than not been called the SAMLA-ADS. Thanks are here therefore duly expressed to SAMLA for making this relationship possible.

The immediate motivation for this collection of papers came from a conversation between Lee Pederson of Emory University and David Shores of Old Dominion University at the 1973 meeting of the SAMLA-ADS. The concern was to use the collection to stimulate greater interest in the SAMLA-ADS annual meetings. The suggestion was presented in the business meeting and endorsed by those in attendance. David Shores agreed to gather, edit, and find a publisher for, the papers. Several university presses expressed interest in the collection, but it was the University of Alabama Press and its director, Morgan L. Walters, who provided the encouragement to complete the collection. Carole Hines later agreed to help with editing.

The unifying aspect of this volume is that all the papers originated at SAMLA. The papers by Grace Rueter and Julia Stanley were not read in the SAMLA-ADS section but in the SAMLA Linguistics section. They are included because both were later presented in annual meetings of the American Dialect Society. Another paper, that of Paul Eschholz, is a replacement for a paper ("Trends and Implications of Current Research in Dialectology") read by James J. Broz, Jr., formerly of the Center for Applied Linguistics, in the 1966 meeting. With these exceptions noted, the editors present the volume as a SAMLA-ADS collection.

All the papers have been revised since their original oral presentations, some have had title changes, and nine have been published. Explanatory notes have been added to the articles to explain these and other matters. The editors owe thanks to all the contributors who wrote and revised their papers at their behest. They regret having been compelled to put aside some papers submitted for the collection.

PREFACE

Thanks are due Paul Eschholz of the University of Vermont, who, though not a member of the SAMLA-ADS, graciously agreed to write a paper for the collection describing current dialectology.

Special thanks are due The University of Alabama Press for providing this kind of opportunity for the SAMLA-ADS group.

Mention should also be made of the Research and Publications Committee of the Department of English of Old Dominion University for granting funds to cover part of the production costs, of Charles Ruhl, John Broderick, and William Riley for help in reading copy and Betty Shores for re-drawing the maps and the tables.

The editors would like to make very special mention of Judith Riley who not only typed the entire manuscript but also gave them very valuable assistance.

The contributors have repeatedly expressed their thanks to the editors for preparing the manuscripts for publication. These expressions are of course appreciated. But for the editors, the chore, and it is a chore, has been in a very real sense a "labor of love."

Finally, the editors and the SAMLA-ADS group are especially proud to dedicate this volume to Woodford A. Heflin, James B. McMillan, and I. Willis Russell for their cheerful presence and dedicated support through the years.

The Editors,

David L. Shores
Carole P. Hines

Old Dominion University

CONTRIBUTORS

John Algeo, a Professor of English at the University of Georgia, is the editor of American Speech and the author of Problems in the Origins and Development of the English Language and the co-author of English: An Introduction to Language. His articles have appeared in American Speech, College English, English Journal, Journal of English Linguistics, and South Atlantic Bulletin.

Jane Appleby is an Associate Professor of English at the University of Georgia.

Jeutonne Brewer is an Assistant Professor of English at the University of North Carolina at Greensboro. She has articles in the American Journal of Sociology and American Speech.

Paul H. Bowdre, Jr., is a Professor of English at West Georgia College. Among his publications are articles in Changing Georgia Education and in Georgia English Counselor.

Frederic G. Cassidy, a Professor of English at the University of Wisconsin, is the director of the Dictionary of American Regional English. He is the author of numerous articles and books on Old and Middle English language and literature and creole languages.

L. Ben Crane is an Assistant Professor of Linguistics at Temple University and the author of a number of papers in social dialects.

Boyd Davis is an Associate Professor of English at the University of North Carolina at Charlotte. She is the co-author of Writing About Literature and Film.

Bethany K. Dumas is an Associate Professor of English at the University of Tennessee. She was the principal fieldworker in the Arkansas Language Survey and has articles on field methodology in Papers in Southwest English I: Research Techniques and Prospects and Orbis.

Howard G. Dunlap, the Administrative Assistant for Curriculum Services with the Fulton County School System, is the author of "Social Aspects of a Verb Form," forthcoming in PADS.

CONTRIBUTORS

Connie C. Eble is an Associate Professor of English at the University of North Carolina at Chapel Hill. She is the author of "Some Broadminded Remarks on Language" in The Writer and the World of Words.

Paul A. Eschholz is an Associate Professor of English at the University of Vermont and the chairman of the American Dialect Society Committee on Regionalisms and Linguistic Geography. He is the co-editor of Language: Introductory Readings and Language Awareness. His articles have appeared in American Speech and the Journal of Popular Culture.

William Evans is an Assistant Professor of English at Louisiana State University. He is the author of several articles about English pronouns that have appeared in Studia Neophilologica and South Central Bulletin.

C. William Foster, the Chairman of the Department of English of the University of North Alabama, is the author of "Folklore and the LAGS Fieldworker," in A Manual for Dialect Research in the Southern States.

Richard Gunter is an Associate Professor of English at the University of South Carolina. He is especially interested in the border region between literature and linguistics and has published several papers in this field. He is also the author of Sentences in Dialog, a collection of papers on conversation.

Robert Howren, the author of articles published in Language, American Speech, and International Journal of American Linguistics, is a Professor of Linguistics and the Chairman of the Department of Linguistics at the University of North Carolina at Chapel Hill.

Raven I. McDavid, Jr., is a Professor of English at the University of Chicago. He is the author of over 300 articles, the co-author of The Pronunciation of English in the Atlantic States and the editor of the Linguistic Atlas of the Middle and South Atlantic States. He was honored on his sixtieth birthday with a festschrift entitled Studies in Linguistics.

James B. McMillan is a Professor of English and a former Chairman of the Department of English at the University of Alabama. He has published variously and extensively in linguistics and dialectology.

Walter E. Meyers is an Associate Professor of English at North Carolina State University. He is the author of Handbook on Contemporary English.

Raymond K. O'Cain, an Assistant Professor of English at the University of South Carolina, is an associate editor of the Linguistic Atlas of the Middle and South Atlantic States. He has published in American Speech, Journal of English Linguistics, Great Lakes Review, and Kansas Journal of Sociology.

Lee Pederson, an Associate Professor of English at Emory University, is the director of the Linguistic Atlas of the Gulf States. He has published extensively in linguistics and dialectology.

CONTRIBUTORS

August Rubrecht, a former Dictionary of American Regional English fieldworker, is an Assistant Professor of English at the University of Wisconsin-Eau Claire.

Grace S. Rueter was a fieldworker for the Dialect Survey of Georgia and the Linguistic Atlas of the Gulf States.

David L. Shores, a Professor of English and the Chairman of the Department of English at Old Dominion University, is the author of A Descriptive Syntax of the Peterborough Chronicle, 1122-1154 and the editor of Contemporary English: Change and Variation. He has published in Neuphilologische Mitteilungen, South Atlantic Bulletin, English Studies, and American Speech.

Julia P. Stanley, an Assistant Professor of English at the University of Nebraska, is the author of a number of papers in linguistics and has published in American Speech and in Linguistics.

Edward A. Stephenson, the editor of the "Miscellany" section of American Speech, is a Professor of English at the University of Georgia. He is the author of articles that have appeared in American Speech, Renaissance Papers, PADS and other scholarly journals.

Gordon Wood is a Professor of English at Southern Illinois University. He is author of Subregional Variation in Vocabulary, Grammar, and Pronunciation.

SPECIAL ACKNOWLEDGEMENTS TO

Journal of English Linguistics and Edward A. Stephenson for permission to reprint "The Beginnings of the Loss of Postvocalic /r/ in North Carolina," Journal of English Linguistics, 2 (March, 1968), 57-77.

Columbia University Press and the respective authors for permission to reprint Gordon Wood, "Dialect Contours in the Southern States," American Speech, 38 (December, 1963), 243-256; Robert Howren, "The Speech of Ocracoke," American Speech, 37 (October, 1962), 161-175; John Algeo, "The Voguish Uses of Non," American Speech, 46 (Spring-Summer, 1971), 87-105; William Evans "French-English Literary Dialect in The Grandissimes," American Speech, 46 (Fall-Winter, 1971), 210-222; Jeutonne Brewer, "Subject Concord of Be in Early Black English," American Speech, 48 (Spring-Summer, 1973), 5-21.

South Atlantic Modern Language Association and the respective authors for permission to reprint William Evans "You and Thou in Northern England," South Atlantic Bulletin, 34 (November, 1969), 17-21; Jane Appleby, "Is Southern English Good?" South Atlantic Bulletin, 35 (March, 1970), 15-19; David L. Shores, "Black English and Black Attitudes," South Atlantic Bulletin, 39 (November, 1974), 104-112.

DIALECTOLOGY: A SUMMING UP AND PORTENT OF THINGS TO COME
Paul A. Eschholz

Although first recognized as a field for legitimate research more
than a century ago, dialect study, until recently, has been limited
to the monumental efforts of a pioneering generation of resourceful,
dedicated dialectologists. These early scholars provided not only
an important personal example but also the necessary methodology and
preliminary foundation studies for the current generation of researchers, those whose first work appeared after 1955. They, in turn,
are training today's students in the new approaches and new techniques of dialectology. Increased interest in the formal study of
regional and social varieties of American English has, in large part,
contributed to the increased interest in language study in general.
Within the last ten years, an impressive list of books has been
published; these include William Labov's The Social Stratification
of English in New York City (1966) and Language in the Inner City:
Studies in the Black English Vernacular (1972), Raven I. McDavid,
Jr.,'s and William M. Austin's Communication Barriers to the Culturally Deprived (1966), and Roger Shuy's Discovering American Dialects
(1967), Carroll E. Reed's Dialects of American English (1967), Hans
Kurath's Studies in Area Linguistics (1972), Walt Wolfram's Sociolinguistic Aspects of Assimilation: Puerto Rican English in New York
City (1974), and J. L. Dillard's Black English: Its History and
Usage in the United States (1972) and All-American English: A History
of the English Language in America (1975). In addition, we have witnessed the long overdue re-issuing of the Linguistic Atlas of New
England (1972), the establishment in February 1965 of a "Clearinghouse
for Social Dialect Studies" by the Center for Applied Linguistics and
the National Council of Teachers of English,[1] and the passing of the
1972 Conference on College Composition and Communication resolution
"Students' Right to Their Own Language,"which acknowledges and accepts
dialect diversity.[2] On our college campuses, courses in dialectology
have been introduced into the curriculum, and two exciting and thorough texts, Readings in American Dialectology (1971) edited by
Harold B. Allen and Gary N. Underwood and A Various Language: Perspectives on American Dialects (1971) edited by Juanita V. Williamson
and Virginia M. Burke, have appeared to meet the needs of students
enrolled in these courses. Also, courses in regional American literature have rekindled interest in regional and local color writers and
their use of literary dialect. At the professional level, membership
in the American Dialect Society has shown steady increases, and attendance at and participation in both national and regional meetings have

1

improved noticeably. Interestingly, sessions at the meetings of other organizations (the National Council of Teachers of English, the College English Association, and the Conference on College Composition and Communication, for example) are now being devoted to issues of dialect study. In short, it would not seem an overstatement to conclude that the field of dialectology is experiencing an impressive renascence.

The innovative, albeit controversial, work of the social dialectologists on Black English, non-standard urban dialects, bi-dialectalism, and the teaching of "Standard English"[3] has tended to overshadow the contributions made by their regional counterparts whose natures are akin to those of historians who observe, identify, record, interpret, and preserve. But the contributions of linguistic geographers are no less impressive. They are in the process of summing up an era that started with the launching of The Linguistic Atlas of the United States and Canada project in 1930 and of assessing future directions and possible contributions. In summing up, regional dialectologists must look to the Atlas projects and the research activities surrounding them, specifically the local and statewide surveys and the Dictionary of American Regional English.[4]

A Summing Up

First proposed and discussed during the late 1920's, The Linguistic Atlas of the United States and Canada project was initiated by Hans Kurath in 1929-1930. It incorporated much of the methodology developed by the Atlases of France and Italy. The New England states, a relatively small region, seemed the most realistic area to survey first. Started in 1930, fieldwork for the New England region was completed by 1933, and the Linguistic Atlas of New England, a work destined to become a model for the systematic study of dialect differences in English, was published from 1939-1943.[5] The relatively smooth and rapid completion of the New England Atlas held promise for the successful completion of the entire project; this promise was not fulfilled. Largely as a result of a lack of financial support, not scholarly interest, Atlas work, and linguistic geography in general, was rather slow and sporadic between 1940 and 1968. Work in this area now seems to have come into its own. The reprinting of the Linguistic Atlas of New England, the first since the original edition of 200 copies appeared more than thirty years ago, together with the publication of the revised Handbook of the Linguistic Geography of New England[6] focused attention once again on the Linguistic Atlas of the United States and Canada and brought new energies and funding to the various regional projects nearing completion.

Although work on the Linguistic Atlas of the North Central States (Wisconsin, Michigan, Illinois, Indiana, Ohio, and Kentucky), under the direction of the late Albert H. Marckwardt commenced in 1933, it was not until 1938 that the bulk of the fieldwork was started. The fieldwork for the project has been completed and, at present, editing of the materials is proceeding slowly as much of the editor's attention is devoted to matters of settlement history and population background.[7] Another project whose status is similar is the Linguistic Atlas of the Pacific Coast. Originally started as two separate projects, David W. Reed's study of California and Nevada and Carroll E. Reed's investigation of the Pacific Northwest (Washington, Oregon, and Idaho), the projects have now joined forces. Although the data has been collected, editing and publication plans remain indefinite.[8]

Dialectologists welcomed the initial volume of the proposed two-volume Linguistic Atlas of the Upper Midwest (Minnesota, Iowa, North Dakota, South Dakota, and Nebraska) edited by Harold B. Allen when it appeared in 1973.[9] It is devoted to regional speech distribution. Also, it includes background materials and methodology needed for an understanding of the Atlas and maps of representative isoglosses and of the distribution of individual items. Harold Allen reports that because of its size, the projected second and final volume of the Linguistic Atlas of the Upper Midwest will be split into two volumes. The University of Minnesota Press expects to publish volume #2, on grammar, late in 1975. Editorial work is currently being directed to volume #3, on pronunciation, which should appear in 1976.

Under the able direction of Guy S. Lowman, fieldwork for the Linguistic Atlas of the Middle and South Atlantic States (New York, New Jersey, Pennsylvania, West Virginia, Delaware, Maryland, Virginia, North Carolina, South Carolina, Georgia, and Florida) commenced in 1933. After Lowman's death in 1941, fieldwork on the project was brought to completion by Raven I. McDavid, Jr. In 1974 a giant step was taken toward the publication of LAMSAS with the formalization of a partnership between the University of Chicago and the University of South Carolina for the financial support of all editorial operations. "Plans for the publication of LAMSAS," according to Editor-in-Chief Raven I. McDavid, Jr., "call for the presentation in finely graded phonetics of the responses of 1210 informants from 516 communities in list manuscript format....This format allows for the expanded treatment of items too complex for a single map, and abbreviation of simpler items....LAMSAS will appear in fascicles of 128 pages; more than enough edited copy for the first fascicle is ready for the compositor."[10]

Since its inception in 1968, work on the Linguistic Atlas of the Gulf States has progressed remarkably well under the direction of Lee Pederson. He reports the acquisition in 1973-1974 of more than 1000 hours of tape recorded conversation which matches the quantity of data gathered in the preceding five years. Also, transcription has now been completed on 125 of the LAGS field records. As a result of accelerated research efforts, data collected through September 1974 includes 407 of an estimated 700 records (700/407) in the following states: Alabama (115/45), Arkansas (50/26), Florida (75/33), Georgia (125/98), Louisiana (65/20), Mississippi (80/69), Tennessee (115/95), and Texas (75/21). These estimated figures, as Pederson indicates, reflect the decision to extend the investigation in Texas across the entire Blackland Prairie and to include the entire state of Arkansas in the basic rural sample, as well as intensifying the survey of urban speech in sixteen cities.

Fieldwork and research on regional Atlases has spawned a whole host of related local and statewide projects. These include Marvin Carmony's work with Indiana dialects, Gary Underwood's Arkansas Language Survey, William Van Riper's Linguistic Atlas of Oklahoma, Lee Pederson's Dialect Survey of Rural Georgia. T. M. Pearce's work in New Mexico, Clyde T. Hankey's work in both Colorado and western Pennsylvania and Ohio, and Gordon Wood's various surveys in the South.[11]

Each of these projects has, in some meaningful way, made a contribution to the larger Linguistic Atlas project.

For many years dialectologists have recognized the fact that they lacked a dialect dictionary for the whole country. Although efforts have been made to document large numbers of American words of a dialectal nature,[12] none of these efforts fulfilled the American Dialect Society's dream of a systematic and comprehensive lexicon of American dialects. Attention is now turned to and excitement is growing about Frederic G. Cassidy's Dictionary of American Regional English project which promises to fill this void. Between the years 1965 and 1970 materials necessary for the Dictionary were collected and put into a computer file. Cassidy now reports that computer processing of the files should begin in 1975. The "hoped-for" completion date is 1978; DARE will be printed and published by Harvard University's Belknap Press.

Taken together, the various Atlas Projects and DARE constitute a systematic study of dialect differences in America, make an impressive contribution to our knowledge and understanding of American speech, and serve as the foundation for future dialect studies. They, in short, open the way and establish the criteria for the study of American speech in a scientific manner. Linguistic geographers have developed questionnaires and other techniques for eliciting responses for the purpose of determining regional variations of a phonological and lexical nature. They significantly contribute to our understanding of the shifts in and regional characteristics of the lexicon and of spoken English through the delineation of dialect boundaries that serve as markers of geographically oriented regional speech differences. Moreover, the Atlas studies, as James J. Broz, Jr., has indicated, serve as a guide for the study of speech and behavior in cities. By adapting the questionnaires of the Atlas and by creating new elicitation techniques to meet a more narrow linguistic investigation, social dialectologists have described not only the phonological, grammatical, and lexical features of urban speech, but also some of their socio-linguistic consequences as well.[13]

A Portent of Things to Come

The Atlas and the Dictionary of American Regional English constitute the foundation upon which future work in regional dialectology will be based. Although the fieldwork and editing for many of the Atlas projects nears completion and the scheduled publication date for DARE approaches, work in these areas will not come to an abrupt halt. We can, I feel, look forward to (1) studies, like several contained in this volume, that are based upon Atlas and/or DARE data, (2) continued discussion of the problems of methodology, (3) research on literary dialects and occupational jargon, and (4) basic studies in problems of usage and, perhaps, a survey of American English usage.

Considering the wealth of information contained in the field records and work sheets of the Atlas and DARE projects, it is not surprising to expect that these materials will be examined and that such examination will result in numerous studies which, for example, consider single features or define dialect areas. In addition, we should look for much activity in the area of dialect revisiting. One such project, the Linguistic Atlas of New England Revisited (LANER),[14] has been undertaken by Audrey R. Duckert and her collaborator David Carlson. Using a questionnaire composed of items from the LANE work sheets and from the Cassidy-Duckert "Method for Collecting Dialect,"[15] LANER, like its predecessor LANE, will have three main objectives: 1) to define the dialect areas of New England, 2) to discover innovations, and 3) to find speech relics.   "The linguistic revisitor," as Audrey Duckert points out, "has much in common with the geneticist: recognizable traits are named and followed; mutations and sports are observed and their possible causes are probed. Diffusion and out-breeding are of a piece. We are all looking for survivals and casualties, and for the reasons behind them."[16]

The areas that can be revisited are many and varied. Regions sur-veyed by the Atlas provide an excellent base for the revisitor; the same will be true for DARE areas when it comes time to resurvey them. "Perfect comparison," as Duckert advises, "is impossible, and prob-ably not really desirable. Since the milieu is different, so must the responses be."[17] Linguistic revisitation does, however, afford the dialectologist the opportunity to record phonological and lexical changes that have occurred, to note changes just as they are beginning to appear, and to monitor these changes as they evolve. These obser-vations, in turn, contribute significantly to our understanding of American English and its history.

Linguistic geographers refuse to separate fieldwork or research from methodology. As a result this important area has not been neglected. The Handbook of the Linguistic Geography of New England (1939, 1972), Method for Collecting Dialect (1953), Studies in Area Linguistics (1972), and A Manual for Dialect Research in the Southern States (1974) are representative works which document sincere interest in and atten-tion to problems of methodology. During the summer of 1972 the First International Conference on Methods in Dialectology was held under the aegis of the University of Prince Edward Island, at Charlottetown, Prince Edward Island. The conference gave interested scholars the opportunity to meet and discuss problems of methodology, data collec-tion, analysis, presentation, and other matters which had a bearing on dialectology. Plans are now set for the Second International Con-ference on Methods in Dialectology to be held in Charlottetown, Prince Edward Island in August, 1975, and there is no reason to believe that this conference will not become a permanent institution. Continued interest in matters of research methodology is important to the field of dialectology for it insures the vitality and flexi-bility so necessary in a discipline which studies the dynamic life and growth of language.

The approaching national bicentennial celebration is stimulating interest in literary dialects and the compilation of lexicons or glossaries of certain highly developed occupational vocabularies. While work has been done on such well-known figures as Edgar Allan Poe, Mark Twain, and Joel Chandler Harris,[18] we can expect studies on lesser-known authors to appear as more and more scholars are attracted to American regional writing, to the "Age of Dialect Fiction." In addition to studies of specific authors, scholars need to develop a sound theory of literary dialect.[19]

In 1949 Hans Kurath, in A Word Geography of the Eastern United States, noted that lexicographers and dialectologists alike had neglected the vocabularies of some basic occupations. Activities in this area have tended toward the colorful slang of the country's colleges and the jargon of the underworld and show business; for example, one immediately thinks of David W. Maurer's The American Confidence Man (expanded and updated 1974), Narcotics and Narcotic Addiction(with V. H. Vogel, 4 ed., 1973), and Kentucky Moonshine (1974), and Sherman T. Sergel's The Language of Show Biz: A Dictionary (1973). Other occupations have not been totally neglected; serious work has been done, for example, with tobacco, fire fighting, truck driving, whitewater kayaking, and sports writing.[20] My own interest is the vocabulary of Vermont sugar-makers, an exciting and colorful part of Yankeedom.

After touring Vermont's sugarbush recently, Sarah Orcate wrote, "...the maple, all of it--trunk, leaves, branches and sap--is as important to Vermont as the cornstalk is to Iowa." She also discovered that "...sugaring off has its own jargon. The men who do it are called 'sappers.' The mountains where they work the maples are 'the sugar bush.' The bore they drill with is a 'bit.' The hole made with the bore is a 'tap.' And the very phrase 'sugaring off' has such all-around sweet connotations that it has become a metaphor for a business deal that winds up well or a relationship that comes off smoothly."

While "sugaring" has long been one of Vermont's most cherished traditions, it, like many of Vermont's other traditions, is rapidly dying out. Significant changes in the vocabulary have accompanied the disappearance of the rude shanties that sheltered the old-time sugar-makers and the appearance of the more technically advanced, profit-oriented, modern sugar-houses with their patent evaporators and automatic feeders. To survey Vermont's sugar-makers at this time would be to preserve an exhaustive listing of their vocabulary. The data from the survey would evidence any changes that the occupation's terminology has undergone as a result of modernization: old terms that have become obsolete, others that have been extended in application, and new terms that have been created. Margaret Bryant's "Maple Sugar Language in Vermont" (1947)[21] offers the opportunity of a limited, yet fascinating, linguistic revisitation. In the future, we should look for glossaries of terms from ranching, mining, cotton growing, dairy farming, and professional football, basketball, and baseball.

Patricia Tway's "An Ethnography of Communication in a China Factory: A Case Study of Occupational Jargon"[22] adds a new dimension to work on occupational vocabulary by bringing together the domains and techniques of the regional and social dialectologist. Based upon a case method of research in a Pennsylvania china factory, Tway's study is concerned with the characteristics and underlying features of occupational jargon and the part they play in reflecting the workers' knowledge of their jobs and their attitudes toward jobs. It describes the ways in which regional and general speech habits contribute to occupational jargon, the ways in which workers change speech styles for different communicative situations on the job, and the manner in which formative elements are combined to create technical terminology associated with a job. By examining the china factory as a speech community, she was able to illustrate dialect boundaries within the plant and show that factory speech habits supersede personal speech habits for job-related terms and that shared technical terminology is

Paul A. Eschholz

related to operational and geographical proximity within the plant.
Another area in which social and regional dialectologists can join
forces is in the study of problems of usage. Despite our tendency
to think otherwise, "usage," as Walter E. Meyers observes, "continues
to be a saleable issue."[23] Contemporary scholars are becoming
increasingly disturbed by the rather subjective, idiosyncratic statements about modern American usage that are being passed off as objective. Thomas J. Creswell reports that "a study of mid-twentieth century American practice in the treatment of problems of usage in
general-purpose dictionaries reveals little real change from the
authoritarian and idiosyncratic practice characteristic of Samuel
Johnson's 1755 English Dictionary. More than two centuries of linguistic and lexicographic scholarship have altered somewhat the tone
of statements about usage in dictionaries, but have had little apparent
effect upon the objectivity of judgments. When the user of a modern
dictionary finds that a locution is censured or assigned a restrictive label, all that he can really be certain of is that the compiler
believes the implied judgment to be accurate."[24] Creswell concludes
that usage labels and discussions of usage should be derived from
the examination of available bodies of language material such as the
Brown University Standard Corpus of Present-Day Edited American English.
Exploratory work based on an examination of the Brown Corpus has
been undertaken by Walter E. Meyers and Virginia G. McDavid.[25] Perhaps
the most ambitious and far-reaching project in the area of usage is
John Algeo's proposal for a Survey of English Usage.[26] Currently
he is grappling with the problems associated with the elicitation of
usage sample from informants and with the distribution of texts within
a new corpus, comparable to the one at Brown, that is being considered.
When seen to its completion, a Survey of American Usage would be
very helpful in eliminating the unfortunate polarization of arguments
about the teaching of English usage and most certainly join The Linguistic Atlas and DARE as a monument in the field of dialectology.

NOTES

[1]See: A. L. Davis, ed., Culture, Class, and Language Variety: A
Resource Book for Teachers (Champaign, Illinois: NCTE, 1972), and
Lester S. Golub, "What Can the English Teacher Do With Dialects" (EDRS:
ED 078 421, 1973). Dialect study, especially with its recent
historical, sociological, and educational application, is a fascinating
and integral part of linguistics. The word dialect, however, is
generally misunderstood, largely as a result of the negative connotations it has acquired. Many Americans, for example, mistakenly view
dialect as an ignorant corruption of the language. Great care must
be taken so that no misunderstandings are propagated in the teaching
of dialects.

[2]The resolution has been published as a Special Issue: "Students'
Right to Their Own Language," College Composition and Communication,

25 (Fall 1974). This issue contains a useful bibliography of literature on dialects for the teacher of composition and reading.

[3]The Summer 1975 number of the <u>Florida FL Reporter</u> is devoted to
"Issues on the Teaching of Standard English."

[4]I am grateful to colleagues who in conversation or in correspondence have supplied me with up-to-date information regarding their
research.

[5]Hans Kurath, Miles L. Hanley, Bernard Bloch, et al., <u>Linguistic</u>
<u>Atlas</u> of <u>New England</u>, 3 vols. in 6 parts (Providence, R.I.: Brown
University Press, 1939-1943). The carbons of the original <u>LANE</u> field
records together with tapes of the recordings made by Hanley and
Lowman are now stored in the Archives at the University of Massachusetts Library. The original field books and the voice recordings made
on aluminum platters will be deposited at the University of South
Carolina.

[6]Hans Kurath, et al., <u>Handbook</u> of <u>the Linguistic Geography</u> of <u>New</u>
<u>England</u>, 2nd ed. (New York: AMS Press, 1972).

[7]Work based on fieldwork for the North Central Atlas includes
Albert H. Marckwardt, "Principal and Subsidiary Dialect Areas in the
North-Central States," <u>PADS</u>, 27 (1957), 3-15; Raven I. and Virginia
G. McDavid, "Grammatical Differences in the North Central States,"
<u>American Speech</u>, 35 (1960), 5-19; and Alva L. Davis, "A Word Atlas of
the Great Lakes Region," Dissertation University of Michigan 1949.

[8]Work based on fieldwork for the Pacific Coast Atlas includes
Carroll E. Reed, "Washington Words," <u>PADS</u>, 25 (1956), 3-11; Carroll
E. Reed, "Word Geography of the Pacific Northwest," <u>Orbis</u>, 6 (1957),
86-93; and David W. Reed, "Eastern Dialect Words in California,"
<u>PADS</u> (1954), 3-15.

[9]Harold B. Allen, <u>Linguistic Atlas</u> of <u>the Upper Midwest</u>, Vol. I
(Minneapolis, Minnesota: University of Minnesota Press, 1973).

[10]Three valuable works based on LANE materials and LAMSAS fieldwork
are   E. Bagby Atwood, <u>A Survey</u> of <u>Verb Forms</u> in <u>the Eastern United</u>
<u>States</u> (Ann Arbor, Michigan: University of Michigan Press, 1953);
Hans Kurath, <u>A Word Geography</u> of <u>the Eastern United States</u> (Ann Arbor,
Michigan: University of Michigan Press, 1949); and Hans Kurath and
Raven I. McDavid, Jr., <u>The Pronunciation</u> of <u>English</u> in <u>the Atlantic</u>
<u>States</u> (Ann Arbor, Michigan: University of Michigan Press, 1961).

[11]For a detailed discussion of early statewide projects, see:
E. Bagby Atwood, "The Methods of American Dialectology," <u>Zeitschrift</u>
<u>für Mundartforschung</u>, 30 (1963), 1-29; and Raven I. and Virginia G.
McDavid, "Regional Linguistic Atlases in the United States," <u>Orbis</u>,
5 (1956), 349-386.

[12]William A. Craigie and James R. Hulbert, <u>A Dictionary</u> of <u>American</u>
<u>English</u>, 4 vols. (Chicago: University of Chicago Press, 1938-1944);

Paul A. Eschholz

Harold Wentworth, _American Dialect Dictionary_ (New York: Crowell, 1944);
and M. M. Mathews, _A Dictionary of Americanisms on Historical Principles_
(Chicago: University of Chicago Press, 1951).

[13] James J. Broz, Jr., "Trends and Implications of Current Research
in Dialectology," unpublished paper presented at SAMLA, American Dialect Society Section, November 12, 1966.

[14] Audrey R. Duckert, "The Linguistic Atlas of New England Revisited,"
PADS, 39 (1963), 8-15. At the July 28, 1974 meeting of the Northeast
American Dialect Society, Raven I. McDavid, Jr., presented a paper
entitled, "The Linguistic Atlas of New England and Black English."
He argued that "although the Linguistic Atlas of New England was
published in 1939 and reprinted in 1972, it has apparently not been
consulted by currently active sociolinguists. An inspection shows
(1) ample detail on many ethnically controversial items such as multiple negation, (2) widespread use among whites of linguistic forms
often attributed to blacks, (3) as controls, field records from blacks
in Connecticut, Maine and Nova Scotia, suggesting the importance of
continuing reinforcements from the South."

[15] Frederic G. Cassidy and Audrey R. Duckert, "Method for Collecting
Dialect," _PADS_, 20 (1953).

[16] Audrey R. Duckert, "The Second Time Around: Methods in Dialect
Revisiting," _American Speech_, 46 (Spring-Summer 1971), 66.

[17] Ibid., p. 72.

[18] Eric Stockton, "Poe's Use of Negro Dialect in 'The Gold Bug,'"
in _Studies in Language and Linguistics in Honor of Charles C. Fries_,
ed. Albert H. Marckwardt (Ann Arbor, Michigan: University of Michigan
Press, 1964), pp. 249-70; Curt M. Rulon, "Geographical Delimita-
tion of the Dialect Areas in _The Adventures of Huckleberry Finn_,"
The Mark Twain Journal, 14 (Winter 1967), 9-12; and Sumner Ives,
"Dialect Differentiation in the Stories of Joel Chandler Harris,"
American Literature, 17 (March 1955), 88-96.

[19] Sumner Ives, "A Theory of Literary Dialect," _Tulane Studies in
English_, 2 (1950), 137-82.

[20] Consult back issues of _PADS_ and _American Speech_ for representative studies of occupational jargon.

[21] Margaret M. Bryant, "Maple Sugar Language in Vermont," _PADS_, 8
(1947), 3-10.

[22] Patricia Tway, "An Ethnography of Communication in a China
Factory: A Case Study of Occupational Jargon," Dissertation Syracuse
University 1974.

[23] Walter E. Meyers, "A Study of Usage Items Based on an Examination
of the Brown Corpus," _College Composition and Communication_, 23 (1972),
155.

9

[24]Thomas J. Creswell, "Usage in Dictionaries and in Dictionaries of Usage," Dissertation University of Chicago 1974. Creswell presented a paper, "Usage in Contemporary American Dictionaries," at MLA in New York, December 27, 1974.

[25]Meyers, "A Study of Usage Items;" and Virginia G. McDavid, "That and Which in Relative Clauses," a paper presented at the annual American Dialect Society Meeting in New York, December 27, 1974.

[26]John Algeo, "A Survey of American Usage: Prospects," a paper presented at the annual American Dialect Society Meeting in New York, December 28, 1974.

I.   REGIONAL VARIATION

WHAT'S NEW ABOUT DARE?*

Frederic G. Cassidy

As most readers are no doubt aware, the Dictionary of American
Regional English has been in preparation since 1965 under sponsor-
ship of the American Dialect Society. Nevertheless, it may be
well to refresh your memories briefly about the project.
From the time of its foundation in 1889, the Society had as one
tangible goal the publication of an American Dialect Dictionary
which, it was hoped, might be an "opposite number" to Joseph Wright's
English Dialect Dictionary. To this end, materials were collected
and studies published in Dialect Notes for fifty years and the Publication of the American Dialect Society thereafter. On several occasions down the years, editors were appointed to push the work toward
the hoped-for publication, but in every instance they were defeated
by lack of adequate materials and lack of money. It became obvious
at last that nothing could be accomplished without ample funds and
full-time direction--the spare-time, shoestring approach had failed
repeatedly.
You may also remember that, 'way back in 1964, the Federal Government had at last begun in a small way to spend money for projects of
an artistic or intellectual kind. In that year we were able to get
the U.S. Office of Education to agree to support the American Dialect Society dictionary project, and DARE was born. It began officially under my direction on July 1, 1965, the U.S. Office of
Education and the University of Wisconsin funding it generously till
the end of 1970. During those five and a half years we succeeded in
processing into a magnetic tape computer file approximately two and
a half million lexical items on the basis of which the Dictionary is
to be made. This filing was finished in 1974, and first steps toward
editing have been taken. The National Endowment for the Humanities
has succeeded the U.S. Office of Education as chief funding source,
and the project continues with a good hope of publishing a first
section, what we call the Data Summary, possibly before the word-by-
word part.
DARE will combine some conventional features with others that are
new to dialect or similar dictionaries. Joseph Wright had to work
almost entirely from wordlists, some of them very good, thorough and
accurate, many others of much lesser quality. Himself a native dialect speaker from Windhill, Yorkshire, as well as a superlative
philologist, he was well fitted for the task and performed it
excellently. Yet even while he was editing the book, the new techniques of dialect geography were entering upon the scene--notably in

13

France with the Atlas Linguistique de la France. These techniques, later applied in England, brought to light many items which Wright had altogether failed to find.

The same is true of dialect collecting in the United States. Many of the wordlists early published in Dialect Notes left a good deal to be desired. Collectors seldom conceived clearly just what the lexicographer needs to know in order to frame an accurate and adequate treatment for the dictionary. They often omitted pronunciation or failed to note down the "social" facts about their informants: age, sex, occupation, social status, race or ethnic background, degree of education, and so on; and they were often quite vague even about geography--the exact places where the items had been found in use or were unknown. It may truly be said that the way to this degree of fullness and accuracy was shown only when the Linguistic Atlas of New England began to do its work under Hans Kurath. The DARE project is fortunate to be able to stand on the shoulders of the American Atlas-- from that vantage point we can see farther and more clearly.

Certainly no dialect dictionary today could do without a large corpus of contemporary speech gathered systematically and with tape recordings. DARE has completed 1002 full questionairs** in chosen communities in all fifty states; also 1843 tapes of spontaneous speech as well as readings of our improved version of "Arthur the Rat." While all the previous collections of the American Dialect Society and many other collections have gone into the general DARE file for use in editing, we can claim that, through our questionairs, filled out within a five-year period (relatively a very short time), we have a virtually synchronic record of the American lexicon, especially the local and regional part of it.

A word about this questionair. While it is not perfect, it has proved out very well in use. The head of the French linguistic Atlas, Jules Gillieron, is famous for the statement that the best time to make a questionair is after the fieldwork has been done. If we were to make our questionair now on the basis of the 1002 completed in fifty states, we could of course improve it. Nevertheless, it was not a hasty concoction. The need of such a questionair was anticipated thirty years ago when, with the help of many American Dialect Society members, I made a file of everything published by the Society up to that time. Professor Audrey Duckert and I then sorted this file by sense categories, made the initial questionair, tested it in fifty Wisconsin communities, revised it in the light of this testing, and published it as PADS 20 (1953). We worked on the theory that since a questionair which tried to cover everything would become impossibly long, we must limit the questions to those subjects which regularly produced regionally varying responses--in a word, maximize the results.

The questionair used for DARE is based on this PADS 20 questionair with subtraction of the least productive questions and addition of others which the Atlas workers had meantime found valuable. Recognizing the fact of the shift of population to the cities we added a number of urban questions--for example on apartment dwelling, cars, gasoline, traffic lights, headlights, toll roads, and so on. We now have evidence on the distribution of the alternatives access road/ frontage road/ service road for the road that connects a big highway with stores and business places set back from it. And for the area between the curb and sidewalk where grass and trees grow, we have the alternatives tree strip/ park strip/ the parking/ devil strip/ boulevard/ tree bank, and so on. No single response or set of responses is by itself earth-shaking, but since the questionair contains 1855 questions, the aggregate from 1002 is quite impressive. Some questions always remain unanswered, but many elicit multiple answers. On the average we have received about 2300 answers per questionair.

Another feature of our DARE questionair is that each question is phrased exactly, and the fieldworkers were instructed to ask each question in exactly that form. With our several revisions, based on field tests, we were able to get these questions phrased so as not to predispose the informant to one alternative answer rather than another. This was not always easy. We had difficulty, for example, with the variants for pancake: wheat cake, griddle cake, flapjack, slapjack, fritter, flitter, and so on. To describe the object briefly so that nobody could misunderstand what it was, and yet not use the words pan, griddle, or cake, became nearly impossible. I cut the gordian knot by asking first, "Do you have 'pancakes' around here?" Of course the answer was almost always "yes"; then the following question--the one which counted--was, "What other names do you have for them?" As with the Atlas, we went on the principle that the first spontaneous reply would be the word the speaker normally used, whatever else he or she might add afterwards. However, a slow or hesitant reply would suggest that pancake was the usual form--and some informants told us so: "Just pancakes is all we ever call 'em." This term is nationwide, it is standard, and standard terms will not be listed in the Dictionary. But we had to get pancake out of the way, so to speak, to allow the regional and local terms to appear.

The exact phrasing of our questions also avoids ambiguities which a fieldworker might at first not even be aware of. He might not know that in some areas a woodchuck is not a marmot but a type of woodpecker, and that though a gopher is, most places, a type of rodent, in other places it is a land tortoise. Further, it may make a considerable difference whether a response takes the form of a noun, a verb, an adjective: even with identical forms they are not the same word. The pre-stated question used in our questionair can help to avoid answers that do not match: to produce responses of nationwide comparability. Yet in pure honesty I must confess that with all the care we put into phrasing these questions, a handful remained unmanageable to the last. Besides, no scholarly ingenuity can forever thwart the human creature's capacity to blunder, to an-swer a perfectly plain question at completely cross purposes.

I hope it is unnecessary to say that the communities we chose to study were not picked at random. The number of 1000 questionairs was more or less arbitrary: it seemed the largest number one could hope to complete within the five-year data collecting period. The number allotted finally to each state was prorated to density of population, the length of time the area had been settled, and similar factors. Thus a thinly populated state such as Nevada was allotted only two questionairs while New York State was allotted eighty-six, California fifty-six. Further, these were chosen to balance as well as possible the existing proportions of rural and urban areas, small towns and metropolises. We sought out stable

15

communities for the obvious reason that regionalisms and localisms
are generally traditional: their continuance depends on social
continuity. To choose the stable communities was thus another step
toward maximization.

In these communities our fieldworkers sought native speakers of
American English, born there or in the near neighborhood and not
having traveled enough to affect their local speech. If their parents
and grandparents had lived there before them, so much the better.
They are of all degrees of education, many and varied occupations, and
so far as possible representative of the ethnic composition of their
community. Facts about the chosen communities and informants will be
presented in the Introduction to the Data Summary.

The mass of living American English gathered by means of the DARE
questionair is very large and we knew from the beginning that the
only way to handle it was to computerize it. All returned questionairs
were therefore pre-edited by our staff and the information put on magnetic tapes. This is now almost fully processed into the Data
Summary, an essential source of information for the editors. We
expect this Data Summary to be the last volume of the completed Dictionary. We will cross-refer to it from the first volumes--the conventional alphabetical word-list--for much fuller detail than would
be appropriate to the treatments of individual words. This feature,
one that other dictionaries do not have, will be made possible by the
way the questionair was set up in the first place and by use of the
computer to tabulate the data.

The Data Summary will present in condensed form, and in proper
sequence, each question of the questionair with all the responses it
received. These responses will themselves be listed in descending
order of frequency so that at a glance the reader may distinguish the
commonest response--usually the standard word--from the less frequent
ones, many of which have been given only once. Facts about the
informants will also be digested and presented with each response:
how many and which of the individuals who gave it were of the old,
middle aged, or young adult generation; which had grade school, high
school, or college education; and how they were distributed geographically within twenty areas. These lists of alternative responses
to the same question will form a sort of synonymy--another unusual
feature of DARE. Tabulation of such a mass of data, even though raw,
should make possible some sociolinguistic correlations. We hope
also to display the best of the geographical information on computer-
drawn maps, thus making it much clearer (for some types of questions
at least) and more usable.

DARE plans to present each word or phrase that is evidently local
or regional, or characteristic of some socially distinct community,
anywhere in the United States; to designate its area of use,
variant forms and etymologies; and to illustrate with quotations or
references to sources. Though what we have gathered with questionairs and on tapes will be the largest part of our corpus, the "Main
File" also includes all that the American Dialect Society has
gathered and published over the years, much from several private
collections donated to us, much from the Atlas sources and recordings
made in New England which were not used for the Linguistic Atlas of
New England, a good deal from diaries, newspapers, folklore and
literary sources, to say nothing of the thousands of random items

Frederic G. Cassidy

that have found their way into our file by every conceivable route.
The computer will process these for us, alphabetize by headword,
sort by part of speech, and chronologize the sources. The print-
out of all this will be used by the editors as the basis for treatments of individual words.

In 1974 one of our chief problems was removed when the Belknap
Press of Harvard offered to publish DARE. The only question that
remains is how soon we can finish the rather large though fascinating
task of editing. We had hoped to see the Dictionary completed as a
contribution to the Bicentennial celebrations of 1976, but this date
cannot be held to. Nevertheless, the growth of this nation has
been a powerful linguistic fact, among others; it deserves to be
shown more clearly than is possible at present, despite the existence of the Dictionary of American English and the Dictionary of
Americanisms, both very fine works, but limited in some respects. We
hope DARE may within a few years take its place alongside them on the
shelves of libraries and of students of American English.

NOTES

*Read at the SAMLA-ADS Meeting, Atlanta, Georgia, November, 1971.
**Cassidy's spelling.

STRUCTURAL DESCRIPTION IN LINGUISTIC GEOGRAPHY*

Lee Pederson

As an application of general linguistic theory, linguistic geography is necessarily conservative in its approaches to the study of
variation in human speech. Both field and descriptive procedures
are derived from established methodology, reflecting the develop-
ments of general linguistics by implementing those techniques that
have been proven thoroughly effective. That image, however, might
be obscured by the very nature of linguistic geography itself. Its
work is slow and deliberate, its projects are often interdependent
and extend over long periods of time, and its findings, more often
than not, lag a generation or more behind contemporary usage. As
Hockett observed, "Dialect geography has the virtues of concreteness and specificity; sweeping generalizations not based on concrete
small-scale facts are bootless."[1] To gamble away those virtues
with unproven methods would be irresponsible. Instead, linguistic
geographers conserve conventional procedures in the collection of
evidence that can be combined and compared with earlier findings.
Ignoring that rationale, casual observers may well interpret that
approach to language investigation as both primitive and unsatisfactory.[2]

Although such criticism is essentially empty, linguistic geographers might have set the record straight years ago with a little
more attention to the place of structural description in the analysis
of data. Apart from McDavid's comparison of the aims and methods
of structural linguistics and those of linguistic geography,[3] little
attention has been given to the bill of particulars recited by
Pickford and others.[4] A rare instance of clarification is McIntosh's
epistemological observation,[5] but this, like McDavid's comparison,
has been roundly ignored.

A substantive criticism of American linguistic geography should
proceed along a very different line. Too much time has been spent
in the composition of autonomous word geographies because we have
failed to absorb the first lesson of American structuralists from
Bloomfield to Harris: descriptive units are most productively
studied within the context of system. As Bloch insisted:

> Only one kind of written record, according to Bloomfield,
> is scientifically relevant: 'a record in terms of pho-
> nemes, ignoring all features that are not distinctive in
> the language'--and ignoring also, if the record be
> strictly phonemic, all features that are distinctive
> but not immediately observable in the stream of speech,

19

such as morpheme boundaries, word structure, and morphophonemic relationships. Such a record is the only safe
and adequate basis for further investigation of linguistic structure; the analyst who attempts to study
the morphemes or the grammatical constructions of a language in terms of a transcription that is either less
or more than phonemic--a raw phonetic transcription on
the one hand, or on the other a transcription that
tacitly relies on non-phonetic evidence--will either
be lost in a confusion of irrelevant details or overlook significant correlations between the phonemic
structure and the structure of other linguistic levels.[6]

Although a rigorous structural approach is inconsistent with the
aims and methods of American linguistic geography,[7] the tacit
assumptions of autonomous word geography, sketchy morphological
glosses, and vowel-dominated phonemic descriptions need to be
amplified and made explicit with essential details. Descriptions
of the phonological system must precede discussions of words, and
those descriptions must be recognized as segmental, suprasegmental,
and extrasegmental units, if the system is to be adequately identified. With the wide range of variation of lax vowels preceding
resonant consonants, especially /l, r, m, n, ŋ/, it is impossible
to discuss preterit and past participial forms of the verbs fall,
bear, swim, run, and drink, without a clear statement of phonemic
incidence of vowels within the idiolects and without a description
of infinitive, preterit, and past participial forms as contrastive
(or noncontrastive) members of the series.

This report is limited to three specific details in the composition of an adequate phonological statement for dialect study. The
aim is to identify the place of phonology in dialect description and
to discuss these three aspects from the perspective of completed
research. Without attention to these details structural description
is impossible, and without structural description linguistic geography cannot make efficient use of the rich materials gathered over
the past forty-five years.

As Bloch indicated, phonemic description involves an inventory and
analysis of the contrastive units in the sound system. Whether distinguished by contrast, phonetic similarity, or distribution, however, these units provide the basis for all subsequent structural
description by reducing speech to writing. Recognizing the fundamental position of this system within the descriptive design, one
should expect to find comprehensive analysis of phonology in all
dialect studies based on direct observations of speech, but this is
not always the case.[8] Three aspects of phonemic description that
deserve attention of American dialectologists are these: 1) the
consonant system (usually discussed only incidentally as orthographic frames for the study of vowels); 2) prosody (virtually
ignored in most studies); 3) paralanguage (not yet considered by
anyone in the context of phonemic description).

Adequate structural description of the consonant system is an
essential preliminary to the discussion of regional and social dialects. As stated before, the conclusions of a survey of North
Georgia social dialects are certainly suggestive:

1. The obstruent system in rural North Georgia is highly

complicated by several recurrent features which usually involve
phonotactic patterning and which invariably result in a higher
incidence of phonemic alternation in these environments--often
involving specific processes of assimilation--and phonemic loss
than are found in other observed dialects of American English.
2. The incidence of these recessive features is considerably
higher among Upcountry Lower Southerners than among South Midland speakers. At least two of these features, however, have
been conventionalized and are widespread throughout the territory of North Georgia, the products of medial and final devoic-
ing of stop consonants in <u>spigot</u> /g/ > /k/ and in <u>salad</u> /d/ > /t/.
3. Overall, but especially in the Upcountry Lower Southern
area, the highest incidence of these recessive features is
recorded among blacks. Those whites with the greatest number
of these recessive forms in their speech live where the black
population is most heavily concentrated--everywhere south of
the Chattahoochee River, but most notably in close proximity of
Atlanta in the southwest quadrant of the area and along the
Savannah River in the southeast.
4. Some of the most complicated problems of phonemic classification within the obstruent system in rural North Georgia involve forms with grammatical functions. The alveolar stops
/t/d/ are regular preterit signals among reflexes of Old English weak verbs; the alveolar fricatives /s/z/ mark tense and
number in all verb paradigms; these same fricatives mark number
and possession in the case system that accommodates most English
nouns. Although these phono-syntactic problems are beyond the
range of a phonemic outline, the implications seem inescapable:
unless a grammar of American English is carefully limited to a
description of "General American," syntactic analysis requires a
much more sensitive phonological interpretation than is currently
available, and future surveys of American English require close
attention to the pronunciation of consonants, as well as the
vowels, and to the distribution of linguistic forms among the
blacks, as well as the whites.[9]
More than a decade ago, McDavid outlined some basic problems in
prosodic description. Answers to all of the questions he raised
(and solutions to all of the problems he posed) are necessary and
must precede any claim of adequate phonological description. He
wrote:

> The problem of an over-all frame of suprasegmental phonemes
> (accepting the point of view that these phenomena are a
> part of the phonemic system) is left in abeyance at this
> time, pending the collection of a body of unrehearsed evi-
> dence for independent analysis. That there may be differ-
> ences in the number, distribution, and phonetic qualities
> of these phenomena would seem a reasonable inference from
> what we know about the segmental phonemes. This inference
> is also supported by such heuristic evidence as:
> 1) The widespread recognition that South Midland and
> Southern dialects--particularly those of the tidewater re-
> gion from Georgetown, South Carolina, to northeastern
> Florida--have speech tunes unlike those of North Midland
> and Northern dialects.

2) Other structural analyses of suprasegmental phenomena, especially
    a) Gage's discovery of five-pitch dialects in upstate New York;
    b) Pike's suggestions that, in some dialects at least, the two Tragerian terminals/ | | / and /#/ may be reduced to one.
3) Interdialectal misinterpretation of suprasegmental phenomena. For example, the sequence /^+⁓/, in such South Midland dialects as Sledd's and mine has been interpreted by Joos as /⁓ | ⁓/, because the phonetic features of Greenville and Atlanta /^+⁓/ resemble those of Wisconsin /⁓ | ⁓/.[10]

Although the analysis of paralanguage is ostensibly beyond the responsibility of phonemic description, a careful distinction must be drawn between primary and secondary linguistic signals. In the case of nasalization, McMillan has demonstrated its role as a primary (phonemic) signal.[11] But to delimit that feature, it is necessary to sort out the secondary (paralinguistic) signals that recur in the same corpus of data. In the transcriptions for the Linguistic Atlas of the Gulf States project, for example, six stylistic contexts of vowel and consonant nasality have been reported. These include 1) intimacy, 2) playful humor, 3) doubt or uncertainty, 4) emphasis, 5) sarcasm, and 6) mild disapproval or disgust. These paralinguistic signals are found most frequently in the speech of those informants who also use vowel nasality as a phonemic signal. It is for this reason that the study of paralanguage must enter any serious consideration of Southern speech, not as an experimental innovation, but rather as a bare necessity in getting at the basic units of the phonological system.[12]

Only with an advance toward coherent structural description will it be possible to accommodate these diverse problems with consistent solutions. These are interdependent problems of the segmental subsystem (consonants and vowels), suprasegmental subsystem (stress, pitch, and juncture), and extrasegmental subsystem (phonemic vowel nasality and paralinguistic vowel nasality). Efforts to solve these problems will refine, not waste, the virtues of dialect geography because "concreteness and specificity" are but strengthened in substance and sharpened in focus through accurate observation and comprehensive description.

NOTES

*The earlier SAMLA-ADS version of this paper was called "Structural Imperatives in Dialect Study." Read at the SAMLA-ADS Meeting, Washington, D.C., November, 1970.

[1]Charles F. Hockett, A Course in Modern Linguistics (New York: MacMillan, 1958), p. 484.

[2]E.g., Glenna R. Pickford, "American Linguistic Geography: A

Lee Pederson

Sociological Appraisal," Word, 12 (1956), 211-33; Samuel J. Keyser, "Review of PEAS," Language, 39 (1963), 303-16; J. L. Dillard, Black English (New York: Random House, 1972); and various contributors to the Center for Applied Linguistics, Urban Language Series.

[3]Raven I. McDavid, Jr., "Structural Linguistics and Linguistic Geography," Orbis, 10 (1961), 35-46.

[4]For a useful perspective, see Lawrence M. Davis, "Social Dialectology in America: A Critical Survey," Journal of English Linguistics, 4 (1970), 46-56.

[5]Angus McIntosh, An Introduction to a Survey of Scottish Dialects (Edinburgh: Nelson, 1961), p. 1. "The scientific study of dialects can be approached in different ways according to the objectives and methods of those who undertake it. Like any other scholarly pursuit, the investigation of dialects is in one sense arbitrary and artificial, because what is collected and analysed is inevitably a comparatively small selection of material: for reasons of practicability and convenience and also because of the particular objectives a scholar has in mind, a mass of related material is either ignored or taken for granted. There is nothing specially disturbing or alarming about this state of affairs, which is common to most fields of study, but the fact must be recognised and kept continually in mind."

[6]Bernard Bloch, "Studies in Colloquial Japanese: Phonemics," Language, 26 (1950), 123-24. Bloch's citation of Bloomfield is from Language (New York: Holt, 1933), p. 85.

[7]As McIntosh correctly indicates, all investigations cannot be organized along uniform lines, and no investigation can reasonably expect to cover all aspects of sociolinguistic problems. As Kurath, McDavid, Sledd, and others have observed, the dominant structural model of descriptive phonology--the binary phonemic interpretation of Bloch, Trager, and Smith--is simply not adequate to the task of describing several varieties of American English in the Southern states. As McDavid (1961) noted, the basic questionnaire, the work sheets for American atlas projects, are unsuited for the collection of data for rigorous structural description. None of these qualifications, however, should discourage one from making the best possible structural statement that his data will allow.

[8]Perhaps the most naive statement to date on this matter comes from a sociolinguist in a publication of the Urban Language Series: "Although it is not the primary task of this study to give a linguistic description of either standard or nonstandard norms, a clear structural understanding of particular features in terms of these norms will be necessary. The theoretical model of language underlying structural descriptions will be that of Stratificational Grammar....The essential aspect of Stratificational Grammar is its recognition of language organization on at least three Strata (semology, grammar, phonology). Each of the Strata has its own inventory of units and tactics, being related to adjacent Strata

23

only through realization rules. Since structural description of features is secondary to their social stratification, no formulaic representation of features will be given as a part of this study." Walter A. Wolfram, A Sociolinguistic Description of Detroit Negro Speech (Washington, D.C.: Center for Applied Linguistics, 1969). He then proceeds to identify phonological and grammatical variables with no attention whatsoever to the systems from which they are drawn, and the sketches of Lamb, Gleason, and Taber, represented in ellipses in the foregoing quotation, are of no help because they do not describe phonological or grammatical systems of British, American, or Detroit English. Wolfram could as well have identified his theoretica⁴ model as Free Will Baptist, for all that model has to do with the "structural descriptions" in question.

[9]Lee Pederson, "Southern Speech and the LAGS Project," Orbis, 20 (1971), 85-86. From the essay, still in press, "Obstruent Consonants in Rural Northern Georgia."

[10]Raven I. McDavid, Jr., "Confederate Overalls; or, A Little Southern Sweetening," mimeographed, Chicago (1960). The reference to (William Whitney) Gage is Grammatical Structures in American Intonation, Dissertation Cornell University 1958.

[11]James B. McMillan, "Vowel Nasality as a Sandhi Form of the Morphemes -nt and -ing in Southern American," American Speech, 14 (1939), 123-25.

[12]Grace S. Rueter reported her work in progress in "Vowel Nasality in Rural Middle Georgia" at the MLA-ADS section, New York City, December 1974.

TOWARD A DESCRIPTION OF SOUTHERN SPEECH*

Lee Pederson

During the past seven years, the Linguistic Atlas of the Gulf
States (LAGS) project has followed a course that could not be
predicted at SAMLA-ADS in 1968. Although much work remains to be
done, the survey of regional and social dialects in the Gulf states
will be completed by September 1975, through the generous support
of several institutions and many people.[1] Three progress reports
have been issued, a research manual has gone through two editions,
and summaries have been prepared to describe the aims, methods, and
preliminary findings of the survey.[2] A review of those writings is
unnecessary here, but the course of that investigation might be
better understood with an outline of the work in progress and a
perspective on its goals and implications.

1. The LAGS Project, April 1975. As an extension of the Linguistic
Atlas of the Middle and South Atlantic States by affiliation, the
LAGS project uses the empirical methods developed by Hans Kurath
and his associates over the past forty-five years.[3] With these
procedures the survey aimed to cover evenly the varieties of indige-
nous American English spoken in the Gulf states of Florida, Alabama,
Mississippi, Louisiana, and Texas, as well as the neighboring
states of Georgia, Tennessee, and Arkansas. From the preliminary
research begun in 1968 to the fieldwork in progress in 1975, the
organization of the LAGS project has been developed through bibliographical and field investigations, conferences and subsequently
revised plans, and a preliminary analysis of materials, all of
which have contributed and have helped to determine the aims and
methods of the work to be done. These considerations preceded
the final delimitation of territory, the identification of the
sample, the composition of the work sheets, the assumption of local
responsibilities, and the plans for the publication of the basic
materials.[4]
    After several reconsiderations, it was finally decided to include
the entire region dominated by the Gulf Coastal Plains, that is,
East Texas (well into the Post Oak Belt that borders the Blackland
Prairie), East and Southwest Arkansas (the Mississippi and Coastal
Plains and the southern fringes of the Ouachita Mountains), all of
Louisiana, Mississippi, Alabama, Tennessee, and Florida, as well as
the area of Georgia south and west of the Ocmulgee and Altamaha
Rivers.[5] This region was divided in four zones, each including four
sectors: 1) Eastern Zone (East Tennessee, Upper Georgia, Lower

Lee Pederson

Georgia, and East Florida), 2) East Central Zone (Middle Tennessee,
Upper Alabama, Lower Alabama, and Gulf Alabama with West Florida),
3) West Central Zone (West Tennessee, Upper Mississippi, Lower
Mississippi, Gulf Mississippi with East Louisiana), and 4) Western
Zone (Arkansas, West Louisiana, Northeast Texas, and Southeast
Texas).[6]

This area includes 590 counties and parishes, which have been
grouped in a grid of 158 units, determined by local settlement history,
population distribution, and topographical distinctiveness.

Each of these 158 units has been taken as a target community, where
at least one elderly white folk speaker will be interviewed, as well
as one middle-aged white informant with a high school education. In
each community where the black population in 1930 exceeded twenty
percent of the local census, an elderly black folk informant will be
interviewed. Black informants with high school and college education, like white informants with college education, will be selected
according to the judgment of the fieldworker, determined by the
history and social composition of the community and the availability
of such speakers for day-long interviews.[7]

Following that selection procedure, approximately 550 records in
rural and non-metropolitan communities will have been completed by
June 1975. To complete the survey in July and August, 112 interviews will be conducted in these urban communities: Atlanta,
Birmingham, Dallas, Houston, Jackson, Jacksonville, Little Rock,
Memphis, Miami, Mobile, Nashville, New Orleans, San Antonio, and
Tampa. In each of these places, four black and four white informants will be interviewed: two folk speakers over age 65, two
common (high-school educated) speakers between 45-65, two cultivated (college-educated) speakers between 20-45, and two teenagers.
With additional records already in hand from Atlanta, Chattanooga,
Knoxville, Shreveport, and several other urban centers, the LAGS
sample will certainly include more than 700 records when the fieldwork is completed.

The work sheets for the LAGS project in their basic form include
approximately 1100 items, and this instrument has been used in all
rural and non-metropolitan communities, as well as in those urban
places already investigated. In Knoxville and Chattanooga, for
example, it was impossible to represent the complicated urban populations without a significantly enlarged sample, even with seventeen interviews representing those two cities. To correct the
problem, we have decided to investigate the speech of the remaining
metropolitan areas of the territory with an urban supplement to the
basic work sheets. This has been developed through work done in
Chicago and by extensive exploratory research in Atlanta. Charles
E. Billiard has directed the Atlanta work and has organized the
urban work sheets. These 250 items will be added to the base form,
providing phonological contexts when urban dwellers are unable to
offer responses to rural lexical matters and initiating approaches
to the neglected general and special vocabularies of urban speech.

Two full time fieldworkers, Barbara J. Rutledge and Edward W.
Crist, have done most of the interviewing for the LAGS project
during the past three years. Their work has virtually completed the
regional sample for the states of Mississippi, Tennessee, and Texas,
and has supplemented the records for upper Florida and lower

26

Lee Pederson

Louisiana, where the research is also nearly completed. Since the
beginning of the project in 1968, Charles W. Foster has directed the
work in upper Alabama, where the work is now complete. In the
summer of 1974, Mary McCall spent three months in Arkansas, recording
thirty interviews, nearly three-fourths of the regional sample for
that state. Additional contributions have been made by Allyne Baird
and Robert Smith in lower Georgia and by Christine Unger in lower
Mississippi. The data collected through March 1975 clearly reflects
those contributions. There are now 510 completed field records of a
projected 700 in these states: Alabama (85 of 115), Arkansas (40
of 50), Florida (43 of 75), Georgia (99 of 125), Louisiana (40 of
65), Mississippi (72 of 80), Tennessee (99 of 115), and Texas (32 of
75).
    Although the LAGS project followed the methodology of other
American Atlas projects, fieldwork here is distinguished by the use
of the tape recorder for the preservation of the entire interview
and for the sole basis of all transcriptions that will be included
in the atlas. In the LAGS project, the taped record is the field
record and the transcriptions are designated as protocols. The
term protocol suggests three aspects of the document previously
identified by American linguistic geographers as the field record.
These scribal notes are 1) the first written draft of an event or
transaction, the tape-recorded interview, 2) a preliminary memorandum prepared to assist auditors of the tapes, and 3) the formal
account of the information included in the tapes. The first of
these aspects indicates that the entire corpus is limited to that
which is on tape and that the entire process of transcription is
limited to that which the transcriber can perceive on the tape--
nothing is manually transcribed in the field. The second aspect
indicates that the transcriptions are aimed at further, more nearly
comprehensive, analysis and that they are subject to correction.
The third aspect indicates that the LAGS methodology remains
squarely in the tradition of conventional linguistic geography and
that all departures from that tradition are accretive and supple-
mental--accretive in that additional information is provided and
supplemental in that a self-corrective capacity is recognized within
the project.[8]
    The transcription of a LAGS protocol requires 20-30 hours of work
by a trained phonetician who must resist the impulse to make a
phonetic transcript of the complete text, and, instead, concentrate
on the primary responsibilities. They include the evaluation of the
record as a legitimate contribution to the LAGS project; the composition of a text equal in all possible respects to the graphic field
records of earlier American Atlas projects; the notation of extensive marginalia that should be far richer in content than the
cursory notes of fieldworkers who operated without the aid of tape
recorders; and the indexing of conversational information on the tape,
indicating the reel and the approximate point on the tape where a
form occurs out of sequence.
    With the field record thus identified, the corpus of the LAGS project
is best represented by the number of hours of Southern speech recorded
on tape. That estimated sample will probably include between 3500
and 4000 hours of recorded speech. Plans are underway to make a

27

duplicate set of the field records to be used by interested students
of American English for additional study of the materials and for
the production of additional copies. As with every other American
Atlas project, all of the LAGS material is available at all times
for scholarly use.

The remaining work in the LAGS project includes three phases to
complete the protocols, the editing of the Atlas, and the description of the data. Since the format of the Atlas will be quite
different from any previous American Atlas project, it will be
possible to complete most of the editorial work during the composition of protocols. Instead of publishing results on maps or in list
manuscripts, the LAGS will be presented on micro cards and will
include all 700 protocols in that medium. A handbook will also be
prepared to provide the backgrounds of the project and a guide to
the use of the micro cards, including a complete index of words and
phrases elicited in the survey. The protocols will be published in
a double set: one set will duplicate the format of the protocols
in order to provide a convenient way to study individual idiolects;
the second set will be arranged according to protocol pagination in
order to provide a convenient way to study specific items across the
entire Gulf-states territory.

If funds are available, typescripts of complete interviews will
also be undertaken, but the number of these and the time it would
take to produce such material cannot be sensibly estimated at this
time. As with all other facets of this program, participants will
do the best they can and settle for that.

The descriptive volumes can be projected with much greater assurance because precedents are available in the classic studies of
Kurath, McDavid, and Atwood. Parallel studies will certainly be
derived from the LAGS material, although the order of presentation
will be reversed: phonology will be described before morphology,
and both of these will precede the description of the vocabulary.

2. Goals and Implications of the LAGS Project. From the outset,
four interrelated goals have been pursued in the study of Southern
speech: 1) to provide an inventory of the dominant and recessive
patterns of usage in the eight-state region, 2) to describe these
varieties of Southern speech in a global fashion, 3) to offer an
abstract of regional phonology, grammar, and lexicon, and 4) to
identify areas of linguistic complexity that will require additional
and more intensive study.

The notion of inventorial research underlies the aims and accom-
plishments of all useful work in traditional linguistic geography,
from the pioneer efforts in Europe during the past century to the
explorations currently underway there, as well as in Asia and
North America. A century of dialect research has demonstrated that
the ranges of linguistic variation must be determined before a few
particulars can be weighed and balanced. A realistic approach to
any set of sociolinguistic problems requires a frame of reference,
a baseline, for the measurement and evaluation of selected features.
Without such work, heuristic observations lack authority and run
the risk of errors, from naiveté to downright absurdity.[9] To avoid
that, the inventory of Southern speech habits proceeded within the
framework of earlier research in the region and expanded that
context with evidence gathered in free conversation and recorded in

full on magnetic tape (providing a foundation for further research).
The notion of global descriptions in conventional dialectology
was offered at SAMLA-ADS in 1970.[10] That approach suggests the
necessity of establishing linguistic contexts for the sensible
articulation of data. These include the contrastive sets that com-
prise the phonemic system, the morphological structures that are
fundamental to the grammatical system, and the general and special
vocabularies that outline the regional lexicon. This aim reaffirms
the inventorial requisite and, when realized, provides the substance of the abstract. Balanced coverage of all components of
language is necessary for both understanding the structures of
idiolects and evaluating the significance of selected isolates,
those autonomous linguistic variables that have become the central
preoccupation of current sociolinguistic research.

No description, of course, can provide an exhaustive analysis of
the full range of sociolinguistic problems or can cover all the
variables within the idiolects of an eight-state region. Instead,
the aim in the LAGS project is to compose an abstract, an outline
that will indicate uniformity and diversity in regional and social
patterns. These points of similarity and difference make possible
sustained discussion of the idiolects, the speech of particular
human beings, everywhere recognized as individual speakers and
nowhere represented as anonymous members of a statistical mass.
The incidence of a given vocabulary item can be described in every
instance in both the phonological and morphological terms of the
idiolects in which it occurs, and characteristics of these idiolects
can be correlated in a baseline pattern of preliminary indices for
the continued study of Southern speech.

A regional dialect survey cannot offer descriptions of all sub-
cultural varieties of speech or of all subregional patterns. As an
exploratory program, however, the LAGS project aims to identify
areas of sociolinguistic complexity suitable for further study.
Problems of bilingualism in Florida, Louisiana, and Texas, the composition of delta speech communities on both sides of the Mississippi River, with a somewhat comparable situation on the Sabine in
both Texas and Louisiana, and the reflexes of intraregional migration offer challenges to all students of American English. As the
LAGS project outlines the principal dialect areas of the region,
identifies the ranges of the major focal areas, and analyzes the
sociolinguistic content of its data, both field and descriptive
procedures will be evaluated in terms of efficacy, sensitivity, and
reliability. These aspects of the work reflect the essence of
baseline research and project implications that are not always
appreciated by students of linguistic variation in the United
States. Every phase of every research project offers a test of
preliminary, field, or descriptive procedures, and the evaluation
of these experiences is central to the development of a viable
theory of general dialectology.

NOTES

*The earlier SAMLA-ADS version of this paper was called "The Linguistic Atlas of the Gulf States: Preliminary Considerations." Read at the SAMLA-ADS Meeting, Jacksonville, Florida, November, 1968.

[1]The major contributors to this project have been the National Endowment for the Humanities and Emory University. Seed funds were provided earlier by ACLS, NCTE, the Ford Foundation, the Rome (Georgia) City School System: Linguistic Research and Demonstration Center, and the Southeastern Education Laboratory. In addition to the continuing efforts of the associate directors, Charles E. Billiard and Charles W. Foster, and the consultant director, Raven I. McDavid, Jr., substantial support came from Harold B. Allen, Allyne Baird, Frederic G. Cassidy, Edward W. Crist, Alva L. Davis, Louise A. DeVere, Howard G. Dunlap, Joan H. Hall, Deborah Hunter, Hans Kurath, Charles T. Lester, Anne Malone, Mary McCall, James B. McMillan, Ronald Midkiff, Margaret Moran, Barbara Respess, A. Hood Roberts, Grace S. Rueter, Barbara Rutledge, William Smith, Rudolph Troike, Christine Unger, William R. Van Riper, W. Gene Watson, Juanita V. Williamson, and Gordon R. Wood.

[2]Lee Pederson, "Southern Speech and the LAGS Project," Orbis, 20 (1971), 79-89; "The Linguistic Atlas of the Gulf States: An Interim Report (1972)," American Speech, 44 (1969), 279-86; "The Linguistic Atlas of the Gulf States: Interim Report Two," American Speech (in press). Lee Pederson, Raven I. McDavid, Jr., Charles W. Foster, and Charles E. Billiard, eds., A Manual for Dialect Research in the Southern States (Atlanta: Georgia State University, 1972); 2nd ed. (University: University of Alabama Press, 1974). Lee Pederson, "Black Speech, White Speech, and the Al Smith Syndrome," Studies in Linguistics in Honor of Raven I. McDavid, Jr., ed. Lawrence M. Davis (University: University of Alabama Press, 1972), 123-34; "Dialect Patterns in Rural Northern Georgia," Lexicography and Dialect Geography: Festgabe für Hans Kurath, eds., Harald Scholler and John Reidy (Wiesbaden: West German Federal Republic: Franz Steiner Verlag, 1973), 195-201; "Tape/Text and Analogues," American Speech (in press).

[3]See Hans Kurath, Studies in Area Linguistics (Bloomington: Indiana University Press, 1972), especially "From Sampling to Publication," 1-23.

[4]A convenient summary of this is Lee Pederson, "An Introduction to the LAGS Project," Manual (1972/74), 1-31.

[5]Supplemental records have been added during the course of the fieldwork to provide full and even coverage for the entire state of Arkansas and for much of east Georgia.

[6]For maps and community identities, see Manual (1972/74), 229-40.

30

[7]Findings in the Dialect Survey of Rural Georgia have demonstrated the necessity of carefully examining black speech in any survey of American English in the Southern states; see Pederson (1972) and those title notes in Pederson (1971). Systematic sampling of black speech, however, must also be realistic and practical, recognizing that where the native black population is limited to the very young (because of recent in-migration) it is wasteful to attempt matching black and white speakers and that in most rural communities (given the reality of rigorous segregation) it is usually impossible to find native black informants over age 65 with much formal education, Manual (1972/74), 23-4.

[8]See "Tape/Text and Analogues" for implications and responsibilities inherent to this approach.

[9]Some of the larger outrages have been reviewed by Raven I. McDavid, Jr., "Sense and Nonsense about American Dialects," PMLA, 81 (1966), 7-17; and by Lawrence M. Davis, "Social Dialectology in America: A Critical Survey," Journal of English Linguistics, 4 (1970), 46-56.

[10]Lee Pederson, "Structural Imperatives in Dialect Study," a paper read at the SAMLA-ADS section Washington, D.C., November 1970. This is revised and restricted to phonological considerations in the present volume under the title "Structural Description in Linguistic Geography."

A DIALECT SURVEY OF RURAL GEORGIA: THE PROGRESS*

Grace S. Rueter

The Dialect Survey of Rural Georgia is nearing completion. The field records are in, phonological interpretations for Northern, Middle, and Southeastern Georgia are finished or nearly finished, and the final report has been planned. The Georgia Survey, directed by Lee Pederson of Emory University in collaboration with Howard Dunlap, Joan H. Hall, and Grace S. Rueter, is providing information about the speech of older black and white natives of rural communities in all parts of the state.

The Georgia Survey was begun in 1968 and described by Pederson in the prospectus as follows:

A realistic program for any academic discipline concerned with the collection, analysis, integration, and description of data requires immediate involvement with that subject matter. A lecture course in descriptive linguistics or dialectology is no less superficial and inadequate than a similar offering in plant systematics or animal ecology. This dialect survey of rural Georgia is designed to provide students at Emory University with an opportunity to do linguistic fieldwork, and with it to gain first-hand experience with the methods of descriptive linguistics. In the present schedule, advanced undergraduates and graduate students will do a specified number of interviews with native rural Georgians over age 65. Descriptive and contrastive analyses of the data collected in those interviews will be reported in course papers, but the material should also lend itself to broader and more significant interpretations.

Concentrated studies of regional and social dialects are badly needed right now because several trends in recent American social history have had a profound effect upon the varieties of English spoken in the United States, and few of the results have been systematically investigated. Mass education, technological advancement, and changing economic priorities have accelerated urbanization and social reformation with improved racial interaction, professional specialization, and social, as well as geographic mobility. These phenomena have affected the regional and social dialects of American English by blurring previously sharp regional boundaries, depleting rural populations and blending formerly discrete social groups in a steadily growing urbanized working class. Nowhere in the United States is this dialectal problem more complicated than in the Urban South where Northern-based

33

industry has had its effect on the entire speech community and where rural inmigration has saturated the lower strata of the population.

To understand the composition of Atlanta speech it will, no doubt, be necessary to evaluate the influences of the insinuative Northern dialects, but population statistics recommend the speech of rural Georgia should be considered first. More than half of the newcomers to Metropolitan Atlanta between 1955 and 1960 arrived from smaller communities, from places other than the Standard Metropolitan Statistical Areas of the United States, and 51,445 of a total of 142,000 came to Metropolitan Atlanta from other parts of Georgia. Several other factors indicate the importance of an immediate investigation of Georgia's rural dialects. First, regional dialect boundaries are more satisfactorily established where the social composition of the communities is less complicated. Furthermore, many rural communities in Georgia are vanishing with their oldest generation and with them disappear many interesting varieties of folk speech. Finally, because there are fewer social variables in rural areas to separate the economically deprived Negro and White than are found in urban centers, valuable information should be available in these isolated communities for measuring the intrinsic distinctiveness of Negro and White speech.

With these considerations in mind, a dialect survey of rural Georgia has been planned to investigate selected features of the vocabulary, grammar, and pronunciation of native Georgians in a network of communities with populations under 2,500 in 30-mile grid squares across the state. This investigation has three immediate aims: 1) to enlarge and strengthen present knowledge of the regional dialect boundaries in Georgia, 2) to make more nearly precise statements about the distinctiveness of Negro and White speech within the context of regional dialects, and 3) to define some of the characteristics of old-fashioned rural speech by comparing the language of cultivated and uncultivated Negroes and Whites.

Since the design of this research project reflects the biases of taxonomic, rather than quantitative, social dialectology, interpretations here must be non-mathematical. This is, essentially, an investigation in area linguistics, and although the pairings of Negroes and Whites of comparable cultivation is intended to provide contrastive data for descriptive sociolinguistics, references to the evaluation of that information are to be taken as non-arithmetic estimations or appraisals. Such a distinction must be observed at the outset because the survey will be based on a judgment, rather than a probability, sample, so its findings will not be amenable to statistical analysis. This priority is necessary because a descriptive inventory of selected characteristics is interesting in its own right, as well as being a requisite for any significant, valid and reliable quantitative analysis of regional and social dialects.[1]

The Survey was carried out within that framework. Target communities were selected within the system of 30-mile grids, with selection beginning in the northwestern corner of the state and proceeding eastward. The community of Ringgold was chosen first, because it was the northwesternmost biracial community in Georgia, and all subsequent choices were made in relation to Ringgold. A more central and southern community was selected in the next grid square to the east; then a more northern community was sought in the grid square which followed. When this pattern was interrupted by the absence of any community, the presence of a city, or the presence of an all white community, the nearest appropriate community was designated.

Items in the questionnaire were drawn from several sources.[2] The format was essentially that of the checklist first developed for use in a regional survey by A. L. Davis,[3] and additional items, including grammatical and morphological forms, were taken from Frederic G. Cassidy's "A Method For Collecting Dialect."[4] The most clearly experimental section of the questionnaire was the phonological sequence. In incorporating a phonological component, and recording interviews on tape, the Georgia Survey went one step beyond Atwood's survey in Texas,[5] combining the use of a checklist with Atlas methods. This combination had been used successfully in small geographical areas,[6] but had never before been applied in a highly complicated regional dialect area.

Several kinds of questions were used to elicit responses in the Survey. For lexical information, questions such as the following were used:

What do you call the shelf over a fireplace?

If a country person goes to town, what do the city people call him behind his back?

What are some different things made out of cornmeal in the kitchen? How are they made?

In designing the lexical section of the questionnaire, an effort was made to tape different aspects of rural Southern culture as well as to include conventional dialect markers. A set of questions was incorporated, for example, which elicited terms of abuse for black people, white people, city people, and country people. Given the social diversity of the informants from whom these terms were elicited, this information should provide interesting insights into social relations, both within and across black-white and urban-rural boundaries. Conventional markers which were used reflect lexical categories described by Atwood, including items relating to the weather, the landscape, goods and chattels, time, the premises, various fauna, edibles, family matters, social and daily life, and other people.[7]

In the morphological section of the questionnaire, the principal parts of strong verbs were elicited by questions which conform to a single pattern. The pattern was easily established with the informants, and it usually elicited the forms rapidly and painlessly:

If we were talking about ringing a bell (riding a horse, climbing a tree, etc.), you might ask, "Has that bell (horse, tree, etc.) ever been ____?" And I might answer, "Yes, yesterday someone ____ the bell (horse, tree, etc.)."[8]

In the phonological section of the questionnaire, where the purpose
was to elicit the same set of words from each informant with comparable
suprasegmentals, the questions were most often of the fill-in-the-
blank sort, and were phrased so as to hold misunderstandings to a
minimum. Examples are:
    You light a match to start a _____.
    Robins, bluejays, and sparrows are_____.
    A wagon has four _____.[9]
The informants were also asked to supply names for parts of the body
and several lists: numbers from one to twenty, days of the week, and
months of the year. Free conversation and extensive biographical
information about the informants were also provided for in the questionnaire. Each interview lasted about an hour and a half and was recorded
in its entirety on tape for subsequent phonetic transcription.

Although the fieldwork went remarkably smoothly, some interesting
problems arose and have been reported in "Biracial Dialectology: Six
Years Into the Georgia Survey."[10] One problem involved finding in
every community four older informants who met the interlocking criteria
of racial membership and level of education. In some communities it
was possible to interview, in accord with the Georgia Survey's plan,
one better educated white, one lesser educated white, one better educated black, and one lesser educated black. In others, however,
informants of all four types were simply not available. When this was
the case, the criteria had to be relaxed somewhat:
    Shortly after the field work began in 1968, it became
    apparent that rapid shifts in population during the
    preceding eight years significantly altered the racial
    distribution in many communities. The black population
    in some north Georgia communities and the white population
    in some south Georgia communities were so small that it
    was impossible to locate appropriate subjects. In all of
    those places, other villages were sought within the county
    or, if necessary, elsewhere in the grid. In one north
    Georgia grid it was necessary to interview three whites
    and only one black, and in one south Georgia grid the
    situation was reversed. A more serious problem of selec-
    tion in middle and south Georgia reflected the system of
    racial segregation and its impact upon these rural communi-
    ties. It was usually impossible to locate black informants
    over age 65 with more than a few years of formal education,
    and virtually all of those better educated blacks who partici-
    pated in the survey were recently retired teachers from
    thoroughly segregated schools. Elsewhere, the criterion of
    literacy was used to distinguish between better and lesser
    educated informants.
By 1973, all of the projected interviews had been completed. To date
(1975), 100 taped records from North Georgia, 68 from Middle Georgia,
and 64 from South Georgia have been transcribed by Pederson, Rueter, and
Hall with the finely graded system used by Atlas workers; only the 75
records from Southwest Georgia remain to be transcribed. Interpretations of phonic data from Northern, Middle, and Southeast Georgia explore phonological systems and regional and social

variation in the speech of the state. Three essays by Lee Pederson which raise questions about sampling procedures, sociolinguistic distribution, and phonological description, have been summarized in "The Linguistic Atlas of the Gulf States: An Interim Report."[11]

1. Concerning regional dialect boundaries: With social caste distinction (black and white) recognized as a constant factor in the linguistic geography of north Georgia, dialect boundaries must be multiple because black speech and white speech have distinctly different patterns of regional distribution. Black folk speech extends the Upcountry Lower Southern dialect northward into the mountains where South Midland forms prevail among whites, and white folk speech extends the South Midland dialect into the plantation area where Upcountry Lower Southern forms prevail among all black and all better educated white speakers.[12]

2. Concerning the uniqueness of black folk speech: Although black speech differed from white speech in all 25 communities on the basis of both statistical incidence and comprehensive patterning of recessive forms, no variety of black speech can be characterized here as either uniform or exclusive in terms of its segmental units. The uniqueness of black folk speech seems to rest in the pivotal position it occupies in the rural community, sharing phonological features with cultivated blacks and whites, grammatical features with white folk speakers, and lexical forms with all members of both castes.[13]

3. Concerning structural description of Southern speech: With full phonic records of all interviews available on tape, descriptions of regional and social dialects can be much more nearly complete than those based exclusively on field notes, but any such description must outline the structure of the dialects in a coherent way. This requires an analysis of extrasegmental phonemes (to account for features like vowel nasality and long consonants), an articulation of phonological rules (to account for differences in the surface structure like devoiced medial and final stops, and in spigot-spiket and salad-sallit), and a morphological statement (to account for such aberrant patterns as N + V + er - V + N + er, in woodpecker-peckerwood and grasshopper-hoppergrass), all of which should precede efforts in word geography.[14]

Two dissertations currently nearing completion at Emory University interpret Georgia Survey records from Southeast and Middle Georgia, Joan H. Hall's "Regional and Social Dialects of Rural Southeast Georgia" and my "Vowel Nasality in Rural Middle Georgia." Hall's work includes an extensive description of the pronunciation of vowel and consonant phonemes in Southeast Georgia and the incidence of the phonemes in forms traditionally used as regional and social markers. The phonological study is followed by an analysis of regional and social distributions of forms. Regarding regional dialects, Hall is finding that there are no striking patterns of phonological features which would indicate that Savannah serves as a focal area for rural speech with particular features being concentrated near there and occurring less and less frequently in communities progressively further south and west.

Instead, there seems to be a dialect boundary running north and south, differentiating coastal communities from inland communities. This line corresponds roughly to the boundary between the coastal plantation culture and the pine barrens subsistence-farming culture. Regarding social dialects, Hall is finding that the Southeast Georgia data do not recommend positing a "black English" for this area. In the Southeast Georgia data there are a few features which occur only in the speech of black informants, or only in the speech of whites, but they have very limited distribution. Most features occur in the speech of blacks and whites. While the incidence of some features varies with the race of the informant, even if all the features whose incidence is very high in black speech are taken together, no one black dialect emerges, for individual speakers have different numbers and combinations of those features. On the basis of these facts, Hall is thinking of proposing for Southeast Georgia not a "black dialect" on the one hand and a "white" or"standard" dialect on the other, but rather several social dialects, used by both black and white speakers, which have different numbers of specified features, e.g., social dialect X with a large number of features, social dialect Y with fewer of these features, and social dialect Z with still fewer or no instances of the features. Hall suggests that given this framework, even if it is true that dialect X is spoken wholly or largely by blacks and dialect Z wholly or largely by whites, the data will be accomodated.

My work with vowel nasality[15] is based on transcriptions of the 68 tapes from Middle Georgia. As was reported to the American Dialect Society,[16] at the time the Middle Georgia tapes were transcribed, no plans had been formulated for subsequent treatments of the data, and thus every effort was made to record in the transcriptions all possible phonetic detail. Had the transcriptions not recorded so much detail, nasality would probably have been overlooked, as it was of no interest to the transcriber at the time. Since Atlas procedures were followed, however, nasality--along with length, labialization, raising and lowering, fronting and backing, and a host of other phonetic minutiae--was recorded and was therefore available for analysis when subsequently it became apparent that nasality was worth examining.[17] It was in the course of an initial phonemic study of the Middle Georgia data that vowel nasality revealed itself to be an interesting phenomenon. Vowel nasality was simply not amenable to conventional phonemic analysis. Some of the problems encountered again and again are, perhaps, best described by means of examples from the speech of one of the Middle Georgia informants, a native of the community of Deepstep in Washington County, who was in many ways typical of the black folk informants of Middle Georgia. He had been born and reared in his rural community and had lived and worked there all his life. When he was a child, he had attended the local school for Negroes for a few years. He told me that he didn't read or write much, but that he could figure, and when called on to do so, he could "scratch" a little. He had spent his life doing manual labor, mostly farm work. He had also worked at the local saw mill, as he put it, "turning logs and toting lumber." He was 66 years old at the time of the interview. He was alert and interested, and evidently enjoyed himself.

Examination of the vowels in this informant's speech revealed frequent instances of nasality in responses such as cents [sɛ̃nt], shrimp [srĭ̃ə̃mp],and shrink [srĭ̃ɪŋk]. In a phonemic interpretation, nasality here must be viewed as a modification of the vowel in anticipation of a nasal consonant, so that the nasal vowel [ɛ̃] of cents would be a positionally restricted allophone of the vowel phoneme /ɛ/, the nasal vowel [ĭ̃ə̃] in shrimp would be a positionally restricted allophone of the vowel phoneme /ɪ/, and so on. Examination of the consonants revealed the occasional absence of nasal consonant segments from responses that might reasonably have been expected to have them, and the presence, instead, of nasality of the vowel. This was the case in since [sĭ̃ət], for example. In such pronunciations, nasality appears to be an allophone of the nasal consonant phoneme /n/. Obviously, this interpretation conflicts with the interpretation of nasal vowels as positionally restricted modifications of vowel phonemes. Compounding the problem was the fact that in items such as since [sĭ̃ət], nasality appeared to be an allophone of /n/, but in other utterances it appeared to belong to other consonant phonemes. In spring [sprɛ̃ɪ], for example, nasality seems to be an allophone of the phoneme /ŋ/; in thumb [t'ʌ̃ẓə], an allophone of the phomene /m/. Thus vowel nasality, in a given instance, might have been interpreted phonemically in any of at least four ways: 1) as a positionally restricted modification of an allophone of any of the vowel phonemes; 2) as an allophone of the consonant phoneme /n/; 3) as an allophone of the consonant phoneme /m/, and 4) as an allophone of the consonant phoneme /ŋ/. Although it might well be possible to devise a phonemic interpretation of vowel nasality using a generative approach with optional rules, the conventional phonemic framework with which the dialect investigator is familiar does not seem to be able to handle the nasals.

One of the problems here is a phenomenon which involves not only the nasals, but which seems to cut across the resonant system. This is redundancy. Redundancy in the nasals is illustrated by a few additions to the data discussed above. Two pronunciations of cents and the pronunciation of since show three actualizations of the phoneme /n/ with identical following segments. In one pronunciation of cents, [sɛnɫ, the phoneme /n/ is actualized as segmental [n]; in the pronunciation of since [sĭ̃əɫ, it is actualized as nasality of the vowel; in the other pronunciation of cents [sɛ̃nɫ, both segmental [n] and nasality of the vowel are present. In the latter case, one of these features is redundant, since either feature alone can signal the presence of the phoneme /n/. Redundancy in the actualization of the phoneme /m/ is illustrated in the pronunciation of gum [gʌ̃əm]. This pronunciation includes the segment [m], which can actualize the phoneme /m/, as in rum [rʌ̣əm]; it also includes vowel nasality, which can also actualize the phoneme /m/, as in thumb [t'ʌ̃ẓə]. Redundancy in the actualization of the phoneme /ŋ/ is illustrated in the pronunciation of rung [rʌ̃ʌ̄əŋ]. This pronunciation includes the segment [ŋ], which can actualize the phoneme /ŋ/, as in string [strɛɪŋ]and it also includes vowel nasality, which can also actualize the phoneme /ŋ/, as in spring [sprɛ̃ɫ. Thus all three nasal consonant phonemes may be actualized by a segmental nasal phone, by nasality of the vowel, or by both the segment and the vowel nasality; and in the latter case, one of these features is redundant.

Redundancy elsewhere in the resonant system is illustrated with examples of pronunciations of /r/ and /l/. Examples of redundancy in pronunciations of /r/ are taken from the speech of a 61 year-old white informant, a native of Laurens County In his pronunciation of car [kʻɑˑɚ], historical /r/ is actualized by the retroflexed segment [ɚ]; in his pronunciation of arm [ɑˑm], the /r/ is actualized in the low back vowel [ɑ]; in his pronunciation of garden [gɑˑɚdn], the /r/ is actualized by both the retroflexed segment and the low back vowel. In the latter pronunciation, one is redundant. Examples for /l/ come from the speech of an 85-year-old black informant, a native of Mountain Hill. In this informant's pronunciation of cloud [klaʔʊd], the phoneme /l/ is actualized by the lateral consonant; in twelve [tweɰv], the phoneme /l/ is actualized by a high back unrounded vowel [ɰ]; in elbow [ɛʊboˇˑʊ], the phoneme /l/ is actualized by both the vowel and the consonant. Again, in the latter case, redundancy is occurring.

A structural solution to descriptive problems raised by vowel nasality in Middle Georgia is considered in the dissertation and the nasal data are analyzed in terms of that solution. On the basis of the analysis several observations regarding the distribution of vowel nasality in its various functions are made. While no clear patterns of regional distribution have been observed in the piedmont of Middle Georgia, the coastal region, or the transition area between them, vowel nasality does appear to be socially distributed. Examination of vowel nasality in the speech of better educated white speakers, lesser educated white speakers, and black folk speakers shows the speech of the black informants to have a much higher instance of nasality than the speech of either white group. Since vowel nasality occurs in a number of West African languages,[18] it is possible that the high instance of nasality in the speech of the Middle Georgia blacks is in some sense a survival from the African past. Between the two white groups, no significant differences in the instance of nasality were observed in any phonological environment except one. This environment occurs in words like can't, shrimp, and ankle which usually have nasal consonants followed by voiceless stops homorganic with those consonants. The environment is defined by the absence of the usual consonant segment after the nasal vowel and the presence of only the homorganic voiceless stop. In this environment, the instance of nasality among the better educated whites was substantially greater than among the lesser educated whites and approached the instance of nasality recorded for the black informants.

Explanations of why this occurs in the speech of the better educated whites, and why it occurs in this environment, are to be sought in the social history of the South which recounts a great deal of contact between blacks and better educated whites. From the early years of settlement blacks have been an integral part of the households of whites of the better classes, and this is still the case among many older Middle Georgians interviewed in the course of the Georgia Survey. Thus it should not be surprising to find points of convergence in Middle Georgia between

the speech of the black folk informants and the speech of the better
educated white informants, points of convergence not shared with
the lesser educated whites, with whom there has been little contact. A possible explanation of why convergence should occur at
one point in the nasal system rather than another is also to be
sought in social history. Because of the stigma traditionally
associated with black culture, one would expect the speech of
the better educated whites to converge with the speech of the
blacks at points where the convergence would not be readily apparent.
Vowel nasality in the environment under discussion might well be
such a point. Malecot, working with acoustic phonetics, has
reported that vowel nasality in this environment is a usual feature
of American English.[19]

As an experimental project, the Georgia Survey is nearing completion. The fieldwork is finished, the initial phonological work is
drawing to a conclusion, and the final report will soon be written.
With phonology in all parts of Georgia reviewed, the report will
interpret morphological and lexical material on a state-wide
basis with phonological descriptions of all forms. A mapping
presentation will be used with grid coordinates identifying the
communities and with positions within each grid identifying the
social types. On these maps, the incidence of forms among the 312
informants in the 78 communities will be indicated.[20] With the
completion of the final report, the immediate aims of the Georgia
Survey will have been met, but the 312 tapes of over 500 hours of
native speech remain intact and are available for further study.

NOTES

*Read at the SAMLA linguistics section, Jacksonville, Florida,
November, 1968.

[1]Lee Pederson, "The Plan For a Dialect Survey of Rural Georgia,"
Orbis (in press).

[2]All the items are listed in Lee Pederson, Howard Dunlap, and
Grace Rueter, "Questionnaire for a Dialect Survey of Rural Georgia,"
Orbis (in press).

[3]A. L. Davis, "A Word Atlas of the Great Lakes Region." University of Michigan Dissertation 1948. For a brief description of
the background of Davis' checklist and his debt to Marckwardt and
McDavid, see Pederson's review of Gordon R. Wood's Vocabulary
Change in Language 49, 184-87.

[4]Frederic G. Cassidy, "A Method For Collecting Dialect," Publication of the American Dialect Society No. 20, 1953.

[5]E. Bagby Atwood, The Regional Vocabulary of Texas (Austin:
University of Texas Press, 1962).

[6]Howard G. Dunlap, "Social Aspects of a Verb Form: Native Atlanta Fifth-Grade Speech, the Present Tense of BE," PADS (in press); Lee Pederson "Middleclass Negro Speech in Minneapolis," Orbis, 16(1967), 347-53.

[7]Atwood, Chapter 2.

[8]The verbs elicited by this pattern, in addition to ring, ride, and climb are buy, eat, drink, do, drag, rise, dive, and grow. Forms of do and be and modals, including negatives, were elicited similarly.

[9]The items elicited by such questions were: ten cents, since, merry, hot dog, Mary, Washington, married, hoarse, write, ride, horse, roots, fire, soot, cow, bulk, father and mother, birds, white, girl, wheels, boy, worms, poor, purse, Billy, wolf, field, garden, Thanksgiving, concrete, Tennessee, help, narrow, can't, car, aunt, nests, desks, fists, mosquito, clouds, house, varmint, shrimp, shrink, point, orange, garage, measure, television, lawyer, judge, flour, wire, church, onions, new, itch, stingy, hour, our, book, sleep, slaves, rabbit, rifle, rice, watch, wasps, spring, water, wash, rinse, brush, temperature.

[10]Lee Pederson, Grace Rueter, and Joan Hall, "Biracial Dialectology: Six Years Into the Georgia Survey," Journal of English Linguistics (in press).

[11]Lee Pederson, "The Linguistic Atlas of the Gulf States: An Interim Report," American Speech, 44 (1969), 279-86.

[12]Lee Pederson, "Dialect Patterns in Rural Northern Georgia" in Lexicography and Dialect Geography: Festgabe für Hans Kurath, H. Scholler and J. Reidy, eds. (Wiesbaden, West Germany: Franz Steiner Verlag, 1973), 195-207.

[13]Lee Pederson, "Black Speech, White Speech, and the Al Smith Syndrome" in Studies in Linguistics in Honor of Raven I. McDavid, Jr., L. M. Davis, ed. (University: University of Alabama Press, 1972), 123-34.

[14]Lee Pederson, "Obstruent Consonants in Rural Northern Georgia" (in press).

[15]Descriptive problems associated with vowel nasality have been discussed by James B. McMillan in "Vowel Nasality as a Sandhi Form of the Morphemes -nt and -ing in Southern American," American Speech, 14 (April, 1939), 120-23.

[16]Grace S. Rueter, "Vowel Nasality in Rural Middle Georgia," a paper read to the American Dialect Society, New York, 1974.

[17]Transcriptional procedures are described in Hans Kurath, Handbook of the Linguistic Geography of New England (Providence: Brown University, 1939), Chapter IV.

Grace S. Rueter

[18]Peter Ladefoged, A Phonetic Study of West African Languages. West African Monograph Series, No. 1 (Cambridge, England: University Press, 1964).

[19]Andre Malecot, "Vowel Nasality as a Distinctive Feature of American English," Language, 36 (1960), 222.

[20]Pederson, Rueter, and Hall.

DARE IN LOUISIANA*

August Rubrecht

    Those who travel between the South and the North in this country come
to expect that they will be served grits for breakfast in small cafes
in Mississippi and hash browns in small cafes in Missouri. They learn
that pork sausage is usually formed into patties like miniature hamburgers in Arkansas and packed in skins like little hot dogs in
Wisconsin. They notice that large houses on prosperous plantations
in Georgia commonly have rambling floor plans and columned verandahs
and that large houses on prosperous farms in Iowa usually have blocky
floor plans and simple doorsteps. Such differences blend so smoothly
into the traveler's sense of changing scene that it sometimes takes a
conscious effort to realize that they cannot really be classified,
along with seashores and live oaks, hillsides and hemlocks, as mere
scenery. Rather, they are manifestations of cultural patterns,
closer kin to dialect differences than to topographical ones. Those
of us who served as fieldworkers for DARE were encouraged to note
such features and mention them in our brief descriptions of the
character of communities. Looking back on my year of fieldwork,
especially the months spent in the 18 Louisiana communities shown in
Figure 1, my chief regret is that it did not occur to me until after
the year was over that it might be possible to map cultural features
in the same way that linguistic features are mapped in dialect study.
Because of this lack of foresight, what I present here is not conclusion but hypothesis, not the result of a study but the idea for one.
    The hypothesis is nothing more than a statement of what dialect
researchers have long held as a working assumption--that dialect
differences are related to other cultural differences. The concern
with settlement history in virtually every study of American dialects
is a reflection of this assumption, as is the attention paid to the
age and social level of informants. But as in the case of scenery,
it can be interesting and profitable to bring to our conscious
attention certain details in our working assumptions. Louisiana
is especially suitable for illustrating such details for dialectologists because a cultural and dialectal sub-region lies almost
entirely within the borders of the state. It consists of the territory which was already comparatively thickly settled by French
speaking people when the United States acquired Louisiana in 1803.
The geographical extent of this region has been defined as a tri-
angle with its apex near the junction of the Red and Mississippi
Rivers and its base along the Louisiana gulf coast, as illustrated
in Figure 2.[1] Realizing that the boundary is not intended to be
anything but approximate, let us accept it for the present and call

45

Figure 1. Communities studied for DARE. Reproduced from August Weston Rubrecht, "Regional Phonological Variants in Louisiana Speech," Dissertation, University of Florida, Gainesville, 1971, p. 58.

Figure 2. French Louisiana roughly outlined.

the area "French Louisiana." The rest of the state, which is linguistically and culturally similar to adjacent parts of Texas, Arkansas, and Mississippi, we can call "Anglo Louisiana."

Our hypothesis leads us to expect that French Louisiana will be set off by both linguistic and cultural features which exhibit the same geographic spread. Our expectation is dramatically fulfilled. The DARE communities are too far apart for us to ascertain boundaries with precision, but they do allow us to see that French and Anglo Louisiana are distinguished by several dialectal features. Figure 3 shows the geographical limits of 12 phonological features that show clear regional variation. The information for these isophones was abstracted from the tape recordings made for DARE. Notice that a bundle of 5 to 7 isophones traces a path along the border communities of Cameron, DeQuincy, LeCompte, St. Francisville, Clinton, and New Orleans, along with Hammond, which is not very close to the border, but is the closest we have in the eastern part of that block of land east of the Mississippi, known as the Florida Parishes. Even though we must not put too much faith in the exact placement of these lines, their general position is so close to our tentative boundary between the regions that they confirm both our expectation of dialect differences and our preliminary borrowed estimate of the boundary.

A more precise idea of the dialect boundary can be gained from E. Bagby Atwood's study of Texas vocabulary.² His investigations extended far enough into Louisiana to show the western part of the line between French and Anglo Louisiana. Figure 4 compares a bundle of 6 to 7 isoglosses from his study to Smith and Hitt's rough estimate. A consideration both of Atwood's dense sampling and of my own impressions during the six months I worked in Louisiana leads me to believe that this isogloss bundle follows pretty closely the western part of the boundary of French Louisiana.

So far we have looked at particular information on dialect characteristics but have not dealt with specific cultural ones. Our next step in comparing the two is to find a cultural or social feature characteristic of one region or the other and find out what its geographical extent is. Such a feature is easy to find. Religious preferences are rather sharply divided in Louisiana: most of those who carry on the French cultural tradition are Catholic and most in the Anglo tradition are Protestant. Figure 5, showing the regional distribution of Catholics and Protestants, illustrates how well-defined the boundary between the regions is. It is especially interesting to note how well the western part of this religious boundary corresponds to Atwood's isogloss bundle in Figure 4.

Another cultural feature often used as an index to these regions is the kind of coffee preferred; a related consideration is the way it is served. The coffee characteristic of French Louisiana is made from beans roasted considerably darker than the coffee most Americans are familair with; it is brewed very strong by dripping hot water slowly through the grounds in a small drip pot, and it is served in demitasse cups. The coffee of Anglo Louisiana is typically the same kind as in most of the rest of the country and is served in the same way. The round dots in Figure 6 show the communities where DARE informants served coffee in demitasse cups; the squares show where DARE informants served dark-roast coffee. In the other communities they either served what the informants in LeCompte called

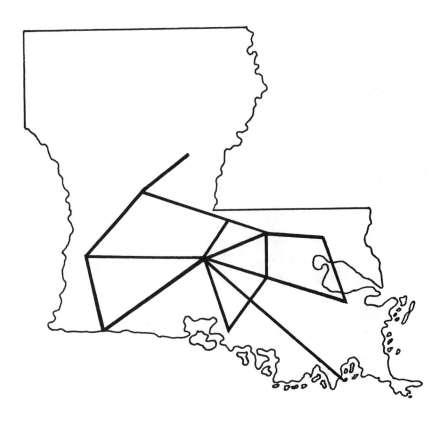

Figure 3. Boundaries of 12 phonological features that show significant regional variation in Louisiana.

Figure 4. Boundaries compared. Dotted line--French Louisiana roughly outlined. Heavy line--Isogloss bundle showing 6-7 vocabulary differences, after Atwood, p. 97.

August Rubrecht

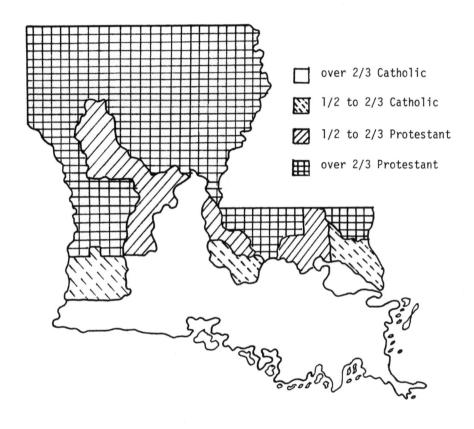

Figure 5. Ratio of Catholics to Protestants. Adapted from Smith and Hitt, p. 136.

51

"Yankee coffee" or some other beverage. The question marks at DeQuincy
and Hammond mean I cannot recall the coffee there, illustrating why I
am distressed that I did not think to begin mapping such features at
the time. Even with the spotty sampling, however, we can see that these
two cultural features are spreading, at different rates, outward from
the region they are associated with.

Another culinary feature associated with French Louisiana has not
spread so far--at least impressions derived from fieldwork lead me to
think they do not. Triangles in Figure 6 show those DARE communities
where freshwater crawfish are eaten by a significant proportion of the
population, as evidenced by restaurant menus, informants' remarks, and
personal observation of crawfish traps or crawfish fishermen. If we
draw lines around the communities noted in Figure 6, as has been done
in Figure 7, we see that these features seem to be related to each
other and to features mapped before, but that they show a different
geographical spread for each feature. For brevity and convenience,
let us term lines like these in Figures 7 and 5 cultural isomorphs.
Those cultural isomorphs presented so far correspond well enough to
the dialectal isoglosses and isophones that have been presented to confirm in a general way our hypothesis that dialectal and cultural
regions should have about the same boundaries.

At the same time, the failure of the cultural isomorphs in Figure 7
to correspond exactly to each other illustrates that it is not in the
nature of things to be as neat and simple as we would like. It leads
to a major qualification of our hypothesis: features associated with
a region may extend outside that region or be restricted to only a
part of it. Spread outside a region is well known to linguistic geographers. It has already been illustrated with cultural features in
Figure 7. At the risk of overworking the subject of coffee, an example
of a cultural feature restricted to only part of a region can be seen
in chicory coffee, which is characteristic of the eastern part of
French Louisiana, in the New Orleans area. People farther west in the
dark-roast area generally prefer their coffee unadulterated.

Figure 8 illustrates with a dialect term the qualification that
features may have boundaries different from those of the region they
are associated with. It maps the area in Louisiana of the French word
poule d'eau, including its anglicized forms pulldoo and pooldoo as
attested on the DARE questionnaires. In the western part of its range,
the word extends a considerable distance into Anglo Louisiana; in the
eastern part, however, it does not extend much outside French Louisiana,
and even failed to appear as a questionnaire response in one French
Louisiana community, Donaldsonville.

Referring again to Figure 3, we see a number of isophones showing
phonological variation within French Louisiana, illustrating once again
with dialectal features that the range of individual features is not
always the same as the region they are associated with.

Now that we see that dialectal features and cultural features may be
related to each other without sharing the same geographic spread, the
twin questions arise: Are there dialectal features that have nothing
to do with cultural regions? And are there cultural regions with no
dialectal features associated with them? Perhaps unfortunately for our
faith in the order and rightness of things, the answer to both questions
is "Yes."

August Rubrecht

Figure 6. Cultural features compared. Squares--dark-roast coffee.
Circles--demitasse cups. Triangles--crawfish used as food.

Figure 7. Cultural isomorphs. Dashes--dark-roast coffee. Dots--demitasse cups. Carets--crawfish used as food.

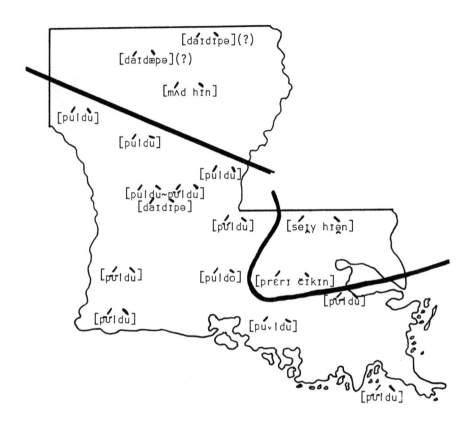

Figure 8. Isogloss for <u>poule d'eau</u> ~<u>pulldoo</u> ~<u>pooldoo</u>, "coot." Based on DARE questionnaires.

First, let us look at a dialectal feature. Figure 9 shows that in a diagonal band across Louisiana, some words which usually have [ɑ] in American English may occasionally have a vowel shifted to or toward [ɔ]. No other phonological feature has the same range in Louisiana; [ɑ] and [ɔ] may fall together in the position before [r] in many of the communities within this band, but the latter feature extends all the way east to New Orleans and Grand Isle and it does not have the same northern and western boundary, either. Nor is any cultural feature that I know of associated with this band.

Now, let us look at a cultural region. The major river valleys of Louisiana, the Mississippi and the Red, are often called the Black Belt because of the large number of Negroes imported there to work plantations established on the rich bottom land. Figure 10 shows that these regions are still characterized by a higher percentage of blacks in the population than the average for the state. Residents of Louisiana consider the part of the Black Belt which is in Anglo Louisiana culturally distinct from the piney woods regions of the north central and southwestern parts of the state. For example, a cultivated resident of Lake Providence, on the Mississippi in the northeast, said that the people of Lake Providence have "an entirely different way of life" from those just across the Parish line to the west. And on a purely impressionistic basis, it seemed to me that Lake Providence showed more similarity to Natchitoches, on the Red River in the west, than either did to Columbia or Ruston, which are about halfway between. Conscious of cultural differences, we naturally expect substantial dialectal differences between the Black Belt and the piney woods. But in this case our expectations go unfulfilled almost as dramatically as they are fulfilled in French Louisiana. Note once again that Figure 3, based on phonetic data from the DARE tapes, shows no isophones that even hint that the Black Belt exists. Furthermore, Atwood's The Regional Vocabulary of Texas shows a number of isoglosses in Louisiana[3] but none of them trace a path along the Black Belt. Furthermore, a study focused specifically on North Louisiana, using a questionnaire similar to Atwood's, revealed no consistent vocabulary differences between the Black Belt and the piney woods. The vocabulary contains a homogeneous mixture of Midland and Southern terms; it varies less according to geography than according to age, education, and community size.[4]

If we stop now and review the cultural and linguistic features that have been discussed and make a concise summary of the possible relationships between them, what we come up with is this: cultural and linguistic features may be either interdependent or independent. It does not make a very impressive conclusion to say, in effect, "Anything can happen." But remember that this paper is not the result of a careful study but the idea for one--or for several. It can be interesting when a study reveals that a particular cultural region is defined partly by its dialectal characteristics, but it is just as interesting and just as important to know that another region is not so defined. There is a lot of material on record concerning dialects that sociologists could well make use of. There is a lot of sociological material that dialect researchers could find relevant to their work. And there are hundreds of unanswered questions for sociolinguists.

And besides these broad questions concerning social and linguistic relationships, there are hundreds of others important chiefly because they pique our curiosity about details of the cultural scenery. I

August Rubrecht

Figure 9. The vowel of such words as <u>job</u>, <u>pot</u>, and <u>clock</u>.

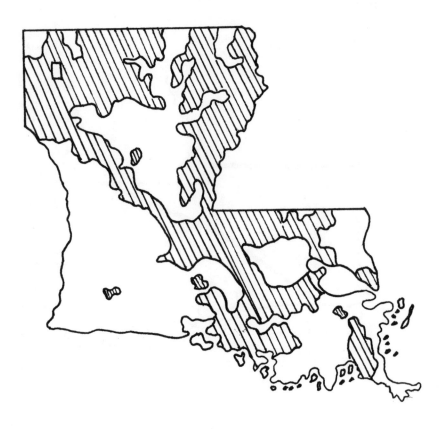

Figure 10. Louisiana's Black Belt. Shaded area--regions in which Negroes make up 36% or more of the population. Adapted from Smith and Hitt, p. 39.

would like to know, for example, whether the shotgun house--so-called because all the rooms and all the doors are in line, so that a person could stick a shotgun in at the front door and shoot all the way out the back--is more common in the Black Belt than the piney woods, as I suspect it is. I would like to know whether the fish known to icthyologists as the bowfin is eaten more frequently in those areas where it is called choupique and green cypress trout than where it is called dogfish, grindle, or mudfish. And I would like to know exactly how far north I can go on any given highway before I have to give up grits for breakfast and settle for hash browns.

NOTES

*Read at the SAMLA-ADS Meeting, Atlanta, Georgia, November, 1971.

[1]Thomas Lynn Smith and Homer L. Hitt, The People of Louisiana (Baton Rouge: Louisiana State University Press, 1952), p. 49.

[2]E. Bagby Atwood, The Regional Vocabulary of Texas (Austin: University of Texas Press, 1962).

[3]See maps 119-125, pp. 249-55.

[4]Mary Lucille Pierce Folk, "A Word Atlas of North Louisiana," Dissertation Louisiana State University Baton Rouge 1961, p. 278.

THE SPEECH OF OCRACOKE, NORTH CAROLINA*

Robert Howren

The Outer Banks of North Carolina, a rope of sandbanks flung out from
the coast in an irregular, 200-mile arc extending from the Virginia
border southeast to Cape Hatteras, which lies some twenty-five miles
from the nearest point on the mainland, and looping from Hatteras back
southwest toward the mainland, have changed in recent generations from
the isolated habitat of a hardy fisherfolk to the popular destination
of tourists in search of the quaint and picturesque. The relative
isolation of the Banks has produced a dialect sufficiently distinct
from the speech of the coastal South that every North Carolinian has
heard--and many believe--that the Bankers speak "Elizabethan English"
(a dialect related, no doubt, to the form of English popularly supposed to be spoken in the more isolated coves in the mountains at the
opposite end of the state). However, the motorcar and the ferryboat--
a combination inevitably fatal to quaintness and picturesqueness--have
brought perceptible changes to the Outer Banks. A good many linguistic
archaisms and localisms perhaps have long since passed from usage, and
inevitably further leveling will eventually result from close and continuous contact with the speech of the mainland. One observer noted
as early as 1910 "greater changes in the speech of the people [of
Hatteras] since the coming of the daily mail in motor boats just ten
years ago, than...in the preceding thirty years, and the songs of the
mothers and grandmothers are well nigh forgotten by the daughters."[1]
The aim of this article is to describe in some detail the speech of
Ocracoke, one of the oldest of the fifteen or twenty villages scattered
up and down the Outer Banks and the latest to succumb to the influences,
both good and bad, of tourism. Ocracoke is the sole village (population
about 600) on Ocracoke Island, which lies in a northeast-to-southwest
position between Hatteras and Portsmouth islands, separated from them
by Hatteras Inlet on the northeast and Ocracoke Inlet on the southwest.
The small fishing village of Ocracoke is located at the southern end
of the island, clustered around Silver Lake a circular harbor opening
into Pamlico Sound. The village originated in 1715, when the North
Carolina Assembly passed a bill providing for settling and maintaining
pilots at Ocracoke Inlet, which had become an important but dangerous
point of entry for shipping. By the end of the colonial period a
sizable community, then called Pilot Town, had grown up around Cockle
Creek[2] (that is, Silver Lake; the natives still refer frequently to
the harbor by its earlier name).
For more than a century the Ocracokers had relatively little contact
with the mainland. The first regular communication was established
sometime after the turn of the century, with the inauguration of mail-
boat service. From that time until 1957, when a paved road was

61

constructed from Hatteras Inlet to Ocracoke village, thirteen miles away at the southern end of the island, the village was most easily reached by means of the mail boat, which made one four-hour trip each morning from the mainland town of Atlantic up Core and Pamlico sounds to Ocracoke, returning to Atlantic in the afternoon. The completion of the road in 1957 made it possible to drive all the way down the Banks from Kitty Hawk, at the mouth of Albemarle Sound, to Ocracoke, crossing Oregon and Hatteras inlets on free, state-operated car ferries. Early in 1960 a private company inaugurated car-and-passenger ferry service between Atlantic and Ocracoke, thus closing the final gap of inconvenience between Ocracoke and the mainland and pointing up the desirability of an early systematic study of the speech of the Bankers.

Because of its long isolation, the Outer Banks dialect should prove valuable in what it may eventually reveal about the development of American English. Since the Banks were not included in the <u>Linguistic Atlas</u> field work, and since there have been no systematic studies of the dialect, this study may perhaps partially fill in this considerable blank space in our knowledge of the speech of the coastal South.[3] It is hoped that the following presentation of the vowel phonology and some of the regionally distinctive lexical features of Ocracoke speech may provide a starting point for a thorough treatment of the Outer Banks dialect.

The system of stressed vowels in Ocracoke speech differs structurally only in minor details from the systems of the other dialects of the Atlantic states, just as these systems differ only slightly from each other. In the following display of the Ocracoke stressed vowel phonemes, I have adjusted my phonemicization to correspond with that used by Kurath and McDavid in their study of American pronunciation[4] and have listed the vowels in such a way that the place of the Ocracoke system in the typology suggested by Kurath and McDavid may be readily seen. In Table 1, the checked vowels /ɪ, ɛ, ʊ, ʊ/ are paired with the free vowels which are phonetically most similar to them. The low-front checked vowel /æ/, the mid-central vowel /ʌ /, and the low-central free vowel /ɑ/ are the only ones not so paired.

Table 1

crib : three /ɪ:i/		/ʊ:u/ wood: tooth
ten : eight /ɛ: e/	/ʌ/ sun/thirty	/o/ road
bag /æ/	/ɑ/ car	/ʊ:ɔ/ crop:law
down /au/		/ʊi/ buoy
		/ɔi/ boil
		/ʊi/ five

A comparison of Table 1 with those of Kurath and McDavid[5] indicates that the dialect spoken in Ocracoke shares with all the major Eastern dialects the nuclei /ɪ/ in <u>crib</u>, /i/ in <u>three</u>, /ɛ/ in <u>ten</u>, /e/ in <u>eight</u>, /æ/ in <u>bag</u>, /au/ in <u>down</u>,[6] /ʌ/ in <u>sun</u>,[7] /ʊ/ in <u>wood</u>, and /u/ in <u>tooth</u>. It also shares the free nucleus /o/ in <u>road</u> with all dialects save that of eastern New England (especially in the speech of older informants), which often, but not consistently, has the checked vowel /ʊ/ in this and a few other words.

In the low-back region, however, where most of the differences in vowel incidence are found, Ocracoke speech aligns itself as follows:

Table 2

/ɒ/ in <u>crop</u>   Ocracoke with eastern New England, western Pennsylvania, and Middle Western and Western derivatives from western Pennsylvania; also Standard British (all others have ɑ /)

/ɔ/ in <u>law</u>   Ocracoke with all (including Standard British) except eastern New England, western Pennsylvania, and Middle Western and Western derivatives from western Pennsylvania, which have /ɒ/.

/ɑ/ in <u>car</u>   Ocracoke with upstate New York, eastern Pennsylvania, South Midland (New York City, upper and lower South, and Standard British have /ɑɹ/;[8] western Pennsylvania and its derivative dialects have /ɒ/; and eastern New England has /a/).

/ɒi/ in <u>five</u>   The phonetic charts in <u>PEAS</u> show no diphthong with an open low-back rounded onset in the word <u>five</u>. The nearest approximation of such a diphthong in this word occurs in the chart for an informant in Georgetown, S.C., who uses the diphthong [ɑ·ɹɪɹ] in <u>five</u>.

/ɔi/ in <u>boil</u> Ocracoke with all except eastern New England and western Pennsylvania and its derivative dialects, which have /ɒi/.

No particular pattern of affinity of Ocracoke speech with the major dialects is evident in the system of vowel phonemes, except that the Ocracoke system aligns itself less frequently with that of the coastal South than with the systems typical of the other major dialects. The frequent lack of affinity with the Southern dialect becomes even more apparent when we turn to the phonetic particulars of the Ocracoke stressed vowels, as presented in Table 3:

Table 3

Phoneme	Principal Allophones	Distribution	Incidence
		1. CHECKED VOWELS	
/ɪ/	[ɪ]	Generally, except as follows	inlet, any, penny, jingle, dip, here, [hjɪɹɚ] (sometimes has /ɛ/), career
	[ɪᷟəᷟ~ɪəᷟ]	Before final or preconsonantal /l/; under terminal contour before apico-alveolars, labials	it, is, went, dip, bit, keelson, hill
/ɛ/	[ɛ]	Generally, except as follows	ever, edge (sometimes has /e/), kept, yet, wreck, Methodist, catch, Mary[10]
	[ɛᶴə~ɛə]	Before final or preconsonantal /l/; before /ð/; under terminal contour before apico-alveolars, labials	ebb, bell, weather, net, bed, kept
/æ/	[æ]	Generally, except as follows	after, half, square, married, dance, aunt, can't, Wahab [ˈweɹˌhæb] (a surname), bad, bat, back, shallow

63

Phoneme	Principal Allophones	Distribution	Incidence
	[æə]	Before final or preconsonantal /l/; under terminal contour before apico-alveolars, labials	half, [hæəf], bass, bad, gal, dance, can't, aunt, have
	[æɪ]	Before /g,ŋ,ʃ/	keg, smashed, tanker, ashes
/ʌ/	[ɜ˞]	Generally, except as follows	up, tubs, husband, lucky, jug, nothing [ˈnɜ˞θɪŋk], Fulcher (a surname), rum, judge
	[ʌ˞]	Before /r/	earth, girl, hurricane, far
/ʊ/	[ɜɪ] [u˞]	Before /ʃ/ Generally, except as follows	Russian, hush one [wu˞n ˜ wɜ˞n], woman full, wood, took, put could
/ɒ/	[ʊɪ] [ɒ]	Before /ʃ/ Generally, except as follows	bush, push otter, hog, log, water box, forwards, Florida
	[ɒɪ]	Before /ʃ/	wash, Washington, the Swash (a section of Ocracoke Island)

2. FREE VOWELS AND DIPHTHONGS

Phoneme	Principal Allophone	Distribution	Incidence
/i/	[ɪ̵˜ɪ̵˜ɪ̧]	Alternate rather freely; [ɪ̧] most frequent; [i˞] generally before dorsovelars	either, east, inch, creek, fish, big, sea, really, lee
	[ɪ̵ə]	Before final or preconsonantal /l/; under terminal contour, occasionally, before final /z,n/	eel, reel, knees, mean
/e/	[ɜɪ˜ɛɪ˜e˞]	Alternate rather freely; [ɜɪ] most common	age, April, days, Hazel weight, sailor
	[e˞ə]	Before final or presonantal /l/	nail, sail
/u/	[u˞u˞˜u˞]	Alternate rather freely; [u u] more frequent and occurs before /r/ almost invariably	school, New Bern [ˈnu˞u˞bən], room, cured, bluefish, crew
/o/	[oe˞u˞˜o˞u˜o˞]	Alternate rather freely; [oe˞u˞] most frequent; frequently [o˞u] before /r/	over, old, Ocracoke [ˈoe˞u˞krɪ,koe˞u˞k] boat, 'course [ko˞us] four, Portsmouth, know
/ɔ/	[oꞱ]	Generally, except as follows	all, on, dog, lost, caught, war, horse, morning, forty, storm, along, draw
	[oꞱə]	Under terminal contour before apico-alveolars, final or preconsonantal /l/	all, across, Claude, ball, called

64

Phoneme	Principal Allophones	Distribution	Incidence
/ɑ/	[ɑ]	(Single major allophone)	honest, fire, calm, barkentine, copper, pond, pa
/au/	[a˔ʊ~aʊ~ɐʊ˔]	Alternate freely, except that (1) [a˔ʊ] occurs most frequently, and is the sole variant before /n/; (2) [ɐʊ˔], in its relatively infrequent occurrence, is found only before voiceless consonants; and (3) only [aʊ] is found before /r/	out, trout, south, sound, flounder, house, now, hour, sour, ourselves
/ʊi/	[ʊ˔ɪ]	(Single major allophone)	ruin, buoy
/ɔi/	[oᵀɪ]	(Single major allophone)	oyster, boys, boil, boiler, Roy
/ɒi/	[ɒɪ~ɑɪ~aɪ]	[ɒɪ] is regular; [ɑɪ,aɪ] occur infrequently in all positions[13]	eyes, island, ['ɒɪᵀlənt], pirate, tide, tight, mile, pilot, high

Several details of Table 3 are worthy of further emphasis. The two most immediately evident phonological features of Ocracoke speech are: (1) the general and regular retention of postvocalic /r/, in contrast with the very mixed patterns of eastern North Carolina;[14] (2) the quality of the diphthong in tight, tide, tie, and so on. Unlike the coastal Southern dialect, Ocracoke speech generally has /r/ in all positions. Moreover, this sound is notable for its sharp constriction in all positions except finally in unstressed syllables. Also, unlike various types of Southern speech, Ocracoke speech has essentially the same diphthong before the voiced consonant and finally in tide and tie that it has in tight and other words ending in a voiceless consonant. The diphthong is further distinguished by its low-back, very slightly rounded onset: ['ɒɪᵀlənt] island, [tɒɪ‚t] tight, [tɒ·ɪᵀd] tide, [mɒɪᵀɫ] mile, [tɒɪ·ᵀ] tie. Though the diphthong /ɒi/ does not occur, in my records, before final or preconsonantal /r/, being replaced in this position by the simplex /ɑ/, it does occur before intervocalic /r/, as in pirate ['pɒɪᵀrət].

A clear distinction between the diphthongs of tie and toy is maintained by the rather close mid-back rounded onset of the latter, as in oysters ['oᵀɪstəz], noise [noᵀɪz], boil [boᵀɫ],[15] and toy [toᵀɪ]. Similarly, the vowel of all, along, draw, hawk, and so on, is a noticeably closer vowel than one is accustomed to hear in mainland North Carolina speech. Moreover, it is normally a lengthened monophthong in Ocracoke speech, without the usual Southern and South Midland back-rounded offglide, except under a terminal contour before an apico-alveolar consonant, where a central-gliding diphthong occurs: thus, under terminal contour, all [oᵀ:ɫ], hawk [hoᵀ·k], dog [doᵀ:g], draw [droᵀ :], but Claude [kloᵀ·əd], bought [bo·ət], across [ə'kro·əs]. Around Albemarle Sound and the mouth of the Neuse River, the PEAS map for the word dog[16] shows a consideralle sprinkling of [ɔ·~ɔ·ə] in this word. The Ocracoke records shows no central-gliding diphthongs before dorso-velars, but perhaps the monophthongal variant in these two areas reflects a vowel related to the close monophthong in Ocracoke speech.

A third distinctive characteristic of Ocracoke pronunciation--and one which, it would seem from an examination of PEAS, is unique--is the centralization of the onsets of the diphthongal allophones of /i/ and /e/ in all positions except after the dorso-velars /k,g/ and the fronto-palatal fricative /ʃ/. The words east, ceased, beach, creek, three, age, same, great, and way are normally heard as [ɨ⁺ist, sᵻist, brᵻitʃ, krᵻ⁺k, θrᵻ⁺ɨ, ɜ·ᵻdʒ, sɜ·ᵻm, grɜɨt, wɜ·ᵻ⁺].

A fourth prominent phonetic feature is the distinctive quality and distribution of the diphthong occurring in words such as house, sound, and so on. This diphthong may be described as beginning at a somewhat retracted low-front position and terminating at an open, slightly rounded, high-central position; thus, the words out, house, flounder, sound, and now are normally pronounced [ɨ⁺ʊt, haᵻʊs, flaᵻʊndɚ, saᵻʊn, naᵻʊ] Occasionally, however, one hears a second allophone of /au/, a diphthong [ɐʊ] with a central onset and a back-rounded glide, before voiceless consonants. One can detect some similarity between the distribution of the variants of /au/ before voiceless consonants in Ocracoke speech and the speech of certain areas of the Southern coast. A diphthong transcribed with an advanced rounded offglide in the Atlas records-- evidently similar to the [aᵻʊ] of Ocracoke--occurs in alternation with [ɐʊ,ɐʊ,ʌʊ] before voiceless consonants in the Charleston area, in most of Virginia, and on Chesapeake Bay.[17] It would seem, however, that nowhere except on the Outer Banks does such a diphthong occur before voiced consonants or finally.

It should be noted here that in Ocracoke speech [aᵻʊ] does not have an unlimited distribution. A variant [aʊ] is regularly heard before /r,l/, and a similar diphthong alternates occasionally with [aᵻʊ] elsewhere, particularly in final position.

The mid-central vowel also exhibits some peculiarities worthy of mention. The first of these is the extreme fronting of the vowel in all positions except before /l/ and /r/, but particularly before the apico-alveolars. Phonetically, this vowel is so closely similar to [ε] that the two are easily confused at first hearing. During my first visit to Ocracoke, I overheard a housewife complaining to the clerk in the community store that the last cornmeal she had bought from him was "mesty." It was only much later, after having heard the same vowel in husband, must, run, and other, that I realized that the woman's cornmeal had not been infected with some exotic blight, but was simply musty (not fresh). This fronted variant of /ʌ/ contrasts with [ε] in such pairs as says [sεz]: husband ['hɜᵻzbən], and rest [rεsɨ]: rust[rɜᵻst].

Before /r/, however, we find a different positional variant of the mid-central vowel. Here the vowel is open central, but more noticeable than its position of articulation is the relative absence of "r-coloring" --the vowel and the /r/ remain quite distinct from each other. Typical incidences are in the words earth, furrow, Burrus (a surname), burned, and far, which are regularly pronounced [ʌᵻθ, 'fʌᵻə, 'bʌᵻəs, bʌᵻnd, fʌᵻ]. A similar variant of /ʌ/ in the word furrow is not infrequent in northeastern North Carolina, eastern Virginia, New York City, the Hudson Valley, and New England,[18] but would seem to be rare in mono- syllables.

In the word one, the mid-central vowel is occasionally replaced by /ʊ/--as relic usage evidently related to the pronunciation of home as /hʊm/ recorded frequently in a wide area of eastern Virginia and in scattered instances in eastern North Carolina.[19] A related usage in Ocracoke speech is the pronunciation of woman with the stressed nucleus /ʊ/ rather than with the more generally current /ɞ/ or /o/. The

pronunciation /'wʊmən/ seems to be more widely current than /wʊn /
one in Ocracoke speech.

The diphthong heard in <u>Ocracoke</u>, <u>boat</u>, <u>show</u>, and <u>froze</u> regularly has
an onset approaching a mid-front rounded position: [ˈoɛʉˀkrɪˈkoɛʉˀk,
boɛʉˀt, ʃoɛʉˀ, froɛˀɪˀz]. This particular diphthong, one of the most
distinctive characteristics of Ocracoke speech, is similar to one
which has considerable currency in the Albemarle Sound area of North
Carolina, along the upper Ohio River, and in the Philadelphia area.[20]
A back-gliding allophone [oᶴu], with a more retracted onset, frequently
occurs before /r/, as in <u>Portsmouth</u> [ˈpoˀʊtsmɛθ], <u>four</u> [foˀʊ], <u>ashore</u>
[əˈʃoˀʊ].

The vocabulary of Ocracoke speech reveals upon examination some
interesting patterns of affinity with the regional dialects of the
Eastern states.[21] Evidently, there are also a number of localisms,
which, however, must await systematic collection before anything
significant can be said of them. I have not yet attempt any attempt to
collect such expressions systematically, and the lexical observations
which constitute the remainder of the present article are confined
largely to the generally established regional expressions included in
Kurath's <u>Word Geography</u>.[22]

In some respects, the regional words used by the Ocracokers are the
regional words of the North Carolina coast, especially the relic area
which lies around Albemarle Sound--the northeastern section of the
state. Of more interest, however, are the numerous points of usage
which distinguish Ocracoke speech from that of the mainland. We may
perhaps approach the lexical features of Ocracoke speech most systematically by examining them under four headings: (1) words predominant
both on Ocracoke and on the mainland, with no significant difference
in usage between the two areas; (2) words predominant in both Ocracoke
and mainland North Carolina speech but current in Ocracoke usage
beside non-North Carolina words; (3) words predominant in Ocracoke
speech but infrequent or apparently nonexistent in coastal North
Carolina speech; and (4) coastal North Carolina words which are lacking
or infrequent in Ocracoke usage.

A few items will illustrate the first group--words current in both
areas alike. Two nautical expressions current throughout the East
Coast area of the United States, <u>the wind is breezing</u> or <u>breezing up</u>,
and <u>squall</u>, are the regular expressions among Ocracokers for "the wind
is rising" and "heavy rainstorm." The words <u>gutters</u> and <u>kerosene</u>
flourish as regional terms among the Ocracoke informants and on the
mainland. The fence made of upright slats, known as a <u>paling fence</u> or
<u>palings</u> throughout the Southern area, is called by those names,
especially the former, by Ocracokers, though a few use <u>picket fence</u>,
which appears as a modern term, in among other areas, northeastern
North Carolina. The word <u>whicker</u> (for the sound made by a horse) and
its variant <u>whinker</u>, both firmly established folkwords in the Carolinas,
and the coastal expression <u>mosquito hawk</u> (for "dragonfly") are regularly
current also on Ocracoke.

The second group of words, those shared by Ocracoke and the mainland
but current in Ocracoke usage beside expressions not found in eastern
North Carolina, are relatively few. One such repression is the Southern <u>quarter to eleven</u>, which predominates in Ocracoke speech beside
the fairly frequent Northern <u>quarter of</u> and the Midland <u>quarter till</u>.
<u>Quarter till</u> was offered by four, and <u>quarter of</u> by three, informants.

Quarter to is the sole usage recorded in the Atlas records for the North Carolina coast from the Virginia line to the Neuse River, with the exception of a single instance of quarter of on Albemarle Sound. Perhaps quarter to and quarter of are the oldest expressions on the Banks, and quarter till may have spread to the Outer Banks from southeastern North Carolina, where the Midland form has come by way of the Cape Fear-Peedee "corridor."

Another instance of a Midland term which crops up in the Ocracoke materials along with a more frequent Southern word is skillet (beside spider). There are three occurrences of skillet in the Ocracoke records; none at all is recorded for coastal North Carolina.

A similar situation may be observed in the occurrence of the term coal hod beside the more frequent coal scuttle and coal bucket, and of corn husks beside corn shucks. Both coal hod and husks are Northern expressions on the mainland. The word husks is not recorded in a single instance in central or eastern North Carolina in the Atlas records, but it appears in the Ocracoke questionnaires seven out of seventeen times. The Atlas records show two occurrences of coal hod in northeastern North Carolina, and the term appears twice in the Ocracoke materials, both times offered by older informants. Possibly coal hod is a recessive form on the Banks, but husks seems as current among younger as among older Ocracokers.

The group of words which represents the greatest difference between the usage of Ocracoke and that of mainland North Carolina is a sizable one; these are the expressions which predominate on Ocracoke but occur infrequently or not at all in the rest of North Carolina. Possibly the most striking example of this group is the Northern term stone wall, in the sense of the fence or low wall constructed of flat stones piled one on another without the use of mortar. This term was offered by thirteen out of seventeen informants; the other four gave stone fence, the usual North Midland expression. Few instances of any name for this particular type of fence are recorded on the Carolina coast, but piedmont and western North Carolina, as well as all of Virginia from the tidewater west, show the Southern and South Midland rock wall and rock fence, especially the latter. A single instance of stone wall recorded on Albemarle Sound suggests the possibility, at least, that there flourishes on Ocracoke a usage that used to be more frequent in northeastern North Carolina than it is today. Ocracokers employ the simple term rock for the throwing-size piece of stone, but the word stone has an equally vigorous currency.

A situation similar to that of stone wall or fence vs. rock wall or fence is seen in the relative frequency of the expressions an armful (of wood), a Northern and North Midland usage which does not occur in North Carolina except sporadically in the west; and a turn (of wood), which is the regular expression throughout the Southern area and the only one in eastern North Carolina. Ocracokers seem to prefer armful; only five out of eighteen offered the Southern expression.

Another Northern term principally found in eastern New England and regularly current on Ocracoke is the form comforter as the name of the thick cotton-padded bedcover. This term, which was offered by all but four of the Ocracoke informants, has no currency at all in the Midland or Southern areas, with the exception of four isolated occurrences across Pamlico Sound from Ocracoke. In all of North Carolina the regular form of the word is comfort.

Finally, we may look briefly at a group of words which, though characteristic of the mainland adjacent to Ocracoke, are evidently employed infrequently or not at all by Ocracokers. The typically Southern coast expressions lightwood (or /láitəd/) for "kindling wood," and curtain for "roller shade," seem surprisingly infrequent on Ocracoke: they occur five and three times, respectively, in the Ocracoke records. The Southern and South Midland dog irons, which is the regular expression along the coastal plain of North Carolina as far south as the Cape Fear River, was not offered by any of the Ocracoke informants, nor were the related forms dogs and firedogs, which are current in the rest of North Carolina. In the total absence of dog irons, dogs, and firedogs in Ocracoke usage, we may consider andiron, which together with one instance of handirons takes their place, a true folkword in Ocracoke usage.

Two peculiarly North Carolina expressions should be mentioned in connection with the group of North Carolina words without wide currency in Ocracoke speech: shivering owl (and its variant shiveling owl), of which there are no occurrences in the Ocracoke records; and tow sack, which was offered by five out of twenty-one informants. The term screech owl, which in eastern North Carolina has less currency than the regional term, was used by all the informants; and burlap bag was generally preferred over the North Carolina expression.

I shall conclude this rather general discussion of noteworthy lexical features of Ocracoke speech by mentioning a handful of expressions gleaned from casual conversation with Ocracokers, and included here simply as interesting points of usage which seem to have a more or less limited geographical distribution. One of these, a usage with a nautical flavor, is the word abreast meaning "across from," employed regularly as a simple preposition, as in "He lives up here abreast the post office" and "She went aground abreast the island."[23] Another term connected with the sea and used quite regularly is fatback, pronounced /fǽd bæk/, the popular name for the menhaden, a fish plentiful in Pamlico Sound. A grove of trees is generally called a hammock /hǽmək/, and two hills on the island which support some vegetation are called "First Hammock Hill" and "Second Hammock Hill," in order of their distance from the village. A single cow is frequently referred to as a cattle-beast. An item of syntax which is particularly interesting in view of its currency also in New England speech and of its similarity in that respect to other Northern terms like coal hod, stone wall, and comforter which are current on Ocracoke, is the use of the preposition to in a locative sense, as in "She was borned up to Buxton" and "the new hospital over to Sealevel." Finally, there is a holly-like shrub which grows wild on the Outer Banks, as well as in some other parts of the South, and which is known by the Ocracokers as yaupon /yópən/. What is interesting about this word is not the name itself but the Ocracoke pronunciation of it, for unless the lexicographers have erred, the pronunciation elsewhere is /yɔ́pən/. It is tempting to speculate that both the first vowel and the slightly stressed second syllable of the Ocracoke pronunciation represent a more authentic rendering of the original Catawba Indian word, yopún.

Much more study of the speech of the Outer Banks must be done before firm patterns emerge; this article is admittedly preliminary and incomplete. However, we may be justified in making a few tentative generalizations about Ocracoke speech on the basis of the foregoing details of vowel phonology and vocabulary.

Robert Howren

It is immediately evident, for instance, that the speech of Ocracoke
in several respects differs markedly from the Southern dialect, particularly in: (1) the retention of postvocalic /r/; (2) the general
occurrence of the stressed nucleus /ɛ/ in both merry and Mary; and
(3) the considerable currency of such non-Southern expressions as
quarter of, quarter till, skillet, corn husks, coal hod, stone wall,
and so on. Moreover, there are certain features of phonology which
seem to set Ocracoke speech apart from all the major dialects--for
instance, the diphthong /ɒi/, the pronunciation of the mid-central vowel
plus /r/ in monosyllables as [ʌˑɹ], and the extreme fronting of the onset
of the diphthongal allophone of /o/ (which more closely resembles
Standard British usage than that of any type of American English). But
these differences should not be permitted to obscure the numerous similarities between Ocracoke speech and that of the upper South, particularly of eastern North Carolina (and more particularly of the Albemarle
Sound area) and eastern Virginia.
Perhaps the most fitting generalization with which to conclude is
that the speech of the Outer Banks is obviously a fertile field for
investigation, and one too long neglected. It should be cultivated at
once, for the Banks are becoming year by year less isolated and more
susceptible to outside linguistic influence.

NOTES

*Read at the SAMLA-ADS Meeting, Atlanta, Georgia, November, 1958.

[1]Collier Cobb, "Early English Survivals on Hatteras Island," North
Carolina Booklet, 14 (1914), 99.

[2]See David Stick, The Outer Banks of North Carolina, 1584-1958
(Chapel Hill, 1958), 298-304.

[3]The field work and the distribution of lexical questionnaires were
aided by grants from the Southern Fellowships Fund and from the Wake
Forest College Research and Publication Fund.

[4]Hans Kurath and Raven I. McDavid, Jr., The Pronunciation of English
in the Atlantic States (Ann Arbor, Michigan, 1961), 3-6. This work will
subsequently be cited as PEAS.

[5]Ibid., pp. 6-7.

[6]/au/ is listed here with the front vowels because its onset is most
generally, in all positions, markedly fronted.

[7]The nucleus of sun is consistently paired with a back vowel in the
PEAS charts. I have placed it in the central column because of its
noticeably fronted articulation in Ocracoke speech. Moreover, I find
no contrasts in Ocracoke speech to justify a phonemic separation of
the stressed nucleus of thirty and the vowel of sun. These words are

70

usually pronounced [θʌˑɟɹɪ] and [sɜˑɑn], with the more retracted vowel occurring before /r/.

[8]However, the degree of retraction of this vowel is considerably greater in New York City and New Orleans speech, for example, than it is in Standard British.

[9]PEAS, p. 91.

[10]PEAS shows considerable currency of /ɛ/ in Mary around Albemarle Sound and in the eastern peninsular area of Carteret County, which juts out between the Outer Banks and the mouth of the Neuse (Map 50). Otherwise, eastern North Carolina usage conforms to the Southern pattern, with some diaphone of /e/ generally current in this name. I have observed that in many respects the speech of the easternmost part of the Carteret peninsula (on the coast of which the town of Atlantic is located) seems quite similar to Ocracoke speech.

[11]A similar diphthongal allophone of /i/ before voiced apico-alveolars is characteristic of the speech of the Charleston, S.C., area (see PEAS, Map 16, showing the pronunciation of grease).

[12]The first syllable of the name of this city is consistently pronounced without the palatal semivowel /y/, but new, due, and so on, are generally /nyu, dyu/.

[13]The diphthong /ɔi/ does not normally occur before a final or preconsonantal /r/, but is replaced in these positions by the phoneme /ɑ/, as in /ɑrn/iron, /fɑr/fire.

[14]See PEAS, Map 156.

[15]The PEAS charts show a somewhat similar diphthong in the word boil in the field records from Atlanta; Charleston and Georgetown, S.C.; Georgetown, D.C.; Cassville and Philadelphia, Pa.; Providence, R.I.; New London, Conn.; and Billerica, Mass.

[16]Map 24.

[17]See PEAS, Map 29.

[18]See PEAS, Map 55.

[19]See PEAS, Map 123.

[20]PEAS, Map 21.

[21]Unlike the phonological data, which were collected in personal interviews with selected informants and by random notes on conversations overheard and engaged in during visits to Ocracoke, the lexical material was collected mainly by means of questionnaires mailed to fifty-three residents of Ocracoke, twenty-five of whom responded by marking the questionnaires more or less completely. The questionnaires consisted of 115 items for which variant expressions occur. The informant was

asked to circle in each group the expression or expressions which he
employed, and to write in any expression which he employed but which
was not included in the group given. Each informant also gave relevant
personal information.

[22]Hans Kurath, A Word Geography of the Eastern United States (Ann
Arbor, Michigan, 1949). All subsequent statements about regional
distribution of terms are based on this work.

[23]The word island here means, as it frequently does in Ocracoke, the
village itself, i.e., the inhabited part of Ocracoke Island. Thus,
"She went aground at about the latitude of the village [but on the ocean
side of Ocracoke Island]."

THE BEGINNINGS OF THE LOSS OF POSTVOCALIC /r/ IN NORTH CAROLINA*

Edward A. Stephenson

To understand the distribution, both geographical and chronological, of the early spellings indicating loss of /r/ in North Carolina,[1] one must consider (if only briefly) the history of the early settlements and population movements within the present boundaries of the state.

According to the leading authorities on North Carolina history, "as early as 1609 a few individuals had pushed westward and southward from Jamestown [Virginia] into the Nansemond River Valley, which borders present North Carolina."[2] As the population of the Jamestown colony began to grow and expand, the desire for fertile land and fresh hunting grounds "caused explorers, hunters, traders, and farmers to follow the streams of southeastern Virginia into the Chowan River-Albemarle Sound area," although the process was gradual. In the 1630's and '40's "hunters, trappers, and traders continued to filter into the region from Virginia."[3] In 1663 Charles II paid a political debt by granting eight Lords Proprietor a charter to "all territory lying between 36 and 31 degrees north latitude and extending westward to the South Seas."[4] Two years later a northward revision of the boundary placed the Albemarle settlements within the limits of Carolina, and in 1670 Albemarle was divided into the four "precincts" (now counties) of Chowan, Pasquotank, Perquimans, and Currituck. But growth was slow, and by 1689 there were only about 3,000 people in the entire Carolina colony.[5]

At about this time, settlers began to move into lands south of Albemarle Sound. Bath County was created in 1696, "embracing the region from Albemarle Sound to Cape Fear."[6] Many French Huguenots from Virginia migrated into the Pamlico Sound region, and the town of Bath--the first town in North Carolina, was incorporated in 1706. In 1708 the president of the Virginia colony's Council remarked that "many of our poorer sort of Inhabitants daily remove themselves into our neighboring colonies, especially to North Carolina," to seek land.[7] The first permanent settlement directly from England was established when the town of New Bern was founded in 1710 by a group of German and Swiss Protestants. This colony was almost wiped out by the Tuscarora Indian uprising of 1711, but with aid from South Carolina the Tuscarora power was broken in 1713, and "New Bern was rebuilt and was incorporated in 1723."[8]

A new phase of settlement began as a result of the Tuscarora War. Some of the South Carolinians had been impressed with the lower Cape Fear Valley "as they marched through it during the Indian Wars, and they, along with some people from Albemarle, became interested in settling it."[9] The town of Brunswick was laid off by Maurice Moore of South Carolina in about 1727, and the town of Wilmington was begun about a decade later. Meanwhile, settlers were moving steadily up the Cape Fear and other eastern rivers. In 1739 a group of Highland Scots landed at Wilmington and settled in the present Fayetteville region. Thousands of Highlanders came to North Carolina after the Scottish defeat at Culloden in 1746, and in 1754 the state legislature created Cumberland County, ironically named for the "Bloody Duke" of Cumberland, who had led the British at Culloden.[10] But since the Highlanders spoke Gaelic, they had no influence on the development of English in the colony.

Meanwhile, North Carolina had become a royal colony in 1729, when George II had bought all but one of the shares of the Lord Proprietor. Under royal government, with its greater stability, population grew rapidly. In 1729 there had been only about 30,000 whites and fewer than 6,000 Negroes in the province; in 1751 the governor reported that "Inhabitants flock in here daily, mostly from Pennsylvania.... They commonly seat themselves toward the West and have got near the mountains."[11] In 1755 the colony's population was 80,000; by 1775 the white population was estimated at 265,000 and the Negro population at 80,000.

This upsurge in population was due in considerable part to the large number of Scotch-Irish and German immigrants, chiefly from Pennsylvania, pouring into the "back country" after 1740. Seeking cheaper land, they came southward over "The Great Philadelphia Wagon Road," which passed through the Valley of Virginia, cut eastward through the Staunton Gap of the Blue Ridge Mountains, then ran southward on to Salisbury (after about 1756) in present Rowan County.[12] The Scotch-Irish made a great contribution to the growth of North Carolina. As Lefler and Newsome remark, "They developed agriculture and a variety of local industries, having among their numbers capable weavers, coopers, joiners, wheelwrights, wagon-makers, tailors, blacksmiths, hatters, rope-makers, fullers, and other skilled workers."[13]

The largest group of Germans in the first stages of settlement was that of the Moravian Brethren, who purchased nearly 99,000 acres of land in present Forsyth County and commenced to settle the tract in 1753. Salem (now part of Winston-Salem), founded in 1766, became the most important Moravian community. By habit and training the Germans were industrious, thrifty, and law-abiding. Unaccustomed to slavery, they were inclined to rely on their own labor and became the best farmers in the province.[14]

Eventually these differences in the settlement of the eastern and western parts of the state were reflected in a dialect cleavage. Norman Eliason puts the matter succinctly:

The eastern half of North Carolina had been settled by people fanning westward from the coast, who thus spread the Southern dialect that had been developing there. The western half was largely settled by immigrants, most of them originally Scotch-Irish or German, who came southward from Pennsylvania bringing with them the Midland dialect that had begun to take form there. Basically this is what accounts for the still very noticeable difference in the speech of eastern and western North Carolina.[15]

To judge from the evidence of the manuscripts, however, this cleavage was merely incipient, in most respects, in the 18th century. The

picture that emerges is one of considerable diversity of pronunciation
in both parts of the state in the 18th century, with neither section
having any marked characteristics that distinguish it clearly from the
other. The extent to which this general statement is applicable to
the forms showing early loss of /r/ will become apparent in the course
of this paper.

As is well known, in Southern speech of what has been called the
"Plantation Type," as opposed to the "Hill Type,"[16] postvocalic /r/
is often or even normally lost, except when another vowel follows the
/r/ in the same word. Thus in describing Virginia pronunciation forty
years ago, Edward F. Shewmake asserted that r "is silent in words of
the type of harm, term, firm, form, churn; and it has the sound of u in
hut (uh), but unstressed, in scarce, fear, fire, course, and similar
words."[17] And a few years later C. M. Wise, basing his remarks
primarily on the educated speech of Louisiana and Mississippi, stated
that r "is silent before consonants and finally, as HARD [hɑ:d], CAR
[kɑ]" or "is replaced by [ə] in words ending in diphthongs plus 'r' and
in a few other cases, as in HOUR [auə],FOUR [oə], FIRE [faɪə], FEAR
[fɪə]."[18] At about the same time, Katherine Wheatley, reporting chiefly
on the speech of Austin, Texas, observed: "In Texas, where the Western
and Southern types meet, the dropped r is characteristic of the speech
of the cultivated classes, at least in Austin and vicinity."[19] Speakers
who retain postvocalic /r/ are probably to be found, nevertheless, in
all parts of the South, even among the most highly educated groups.
And in recent years there seems to have been a trend toward restoration of the /r/, as Professor Wheatley and a collaborator found in
the speech of a group of natives of Nacogdoches, Texas (in the extreme
eastern part of the state). They discovered that "the following features of old-fashioned plantation speech have apparently disappeared
altogether from the speech of the younger generations: [ɑ:] as in card;
[ɛə]as in clear; and [ɜɪ] as in bird."[20]

Granting, however, a widespread loss of /r/ in the South--a feature
of pronunciation that sets the "r-dropping" Southerners rather sharply
apart from their nearest Northern neighbors--one would like answers
to these closely related questions: When was the /r/ lost? By what
process was it lost?

Before answers to these questions can be properly attempted, it is
necessary to make several important distinctions, which most writers
on this subject fail to make. The general loss of postvocalic /r/ in
those dialects in which it occurs must be distinguished from three
other types of loss of /r/: (1) loss of /r/ in unstressed syllables,
(2) loss of /r/ through dissimilation, and (3) an earlier loss of /r/
in certain words through assimilation to a following tongue-tip consonant. Since the /r/ lost under any of these conditions also usually
followed a vowel, scholars sometimes incorrectly assume that the loss
belongs to the general loss of postvocalic /r/ in which the /r/ was
gradually absorbed into the preceding vowel.

It is instructive to compare the dialect in question with other
dialects in which postvocalic /r/ is generally retained--the exceptional losses of /r/ being assignable to one or more of the three
types listed above. For example, in the dialect of Ithaca, New York,
as described in 1891, a distinct /r/ was heard in all positions and
final /r/ never became /ə/. But /r/, though preserved as a rule, was
lost quite commonly in unstressed syllables, as in adve(r)tise,

info(r)mation, prope(r)ty, yeste(r)day, Ve(r)mont, and many other words.[21]

Early North Carolina spellings indicating loss of /r/ in unstressed syllables include the following (arranged chronologically): ORCHARDS: orchads (2: 1730/B2-1732/B2);[22] ELLERBEE (personal name): Ellebee (1737/E2); FORMERLY: formily (3:1737/H8, 1765/E3, 1792/C6), formely (2: 1784/M4-1799/L5); PERSIMMON: pissimon (1762/M9 regularly), posimon (1778/M18), possimmon (1786/N4); SUBALTERN: Subalton (1777/B14); GOVERNOR (-S): Govener (1781/B13), Govenor (2: 1782/B13-1787/L5), goveners (1794/L5); OPPORTUNITY: opputunity (2: 1782/B13-1786/H10, the latter by former governor Abner Nash; CERTIFICATE: Setificate (1791/H10), setiffeget (1797/C1); SURPRISED: supprised (1792/H14); REGULARLY: regulaly (1797/G6); DISORDERLY: disordily (1797/P4); PATTERN: patton (1799/L5); CUMBERLAND (County): Cumbuland (1799/M10); ERROR: Errow (3: 1799/L2-1800/L2 twice).[23]

Some of the words in the foregoing list contain two instances of postvalic /r/ in those dialects in which /r/ is retained: orchards, formerly, governor, etc. In these words the ousting of the /r/ from an unstressed syllable may have been aided by the process of dissimilation--the presence of the one /r/ tending to cause the disappearance of the other /r/. Illustration of this type of exceptional loss of postvocalic /r/ is found in George Hempl's 1893 report of a "very common" loss of /r/ by means of dissimilation in his own southern Michigan dialect, in which /r/ was normally retained. Even in stressed syllables, the loss occurred in such words as fa(r)ther, fo(r)mer, co(r)poration, qua(r)ter, co(r)ner, and many others.[24] In the North Carolina manuscripts, I have found only two 18th-century spellings which could reflect a dissimilative loss of /r/ in a stressed syllable, paralleling the Michigan examples: QUARTER: quater (1781/B13); LARGER: Lager (1799/B7). The first of these spellings is unlocalized; the second is from Lincoln County in western North Carolina.

Examples of the third type of exceptional loss of postvocalic /r/ can be found in the Smoky Mountain dialect. Joseph Hall says that "r in the Smokies is usually a distinctly retroflex sound with little difference from its counterpart in western American speech....and shows no influence of the suppressed or lost r of Southern 'plantation' speech."[25] But the omission of /r/ is "fairly common" in the Smokies, especially among the older generation, in horse, mercy, nurse, nursery, parcel, burst, first, worst, cartridge, partridge, north, farther, and further.[26] In these examples the /r/ is lost before /s/, /t/, /θ/, and /ð/. Except for the last two words (in which dissimilation could have played a part), these /r/-less pronunciations almost surely reflect a very old loss of /r/ that antedated the first American settlements and caused a number of such /r/-less variants to be imported into the American colonies. This loss of /r/ has been brilliantly and exhaustively studied by Archibald A. Hill, who has shown that during the period 1300-1500 /r/ was frequently assimilated to a following dental, alveolar, or alveopalatal consonant.[27] Inasmuch as a preceding short vowel was not lengthened as a result of this loss of /r/, a pronunciation like [bʌst] 'burst' presupposes a loss of /r/ (in some dialect or dialects) before ME [ʊ]>ModE [ʌ]. The pronunciations [bɜɪst] or [bɜːst], on the other hand, probably originated in the later 18th century loss of postvocalic /r/, in which the /r/ was vocalized to form a diphthong with the preceding vowel or was entirely absorbed into the vowel, with attendant lengthening of the vowel.

Hill's study has some important implications for spelling-evidence. Does an 18th century spelling like <u>fust</u> 'first' (e.g., 1779/M8) represent the old popular form [fʌsɫ, with assimilation of /r/ to the following /s/? Or does it stand for the newer and more cultured [fɜːst], reflecting the general loss of postvocalic /r/? Probably the former, but we cannot be sure. Occasional spellings seldom reveal the quantity of a vowel, and too often we can only make an informed guess about the quality. A spelling like <u>Cattridge</u> 'cartridge' (1777/B14, unlocalized) seems to indicate [ˈkætrɪʤ] (old type); and <u>posal</u> 'parcel' (1795/H14) probably stands for [ˈpɑːsəl] (new type); but most of the spellings are inconclusive as to the vowel. Thus every spelling given by Henry C. Wyld to establish early loss of /r/ in stressed syllables could be an instance merely of the consonant-assimilation type.[28] Since Hill has shown that this assimilation did not occur before labial and velar consonants, what is required in order to prove the new loss of /r/ is evidence from words like <u>herb</u>, <u>carp</u>, <u>harm</u>, <u>worm</u>, <u>curve</u>, <u>wharf</u>, <u>work</u>, <u>lurk</u>, <u>target</u>, etc. And, of course, evidence of the loss of final /r/ in words like <u>star</u>, <u>fur</u>, <u>door</u>, etc., will serve the same purpose.

Bearing in mind, then, that /r/ may be lost in any dialect in an unstressed syllable and that /r/ may be suppressed in any dialect if another /r/ follows in the next syllable, we may rephrase the questions raised earlier: In Southern speech, when and why was postvocalic /r/ lost in a stressed syllable not followed by another /r/?

To the first half of this question--<u>when</u> was postvocalic /r/ lost?-- at least a qualified answer can be offered with a considerable degree of certainty. We cannot say precisely when the loss began nor how long the spread of the loss may have continued, but we can say with confidence that a loss of /r/ was in progress in North Carolina in the 18th century. Even if we temporarily set aside those r-less spellings that <u>may</u> represent "old" pronunciations of the type described by Hill (or, alternatively, the "new" general loss of postvocalic /r/), there is both direct and indirect evidence to support this statement. The direct evidence is slight but clear. The spelling <u>posal</u> 'parcel' (1795/H14), from Lincoln County, has already been mentioned. This would be a strange way to spelling [ˈpæsəl], the well-known dialect pronunciation resulting from early loss of /r/ before ME [ɑ]>ModE [æ], which no doubt underlies the spelling <u>passell</u> that occurs in the town records of Watertown, Massachusetts, in the entries for the year 1651.[29] The <u>o</u> in <u>posal</u> is in all likelihood a symbol for [ɑ] or [ɑː], and the indicated pronunciation of the word is probably the result of the general loss of postvocalic /r/ that is usually assigned to the 18th century. There is even better evidence that the "new" loss of /r/ had reached North Carolina in the 18th century. Since the early loss due to assimilation to a following consonant obviously could not affect final /r/, the following spelling must reflect the new, general loss: SYCAMORE: <u>sycermo</u> (1800/M15--in the phrase "sycermo bark"). This is a North Carolina spelling, but unfortunately its provenience cannot be determined any more specifically. The early, assimilative loss of /r/ also did not affect /r/ preceding a velar consonant; hence the following spelling equally signifies the new, general loss of postvocalic /r/: CORKSCREW: <u>caulkscrew</u> (1791), reported from Currituck County, on Albemarle Sound, by Norman Eliason.[30] In view of the evidence still to be presented, the surprising thing is that so little direct evidence of the above types has been discovered in the 18th century manuscripts.[31]

Edward A. Stephenson

But perhaps the paucity of direct evidence is significant. If the Southern loss of postvocalic /r/ ("new" type) was originally a feature of upper-class speech, then we can hardly expect to find very many naive spellings indicating the sound-change: the conventional spelling (as a rule) of the upper-class documents effectively conceals the underlying pronunciations. And, it should be further noted, the words that could yield evidence of the new change are mostly short and easy to spell: harm, work, door, etc.

Certainly we cannot sustain an hypothesis that the new loss of /r/ had not begun, or had barely begun, in North Carolina in the 18th century. If this were so, we would be unable to account for the many spellings with intrusive or excrescent r, regardless of whether these are interpreted as inverse spellings (with analogical "silent r") or phonetic spellings (showing addition of /r/). Though these examples provide only indirect evidence that a general loss of /r/ was in progress, they are impressive in their cumulative effect. I list them by regions of the state (chronologically within regions), since their geographical distribution may have some significance.[32] The counties of provenience are given according to their present boundaries.

Eastern counties:

WATER (-S): Warters (1767/C11, Beaufort), warter (1799/H10, Craven).
FOLLOWS: follars (1787/N3, Bertie).
DEATH: dearth (1792/W2, Craven).
DUST: Durst (1795/C1, Halifax).
POSSESS: persess (1800/J4, Craven).

Central counties:

FATHER: farther (3: 1767/B13, Orange; 1794/M10, Cumberland; 1800/L2, Caswell).
MINISTER (-'S): Minnarstar (1785/M8, Rockingham), minirsters Stipend (1795/M10, Cumberland).
HANNAH: Hannar (1787/M8, Rockingham).
DEPRECIATION: derpreciation (1788/C1, Orange).
WATERS: Warters (1789/G7, Orange).
ESTIMATION: Estermation (2: 1792/G8 twice, Warren).
COMPASSES: comperses (2: 1792/C1 twice, Orange), Coumpersis (1799/L2, Caswell).
AUGERS: Orgers (1798/L2, Caswell).
WINDOW: winder (1799/L2, Caswell).
POTATOES: petators (1800/L2, Caswell).
UMBRELLA: umbraler (1800/H10, Wake).

Western counties:

HOLLOW (-S): hollars of the Mount[n]. (1779/B8, Wilkes), Hollar (1796/P1, Wilkes).
TALLOW: Taller (1785/H2, Rowan).
CATAWBA: Catawber (1785/L5, Wilkes).
WAGES: wagers (1787/L5, Wilkes).
SUPPOSE (-D, -ING): Surposed (1792/J3, Caldwell), Surposing (1792/J3, Caldwell). Both spellings by the same writer.
DEATH: dearth (1795/L5, Wilkes).
WATER (-S, -COURSE): warters (1796/P1, Wilkes), Warthers (1797/P1, Wilkes), wartercours (ca. 1796/P1, Wilkes).
CAROLINA: Caroliner (1799/P1, Wilkes).

Most of the foregoing are probably phonetic spellings, for some of which the implied pronunciations are well attested in many dialects.

Edward A. Stephenson

John S. Kenyon long ago explained how such forms originate:
    When the dropping of [r] not followed by a vowel...began, probably
    in London near the end of the eighteenth century, it did not take
    place suddenly. Hence for a period there must have been people
    who kept the old [r], living in proximity to those who were
    losing it or had lost it. A similar state of affairs is a per-
    manent one on the borders of the r-less regions, and in cities
    where people from different regions mix. People who say [fɑrm
    are in contact with those who say [fɑ:m]. To suppose a
    specific case: it is not unlikely that a child accustomed to
    say [fɑrm] should hear another accustomed to [fɑ:m]use some
    word new to him like...caucus, and suppose that in the speaker's
    dialect it represented what in his own he would call...[kɔrkəs].
    The process would be largely unconscious.[33]
It is enlightening to compare my findings with those of Eliason in this
matter of the addition of r. From the period 1796 (his earliest example)
to 1863, he cites eighteen words spelled one or more times with an
unhistorical r--e.g., pillar 'pillow' (1812), wider 'widow' (1819),
winder 'window' (1833), farther 'father' (1835), horling 'hauling'
(1843), orfered 'offered' (1852), surply 'supply' (1853), foller 'follow'
(1855), etc.[34] He then concludes that "the evidence shows pretty
clearly that intrusive r was formerly much more common than it is today.
This is what we would expect at a time when the newer r-less type was
actively conflicting with the r type." On the basis of the dates of
Eliason's citations, one might reasonably infer that the period of
active competition between the two types of treatment of historical /r/
(loss vs. retention) was the first half of the 19th century. However,
the evidence that I present (of at least equal magnitude) shows that
we must push back the date of the competition to encompass at least the
last third of the 18th century in North Carolina. This line of reasoning
yields a tentative answer to the question of the time of the beginning
of the general loss of postvocalic /r/ in North Carolina.[35]
    But why was postvocalic /r/ lost in those Southern regions in which it
was lost?
    Two main theories have been offered in answer to this question; for
convenience we may label them "the Krapp theory" and the "Kurath-McDavid
theory"--though it is not claimed that these scholars are the originators
of the theories.
    George Philip Krapp expressed his opinion as follows:
    The loss of [r] in typical Southern speech must have been due
    to the same causes as the loss of [r] in New England speech. In
    the lack of any positive evidence to show that this feature of
    American speech was the result of imitation of British speech,
    one must assume the contrary. The burden of proof certainly
    falls on him who would maintain that American speech between
    the close of the Revolution and the War of 1812 was so re-
    spectful of British example that it took over so marked a
    feature of pronunciation as the one under consideration....
    The only reasonable conclusion, is, therefore, that the loss
    of the [r], both in American and in England, was a natural and
    early change in language which took place in popular speech
    unaffected by learned or standard influences.[36]
Hans Kurath's view, however, is that the Southern plantation aristocracy
and cultivated classes in and near the seaports imported the /r/-less

79

Edward A. Stephenson

pronunciations from England, where the loss of postvocalic /r/ is
supposed by most scholars to have become established in the standard
language during the 18th century. The method of transmission, in this
view, might have been as follows:

> In the southern seaports the social grouping was similar to
> that in the New England ports, but as far as the social elite
> was concerned the connections with England were even closer.
> The Southern merchants and planters belonged to the Church of
> England, they were received as equals in London society, and
> their sons were admitted as students to the English univer-
> sities, a privilege that was denied to the dissenters of New
> England and of Pennsylvania. The College of William and Mary
> was founded early in Williamsburg,...but the great majority
> of the sons of Southern gentlemen got their education in
> England or from imported English tutors. In this manner the
> speech ways of this social class conformed to those of
> London to a considerable extent.[37]

Kurath and McDavid have later amplified this theory, insofar as the loss
of final /r/ is concerned, in a way that would make allowance for very
early occurrences of /r/-less forms in the American colonies while still
denying to folk speech (or "popular speech," in Krapp's phrase) any
influence in the spread of the type:

> In English folk speech of today, door, care, ear end in un-
> syllabic /ə/ in the eastern counties north of the Thames, in
> /r/...in the south and the west. In all probability both types
> came to this country with the first colonists and could be heard
> in all of the colonies. With the acceptance of /doə,keə,iə/
> in Standard British English during the eighteenth century, it
> would seem that this type acquired prestige in the chief American
> seaports on the Atlantic coast--Boston, New York, Richmond,
> Charleston--and spread from there to the hinterland. In the
> inland, on the other hand, the postvocalic /r/, common from the
> beginning, came to be generally established, as also in the
> Quaker-dominated port of Philadelphia and vicinity.[38]

What can be said for these two conflicting theories? Much of the
(chiefly New England) evidence that Krapp cites for his theory is less
significant than he supposed. For example, Washbon 'Washburn' (Plymouth,
1694 or earlier) merely illustrates the loss of /r/ in an unstressed
syllable; Parkis 'Parkhurst' (Watertown, 1678) is either the same or
else a reflection of the dissimilative loss of /r/.[39] Krapp has
probably misinterpreted the intrusive r in wartering 'watering'
(Southold, 1704), which he takes to be a "silent r" (his usual interpretation of such spellings); six words with intrusive r from the
Hempstead Records in the brief period 1790-92 (e.g., marsters 'masters')
can plausibly be taken to indicate an active competition between the
two types of pronunciation (with and without /r/), but the date is too
late to favor Krapp's theory--as is true also of Fobes 'Forbes'
(Hanover, New Hampshire, 1786, 1789, 1792).[40] The fact that this
spelling reflects a loss of /r/ before a labial consonant suggests
that the new wave of /r/-loss had begun to take effect in New England.
However, Krapp offers no examples of the loss of final /r/. He probably
did not perceive the significance of this lack, inasmuch as he was
under the disadvantage of writing prior to Hill's 1940 article, which
clearly distinguishes the two main types of loss of /r/. To Krapp, all

losses of /r/, of whatever kind, were on the same level and were already
well established in popular speech in the colonies in the 17th century,
as supposedly attested by such spellings as the following: Bastow
'Barstow' (Dedham, 1652), Bud 'Bird' (Huntington, 1675-76), Passen
'Parson' (Watertown, 1649), Moss 'Morse' (Watertown, 1659), Chals
'Charles' (Hempstead, 1668), Haughton 'Horton' (Southold, 1691), and
others.[41] What these spellings do seem to show is that a loss of preconsonantal /r/ (except before labials and velars) was widespread in the
New England colonies. Beyond that, they do not testify.

Kurath's theory of an upper-class origin for the American loss of
postvocalic /r/ appears to be more applicable to the South than to New
England. In a study that may have prompted Kurath's view of British
influence on the Southern planters, Raven I. McDavid, Jr., has shown
that the social distribution of postvocalic /r/ in South Carolina is as
significant as the geographical distribution.[42] In those areas of the
state in which postvocalic /r/ is pronounced with constriction (i.e.,
retroflexion or other tongue movements producing friction), the amount
of constriction decreases with the increase of the education of the
informant, and urban informants have less constriction than rural ones.[43]
On the basis of the present distribution of the sound, McDavid con-
structs this theory:

> Only in Beaufort, Charleston, and Georgetown districts--and only
> in the tidewater riceland sections of those districts--were the
> southern British settlers, in whose dialect constriction would
> have first been lost, the dominant group in 1790; and in those
> same sections plantation agriculture and large slave majorities
> prevailed. Clearly, the spread of the loss of constriction
> accompanied the spread of the plantation system.[44]

This theory offers a plausible explanation for the spread of the /r/-less
pronunciations in South Carolina.

That a similar explanation will suffice for North Carolina is not so
clear. According to Map 156 in Kurath and McDavid, The Pronunciation of
English in the Atlantic States, in North Carolina the /r/-less pronunciations of door (whether /doə/ or /do/) are now concentrated chiefly
in the section--less than half of the state--lying north and east of the
Cape Fear River and its upper extension, the Haw River. Outside this
area a few examples occur near the west bank of the Cape Fear and the
Haw, and a few more between the Pee Dee River and Charlotte to the west.
Between the Cape Fear River and the Neuse River to the north, the /r/-less
types seem to be slightly in the minority. North of the Neuse the /r/-
less types predominate, except in a strip (including a good deal of
marshland) along the coast by Pamlico Sound and Albemarle Sound. The
most solidly /r/-less part of the state is the area north of Raleigh
between the Haw River to the west and the Roanoke River to the east.
Kurath and McDavid give no examples of the retention of /r/ in door in
this section--in striking contrast with the area west and north of
Charlotte, in which there are no examples of the loss of /r/ in door.
Unless the pattern of geographical distribution has changed radically
in the last century and a half, evidently Wilmington--the chief seaport
of North Carolina then as now--was not a major focal point for the
dissemination of these /r/-less forms. Since Wilmington lies at the
mouth of the Cape Fear River, it would seem (according to a strict
application of the Kurath-McDavid theory) that the fertile plantation
lands of the Cape Fear Valley should have been a natural transmission

belt for the spread of the loss of /r/. But even in this area usage is divided, with retention of /r/ dominant. As for the /r/-lessness of north-central North Carolina, for its principal source we must apparently look to the equally /r/-less neighboring region in southside Virginia.[45]

Since the Kurath-McDavid theory has a social as well as a geographical aspect, it will be pertinent here to examine the remaining localized North Carolina spellings that indicate 18th-century loss of /r/ in a stressed syllable, distinguishing wherever possible cultivated usage and popular usage. As mentioned earlier, these spellings could result from either the (earlier) assimilative loss of preconsonantal /r/ or the (later) general loss of postvocalic /r/. In the instances in which parallels are recorded from earlier times in other dialects, it is probable that the /r/-less pronunciation was imported into North Carolina and did not develop there independently.

Eastern counties:

COURSE: couse (1737/H8). From a deed to land in Edgecombe County. Joseph Wright's English Dialect Grammar (1905) cites [kos] from one Midland county of England. Popular usage.

FOURTH: fouth (1739/M11). From a Bladen County indenture. Krapp (ELA, II, 228) cites the Massachusetts spelling fouth (Groton, 1693). Eliason (TT, p. 311) has found an example of fouth in 1799 from Caldwell County in the west. Popular usage.

VIRTUE: Vatue (1760/W8). From a Tyrrell County deed. This spelling implies derivation from vartue (from ME vertu), of which I have found three occurrences, in central and western counties: e.g., "power and vartue" (1782/W4, Warren County). Eliason (p. 320) cites a 1773 example of vartue from Mecklenburg County in the west. Popular usage.

NORTH: Noth (1764/B4). From a Duplin County indenture (a deed of sale). Orbeck (p. 85) lists the Massachusetts spelling noth (Groton, 1663). Hill (p. 335) cites scholarship reporting /r/-less pronunciations of north from three counties of England. Popular usage.

GIRLS: galls (2: 1790/B10-1790/C5). From two different copies of the will of William Borden, Sr., planter, of Carteret County. Hill (p. 33) quotes a 1795 occurrence of gal in Massachusetts. Cleanth Brooks cites the Uncle Remus spelling gal.[46] Joseph Wright's EDG reports [gæl] from many counties of England. Though evidently this pronunciation has been common in folk and popular speech, the present instance should perhaps be classified as cultivated usage.

WORSTED: woosted (1797/C10). From a general-store account book in Bertie County. The loss of /r/ in this word is very old: the OED cites wusted from the 15th and 16th centuries. Hill (p. 340) cites scholarship reporting /r/-less variants from many counties of England. Popular usage.

Central counties:

FIRST: fust (3: 1779/M8, 1796/H10 twice). The first instance is from the Record Book of a Primitive Baptist Church in Rockingham County; the other two are unlocalized. Wyld (p. 299) reports an English spelling fust in 1642, Orbeck (p. 85) cites fust (Groton, 1704). Hill (p. 328) cites scholarship reporting /r/-less variants from many counties of England, and Wright's EDG gives [fʌst] for many counties of England. Popular usage.

WORSTED: Wosted (2: 1786/C1-1790/C7), Wostead (1791/C1). From general-store account books in Orange County (C1) and Chatham County (C7). See comment above. Popular usage.

QUART (-S): 2 <u>Quats</u> Rum (1790/C1), <u>quat</u> (1799/L2 twice). From general-
store account books in Orange County and Caswell County respectively.
Wright's <u>EDG</u> gives /r/-less variants from two counties of England.
Popular usage.

SHORTLY: <u>shotly</u> (1795/C1). From a letter written by Rebecca Bennehan,
daughter of a prominent planter and merchant of Orange County. Hill
(p. 337) quotes /r/-less variants of <u>short</u> with the vowel [o] from
three England counties; the vowel used by Miss Bennehan was more
likely [ɔ]. Cultivated usage.

SHORTNESS: <u>shotness</u> of my letters (1795/C1). From the same letter as
the above, Miss Benneham apologizing to her brother Thomas at the
University of North Carolina for her brevity. Cultivated usage.

BARCELONA: 1 Black <u>Bassolona</u> handf. (1785/H2), 1 Black <u>Basseloney</u> handf.
(1786/H2), 1 Black Silk <u>Basalona</u> handkerchief (1786/H2). All from
the same general-store account book in Rowan County. Popular usage.

TARLETON: <u>Talton</u> (1788/J3 twice). From a manuscript poem about the
Revolutionary War written and apparently composed by Edmund Jones,
a boy from Caldwell County who later became a brigadier general in
the War of 1812. Krapp (pp. 229-30) cites a New England example of
<u>Talton</u> (Hanover, 1803). Cultivated usage.

PROPORTION: <u>propotion</u> (1792/J3). Also by Edmund Jones. Orbeck (p. 84)
gives an early Massachusetts example of <u>propotion</u> (Dedham, 1677), as
well as <u>proposhans</u> (Groton, 1691). Krapp (p. 229) cites an instance
of <u>propotion</u> (Hanover, 1790) nearly contemporary with Jones's.
Cultivated usage.

NORTH: <u>noth</u> (1796/P1 twice). Both from Wilkes County land entries. See
comment above on <u>Noth</u> (1764/B4). Popular usage.

The first point to observe about these spellings is that they are not
heavily concentrated in any one section of the state. If they had been,
the concentration might have been a clue as to where in North Carolina
the loss of /r/ first became general. To be sure, the number in the
"Midland" (western) counties is much smaller than the number in the
"Southern" (central and eastern) counties, but this fact may be
primarily a consequence of my having read considerably more manuscripts
from the eastern and central counties (more having been preserved) than
from the western counties. Greater importance in this respect is to
be seen in the distribution of the spellings with intrusive r (like
<u>Orgers</u> 'augers') or excrescent <u>r</u> (like <u>winder</u> 'window'), cited earlier.
Despite the fact that I have read fewer manuscripts from the central
counties than from the eastern, such spellings from the central counties
outnumber those from the eastern counties by a ratio of almost three
to one (and the western counties by three to two). The central counties
involved, with the exception of Cumberland, are either adjacent to
Virginia or adjacent to counties bordering Virginia--Rockingham, Caswell,
and Warren in the former instance, Orange and Wake in the latter. It
certainly looks as though these spellings result from a division of
usage ensuing from an active penetration into the north-central counties
of /r/-less pronunciations from southside Virginia. In the Albemarle
Sound area to the east, where evidently a more settled type of speech
prevailed, competition was less active. In the north-central counties
today, with the triumph of /r/-lessness long established, there is no
competition; hence, Map 155 in Kurath and McDavid shows no examples
of excrescent /r/ in <u>widow</u> north of Raleigh between the Haw and the
Roanoke, though instances occur both east and west of this area.

In considering the spellings of the above list, not much weight should be given to the fact that all four /r/-less spellings of pre-Revolutionary date come from eastern counties. The earlier occurrences of fouth and noth in Massachusetts make it probable that the implied pronunciations are the "old" type and were brought into the colonies with the first settlers; this supposition is practically confirmed by the occurrence of these two spellings also in western counties of North Carolina in the 18th century. Of the other two spellings, there is a fair chance that the unparalleled Vatue (1760) is a reflection of the "new" loss of /r/.

Among other spellings that apparently reflect the "old" type of /r/-loss are woosted (etc.) and fust. Thus from the central counties the best candidates for examples of the "new" loss are quat(s) (1790-99) and--especially--Miss Bennehan's shotly and shotness (1795). That these last two come from the level of cultivated usage may be significant, as may be the fact that they occur within fifty miles of the Virginia state line.

The social distribution, however, of these twenty-five r-less spellings (in thirteen different words) is more revealing than their geographical distribution. Whatever their origins may have been, most of them come from the level of popular usage. And collectively they suggest a fairly widespread loss of preconsonantal /r/ in 18th-century North Carolina.[47] Edmund Jones's Talton and propotion are also instructive: pronunciations that probably originated in popular speech (propotion, at least, seems to represent the "old" type) have spread to the cultivated level. I do not insist, as Krapp does, that the general loss of /r/ originated in "popular speech unaffected by learned or standard influences," but I believe that in North Carolina a loss of preconsonantal /r/ in popular speech was a factor that ought not to be ignored. A further obstacle to unqualified acceptance of the Kurath-McDavid theory, as applied to North Carolina, is the fact that the field records on which it is based include only eleven cultivated informants from the entire state of North Carolina, only three of whom come from the most /r/-less area, the north-central counties.[48]

This subject is obviously one in which there is no room for dogmatism, and any explanation of the data will be conjectural to a certain extent. The following formulation, nevertheless,is at least compatible with all the known facts:

1. By the end of the 18th century, many speakers in North Carolina did not pronounce postvocalic /r/, preconsonantal or final, in unstressed or stressed syllables, in at least certain words. Probably a number of speakers had no postvocalic /r/ at all, except before a vowel. Though it would be extravagant to claim that the /r/-less type of pronunciation had already become majority usage in any part of the state, the /r/-less pronunciations were in all likelihood most prominent in the north-central counties--and to a lesser extent in certain parts of the eastern section.

2. Chronologically, we must distinguish two stages in the loss of /r/ in North Carolina. First, some /r/-less pronunciations--specifically those in which /r/ had been lost before certain consonants or in unstressed syllables--were doubtless brought into the state in the earliest days of settlement; both of these types are exemplified in the spellings as early as the 1730's. Since these pronunciations were fairly numerous, they must have prepared the way for the second stage, in which the loss

of postvocalic /r/ became generalized: a speaker who already pronounced
north as [nɔθ] and Cumberland as ['kʌmbələn(d)] would be the readier
to accept [wɔ:m] for warm and [doə] for door. To draw an inference from
mainly indirect evidence, this later stage seems not to have begun in
North Carolina before about 1760, possibly a little later (unambiguous
direct evidence has not been found from before the 1790's). During the
1780's and 1790's the /r/-less pronunciations were gaining momentum,
and they doubtless continued to spread for several decades of the 19th
century.

3. The causes of the loss of postvocalic /r/ in North Carolina were
complex, and no simple version of either the Krapp theory or the Kurath-
McDavid theory will suffice to account for the development. The combined
evidence of 18th-century spellings and 20th-century linguistic geography
strongly indicates that the later, general loss of postvocalic /r/ spread
into North Carolina primarily from Virginia, probably emanating from
Richmond and Petersburg and their dependent territoiies,[49] moving south
and southwest into north-central North Carolina but being rather
effectively blocked from expansion into the Albemarle Sound area by
the Great Dismal Swamp of southeastern Virginia and northeastern North
Carolina. Although this new style may well have been adopted first by
the Richmond aristocracy (as Kurath would have it),[50] by the time it
reached North Carolina it had apparently spread through all classes of
society.[51] It is very doubtful that the North Carolinians of the
hinterland were aware that the /r/-less type was a fashionable British
pronunciation, or even that it ultimately had a British origin.

4. From the evidence offered in this paper, it now seems that the
loss of postvocalic /r/ may have been the first characteristic of the
"Southern accent" to become established.[52] In order to throw more
light on this problem and others concerning the development of the
Southern dialect, careful studies should be made of 17th and 18th century
manuscripts from South Carolina and Virginia. Very likely they could
tell us much.[53]

NOTES

*Read at the SAMLA-ADS Meeting, Atlanta, Georgia, November, 1965.

[1]The spellings cited in this article are taken from manuscripts
written by North Carolinians in the period 1700-1800. These manuscripts
are found in individual manuscripts collections in the great Southern
Historical Collection of the University of North Carolina Library. For
an assessment of the usefulness of some of this material for linguistic
research, see my article "Linguistic Resources of the Southern Historical
Collection," American Speech, 31 (1956), 271-77. See also Norman E.
Eliason, Tarheel Talk (Chapel Hill, 1956), Ch. 2, "The Writings."

[2]Hugh Talmage Lefler and Albert Ray Newsome, North Carolina: The
History of a Southern State (Chapel Hill, 1954), p. 12.

[3]Ibid., p. 13.

[4]Ibid., p. 30.

[5]Ibid., p. 47. My notes on the Edenton Papers, from Chowan County, begin with the year 1717.

[6]Ibid., p. 49. I have found the Bath County Court Records (1727-34) to be of some linguistic value.

[7]Ibid., pp. 50-51.

[8]Ibid., p. 62. My earliest notes from this district (Craven County) date from 1721, from the Emma Henderson Dunn Collection.

[9]Ibid., p. 65.

[10]Ibid., pp. 73-74.

[11]Ibid., pp. 70-71.

[12]Ibid., pp. 77-78. My earliest notes from Rowan County date from 1770

[13]Ibid., p. 79.

[14]Ibid., pp. 80-81. The Click Papers (with North Carolina documents dating from 1784) are representative of the German strain. A branch of the Glück family settled in Rowan County, anglicized the name to Click, and became substantial middle-class farmers.

[15]Tarheel Talk, pp. 11-12.

[16]These useful terms seem to have been originated by W. Cabell Greet; see Oma Stanley, The Speech of East Texas (New York, 1937), p. 1. They are not quite synonymous with Kurath's "Southern" and "South Midland."

[17]English Pronunciation in Virginia (Davidson, North Carolina, 1927), p. 29.

[18]"Southern American Dialect," American Speech, 8 (1933), 39.

[19]"Southern Standards," American Speech, 9 (1934), 39.

[20]Katherine Wheatley and Oma Stanley, "Three Generations of East Texas Speech," American Speech, 34 (1959), 94. In their best representative of "old-fashioned plantation speech," a well-educated banker of the age of 71, the vowels in these key words were pronounced as given in the quotation, with no postvocalic /r/; see the tables on pp. 85-86 of the article. My own observations of the speech of my students at the University of Georgia tend to support this evidence of a trend: in (unsystematic) surveys made during 1965-67, more than half of the young native Georgians normally pronounced a postvocalic /r/. Farther to the east, an opposite trend has been detected among cultured and younger speakers: see Hans Kurath and Raven I. McDavid, Jr., The Pronunciation of English in the Atlantic States (Ann Arbor, 1961), p. 171. The evidence, however, come from field records made not later than 1948,

and since that time the influence of television (and other factors) may have caused this trend to be checked or reversed.

[21]O. F. Emerson, "The Ithaca Dialect," Dialect Notes, 1 (1891), 163.

[22]The number before the virgule, in each instance, is the date of the occurrence of the spelling; the letter plus number is my designator for the manuscript collection from which the spelling is cited. (The translation of a designator can be found in the list of manuscript collections given in the final note to this article.) If a spelling occurs more than once, the number of occurrences is placed first, separated from the dates by a colon. The earliest and latest dates of occurrence are always given when there are multiple occurrences.

[23]This spelling indicates a hypercorrect pronunciation ['ɛro], which doubtless originated from some such reasoning as the following: If ['wɪndə(r] is "wrong" and ['wɪndo] is "right," then ['ɛrə(r] must be "wrong" and ['ɛro] is "right." According to M. M. Mathews, The Beginnings of American English (Chicago, 1931), p. 119, Adiel Sherwood's Gazetteer of the State of Georgia (1837 edition) reports Erro as a Southern provincialism for 'error.' And Vance Randolph and George P. Wilson, in Down in the Holler: A Gallery of Ozark Folk Speech (Norman, Oklahoma, 1953), report that this pronunciation is still to be found in the Ozarks: "At least a score of times I [Randolph] have heard back-woods orators say errow or urr-o when they obviously meant error, pronouncing the long o very distinctly" (p. 18).

[24]"Loss of R in English Through Dissimilation," Dialect Notes, 1 (1893), 279-80.

[25]The Phonetics of Great Smoky Mountain Speech (New York, 1942), pp. 105-106.

[26]Ibid., p. 89.

[27]"Early Loss of [r] Before Dentals," PMLA, 55 (1940), 308-59.

[28]History of Modern Colloquial English, 3rd ed. (Oxford, 1936), pp. 298-99.

[29]Anders Orbeck, Early New England Pronunciation (Ann Arbor, 1927), p. 85.

[30]Tarheel Talk, p. 309.

[31]Eliason has discovered a few more from the first half of the 19th century--e.g., poke 'pork' (1844) and foe 'for' (1853), pp. 316, 310. Others that he lists (p. 209) are inconclusive, being assignable to one or another of the three exceptional types of /r/-loss discussed above: e.g., audered 'ordered' (1852), probably the result of dissimilation; con 'corn' (1853), perhaps an example of the assimilation of /r/ to a following /n/.

Edward A. Stephenson

32For my division between the "western" and "central" parts of the
state, I follow the dialect boundary between the South Midland area
and the Southern area lying to the east of the former, as established
on the basis of lexical evidence by Hans Kurath; see Figure 3 in his
Word Geography of the Eastern United States (Ann Arbor, 1949). In
The Pronunciation of English in the Atlantic States, Kurath says (p. vi):
"Features of pronunciation clearly exhibit the same types of regional
dissemination as features of the vocabulary, the same expansive and
recessive subareas, and the same transition belts," although there are
some differences in relative importance of the phonetic boundaries
between subareas. For my division between the "central" and "eastern"
parts of the state, I follow the isogloss marking off the coastal subarea of North Carolina, as given in Figure 2 in Kurath's Word Geography.
It is not claimed that these 20th-century boundaries have any linguistic
validity for the 18th century, but they conveniently divide the state
into three roughly equal parts and at least are a forecast of things to
come.

33"Some Notes on American R," American Speech, 1 (1926), 337. As
a further example, I once noticed by younger daughter, then five years
old, speaking of someone's [ɑrnt] 'aunt.' At the time, she was attending
a mixed-dialect kindergarten in Charlottesville, Virginia, with some
children who retained postvocalic /r/ and some who dropped it.

34Tarheel Talk, pp. 209-10. The dates of the spellings are to be
found in the alphabetical list of significant spellings given in
Appendix B, p. 306 ff.

35This is not to say, of course, that the general loss of postvocalic
/r/ could not have begun earlier elsewhere in the colonies. In his
Early New England Pronunciation, among a number of other spellings in
which the lack of r is assignable to one or another of the three exceptional types discussed in this paper, Orbeck (pp. 84-85) does give
three spellings that may be significant, if indeed they are authentic
(Orbeck worked with 19th-century printed editions of the town records
that he used, instead of the original documents): whe 'where' (Groton,
1699), which conceivably could be merely an abbreviation; woks 'works'
(Groton, 1699), which looks more like an accidental miswriting than a
phonetic spelling; and clack 'clerk' (Groton, 1703). Orbeck also cites
a few examples of intrusive r, as in parth 'path' (Dedham, 1662),
in which he thinks that the r "is probably merely an orthographic
device, perhaps to indicate vowel length" (p. 85). It is an interesting
fact that Dorothy Cox Moore, in her article "A Glimpse into Records at
Surry Courthouse, Virginia," American Speech, 40 (1965), 235-38, cites
only one spelling implying an early loss of a postvocalic /r/ in Surry
County (southeastern Virginia): hose 'horse' (1728). And this loss
could, of course, be the consonant-assimilation type.

36The English Language in America, 2 vols. (New York, 1925), 2,
226-27.

37Kurath, Word Geography of the Eastern United States, p. 5.

[38]_The Pronunciation of English in the Atlantic States_, p. 171. On the loss of /r/ in Standard British English, cf. Otto Jespersen, _A Modern English Grammar on Historical Principles_ (7 vols.; Heidelberg and Copenhagen, 1909-1949), "Part I: Sounds and Spelling" [=Vol. 1], 4th ed. (Heidelberg, 1928), para. 13.25: "The weakened /r/ after a vowel must have disappeared in the 18th c....The oldest Englishman to admit the muteness is, I believe, Walker, who in 1775 says, 'aunt, pronounced nearly as if written arnt' and 'haunch...nearly as if written harnch,' and in 1791: 'In England and particularly in London, the r in...bard, card, regard, etc....is pronounced so much in the throat as to be little more than the middle or Italian a, lengthened into...baad, caad, regaad...in London...it is sometimes entirely sunk.'" The spellings cited by Helge Kökeritz, _Shakespeare's Pronunciation_ (New Haven, 1953), pp. 315-16, are no more relevant to the general loss of postvocalic /r/ than are those cited by Wyld mentioned above. E. J. Dobson, _English Pronunciation, 1500-1700_, 2 vols. (Oxford, 1957), 2, 992, expresses a perhaps unduly conservative belief that the change could not have occurred "in good speech" much before ca. 1800. Referring to Wyld and others, he goes on to state that "there is no evidence at all of the StE vocalization and loss of [r] in stressed syllables in any of these fifteenth- to eighteenth-century sources which are alleged to show it" (p. 993).

[39]_The English Language in America_, 2, 229.

[40]Ibid., p. 230.

[41]Ibid., pp. 229-30.

[42]"Postvocalic /-r/ in South Carolina: a Social Analysis," _American Speech_, 23 (1948), 194-203.

[43]Ibid., p. 198. And within these areas, younger informants are said to have less constriction than older informants--a circumstance from which the inference can be drawn that the loss of postvocalic /r/ is still spreading (though perhaps the influence of television has by now checked this tendency). Eighty years ago Sylvester Primer reported in "Charleston Provincialisms," _Phonetische Studien_, 1 (1888), 240, that he always heard "a perceptible r-sound" in Charleston. This statement is scarcely credible, even when allowance is made for increasing disuse of /r/ in Charleston since 1888. In all probability, either Primer exaggerated or else he was less acute in perceiving phonetic distinctions than he was in a later article, "The Pronunciation of Fredericksburg, Va.," _PMLA_, 5 (1890), 185-99, in which he remarks on the pronunciation of r in Fredericksburg as follows: "Here it seemingly disappears in words like door, more, floor, before, war, etc. The disappearance, however, is only partial. The vocal organs assume the proper position for pronouncing the soft r and then stop before producing the sound" (p. 199).

[44]"Postvocalic /-r/ in South Carolina," p. 200. However, of the six words mapped by McDavid (p. 197), worm is the only one in which loss of /r/ was necessarily a reflection of the general loss of postvocalic /r/.

Edward A. Stephenson

[45]Doubtless Kurath and McDavid would agree with this statement. In _The Pronunciation of English in the Atlantic States_ the Virginia Piedmont is called "the geographic and historic center" (p. 19) of the dialect of the Upper South; the area of this dialect "extends from Baltimore, Md., to north-central North Carolina and westward to the Blue Ridge" (p. 20); and their description of this dialect "is based upon the usage of cultured speakers and applies most fully to the focal area centering on Richmond, Va." (p. 21). Yet their "seaport" theory on the loss of /r/ seems to accord with this picture only by omission of reference to any Southern seaports other than Charleston and Richmond. Why not Wilmington? Why not Norfolk, which has always been a more important seaport than Richmond?

[46]_The Relation of the Alabama-Georgia Dialect to the Provincial Dialects of Great Britain_ (Baton Rouge, 1935), p. 39.

[47]The collection of occasional spellings is essentially a sampling technique; in at least some instances there must have been hundreds of speakers who customarily used an /r/-less pronunciation attested in perhaps only one or two spellings that have been recovered. Cf. Krapp's opinion: "The naive spellings...of the early town records indicate a loss of _r_ which must have been much more general than the mere numbers of spelling with _r_ omitted might lead one to suppose" (_ELA_, 2, 228).

[48]_The Pronunciation of English in the Atlantic States_, p. 26, informants 119 through 129.

[49]Some of the general-store account books and records from the north-central counties of North Carolina show that the merchants bought many of their goods in Petersburg, Virginia.

[50]It must be admitted that not only in South Carolina (as McDavid has shown) but also in other places in the South where usage is divided, the /r/-less type of pronunciation is the style with the greater social prestige. This is true of Athens, Georgia. Cf. also Katherine Wheatley's comment on the speech of Austin, Texas, quoted earlier in this paper.

[51]Map 156 in Kurath and McDavid shows that this statement is not a mere guess. When final /r/ is lost, as in _door_, the sequence of change is as follows: [doɚ]>[doə]>[do]. The intermediate pronunciation is characteristic of cultivated usage. And as Kurath and McDavid remark (p. 171): "In Southern folk speech, /ə/ is often lost, _door_, _four_, _poor_ /doə,foə,poə/thus becoming /do, fo, po/. This pronunciation has also some currency among the middle class, but is avoided by cultured speakers." On Map 156 about one-third of the /r/-less pronunciations indicated for the north-central area of North Carolina are of the folk type, and in southside Virginia the percentage of the folk type is even higher. If this Virginia loss of final /r/ did indeed begin at the top of the social scale, it evidently spread to the lower levels as well with little delay. Any other interpretation would be less compatible with the North Carolina spellings.

[52]The chief competitor for this distinction is the Southern use of [ju] instead of [u] after [t,d,n] (and formerly some other consonants)

Edward A. Stephenson

in words like <u>tune</u>, <u>duty</u>, <u>new</u>. Krapp (ELA, 2, 157-58) cites evidence
dating from 1795 showing that this Southern characteristic had been
noted. James Carrol (Krapp reports) in his book <u>The American Criterion</u>
(New London, 1795), based on New England speech, says that <u>u</u> when
preceded by <u>r</u>, <u>l</u>, <u>s</u>, <u>n</u>, <u>t</u>, <u>d</u> has the long sound <u>oo</u>, as in <u>rude</u>, <u>Luke</u>,
nude, tune, etc. He goes on to say, however, that "the dialect of the
southern states is an universal exception to this...rule. For, when
[one of the letters mentioned] precedes <u>u</u> in the same syllable, they
sound it like <u>eoo</u> or <u>yu</u>; thus <u>duty</u>,<u>luminous</u>, <u>tune</u>, they pronounce,
<u>dyuty</u>, <u>lyuminous</u>, <u>tyune</u>" (quoted by Krapp, 158).

[53]The following manuscript collections from the Southern Historical
Collection were cited in this article:

B2	Bath County Court Records
B4	Mrs. Harvey Boney Collection
B7	Brevard-McDowell Papers
B8	Hamilton Brown Papers and Books
B10	Bryan Papers
B13	Thomas Burke Papers
B14	John Bush Orderly Book
C1	Cameron Papers
C5	David M. Carter Papers
C6	Caswell County Papers
C7	Chatham County Miscellaneous Books
C10	Bruce Cotten Account Books
C11	Mary Farrow Credle Papers
E2	William Eaton Papers
E3	Edenton Papers
G6	Globe Church Record
G7	William Alexander Graham Papers
G8	Benjamin G. Green Papers
H2	Peter W. Hairston Plantation Books
H8	Hatcher Deeds
H10	Ernest Haywood Collection
H14	William Alexander Hoke Papers
J3	Edmund Jones Ciphering Book
J4	Alexander Justice Papers
L2	Solomon Lea Books
L5	Lenoir Family Papers
M4	Julian S. Mann Papers
M8	Mattrimoney Creek Baptist Church Records
M9	Henry Eustace McCulloh Survey Book
M10	McDougald Papers
M11	Thomas D. McDowell Papers
M15	Miscellaneous Papers
M18	George W. Mordecai Papers
N3	Norfleet Papers
N4	North Carolina Assembly Propositions and Grievances Committee Report

Edward A. Stephenson

P1   Lindsay Patterson Papers
P4   Person County "Wardens of the Poor" Records

W2   James Webb Papers
W4   Webb-Moore Papers
W8   W. H. Wills Papers

"YOU" AND "THOU" IN NORTHERN ENGLAND*

William Evans

Although the old second-person singular pronoun, thou, became
obsolete in standard English--except for prayer--in the eighteenth
century, it lingered on in the dialects[1] and is still heard in various
parts of England today. Until recently, material for the systematic
study of the dialectal use has been rather limited; Joseph Wright's
English Dialect Dictionary[2] was long the chief source of information.
Now, however, the new Survey of English Dialects[3] gives us the opportunity to make more precise statements about the extent of the
survival of thou in the twentieth century and about the nature of
its use in the areas, like the North, where it seems particularly
strong. There are eighteen items in the Survey that are intended to
elicit some form of the second-person singular pronoun.[4] One item,
for example, directs the fieldworker to say to the informant, "A
little boy comes up and talks to you in the street, and you are not
sure you know him, so you say: Tell me, ..." And the informant is
expected to take it from there. The responses from northern England
in this case ranged from "What do they call you?" to "Whose bairn art
thou?"[5] But practically all of them included some form of the second-
person singular pronoun, and so with the other seventeen items. Several
of them, like the one cited, were deliberately framed to suggest to the
informant a specific situation in which he might be expected to use
thou, the historical singular, rather than you, the standard modern
form.[6]

There are certain limitations on the information obtained from the
Survey about the northern counties. It is not really adequate to say
that we find here a picture of pronoun usage in northern England in
the mid-twentieth century. For one thing, although the eighteen
items are revealing, they do not present all the possible situations
where thou might occur. Furthermore, the Survey embodies the results
of what was largely an investigation of the speech of old countrymen;
and each element of the phrase "old countrymen" suggests a limiting
factor. Almost all of the informants were at least sixty; so the
pronoun forms tend to reflect the usage of the oldest generation and,
presumably, often the earlier part of the century. Most of the
informants were also from small country villages; thus the emphasis
is largely rural. And, as might be inferred, the exposure of these
informants to formal education was generally rather limited, extending
typically to the age of twelve or thirteen. Finally, most of the
informants were men. Both Harold Orton, the original director, and
Stanley Ellis, one of his principal collaborators, felt that men in
England made better dialect informants than women because, in Ellis's

words, "it is the women who try to smarten up their children and their husbands, both in appearance and in speech; who rebuke their families for using old, broad forms of speech; who, that is, try to refine their families."[7] The picture is thus incomplete in some ways, but it is still illuminating. Although the basic pronoun material is not, in a sense, as comprehensive or as up-to-date as we would like, it still has value as a reflection of the usage of old country folk--the ones, after all, who would be most likely to retain the archaic thou and its various implications, if anyone would. Hence, we can still obtain some significant information about the geographical extent of the singular pronouns you and thou and about their extra-lexical meanings in modern dialectal English.

The northern volumes of the Survey cover the six northern counties--Northumberland, Cumberland, Durham, Westmorland, Lancashire, and Yorkshire--and also the Isle of Man (see Map 1); in all, there were seventy-five localities investigated. And it appears that, with the limitations mentioned, thou is the predominant singular in most of the northern area. For practically every item, thou is the response from the majority of localities. The exceptions to this generalization are two. One of them is the Isle of Man. Thou does not occur at all in the responses from the two localities surveyed there, but is commented on as having died out in the earlier part of the century.[8]

What is most striking geographically, however, is that in the northern-most tip of England--that is, in the greater part of the county of Northumberland--thou seems to be virtually nonexistent--except, presumably, in prayer. The you form predominates, with very few exceptions, in the responses of six of the nine informants in Northumberland--those in Lowick (#1),[9] Embleton (#2), Thropton (#3), Ellington (#4), Earsdon (#6), and Heddon-on-the-Wall (#8). It occurs somewhat less frequently in two localities farther to the West--Wark (#5) and Haltwhistle (#7). And it occurs less often, but still significantly, in north and central Durham--in Washington (#1), Ebchester (#2), Wearhead (#3), and Witton-le-Wear (#4). The only locality within the county of Northumberland where thou, not you, seems to prevail is the southernmost one--Allendale (#9). The fact that the informant in Allendale who responded to all the pronoun items[10] was a lay preacher--and thus probably particularly familiar with the Biblical use of thou--may have some bearing on his responses. In any case, it seems obvious that the standard singular you has made more headway in this northern tip than in the rest of the northern region generally.[11]

It is more difficult to discover how long this situation has existed and why it should exist. There is some evidence in Wright's English Dialect Dictionary, already referred to, that you prevailed in this area already in the middle of the nineteenth century. Wright's Dictionary has about twenty citations from Northumberland illustrating the use of thou forms--thou, thee, thy, and thyself; judging primarily from the titles of the source works,[12] about three-quarters of the citations seem to be from the Newcastle or River Tyne area, that is, from southern Northumberland. In other words, there is relatively little evidence in the Dictionary for the occurrence of thou north of the southern part of the county; on the other hand, the few citations for thou north of the Tyne area may simply reflect the fact that--again judging by the titles--relatively few of Wright's sources represent the northern part of the county. Thus, while there is nothing in Wright to

THE NORTHERN COUNTIES OF ENGLAND

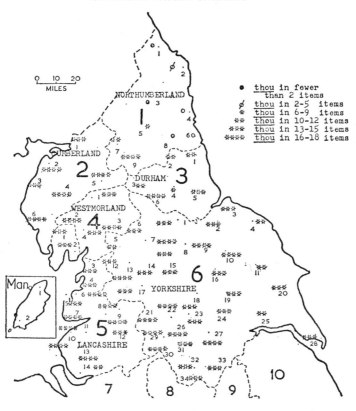

MAP 1

counter the idea that you prevailed in the northern tip earlier, there
is, at the same time, little positive evidence to support that conclusion.
There is also some relevant commentary in Alexander V. Ellis's The
Existing Phonology of the English Dialects.[13] But it is not much more
satisfactory than the evidence in Wright, partly because the information
about pronoun forms was obtained from the informant's reading of a set
passage that was in standard English. The information, nevertheless, is
interesting. The part of the passage which includes the pronoun is this:
"Well, neighbor, you and he may both laugh at this news of mine....How-
soever, these are the facts of the case, so just hold your noise, friend,
and be quiet till I have done."[14] Four informants in the Northumberland
area read this passage; but only one of them changed the forms you and
your to thou and thy. Interestingly enough, though, he was a reader
from Knaresdale,[15] Northumberland--a town very close to Allendale (#9),
which is the only locality in Northumberland, according to the Survey,
where thou may still prevail. The other three readers were from towns
along the coast: one from Berwick-upon-Tweed in the northern tip of
Northumberland, and one from Newcastle in southern Northumberland, and
one from South Shields in northern Durham. In all three places the
forms recorded were you, ye, and your. In addition, and perhaps more
significantly, Ellis also included a dialect story told him in coastal
Warkworth, a town in Northumberland about half way between the Survey
localities Embleton (#2) and Ellington (#4). The second-person pronoun
occurs several times in the story; and each time the pronoun used by
the speaker is you.[16] Ellis's evidence, like Wright's, is somewhat
inconclusive, but it does not contradict the possibility that thou had
greatly declined in much of Northumberland by the mid-nineteenth
century.
    Although a decline is, of course, clearly evident by the twentieth
century, the cause--like the chronology--is not easy to establish. But
it is, perhaps, noteworthy that the area where thou begins to fade out--
roughly a band across southern Northumberland and northern Durham--is
approximately parallel with the northern limits of the densest Scandinavian settlement during the Anglo-Saxon period, as suggested by a study
of Scandinavian place names.[17] It also seems significant that this belt
coincides roughly with the number of isoglosses that also parallel the
northern limits of the densest Scandinavian settlement. Eduard Kolb,
in a recent article,[18] graphically demonstrates that the northern limit
of the old Danelaw seems to constitute a major dialect boundary, which--
on the basis of several aspects of sound, grammar, and vocabulary--
distinguishes Northumberland and northern Durham linguistically from
most of the rest of the North Country. The implication is not that the
presence of the Scandinavians caused the pronoun thou to be retained
longer in most of the North, but rather that its strong retention there--
and not in Northumberland and northern Durham--reflects the same geographical and political separateness that is reflected also in the other
isoglosses.
    Despite the distinctive situation in the Northumberland area though,
we can still say that--at least in the speech of those surveyed--the
old historical singular thou maintains a very vigorous existence in
most of the northern region. And, in general, the old distinctions that
we might expect still exist between thou and you.[19] Traditionally the
choice between the two pronouns depended on the relative rank of the
people concerned, or--in cases of approximately equivalent rank--on the

relative distance or closeness of two people. A speaker said you to
someone of greater consequence--in age, or in social or political
power--but thou to someone of lesser consequence. And to someone of
approximately equal consequence, the speaker varied his pronoun typically
from you--in the case of a comparative stranger--to thou--in the case
of a close friend of a member of the family. The Survey gives us an
opportunity to observe the pronoun, to some extent, in all four of these
relationships--superiority, subordination, distance, and closeness. We
do not find all the information that we might want: sometimes, for
instance, a pronoun form does not occur in a response for a certain
locality.[20] But there is enough material to draw some tentative conclusions since, as suggested earlier, in a number of the eighteen items
the informant is asked to imagine himself a participant in different
situations--an old man talking to a little boy or a mother talking to
her child, for example.

The pronoun usage to someone of more consequence than the speaker is
elicited in a rather indirect way: the informant (IX.7.2)[21] is simply
asked if he would use thou to an older man. Hence, the response is
something less than spontaneous; furthermore, the fieldworker sometimes
neglected either to ask the question or to record the answer. Nevertheless, what emerges is, for the most part, what we might expect: the
informants in most of the localities where an answer is recorded responded
that thou was not to be used to someone older or someone of particular
consequence, like a parson or a vicar,[22] the implication being that the
form would be considered distinctly impolite. The informant from
Longtown, Cumberland (#1), for example, reported that children were often
told not to thou anyone older than themselves.[23]

One sidelight revealed by the Survey is that in a few localities in
Yorkshire thou can apparently be used, quite untraditionally, to older
people--sometimes with reservations, sometimes, presumably, without.
The informant at York (#19) indicated that though thou could be used to
anybody, it was considered "rough" in some cases.[24] On the other hand,
from the informants at Stokesley (#2), Dent (#5), and Askrigg (#7), the
response was simply that thou can be used to anybody. And this is
interesting, not just because it is rather untraditional, but because
it seems to represent an expansion of a form which has, in general,
been contracting--even in the North. It is interesting also in view of
a tendency that Roger Brown and Albert Gilman have recently observed
in regard to the second-person pronoun in other modern languages--a
tendency they have called an "extension of the solidarity ethic."[25]
They conclude that pronoun distinctions in French, German, and Italian
are being made more often nowadays on the basis of closeness or lack
of it, and less often with regard to power or rank; and they contend,
further, that the pronoun of closeness or "solidarity"--the pronoun
corresponding to English thou--is being extended more widely than ever
before. The dialect use of thou to anybody by some informants in
Yorkshire seems to reflect such a tendency, on a fairly small scale.

There are three items in which we may observe pronoun usage in speech
to someone of less consequence than the speaker. Two of them involve
an old man talking to a small boy. The first (VI.5.8) asks the
informant to imagine a boy sitting with his hand to his jaw. The
typical response--with several variations--is something equivalent to
"Have you got a toothache?"[26] And the pronoun is thou almost 75% of
the time. The second item (IX.9.4) suggests an encounter with a small

boy who is vaguely familiar. And the responses range widely; but thou
occurs about 80% of the time. In both cases the high percentage of thou
is what we might expect, in view of the traditional use of thou to the
young.
    But the third item (VI.5.3) involving pronoun usage to a person of
less importance offers something of a contrast. The informant is placed
in the position of a mother scolding a child who has just gotten his
mouth all smeared with jam. The responses vary from "Rub thy gob!" to
"Wipe your mucky mouth!"[27] But they contain thou only about 65% of the
time. The standard you thus occurs here in about 35% of the localities,
whereas in the speech of man to boy it is only found in about 20% to
25% of the localities. Whether or not this difference has something
to do with the refining tendencies that the Survey attributes to women,
it does suggest that the standard form is gaining ground more rapidly in
the speech of a woman to a child than in the speech of a man to a boy.
    Several items in the Survey enable us to arrive at some generalizations
about pronoun usage between those who are of approximately equal consequence. There is one item (VI.5.4) that clearly compels the informant to speak directly to the fieldworker. It is a rather striking
question in that the fieldworker is instructed to stick out his tongue
at the informant and ask, "What am I doing now?"[28] The variety of
verbs in expressions for sticking out the tongue is remarkable.[29] But
only about 25% of the responses contained a form of thou, while more
than 35% had a form of you. Inasmuch as the fieldworker would be a
comparative stranger to the informant, the low percentage of thou and
high percentage of you seem quite understandable and in keeping with
traditional usage. In the rest of the responses to the fieldworker--
roughly 40%--no second-person pronoun is used. But strangely enough,
almost three-quarters of these contain a form of the third-person
pronoun his--in the phrase "sticking his tongue out,"[30] for example.
What this implies is not clear: the editors confess their bewilderment.
But it seems possible that the his may reflect the distance between
comparative strangers even more forcefully than the you form. He,
instead of you, as a pronoun of address has been recorded by Wright
with varying implications, one of them being a particularly respectful
attitude.[31] Hence, it may be that the proportion of responses equivalent
to you is much higher than it seems to be.
    The pronoun to friends, particularly good friends, presents a strikingly
different picture and is suggestive of the usage between those with
relatively equal status and a close relationship. First of all, there
are eight items--IX.5.4, IX.7.2/3/5/6/7/9, and IX.8.5--that are somewhat
ambiguous in the situations they suggest.[32] Several of them seem to
imply that the fieldworker himself is to be addressed, but all of them
are repeated more than once to elicit other personal pronoun forms--she,
they, and the like. Hence, it seems likely that the informant was under
the impression that he was supposed to be speaking to a somewhat
generalized listener of his acquaintance and not primarily to the fieldworker.[33] Appropriately, the proportion of thou forms is much higher
than in the item directed to the fieldworker, averaging in general about
70%.
    More specifically, there are four items--items other than these
generalized ones--which clearly set up a situation where the informant
is supposedly speaking to some friend or acquaintance. In one item
(VI.14.2) the informant speaks to someone whose voice is familiar; and

thou occurs in almost 70% of the localities. In another (VIII.2.8),
the informant meets a friend on the street and inquires about his
health; the pronoun is thou a little more than 70% of the time. And in
the two remaining items in this category, the informant is supposedly
conversing with someone who is not just a friend, but an old friend--
one of many years standing. In the one case (VIII.3.2) the pronoun thou
occurs in more than 70% of the responses; in the other (VIII.3.7), in
more than 80%. And in the first case, it happens that three of the you
responses were from women, and five of the responses did not include a
pronoun; so it is possible that thou would occur more than 80% of the
time in both responses to old friends. The only other situation, it
will be recalled, where there was an equally high incidence of thou was
in the speech of an old man to a little boy.[34]
   The final item (VI.14.2) involving speakers of approximately the same
rank is one that asks the informant to imagine he is speaking to his
wife. Supposedly she has just put on a new hat that is very becoming;
and the informant is instructed to tell her what she would like to hear
him say. In this item the responses included a form of thou only about
50% of the time--or less frequently than in any response except that
directed to the fieldworker, where the figure was 25%. And you occurred
more than 35% of the time--or more often than in any other responses
except those of the informant to the fieldworker, and of a mother to
her child, which were both about 35% also. The relatively low proportion of thou and the relatively high proportion of you from husband to
wife is interesting,[35] for it was long the tendency for a wife to say
you to her husband and for a husband to say thou to his wife--in
keeping with the hierarchical notion of male superiority that was
current in the earlier centuries.[36] This pronominal double standard
had somewhat weakened by the seventeenth century, however, so that
women in that era sometimes addressed their husbands as thou.[37] But
in dialect speech up through the nineteenth century, according to
Wright,[38] the old one-directional thou by the husband was still current.
Hence, the fact that thou occurs only about 50% of the time from husband
to wife here may suggest, again, the refining influence of women.
Perhaps the husband uses thou less often to his wife because, in many
cases, she tends to avoid it herself and does not wish to hear it from
him--any more than she wants to hear a disparaging remark about her
new hat.
   Despite certain limitations on the information about the pronoun in
the Survey, then, we can draw a few conclusions about the extent and
usage of the historical thou singular. It is an integral part of the
speech of most of the localities surveyed throughout the northern
region, with the exception of the Isle of Man and the greater part of
Northumberland. Among the oldest dialect speakers in the North, you
still prevails in address to those who are superior in rank or age--with
perhaps some weakening of the traditional prohibition against thou in
some parts of Yorkshire. And you forms still outnumber thou forms in
speech to comparative strangers. On the other hand, where a woman is
involved as speaker or listener, thou--though still occurring much of
the time--seems to be losing ground noticeably. But in speech from
man to boy and in speech between men who are friends--particularly old
friends--thou seems to have its staunchest strongholds. The traditional
singular would seem to persist in these relationships almost as strongly
as it does, on another plane, in the language of prayer. In other

words, for the informants studied, the persistence of the traditional
thou in Northern dialect speech from man to boy and from friend to
friend is presumably exceeded only by its persistence, in both dialect
and standard language, in address to God.

NOTES

*The earlier SAMLA-ADS version of this paper was called "Thee and
Thou in Northern England: What the Survey of English Dialects Reveals."
Read at the SAMLA-ADS Meeting, Atlanta, Georgia, November 1968.

[1]Thomas Pyles, The Origins and Development of the English Language
(New York, 1964), p. 187.

[2]Six vols. (London, 1898-1905). His English Dialect Grammar (London,
1905) also has some relevant comments on the pronoun.

[3]Basic Material, Vol. I: The Six Northern Counties and the Isle of
Man, ed. Harold Orton and Wilfred J. Halliday (Leeds, 1962-1963).

[4]They are Items VI.5.3/4/8/17, 14.2; VIII.2.8, 3.2/7, 7.9; and
IX.5.4, 7.2/3/5/6/7/9, 8.5, 9.4. The items are arranged in books, e.g.,
Book VI "The Human Body"; each book is divided into parts, e.g., Book
VI, Part 5 "The Mouth"; and each part contains a number of items, e.g.,
Book VI, Part 5, Item 3 (or VI.5.3) "Wipe your mouth!" (the response
that is to be elicited in some form).

[5]Survey, p. 1081.

[6]Unless otherwise indicated, references to you and thou in the text
are intended to include the other case forms of these pronouns as well.
In quotations from the informants' responses, the exact case forms are
of course retained.

[7]"Fieldwork for a Dialect Atlas of England," Transactions of the
Yorkshire Dialect Society, IX (1953), 20.

[8]Survey, p. 1053. One of the informants does mention that thou is
still heard in one town on the southern edge of the island.

[9]Numbers in parentheses after localities refer to Map 1.

[10]In Allendale, as in most of the other localities, there was more
than one informant. The items were divided up among the various individuals. Thus, in many cases, there are at least two informants
reflected in the responses to the eighteen pronoun items; but each item
was answered by only one person. In Allendale, as it happened, one man
replied to all of the pronoun items, although four informants were used
altogether. (See Survey, p. 14.)

[11]As Map 1 indicates, _you_ occurs in a few other scattered localities about as frequently as it does in northern Durham. Two of these localities--Halewood, Lancashire (No. 14) and Newbald, Yorkshire (No. 25)--are very near the southern edge of the northern region, a fact which may turn out to be significant when the basic material for the midland counties becomes available. The other localities--the Yorkshire towns of Egton (No. 4), Dent (No. 5), and Rillington (No. 11)--do not seem to form a part of any larger pattern.

[12]Titles such as Thomas Bewick's The Howdy and the Upgetting: Two Tales of Sixty Years Sin Seyne, in the Tyneside Dialect and Joseph P. Robson's The Song of Solomon in the Newcastle Dialect. Wright's Northumberland sources are listed in Vol. VI of the Dictionary, pp. 17-19.

[13]On Early English Pronunciation, Vol. V: The Existing Phonology of the English Dialects, Early English Text Society, Extra Series, No. 56 (London, 1889).

[14]Ellis, p. 7. In all quotations where the second-person pronouns are italicized, the italics are those of the present writer.

[15]The pronouns for the Knaresdale informant are found in Ellis, pp. 564 and 568; those for the other three informants are on pp. 645-646.

[16]Ellis, pp. 666-667.

[17]P. H. Sawyer, The Age of the Vikings (London, 1962), p. 157.

[18]"Skandinavisches in den nordenglischen Dialekten," Anglia, LXXXIII (1965), 127-53.

[19]The classical formulation of the distinctions is set down by Walter W. Skeat in his introduction to a Middle English poem, The Romance of William of Palerne (Early English Text Society, Extra Series, No. 1 [London, 1867], p. xliii).

[20]We do not find all the information we might like about case forms of the pronouns either. Most of the eighteen relevant items, not unreasonably, elicit unstressed forms of the pronouns. Only two items (IX.7.7/9) are set up so that a stressed form is practically inevitable as a response. Both of these items involve the pronoun in a subject function; and the responses suggest that the historical nominative thou is the usual case form in this function. There are, in fact, no examples in the two items of the historical objective form thee as a subject. For the pronoun _you_, the information is even less comprehensive since the pronoun occurs so infrequently outside the Northumberland area and the Isle of Man. The responses in these areas suggest, however, that both the historical nominative ye and the historical objective _you_ can occur as subjects. Finally, there is, of course, no basis in these items for deciding what forms occur in the object function, for either pronoun.

[21]Numbers of this sort in the text refer to the specific items in the Survey which are the sources of the observations. (See Footnote 4.)

[22]An answer occurs for almost 70% of the localities; and about four-fifths of the answers indicate that thou was felt to be inappropriate in speaking to older people.

[23]Survey, p. 1052.

[24]Survey, p. 1053. The immediately following information about York-shire is also from p. 1053.

[25]"The Pronouns of Power and Solidarity," in Style in Language, ed. Thomas A. Sebeok (New York, 1960), pp. 253-76.

[26]Survey, p. 621.   [27]Survey, pp. 615-16.   [28]Survey, p. 616.

[29]Among them are lagging, lapping, slaking, slapping, slicking, and slarking (Survey, pp. 1617-1618).

[30]Survey, pp. 616-18.

[31]English Dialect Grammar, p. 274.

[32]Item IX.7.2 has already been referred to in connection with the use of the pronoun to older people. In addition to commenting on his usage in such a situation, the informant here was also asked to give certain pronoun forms directly.

[33]In Item IX.7.6, for example, the question asked is "We could say: We were late, weren't we? You could say of yourself: I was late,...?" The first response, of course, is to be in the first-person singular--something equivalent to "wasn't I?" But the question is to be rephrased to elicit not only a second-person singular, but also a feminine third-person singular and a third-person plural.

[34]Occurrence of thou is also fairly frequent (more than 70%) in one item not yet mentioned--Item VIII.7.9--which calls for the informant verbally to chase away someone who is a nuisance. The relative rank and relationship of the person to be addressed are not made clear. But the nature of a number of the responses (e.g., "gan to hell," p.950) suggests that to many of the informants the imagined listener was neither a superior nor an absolute stranger.

[35]The proportions might vary slightly since there was no pronoun recorded in about 10% of the localities. But the relative proportion of you would still seem high enough to be significant.

[36]In some medieval mystery plays, for example, even Mary uses you to her husband, Joseph, while he uses thou to her (The Towneley Plays, ed. George England, Early English Text Society, Extra Series, No. 71 [London, 1897], pp. 160-65).

[37]Anne Carvey Johnson, "The Pronoun of Direct Address in Seventeenth-Century English, "American Speech, XLI (1966), 268.

[38]English Dialect Dictionary, s.v. thou.

DIALECT CONTOURS IN THE SOUTHERN STATES*

Gordon R. Wood

The continuing study of American English dialects has clarified some
of our ideas about the true nature of our language. It used to be
thought that the tangled pattern of migration and settlement had produced a "general American" dialect west of the Appalachians. Now,
because of the work of many linguistic geographers, we know that
southern limits of the Northern dialect can be traced from the
Atlantic states west to Nebraska and the Dakotas.[1] Furthermore, we
know that Midland words occur in parts of the former Confederate
States and that these words can be found as far west as the Oklahoma
panhandle.

This article deals with the presence of Midland and Southern words
in those parts of the South which were settled after 1800. Its main
purpose is to show the diversity of regional vocabulary found in
Alabama, Arkansas, Florida, Georgia, Louisiana, Mississippi, Oklahoma,
and Tennessee, a vocabulary investigated by means of postal questionnaires.[2] For convenience in explaining this diversity, we will say
that the events of the nineteenth century have three phases in this
region: first, the advancing frontier; second, the growth of towns
and permanent settlements; and, third, the increase of regional
communication. Each of these can be associated with certain aspects
of twentieth-century regional vocabulary in the South.

The first stages of advance into the interior South were by way of
the Appalachian mountain valleys and gaps. By 1820 Daniel Boone and
his contemporaries had pushed the frontier into Tennessee and Kentucky,
south to the Gulf of Mexico, and northwest along the rivers of
Louisiana and Arkansas. The general direction of this advance, then,
is from Pennsylvania southwest along the Virginia mountain corridors
into Tennessee and Kentucky, and then south or west again; it was
soon joined by movement down the Ohio River. Travel directly west
from settled parts of South Carolina and Georgia was blocked by
mountain barriers and by hostile Indians.[3]

Thus, at this stage, the migrant from Pennsylvania had a series of
ways to reach the interior, while the South Carolina or Georgia
migrant was blocked. In short, the first stage favored the introduction of Midland or Northern dialect words at the expense of coastal
Southern words. The term tow sack has served to illustrate this
point before and will serve here. It is a North Carolina term for
'burlap bag' and obviously went with North Carolinians when they moved
west to settle Tennessee. When we superimpose the southern isoglosses
of tow sack on a map of the first lines of migration into the interior
of the South, we see (on Map 1) that the present regional occurrence

Gordon R. Wood

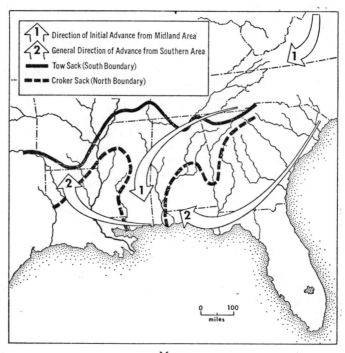

Map 1

follows those lines southward; its occurrence in Louisiana and Arkansas
is complicated by later migrations of Tennesseeans across the Mississippi
River.
Of course, <u>tow</u> <u>sack</u> might have come into this region later. Its
occurrence along the line of pioneer advance into the region could be
merely a coincidence. But, whether my explanation of the presence of
<u>tow</u> <u>sack</u> as a consequence of early migration is valid or not, the
present distribution shows how far south and west one word has gone which
entered the region along the same corridors that the Midland vocabulary
entered. It can stand for the regional introduction of Midland words
by 1820.
At the time that Midland words were being brought southwest, the inven-
tion of the cotton gin caused Southerners to become interested in
raising upland cotton. The Virginian, Carolinian, or Georgian living
east of the Blue Ridge Mountains left his rice or tobacco plantation
and secured for himself new lands in the wilderness. And thus the
Southern vocabulary was brought into the interior of the South, an event
which presents a very real difficulty for those who would discuss the
regional language of the interior states. In this article I shall use
"coastal Southern" as the technical term for that vocabulary which
Kurath, McDavid, and others call "Southern."
The general advance of coastal Southern was west and north, though in
far too erratic a fashion to describe here. The extent and direction
of this advance is across and into the Midland region which we have
already discussed. It can be illustrated by the current distribution
of <u>croker</u> <u>sack</u>, <u>crocus</u> <u>sack</u>, a coastal synonym of <u>tow</u> <u>sack</u>. The arrows
marked 2 on Map 1 show in a schematic way how <u>croker</u> <u>sack</u> and some
other coastal Southern words commingle with <u>tow</u> <u>sack</u> and the Midland
influences moving south (arrows number 1).
In discussing the second phase, the period in which towns, villages,
and plantations were established, we cannot say how the forces of
stability acted upon a particular element in the regional vocabularies.
But we can delimit those regions in which Midland or Southern became
the distinctive vocabulary.
Let us begin with Midland again. The mountain dialect of colonial
Virginia and of the Carolinas was Midland, or more narrowly South
Midland. After the American Revolution, migrants from these states
moved on to the uplands of eastern Tennessee and Kentucky, or northern
Georgia, Alabama, and Mississippi; later they settled in Arkansas,
Oklahoma, and Texas.
The area in which this Midland dialect is prominent can be delimited
by drawing the combined isoglosses of <u>French</u> <u>harp</u>, <u>pack</u> 'to carry,'
<u>clabber</u> <u>milk</u>, <u>red</u> <u>worm</u>, <u>sugar</u> <u>tree</u>, and <u>fireboard</u>, 'mantelpiece.'
The resulting boundary (see Map 2 below) places this aspect of Midland
in eastern Kentucky, east and middle Tennessee, north Georgia and
Alabama, northeast Mississippi, and, west of the Mississippi River, in
northwest Arkansas. The southern point of origin for this line is at
that terminus which Kurath established when he drew the main boundary
between Midland and Southern along the crest of'the Blue Ridge Mountains until it entered the upland counties of South Carolina. From
that point the evidence enables us to extend the boundary west in the
hill country of Georgia, Alabama, and Mississippi, turning it north and
east in Tennessee along the Cumberland Plateau. West of the Mississippi
River, this evidence points to no specific part of the southern Arkansas

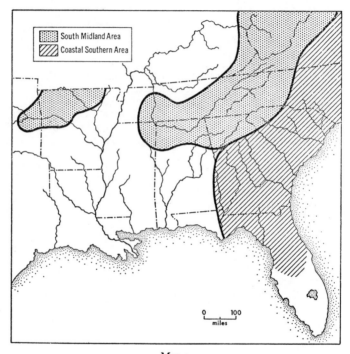

Map 2

uplands as being significantly South Midland in dialect traits; in
northwest Arkansas, however, we can delimit an area which has these
specific Midland features already mentioned.

With Midland restricted to the mountain regions, we could hope that
the vocabulary of the rest of the South is entirely Southern. But the
evidence tends to dash that hope.

The combined isoglosses of eight coastal Southern words will enable us
to draw a second significant boundary in the South. These words are
lightwood 'kindling,' low 'the sound made by contented cows,' tote 'to
carry,' co-wench 'a call to cattle,' snap beans or snaps, harp or mouth
harp 'harmonica,' turn of wood 'an armload,' and fritters. These isoglosses form a wide band in north Georgia, its outer edge touching the
Midland isogloss which I constructed earlier; for convenience, the band
is drawn as a single line. As the isoglosses move westward, they converge and then turn south. Generally the boundary follows the valley of
the Chattahoochee River as it flows west and south. This river line
and part of the political boundary of Georgia coincide with the boundary of coastal Southern (see Map 2). A small island of coastal words
in south Mississippi will interest us later in this article. At the
moment, however, we can say that Southern comes to an end along the
Chattahoochee River in much the same way that Midland comes to an end
along the Cumberland Plateau. The main boundary which divided the two
in the Blue Ridge splits in north Georgia, the Midland half continuing
west and the Southern half turning abruptly south.

While some events served to stabilize the pattern of word distribution, other events introduced change. During the nineteenth and twentieth centuries, movement from place to place became easier. To cite
but one factor that disturbed the elements of linguistic stability in
the interior South, steamboats, trains, automobiles, and airplanes
increased the degree of movement from one region to another. Back-
woodsmen came to town; city slickers went into the country; mail order
catalogs appeared everywhere. Increasing ease of communication introduced abrupt shifts in the standing of regional words. The terms tote
sack and shelly beans suddenly became commercial names to be used
nationally; fireboard, on the other hand, gave way to the mail order
catalog choice of the regional words mantel or mantelpiece.

There are evidences that these more startling events are accompanied
by quieter but probably more significant linguistic movements, our
third phase in this study. To describe this third linguistic development, we need to use a different kind of map, one that stresses the
frequency with which particular groups of words occur within a region.
This sort of density map is initially drawn in the same way that our
earlier maps of Midland and Southern distribution were drawn. But,
instead of trying to establish a general outer boundary from the isoglosses, we seek to generalize and delimit the areas of increasing
overlap among the words mapped. An example may help clarify this
procedure. If we put one coin on top of another so that the edge of
one covers about half of the other, we could draw a line around the
two which would resemble a figure eight, the isogloss of the region
covered by both coins. If we draw only the area of overlap, however,
our figure would resemble a pair of parentheses, the density map of
the region covered by parts of both coins. We would put the number 2
in the center of these parentheses to show that the density at that
point is composed of two elements.

Now to the evidence from the regional vocabulary. In an earlier paragraph I wrote that the coastal Southern vocabulary formed a broad band
in north Georgia. Such a band comes into being when isoglosses do not
occur close together. Or to put it another way, as we move from north
Georgia southward we find an increasing number of Southern isoglosses.
The increasing density of coastal Southern words can be demonstrated
from the maps of mosquito hawk 'dragon fly,' press peach, fatwood
'kindling,' spider 'skillet,' whicker 'a sound which horses make,' and
the cattle call co-wench. The resulting pattern of densities (Map 3)
shows that all six of these words occur within a limited area and that
adjacent to it is a wide zone in which four of the six words occur;
these densities are shown by the numerals 6 and 4 respectively. Outside
that area the numbers decrease rapidly, the degree of rapidity depending
on the direction in which one moves.

From this map we learn that the heaviest current concentration of
coastal Southern words is several hundred miles south of the boundary
which we first established between Southern and Midland in Georgia. We
can draw other conclusions from the map. To do so, however, we must
assume that these six words were a part of the colonial vocabulary in
the English settlements along the Savannah River. With that agreed on,
we then notice that Savannah and its adjacent counties are in the zone
of lesser density. To rephrase the matter, the center of coastal
Southern vocabulary has shifted west of its colonial origins and is now
located between Albany, Georgia, and Tallahassee, Florida. Its chances
for expansion are severely limited by the geography of the region and
because it is far removed from newer centers of activity such as Atlanta.

The continuity of coastal Southern even in this region is threatened
by Midland influences. We noted earlier that the main Midland boundary
passed through the mountains of north Georgia. This boundary now becomes
a kind of line of departure for a southward penetration. The evidence
for this advance comes from the density map of the Midland Jew's harp
or juice harp, comforter, fatback 'a kind of bacon,' dog irons,
middling(s), and ash cake, and from a composite formed by the responses
cock, hay cock, rick, hay rick, and hand stack. One edge of this
density map (Map 4) touches the Savannah River in east Georgia; the
other edge lies in eastern Alabama. The zone of greatest density,
however, has its axis in Georgia along the valleys of the Flint,
Ocmulgee, and Suwannee rivers. All seven of the mapped terms have
followed the river and valley complex southward through Georgia to its
southern political boundary; five of the same terms have gone on into
Florida; a smaller number of the terms have come south on either side
of this main corridor.

We will understand the significance of this penetration a little better
if we superimpose the map of Midland densities on that which we have
drawn of coastal Southern densities. When we have done this (see Map 5),
we find that the zone of greatest Midland density has split the Southern
zones.

As we follow Jew's harp and the other Midland words southward on Map 5,
we see that in the vicinity of Atlanta all seven of the examples enter
and cross the zone in which four coastal words such as mosquito hawk
are located, and that the same seven words then enter and cross the zone
in which all six coastal words are concentrated. The words form zones
of concentration with eleven and thirteen words of a composite Midland-
Southern dialect. On either side of this corridor of greatest density,

Gordon R. Wood

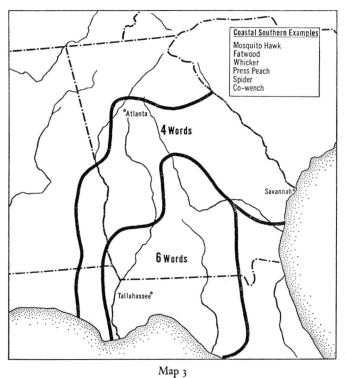

Coastal Southern Examples

Mosquito Hawk
Fatwood
Whicker
Press Peach
Spider
Co-wench

°Atlanta

4 Words

Savannah°

6 Words

Tallahassee°

Map 3

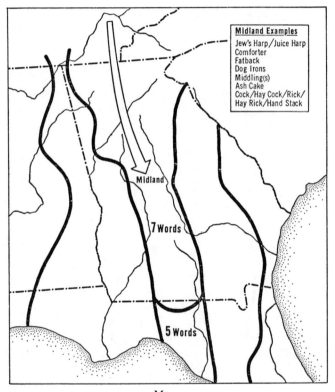

Map 4

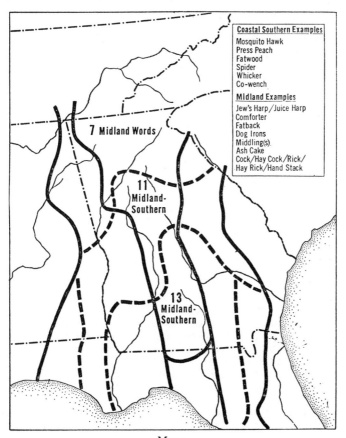

Coastal Southern Examples
Mosquito Hawk
Press Peach
Fatwood
Spider
Whicker
Co-wench

Midland Examples
Jew's Harp / Juice Harp
Comforter
Fatback
Dog Irons
Middling(s)
Ash Cake
Cock/Hay Cock/Rick/
Hay Rick/Hand Stack

7 Midland Words

11
Midland-
Southern

13
Midland-
Southern

Map 5

the Midland-Southern pattern changes, decreasing in variable ways. The relative densities of these adjacent zones have been omitted in order to emphasize the conditions along the main corridor.

The significance of this development for Georgians living within the bounds of the main corridor is that north of Atlanta the Midland vocabulary predominates, from Atlanta for a hundred miles or so south the Midland is evident more frequently than is the Southern, and chiefly in the extreme south central part of the state the two dialects are approximately equal in frequency of use. The areas of lesser Midland density east and west of this central corridor do indicate that Midland influences are spreading in both directions, so that natives of Georgia and Alabama have used and are using an increasing number of words from this regional dialect.

No other linguistic corridor appears in Alabama until we reach its western political boundary. But there, in Alabama and Mississippi, we find a similar pattern of Southern and Midland densities. Coastal Southern appears to have been established in Mississippi when the first planters occupied lands south of the thirty-second meridian; Alabama was settled later and thus does not provide the events which would link the coastal Southern dialect of Georgia with that of Mississippi.

The density pattern in Alabama-Mississippi is made up of the coastal words mosquito hawk, press peach, and whicker combined with gallery 'porch,' and pull bone. For lack of better labels we can call the last two "Mississippi Valley words." They occur in densities of two or more and are shown on Map 6 between the broken lines. Midland words enter this region along the Tennessee state line and generally advance south, following the trace of the Tombigbee River. This is a surprising development when we notice that no similar advance can be discovered along the Mississippi River. My explanation, a guess, is that travel and commerce from Memphis to Mobile was easier along the Tombigbee than it was on the more violent Mississippi; the ease of movement up and down river is thus reflected by the linguistic corridor which developed in the Tombigbee Valley.

The evidence for this corridor is derived from the density patterns of the Midland words clabber cheese, coverlet or coverlid, Jew's harp or juice harp, comforter, fatback, middling(s), jackleg preacher, ash cake, red worm, plum peach, water gutter, and whet stone. On Map 6, we see that the density pattern of seven of these words forms a narrow corridor extending south from the Tennessee border and that four of them form a somewhat wider corridor extending in the same direction and reaching Mobile. In northeast Mississippi they form a composite Midland-Southern density pattern of nine words along the main corridor. Near the confluence of the Tombigbee and Black Warrior rivers they become a Midland-Southern zone of twenty words, and to the southwest a second zone of seven words.

From this evidence we can draw almost the same conclusions that we drew from the evidence in Georgia. The only real problem is to explain the difference in relative width of the two linguistic corridors if we compare the distances between their respective outer edges. The difference may be explained simply as the consequence of the geography of rivers: in Georgia there are many avenues southward; in Mississippi proper there is the one key river leading in the same direction. On the other hand, the differences in width of the two linguistic corridors may be explained as history: the Midland vocabulary entered Georgia earlier and thus has had time to penetrate south and to expand east and west;

112

Gordon R. Wood

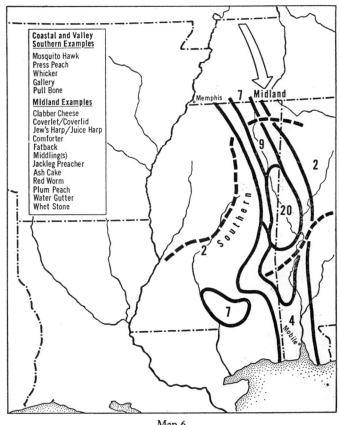

Map 6

it entered Mississippi later and, having advanced along a main avenue of communication, has not had time to expand laterally to the same extent that it has in Georgia. Whatever the explanation may be, we have evidence that Midland densities have been superimposed on Southern densities in this region. Where the Midland densities are greatest, the native speaker has the widest range of choice between competing dialectal vocabularies.

We have seen that the zones of Midland density have taken linear or tubular shapes east of the Mississippi River; west of that river, the density pattern has corpulscular shapes--free forms with boundaries advancing irregularly south and west. Words found in northwest Arkansas will serve to introduce us to the new shapes.

The South Midland dialect has already been reported for Arkansas (Map 2 In the same general region we find a few coastal words also, but mainly Midland words. A concentration map of mosquito hawk, spider, big house 'living room,' tin panning, blinds 'window shades,' worm fence, jerked beef, pressed meat, coal hod, snake feeder, tied quilt, coverlet or coverlid, ridy horse, breaking off 'clearing skies,' sow belly and fatback, head cheese or hog's head cheese, sallet or salad, corn dodger, smearcase, and the complex formed of cock, hay cock, rick, hay rick, and hand stack shows that all these items are reported from Washington County (see Map 7). There all twenty items are known. Ten are reported from the counties immediately to the north and fourteen from the counties to the east. To the west the count is zero. This gradual increase from four to twenty items as we move west or from ten to twenty as we move south seems to present no great difficulty. These are signs of movement into the area by speakers who were able to travel either overland or along the river. The abrupt southern and western loss of density is another matter. The southern edge is in the Ozark Mountains, a linguistic and physical barrier to entrance into the valley of the Arkansas River. The western edge may be as it is because of the reservation of Oklahoma lands for the Indians until the end of the past century.

A larger configuration comes from the density patterns of dog irons, snake doctor, flying jenny 'merry-go-round,' red worm, tow sack, fairing off, side meat, and the composite maps of wheel horse and line horse (see Map 8). These eight words have a center of density near Little Rock, Arkansas. One axis extends along the Arkansas River and presumably is advancing along that historic travel route; the other axis extends south or southwest across five counties. Six of the words form a second density zone which covers most of Arkansas and enters eastern Oklahoma, with an island forming in the south central part of the same state. Zones of lesser density form outer arcs in Louisiana, Arkansas, and Oklahoma. The recent publication of Atwood's The Regional Vocabulary of Texas[4] will enable readers to extend the density patterns into Texas itself. If and when a study of local words in Missouri appears, we will be able to trace the same patterns in that state too.

West of the Mississippi the Midland vocabulary is widespread in Arkansas, Oklahoma, and Louisiana. In some localities the density of Midland words in use is greater than in others, but the shape of the contours suggests that this vocabulary is moving steadily south and west. Of course, there are words from other regional vocabularies scattered here and there--witness the occurrence of mosquito hawk. But, from the evidence thus far examined, I have not found indications

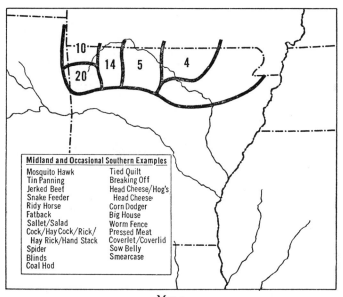

Map 7

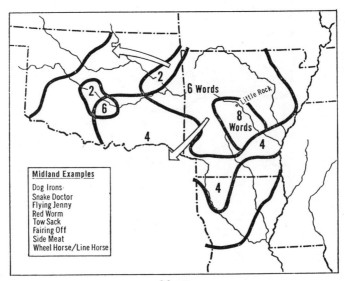

Map 8

that Midland has penetrated another dialect in the way that it penetrated coastal Southern in Georgia.

In considering these aspects of regional vocabulary in some of the states of the former Confederacy, we have seen that change and dialect mingling have been common in those parts of the land settled after 1800. The earliest migrations from the Atlantic states brought Midland into the deep South and then superimposed coastal Southern on it at some points but not at others. In time the interior settlements developed distinctly Midland traits in the uplands of Georgia, Alabama, Mississippi, Tennessee, and northwest Arkansas. (Kentucky and West Virginia have these same traits, but they are not a part of this study.) Coastal Southern has a western boundary along the Chattahoochee River in Georgia and a few isolated outposts further west. It is convenient to say that the forming of the South Midland and Southern dialect areas is the second stage of linguistic history in the interior; obviously, however, this development is simply a part of an ongoing process. While some activities or events serve to establish the boundaries of Southern and Midland in the states west and south of the Appalachians, other events introduce change. Among these events is the increasing ease of movement from place to place. East of the Mississippi River, the avenues of travel and communication led southward in Georgia and Mississippi; along these avenues Midland words moved into areas where coastal Southern had already been used. The density maps show this change in the available vocabulary, a kind of tubular thrust into the coastal plains. West of the Mississippi, the Midland vocabulary, with an occasional Southern term included, appears to be steadily expanding west and south in wide zones. If we consider that these density patterns mark the third and latest stage of development, then we must say they show that in the interior regions of the South dialectal patterns have not stabilized themselves. Furthermore, the density patterns indicate that Midland is actively intruding on other dialectal traits that may have been in the region earlier.

NOTES

*The earlier SAMLA-ADS version of this paper was called "Regional Word Distribution in the South." Read at the SAMLA-ADS Meeting, Atlanta, Georgia, November 1963.

[1] Maps showing the westward advance of Northern and Midland words are in Harold B. Allen, Minor Dialect Areas of the Upper Midwest, PADS, No. 30 (November, 1958), particularly Map 1, p. 4.

[2] Details of preparation, distribution, and analysis of the findings were published by the American Philosophical Society. See Gordon R. Wood, "A Word Geography of the Interior South," Year Book 1961 (Philadelphia, 1962), pp. 602-4.

[3] A fuller discussion of the geographical and human influences is in Gordon R. Wood, Word Distribution in the Interior South, PADS, No. 35 (April, 1961), 1-16.

Gordon R. Wood

[4]E. Bagby Atwood, The Regional Vocabulary of Texas (Austin, 1962).

THE NAMING OF AMERICAN DIALECTS*

James B. McMillan

Although the compilers of dictionaries and glossaries have used
geographical labels for nearly two centuries, the historical
dictionaries, the Dictionary of American English, the Dictionary of
Americanisms, and the Oxford English Dictionary (hereafter DAE, DA,
OED) have not treated such terms as Midland, New England, Northern,
and Southern as names of regional dialects, and general dictionaries
(except, predictably, Webster's Third New International Dictionary)
have done little better.

The DAE defines and illustrates eight senses of the word Northern
and has entries for nine combinations beginning with Northern, but none
with reference to regional speech. The DA cites a 1799 "New England
dialect" among its combinations s.v. New England along with New England
boiled dinner, primer, shilling, states, etc., and it has entries for
New Englandism (1831-), Southernism (1882-), Westernism (1838-), and
Yankeeism (1806-), but the only term for a regional type of speech
entered is Yankee, meaning (eastern) New England, from 1772.

The three historical dictionaries were published too early to
recognize the names of major regional dialects in the United States
adopted by dialectologists using the findings of the Linguistic Atlas
of the United States and Canada, but not one of the names for a major
region was coined de novo in the 1950s; all were in use earlier and
were given more precise definitions as Atlas records were completed.
The terms New England, Middle States, Northern, Southern, and Western
were commonly used by such pre-twentieth century word-watchers as
Bartlett, Clapin, Dunglison, Farmer, Schele de Vere, and Witherspoon
as labels, and Midland got into the nomenclature in the 1890s after
the organization of the American Dialect Society, undoubtedly as a
transfer from Midland as the name of a Middle English dialect and a
Modern English dialect, mentioned in a note but not dated in the OED.

The 1972 Supplement to the Oxford English Dictionary, Vol. I enters
Eastern as applied to "the (north)eastern parts of the United States,"
but not as a dialect name (synonym for Eastern New England). The
Supplement does have a subentry for General American, wrongly defined
as "a form of U.S. speech without marked dialectal or regional characteristics," in spite of the regional limitations in all of the
citations given. (For a fuller discussion see "Of Matters Lexicographical" in American Speech 43:289-92.)

Without question the semantic history of the name of an American
dialect is a problem for the historical lexicographer. When Noah
Webster in his Grammatical Institute of the English Language (1783)
1:6 wrote "The language in the middle States is tinctured with a

119

James B. McMillan

variety of Irish, Scotch, and German dialect," he was using "Middle
States" as a syntactic phrase, but later writers clearly used the term
as a regional dialect label (see appended glossary). Similarly such
terms as Northern and Southern were narrowed and specialized to mean
"a dialect with X features, spoken in Y area." The problem is not
different from that posed by the development of other combinations
including a geographical term, for example Southern crabapple or
Southern Pine Finch.
  A further compilation in recording dialect names is the changing that
has gone on as American dialect study has developed. For some years
after Hans Kurath delimited "Southern" in his 1949 Word Geography of the
Eastern United States most dialectologists assumed that eastern seaboard
"Southern" would include the Gulf states subsidiary area. However,
students like Bagby Atwood and Gordon Wood began to find it necessary
to distinguish Coastal Southern from inland Southern; and when Lee
Pederson completes his Linguistic Atlas of the Gulf States, the term
"Southern" may have to give way to several more specific names. Then
Southern, like earlier Eastern, may lose its status as a name for a
major dialect region.
  The following glossary, which includes dated citations, lists only
the names given to major dialect regions of the United States, some of
which (e.g. New England) are no longer so regarded.

GLOSSARY

Central, Central-Western. Tentative names for the English dialect(s)
    outside New England and the South, abandoned by dialectologists after
    the Northern-Midland boundary was established by Hans Kurath, H. B.
    Allen and A. H. Marckwardt.
1933 Leonard Bloomfield in Language 49: "In the United States we have
three great geographic types of standard English: New England, Central-
Western and Southern." 1940 Raven I. McDavid, Jr., in American Speech
15-144: "The former corresponds generally with both the low-front [a]
and the low-back [ɑ], unrounded Central-Western (CW) vowels." 1944
Hans Kurath in Language 20-155: "I hope to be able to show before long,
on the basis of the Atlas materials, that we must recognize a large
Central or Midland speech area in addition to the Southern, the Northern,
and the Northeastern (eastern New England)."

Coastal South(ern). Alternate name for the dialect area defined and
    labeled Southern by Hans Kurath in 1949.
1962 Robert Howren in American Speech 37-168: "Unlike the coastal
Southern dialect, Ocracoke speech generally has /r/." 1963 Gordon Wood
in American Speech 38-245: "I shall use 'coastal Southern' as the
technical term for that vocabulary which Kurath, McDavid and others call
'Southern.'" 1968 Standard College Dictionary (Text Edition) xxi
"Coastal Southern"[in map legend]. 1972 Lawrence Foley in Publication
of the American Dialect Society 58-8: "Ridy-horse occurs in the Coastal
South." Ib. 17 "Coastal Southern and Northern Lowlands was given."
1972 Hans Kurath, Studies in Area Linguistics 56: "Atwood is inclined
to attribute greater influence upon the regional vocabulary of Texas
to the South Midland dialect than to Coastal Southern."

East(ern). The dialect area east of the Connecticut River; Eastern
    New England.
1872 Maximilian Schele de Vere Americanisms 441: "Better far more

120

James B. McMillan

prevails in the East." 1919 G. P. Krapp, Pronunciation of Standard
English in America viii: "We can distinguish with some certainty
Eastern and Western and Southern speech." 1928 H. Kurath in SPE Tract
30-288: "The Eastern type is spoken by a majority of the inhabitants
of the Atlantic seaboard of New England with Boston as its center."
1930 John S. Kenyon American Pronunciation (1946) viii: "Eastern,
Southern, and General American."

General American. American English exclusive of New England and the
   South. Discredited as a label by dialect geographers.
1925 G. P. Krapp English Language in America, 2-29: "Western or General
American English." 1961 Webster's Third New International Dictionary,
passim. 1971 Albert H. Marckwardt in Readings in American Dialectology,
ed. H. B. Allen and Gary Underwood, 74: "Kurath disposed once and for
all of such negatively conceived catch-all categories as General American."

Hoosier. The (presumed) dialect of the Middle States, q.v.
1871 E. Eggleston, Hoosier Schoolmaster (cited by DA): "The 'big road'
(Hoosier for highway)." 1890 Richard L. Dawson in The Writer 4-28:
"Among the natives we have...the Hoosier dialect of the Middle States."
[In its early uses hoosier was not restricted to Indiana. See the DA,
s.v.]

Inland North(ern). The Northern Dialect (as defined by Kurath in 1949)
   exclusive of New England and the Hudson Valley.
1951 Raven I. McDavid, Jr., in Language Learning (1954) 4-103: "The
Inland North is the northern area exclusive of the Hudson valley and
eastern New England." 1956 Raven I. McDavid, Jr.,and Virginia McDavid
in Orbis 5-361: "Inland Northern" (rubric). 1968 Standard College
Dictionary, Text Edition xxi (map legend). 1973 Charles B. Martin and
Curt M. Rulon, The English Language 192: "Inland North (western Vermont,
Upstate New York & derivatives)." Ib. 193 "Inland Northern."

Middle States. The area (and the dialect of the area) including New
   York, Pennsylvania, New Jersey, Delaware, and Maryland. With no
   reference to dialect, the DA and the DAE define the term (1) as above,
   and (2) as the states between the Alleghany mountains and the
   Mississippi River.
1781 John Witherspoon in The Druid (quoted in M. M. Mathews, Beginnings
of American English, 1931, 25): "He will once in a while, i.e. some-
times, get drunk. The middle states." 1783 Noah Webster, A Grammatical
Institute of the English Language 1-6: "The language in the middle
States is tinctured with a variety of Irish, Scotch, and German dialects.
1829-30 The Virginia Literary Museum quoted in M. M. Mathews, The
Beginnings of American English (1931) 104: "Creek. 'a small river'
Southern and Middle States." 1893 C. H. Grandgent in Modern Language
Notes 8-137: "My 'Middle States' are New York, New Jersey, Pennsylvania,
Maryland."

Middle West(ern). Alternate term for 'General American.'
1926 Josephine M. Burnham in Dialect Notes 5-391: "Some Observations
Upon Middle Western Speech." 1958 Albert H. Marckwardt, American
English 135: "The concept thus eliminated has been variously known as
Middle Western, Western, or General American." 1958 Charles F. Hockett
Course in Modern Linguistics 346: "In the Middle West, all the words
listed usually have /ar/." Ib. 348 "Middle Western English also has

121

many words with /oj/." 1967 Carroll E. Reed Dialects of American English 24:"In the Eastern States the familiar Middle Western and Western word teeter-totter."

Midland. 1. The dialect of the Middle Atlantic States, 'the Middle States and derivative areas to the west.
1890 Sylvester Primer in Dialect Notes 1-57: "But the differences in the different sections of the country are not so great that we can properly speak of a New England dialect, a southern dialect, a midland dialect." 1896 George Hempl in Dialect Notes 1-438: "Midland: a belt separating the North from the South and extending from the Atlantic to the Mississippi (including Long Island, New York City and the adjoining counties, New Jersey, Del., all but the northern strip of Penn., the upper prong of West Virginia, southern Ohio, middle Ind., middle Ill., and St. Louis county, Mo.)." 1902 O. F. Emerson in Dialect Notes 2-273: "We ought to have some such studies for each of the great dialect divisions of the country: New England, the North Central region, the South Atlantic states, the South Central states, the Midland district paralleling Mason and Dixon's line on both sides, and the extreme West."
  2. The dialect lying between the Northern and Southern dialects as defined by Hans Kurath in 1949.
1944 Hans Kurath in Language 20-151:"I hope to be able to show before long, on the basis of the Atlas materials, that we must recognize a large Central or Midland speech area." 1948 Raven I. McDavid, Jr., in American Speech 23-197: "The concept of the Midland group of dialects, spreading westward and southward from the Philadelphia area, is perhaps the most fruitful contribution Kurath has made to the study of American dialects. 1949 Hans Kurath A Word Geography of the Eastern United States, Fig. 3, "The Midland." 1963 Harold B. Allen in Readings in Applied English Linguistics (2nd ed. 1964) 231: "The major bundle of Midland-Northern isoglosses stretches west to the Mississippi. 1965 Lee Pederson in Publication of the American Dialect Society 44-71: "Studies of speech characteristics of the very young with particular emphasis upon such apparent trends as the influences of Midland and Southern speech." 1967 Carroll E. Reed, Dialects of American English 47: "The northern limits of Midland sook!"

Midwest(ern). The dialect assumed to be prevalent in the North Central states.
1941 Bernard Bloch in American Speech 16-279: "These are all taken from varieties of Midwestern American English." 1941 G. L. Trager and B. Bloch in Language 17-22: "/o/ is less common than the other simple vowels in Midwestern American." 1944 Harold Wentworth American Dialect Dictionary 129: "confided, pret. Confined...Midwest."

New England. The speech area comprising the six New England states. Formerly considered a major dialect region, now treated as a subarea of Northern.
1781 John Witherspoon in The Druid (in M. M. Mathews The Beginnings of American English, 1931, 25): "Shall I have occasion, i.e. opportunity to go over the ferry. New England." 1788 in DA: "She spoke much in the New England dialect." 1848 J. R. Bartlett Dictionary of Americanisms 9: "New England." 1872 Maximilian Schele de Vere Americanisms 519: "New England." 1889 John S. Farmer Americanisms Old and New, passim. 1902 Sylva Clapin A New Dictionary of Americanisms, passim. 1936

James B. McMillan

H. L. Mencken The American Language (4th ed.) 358: "The chief characters
of Western, or General American and of New England and Southern American
have been identified.

North(ern). 1. The U. S. Outside of New England and the South. Also
    labeled North-and-West, Western, and General American.
1781 John Witherspoon in The Druid (reprinted in M. M. Mathews The
Beginnings of American English, 1931, 25): "This means of speaking
prevails in the northern parts." 1829-30 The Virginia Literary Museum
(reprinted in M. M. Mathews The Beginnings of American English, 1931,
108): "Lumberer. 'A seller of timber'. North." 1893 C. H. Grandgent
in Modern Language Notes 8-137: "My 'North' includes W[estern] N[ew]
E[ngland], the Middle States, Ontario, Michigan, Ohio, Indiana, Illinois."
1944 J. S. Kenyon and T. A. Knott Pronouncing Dictionary of American
English xxxii: "The North includes the rest of the US [exclusive of
the South and eastern New England]."
    2. The dialect of the area discriminated by Hans Kurath in 1949
    including New England, New York, northern New Jersey, and the deriva-
    tive settlement regions to the west (Inland Northern).
1949 Hans Kurath Word Geography of the Eastern United States 12: "The
Northern speech area corresponds to the New England settlement area,
together with the Dutch settlement area which lies embedded in it....
The subareas of the North." 1957 Albert H. Marckwardt in Publication
of the American Dialect Society 27-4: "Less frequently have the southern
limits of distinctly Northern terms been employed to establish the
Northern-Midland boundary." Ib. 5 "Sweet corn, though concentrated in
the North, is found throughout the area."

North-and-West. The U.S. exclusive of eastern New England and the South.
    Also North-and-Western, Northern, Western, and General American.
1892 C. H. Grandgent in Dialect Notes 1-269: "The rest of the country
will be called 'North and West'." 1928 Hans Kurath in Modern Philology
25-389, n. 5: "The North-and-West extends westward from the Hudson
River, in some respects even from the Connecticut River, and southward
to the Potomac and the Ohio, although southern traits are found for a
considerable distance to the north of these rivers." 1947 C. K. Thomas,
The Phonetics of American English 144: "General American--sometimes
called Northern, or Western, or Northern and Western."

South(ern). 1. The region south of Mason and Dixon's Line and the Ohio
    River, formerly assumed to be a major dialect area.
1781 John Witherspoon in The Druid (reprinted in M. M. Mathews, The
Beginnings of American English, 1931, 25): "Raw salad is used in the
South for salad." 1829 Virginia Literary Museum (quoted in M. M.
Mathews, Beginnings of American English, 1931, 105): "Evening. 'After
dinner.' Southern States." Ib. 109 "Mush. 'Food of cornmeal, boiled.'
Southern States." Ib. 108 "Means. Medicine. South." 1889 John S.
Farmer Americanisms Old and New, passim: "Southern term." 1894 E. H.
Babbitt in Dialect Notes 1-362: "The special works say 'New England',
'Southern', or 'Western', and rarely go any farther." 1936 H. L. Mencken
The American Language (4th ed.) 357: "The Southern form of American
occupies the area south of the Potomac...."
    2. The region east and south of the Blue Ridge, extending through
    the Gulf States.
1944 Hans Kurath in Language 20-151: (See Central, above.) 1955
Raven I. McDavid, Jr., in Publication of the American Dialect Society

James B. McMillan

23-41: "Southern, the plantation settlements from Chespeake Bay to northern Florida, plus their immediate derivatives." 1964 Janet B. Sawyer in Publication of the American Dialect Society 41-8: "San Antonio English is not so strikingly Southern, partially because many of the words known to be characteristic of the South, such as lightwood, chitterling, and co-wench, are obsolescent in this urban community."

West(ern). The dialect(s) spoken outside New England and the South, usually what is now called Midland, General American, etc. 1829 Virginia Literary Museum (quoted in M. M. Mathews Beginnings of American English, 1931, 103): "Cavault or Cavort. Ranting, highflying: --West." 1948 John R. Bartlett Dictionary of Americanisms, passim: "Western." 1893 C. H. Grandgent in Modern Language Notes 8-137: "My 'West' includes the rest of the United States." 1894 E. H. Babbitt in Dialect Notes 1-362: "The special works say 'New England', 'Southern', or 'Western', and rarely go any farther." 1919 G. P. Krapp The Pronunciation of Standard English in America viii: "We can distinguish with some certainty Eastern and Western and Southern speech." 1936 H. L. Mencken The American Language (4th ed.) 358: "The chief characters of Western, or General American." 1939 P. G. Perrin An Index to English 204: "Three American dialects are...and Western, the most extensive of the three, sometimes called General American."

Yankee. The DA, in addition to seven quotes illustrating this term in the sense "the English used by Yankees; American English," has two quotes illustrating Yankee dialect (1832, 1881) meaning New England dialect and five quotes illustrating Yankee with other words referring to eastern New England speech (1803, 1828, 1847, 1866, 1880). Other citations are not hard to find, e.g. Maximilian Schele de Vere, Americanisms 491: "Hull is Yankee for whole." 1895 Willis Boughton in The Dial 18-68: "The Christmas story, Mr. Howells asserts, is written in the 'Yankee dialect and its Western modifications'." 1896 (Miss) E. F. Andrews in The Chatauquan 23-88: "As Georgia English runs into Chaucer English on the one hand, so it runs into Yankee English on the other." 1933 Vida R. Sutton in American Speech 8:1-11: "Some attention is given to the most typical dialects-- Yankee, Western, Southern, and foreign." Although Schele de Vere, Willis Boughton, and Miss Andrews were college professors and Miss Sutton worked for the National Broadcasting Company, Yankee was not a formal or technical term for a dialect; it was on a par with labels like Cracker, Hill-billy, and Down East, informal or jocular.

NOTES

*Read at the SAMLA-ADS Meeting, Atlanta, Georgia, November 1973.

EVIDENCE*

Raven I. McDavid, Jr.

One of the pleasanter aspects of academic buncombe is the custom by which a visitor from afar produces credentials to show that he is familiar with the locality where he is speaking. And so it is with me, at a SAMLA-ADS meeting in Atlanta. Despite the fact that Strom Thurmond revoked my Confederate passport in 1948 when he became the self-appointed spokesman for Southern interests, I am a native South Carolinian; I belonged to SAMLA for more than a dozen years beginning with 1936, and offered at least four papers at previous meetings. In fact, for some two hundred years the McDavids and those with thom they intermarried have been living a few tornadoes away from Atlanta, in Greenville County, South Carolina; I sometimes feel that my grandfather McDavid must have been the only private from the county in the Confederate army. What is more, some of the family connections had come to Charleston well before 1700. All of my education through the doctorate was obtained in the Carolinas; I made my first long foray north in the summer of 1937, and until 1942 spent only one winter north of the Smith & Wesson line. Following the Axis War, I returned South for two and a half years of dialect field work in South Carolina, Georgia and Florida--not merely such idyllic retreats as Clayton, Darien and MacRae (the last the ancestral seat of the sacred Talmadge family), but such Gomorrahs as Charleston, Savannah and Atlanta, That is, whatever the value of my 'intuition' as a native speaker (and I have skepticism about arguing from it, for reasons I shall make plain), I have added a modest amount of systematic observation.

I have one further advantage, of pure serendipity. For nearly thirty years my father was the South Carolina lobbyist (euphemized as a 'field engineer') for the Portland Cement Association, which then had its regional headquarters in the Hurt Building in Atlanta. He spent as much time in Columbia and elsewhere as he did at home; and on those trips I was often a passenger, and was introduced to dozens of politicians, some of whom foregathered at times around our dining room table to help develop the state highway program. I feel that my father's network of political relationships was the greatest single force in developing my skills as a fieldworker, for not only did they create an effective posse of talent scouts in South Carolina, but their official roles suggested analogues which I could utilize in Michigan and Upstate New York, where my family were unknown.[1]

But even more important, my father had gone into politics himself before he began lobbying, and served six fairly successful years on the Ways and Means Committee of the South Carolina General Assembly. Since my mother didn't want to be left alone with three temperamental children

125

Raven I. McDavid, Jr.

when he was out speaking at campaign meetings, we usually went along, supposedly to sit in the car and even go to sleep. But soon we began to slip into the crowd, and watch and listen to the performance--several dozen candidates, for offices ranging from Congressman to mill magistrate, speaking in succession from the same stump. By the time my father gave up campaigning in his own behalf, we were well hooked on such meetings as entertainment; through high school I attended more campaign meetings than movies, because movies cost money. And I became so attuned to the rhythms of Southern campaign oratory that after three decades I have no difficulty in recognizing the rhetorical style of Cole Blease and Gene Talmadge in the political pronunciamentos of Jesse Jackson and others of my Landsmänner translated to the South Side of Chicago. What is more I learned a good deal about the rhetoric of advocacy: otherwise godly, righteous and sober citizens displayed amazing ingenuity in twisting facts in order to induce the voters to put them on the public payroll and keep them there (it is possible that such ingenuity is not unknown elsewhere in the SAMLA area).

Since many of these worthies were lawyers by profession, I grew up with a pardonable suspicion of the operations of the law. Yet when I actually found myself--much later--called on to testify in a few legal cases, I discovered that there were certain rules under which, in the exercise of their profession, lawyers were compelled to proceed. For instance, when Frito-Lay of Atlanta and Dallas invited me to testify for them in a trade-name case against Jay's Potato Chips of Chicago, their attorneys were under an obligation to apprise their opponents of all of the documents which they had asked me to examine. And Jay's counsel had a reciprocal responbility. My own legal colleagues were under no obligation to show me all of the documents which Jay's counsel had assembled, but they could not prevent their being introduced in cross-examination to the detriment of our case. Indeed, at the preliminary hearing Jay's counsel had actually shown their own expert witness (a distinguished professional colleague of mine, now deceased) only a carefully winnowed selection of the documents both sides had assembled; but the others were made available during the cross-examination, with the result that he had to reverse himself.

The general rules of evidence, in law, are clear and simple:
1) Facts must be relevant to the issue.
2) The evidence must be the best obtainable under the circumstances.
3) Hearsay is not evidence.
4) Opinion is not evidence.
And in short, he who alleges a fact must prove it.

Additional safeguards are introduced for each of several kinds of evidence. In positive testimony the credibility of a witness may be challenged on the grounds of reputation and interest. A business man's secretary may be allowed to testify that her boss's wife was conspiring to murder him. But jurors may be ordered to discount this if it is brought out that the boss had given the secretary many expensive presents and had often found it necessary to stay overnight in her apartment. For expert testimony, an engineer's evaluation for the Lockheed C-5A might be discounted if it were disclosed that he has been on the payroll of a company which supplies parts to Lockheed--or to Lockheed's competitor, McDonnell-Douglas. A linguist testifying in a trade-name case must establish his professional credibility by supplying a complete bibliography, to demonstrate the range of his knowledge. When circumstantial

Raven I. McDavid, Jr.

evidence is introduced, it must fit together; as intriguing as great
theoretical leaps may be, they are properly disallowed when life,
liberty and property are at stake.

The principles of evaluation of evidence in courts of law have been
codified over the centuries, and each person who studies the law knows
that in his practice he disregards them at this peril. Other disciplines,
however, are not so rigorous; and among them is the study of language
variation, whether we call it dialectology, areal linguistics, or
something else. There are no professional examinations: it is easier
to set up in business in this field than to become an ordained minister
in a Southern Pentecostal sect. Nor does every practitioner of this
calling realize the need to separate the various professional roles he
may be called on to play at various times:

1) That of the experimental linguist--to use a term of Lawrence M.
Davis--who gathers and classifies and evaluates the evidence.

2) That of the theoretician, who first posits hypotheses of the inter-
relationships of language varieties, and then--with respect for the rules
of evidence--confirms, modifies or rejects them.

3) That of the teacher or textbook writer, who utilizes this information, or parts of it, for pedagogical purposes.

4) That of the propagandist or politician, with other ends.

Most of my professional work has been of the first type. I am basically
what the Right Reverend Robert B. Lees, of the Lower Charles River
Apostolate, calls a "dull cataloguer of data," and the custodian of
collections of such data. My first duty is to keep the collections in
order, to make them available to serious scholars, and to increase their
accessibility by getting them into print. And as I go about my pedestrian
tasks, I set up my own rules of evidence, derived by common law from the
linguists from whom I learned my trade.

1) One of the first rules is that to argue from silence may be to
argue from ignorance. We can sometimes date with extreme accuracy the
origins and first appearance in English of a word like sputnik or
appendicitis or kerosene or piazza, or tolerably well that of a
grammatical form like the genitive its, but for many forms the record is
obscure, and not merely for the common and lowly.[2] In 1937 I discovered
that I had unwittingly included in my dissertation on Milton's political
theory a citation for a sense of sovereignty not attested by the Oxford
English Dictionary before the mid-Nineteenth Century writings of John
Stuart Mill. The argument from presence is another matter: even a oncer
may be suggestive, and a cluster is illuminating.

2) The best direct evidence is that of an informant himself, preferably
under conditions when he is off guard--a holograph letter to a close
friend, or recorded stretches of continuous unguarded discourse. The
thousands of tapes in the folklore archives of the Memorial University
of Newfoundland also contain priceless materials on phonology and grammar
and a great deal of vocabulary--all with identification of speaker,
community and family background. Taped field interviews, where transcriptions can be checked against the original recording, are another
kind of valuable evidence, accessible in many archives. So, too, are
field transcriptions, in phonetic notation, of comparable responses
elicited by a uniform questionnaire. All of these records are subject
to certain qualifications when they are used--the general competence of
the field investigator, the rapport of the investigator with the informant, the skill in eliciting responses, the accuracy of the transcription.

127

It is the business of the investigator and his colleagues to make this ruthlessly clear--as Hans Kurath does in the Handbook of the Linguistic Geography of New England. None of these kinds of evidence is without limitations: a folklore questionnaire may deal with subjects of limited interest; a questionnaire, however long, is bound to be selective. Again the presence of evidence is what we must look for; incidental information on pronunciation and grammar, picked up outside the formal limits of the questionnaire, is suggestive of more frequent use.

3) Documentary evidence, as in legal cases, must be handled gingerly. The less tampering by editors, the greater the likelihood that the record represents the informant's natural usage. Such collections as the Paston Letters, in an edition like that by Norman Davis, are invaluable, though--as with all documentary evidence--the phonological interpretation is a complicated operation.

4) Reported evidence by laymen, especially literate laymen, is very treacherous, inasmuch as it is likely to assume the uniqueness of casual information, and to report as novelties things that are simply not familiar to the observer, ignoring what may be common to him and the person he has been listening to. A generation ago Kurath pointed out that the popular picture of American dialects was badly distorted by the fact that many New England professors took their vacations on Cape Cod and many Southern ones in the Appalachians, where they could daily observe the speech of a class of people they would not ordinarily encount in Cambridge or Charlottesville.

5) Literary dialect is a specially difficult variant of documentary evidence presented by literate laymen, since its purpose is not so much to mirror speech varieties as to suggest them. Sometimes the most pretentious claims to accurate representation prove to be the least reliable. A careful reading of Huckleberry Finn discloses that the narra tor (and almost no one else) is represented as consistently using the -ing ending of present participle, an unlikely practice in view of his region and social class. Not even William Gilmore Simms, as painstaking as he was in attempting to portray varieties of Southern speech, represented one of the most characteristic features of Charleston usage-- the ingliding /e/ and /o/ in date and boat.

6) Personal intuition is valid only for the acceptance of linguistic forms, never for their rejection. This is particularly true of forms that have somehow been stigmatized by schoolmarms and other professional guardians of linguistic chastity, an attitude encapsulated in James Sledd's oft-quoted observation that any red-blooded American would prefer incest to ain't. The invalidity of these judgments of inacceptability is most notorious among the newly risen lower middle class, such as clerical workers and elementary school teachers.[3] Yet on the 'intuitive authority' of informants of this type it has been widely bruited that such forms as might can't and used to didn't are never used by educated Southern whites except when "talking down." However, a glance at the Atlas field records, to say nothing of the studies of verb forms by Bagby Atwood and Virginia McDavid, presents an entirely different picture. What is more, I can cite examples from the speech of lawyers, doctors, and engineers, to say nothing of my father, a liberal arts graduate of Davidson College. Finally, I encounter plenty of further examples in white speech of these and other allegedly non-white usages every time I visit my peers in the South and engage in serious familiar conversation.[4] The tenuousness of intuitive judgments is borne

out every day I work with grammatical materials in the archives of the
Linguistic Atlas of Middle and South Atlantic States. It is not
uncommon for informants to dismiss as the usage of "ignorant folks" or
of another race their own habitual speech-forms, as attested in free
conversation in the course of an interview. Or, in eastern Virginia,
an informant will deny that a folk preterite such as clim is used by
whites, though the other white informants in the same county, to say
nothing of adjacent counties, may normally use it and admit the usage.
And had I not been married to a Minnesotan, and a frequent dinner
companion of a Nebraska-reared colleague of hers, I might never have
known how frequently I uncouple the copula (the verb to be)--a dialect
feature that has often been proclaimed a characteristic of a type of
English I am territorially and technically unable to speak.[5]
   7) Psychological explanations must be ruthlessly checked against the
best available data. It is frequently alleged that two widespread
Southern usages--(1) -s as an inflectional ending in the present indicative plural, as we runs;(2) plurals of -st nouns in /-stəz, -stɨz/
as postəz, fistəz/ are hypercorrective reactions against he do and
/fisəz/. Yet the generalized -s present is documented in Northern
British English from 1300; one need read only the beginning of the
Cursor Mundi. And both /postəz/ and /posəz/ are found in Southern
England, their territories being set off by a line from the Wash to the
Bristol Channel, the former to the Southeast, the latter to the Northwest.[6]
   Finally, in the use of circumstantial evidence, it is well to be
circumspect. Many linguists, including Leonard Bloomfield, have pointed
out the accidental phonetic similarity between the words for 'eye' in
Modern Greek and Modern Malay, mati and mata respectively. Brought up
in a den of Southern Baptists, I could argue plausibly that the pervasive O.K. was derived from Burmese hou'-keh 'it is so,' brought back
to the American South by St. Adoniram Judson, missionary and lexicographer; but my cultural particularism yields to the sober and methodical
cases built up by Allen Read and Woodford Heflin, however much they may
disagree about particular details. Nor do I now get angry when men
who should know far better suggest linguistic evidence based on flimsy
circumstantial evidence. Those who have examined Visser's Historical
Syntax may note (Vol. III, Part 1, p. 1923) a suggestion that hadn't
ought, in Northern American English, may be derived from similar constructions in Dutch, German and French. Remembering that courtesy is
due one's elders--a lesson I learned at my mother's hairbrush--I wrote
him a gentle note, reminding him of the existence of Bagby Atwood's
Verb Forms in the Eastern United States (Ann Arbor, 1953), which shows
the Atlas evidence on hadn't ought--not only in the most persistent
WASP nests of rural New England but also in the Albemarle Sound area of
North Carolina (its absence in the Pennsylvania German area is also
suggestive, though as we have pointed out, not conclusive). I also
enclosed a map of the evidence from Southern England, based on the
records by Guy S. Lowman, Jr., in 1937-8 and a summary of the evidence
in Harold Orton's Survey of English Dialects. That Mr. Visser still
argues for his theory is his privilege, but not enough to disregard the
evidence. Consequently, when bright intuitive visions of the origins
of American speechways dance in our heads, we should take some long
hard look at all the available evidence: the previous dialect surveys
by A. J. Ellis and Joseph Wright, the recent one by Orton, the American

Raven I. McDavid, Jr.

archives (the regional linguistic atlases and Cassidy's Dictionary of
American Regional English), the Newfoundland materials, and the host
of well-edited texts for the eleven centuries of written English. We
will have a great deal of work, many surprises and some disappoint-
ments, but in the end we will derive greater satisfaction from our
conclusions, however tentative. For all conclusions are subject to
revision as more detailed and more accurate evidence comes in. If
pedagogues and politicians choose another course, they have the privilege;
but if they do, they should not pretend to be scholars.

I speak of course as a linguistic geographer, conscious of the role of
my discipline. It is a branch of historical linguistics, designed to
set out the affiliations of present-day regional and social varieties of
a language, with a long-term view toward working out the historical
affiliations of these varieties with those varieties spoken earlier and
perhaps in other lands. The operations of this work may suggest social
dimensions and directions of future linguistic change, but only tentative
for any single community may have from six to twelve social classes,
let alone castes and ethnic subcultures: It is the role of other types
of investigation to examine particular communities intensively.
Linguistic geography properly selects natives, long-resident families,
and the least educated, in greater numbers than statistics might indicate;
for it seeks to establish benchmarks against which one may evaluate the
forces of change. A linguistic geographer using random encounters in a
community would be like a surveyor choosing as a reference point the top
of an automobile in a parking lot. Responsible investigators with other
interests recognize this fact: however different may be his methodology,
his selection of informants, his representations of social classes, his
interviewing techniques--William Labov concedes that without the framework of the Linguistic Atlas of the Middle and South Atlantic States,
his own work in New York City would have been impossible.

As editor-in-chief and custodian of the materials for the Middle and
South Atlantic States, I once more invite scholars to use them, even
as the process of editing continues.[1] I hope I may live to see the data
in print, even as I have helped arrange for a reprinting of the Linguistic
Atlas of New England (1972) and a new edition of its accompanying
Handbook (1973); what the interpretations of the data may be, I am
leaving to others. For in a discipline as intimately concerned with human
behavior as the study of dialects happens to be, we need less political
oratory and more attention to providing and using the best evidence
possible.

NOTES

*Read at the SAMLA-ADS Meeting, Atlanta, Georgia, November 1971.

[1]My father died September 13, 1973, and never saw this paper; fortunate
however, I was able to make known to him well before then my appreciation
of the magnitude of his contribution to my career. I am indebted to
Hans Kurath and Albert H. Marckwardt for involving me in the Atlas
project, and to the American Council of Learned Societies for their suppo
and for permission to cite evidence from the Atlas files.

Raven I. McDavid, Jr.

[2] Such a common word as whoa! 'call to stop a horse' is attested rather
late, though it is likely of Old English derivation. The lack of bulk
in Old English dictionaries is due less to the intrinsic size of the
vocabulary than to the limited range of material covered by what was
written in Old English, and to the limited rate of survival of the
documents.

[3] In the fall of 1943, when I was working on Burmese at Yale, George
Trager invited me to be an informant in his seminar on phonology.
One of the pieces de resistance in my performance was the set hod, hard,
hide, hired, Howard. Though contrasting as I say them, and easily
distinguished by those who are familiar with Up-Country South Carolina
speech, as I pronounce them they were--and still are--confusing to
Ausländer (from which one may derive morals about tests to determine
"auditory discrimination," and even develop such tests based on
Southern distinctions for the benefit of Northern Caucasoids). After
I had gone through the series a few times, there was an outburst of
indignation from a well-dressed young lady at the back of the room, to
the effect that she had never heard anything so fantastic in her life.
Some weeks later I learned that she had grown up in Hickory, North
Carolina, but had moved away, had studied singing and elocution, and
had married up--a Vanderbilt professor. Not only had she certainly
heard my patterns of pronunciation; she had probably once used something
of the kind. Her 'intuitive response' to the pronunciations I used was
in effect a resentment at being reminded of something she thought she had
put behind her.

[4] Two days after this paper was presented, I informally elicited the
intuitive responses to such items as these from a group of English majors
at Furman University. A large number--I was not keeping score--admitted
that they themselves used such grammatical forms, though probably oftenest
in informal discourse. Perhaps, in the situation in which I was
eliciting responses, the admission of usage posed no threat to their egos.

[5] This feature is very common in the speech of my oldest daughter--
Tennessee-reared, a concert singer, and a Ph.D. in English; and in
that of my oldest niece--South Carolina reared, widely traveled,
daughter of a successful corporation executive (East Tennessee WASP,
himself a user of the form), M.A. in history, a member of the Junior
League, and active in the Republican Party. The failure of some sociolinguists to recognize the existence of an upper class, let alone
examine its speech (whether my family belong is irrelevant), is indicative of the perspective which they bring to their research.

[6] The only area in which these forms do not occur is East Anglia--
the seedbed of Northern American English. Attribution of these forms
to an ethnic background is found among sociolinguists who come from the
Northern region, not among native Southerners of whatever background.

[7] Editing is progressing at the University of Chicago and the University
of South Carolina, with composition taking place at the latter. At
present, more than two-thirds of the material is past the first stage of
editing, about a sixth in the hands of the compositor or ready for final
proofreading. Publication, by the University of Chicago Press, will be

Raven I. McDavid, Jr.

in fascicles of 128 pages each. Work on the accompanying <u>Handbook</u> is also in progress.

II. SOCIAL VARIATION

A DIACHRONIC VIEW OF THE SPEECH OF CHARLESTON, SOUTH CAROLINA*

Raymond K. O'Cain

With its relative antiquity of settlement (1670), its well established
class and caste system, and its special place at the head of culture and
affairs in South Carolina, it would be indeed surprising if there were
not distinctive speechways in Charleston, South Carolina.

Sylvester Primer, several years Professor of French and German at the
College of Charleston, was the first to make a scholarly report on the
speech of Charleston. His paper "Charleston Provincialisms" appeared
in 1887 and was followed two years later by "The Huguenot Element in
Charleston's Pronunciation." He promised papers on the influences of
German and of Negro speech on the speech of the city, but they apparently
never materialized.

"Charleston Provincialisms" treated what Primer considered noteworthy
phonological characteristics of local speech, yet made no claim to
exhaustiveness. Primer presented his data in phonetic transcription and
made occasional comments on the social distribution of the phenomena he
observed, stating that the "provincialisms" were most characteristic of
those outside the upper class, who by no means, however, took special
pains to avoid them. Neither did Primer overlook the desirability of
placing his observations in the larger contexts of the history of the
language and the history and character of the community. Still, we have
no clue that Primer's investigation of Charleston speech was systematic,
for he gives neither an account of his informants, their number, and
their several idiolects, nor a plan to elicit data for orderly comparisons.

Systematic study of Charleston speech began in 1933 with the late Guy
S. Lowman's two field records for the Linguistic Atlas of the Middle and
South Atlantic States (LAMSAS). Between 1946 and 1948 Raven I. McDavid,
Jr., completed nine more LAMSAS field records in the city itself and four
field records in rural Charleston County. Lee A. Pederson added another
urban field record in 1965.[1] Only New York City was more intensively
studied for LAMSAS.

The first analysis of the LAMSAS archives was McDavid's (1948) "Postvocalic /-r/ in South Carolina: A Social Analysis," which sought to
account for the distribution of postvocalic /r/ in areas where it had been
assumed not to exist. McDavid demonstrated how /r/-lessness had spread
from the Charleston focal area to wherever the plantation system had
prospered and to wherever regular contacts with Charleston were a normal
part of local life. McDavid went on to predict, on the basis of socio-
economic change he had observed, that postvocalic /r/ might regain
respectability in Charleston. He (1955) further established Charleston
as a focal area by examining systematically the characteristics of its
speech in the context of the LAUSC[2] archives.

135

The intent of LAUSC was not to foreclose but to stimulate further studies on specific features, regions, and groups. Consequently, field-work for a follow-up study of Charleston was carried out in 1969.[3] The year 1969 was felt to be an opportune time for the resurvey of Charleston. Since the LAMSAS field records were completed, profound changes in the socio-economic character of the city had occurred and linguistic changes seemed to be rapidly altering the former distinctive speechways of Charleston.

Informal preliminary observations for a social dialect survey of Charleston indicated a variety of types and sub-types of speech between completely traditional and completely innovative usage. This incomplete mutual linguistic accomodation between long-term and short-term residents of Charleston meant that before a questionnaire could be constructed it would be necessary to examine the LAMSAS records from Charleston proper and from the surrounding territory as well. Thus the questionnaire was prepared to include tests not only of forms characteristic of or in variation in Charleston, but characteristic of or in variation in the surrounding territory as well.[4]

Each of the one hundred informants interviewed was a lifelong[5] resident of Charleston.[6] Though some informants were born elsewhere or had spent time away from the city, each considered himself, and was considered by others in the community, to be a native.

The social position of each informant was ascertained by seeking the judgments of persons living in the community. So-called objective criteria of social position would give a false picture of the social structure of Charleston since there is an aristocratic upper class defined in terms of family and connections. Such matters as education, occupation, and the condition of the plumbing are of secondary significance. And in addition to the normally complicating factor of race, Charleston has a Negro elite[7] that has identified its interests with those of the White aristocrats for over a century, and membership is partially based on family connections to persons free during slavery times.

The social ranking of informants was first done by the intermediaries who provided introductions to prospective informants. After identifying the prospective informant as a long-term resident of Charleston, the intermediary gave an account of his acquaintance with the prospect and an evaluation of the prospect's social standing. At various times an intermediary recommended more than one prospect, and the same prospect was recommended by more than one intermediary. Informants themselves occasionally served as intermediaries. In addition, useful comments about membership in certain churches, attendance at certain schools, residence in certain neighborhoods, and ethnicity were gained not only from contemporary Charlestonians, but also from historical sources as well.

It was also the judgment of Charlestonians that three strata of Whites and two strata of Negroes were necessary to encompass the most important social divisions of the community. These classes reflect the consensus that persons outside the two upper classes could or could not be subdivided and that all the members of any of the classes were of the same rank. Furthermore, the consensus was that classes need not be of equal latitude of membership. For example, it is easier for a Negro to enter the elite than it is for a White.

An informant was not considered adequately judged unless at least two other members of the community had evaluated his rank; no inadequately judged informant was included in the analysis of Charleston speech. Also excluded from the analysis were informants about whom judgments were in conflict or who were judged not to be decisively in one of the major social groups. Twenty-three such records were set aside, leaving a total of seventy-seven for analysis. Only here did the judgment of the researcher come to bear on assessing social position, as a coordinator of the opinions of others. A lifelong acquaintance with the city, lifelong residence in its cultural dominion, two years' recent residence (excluding residence during fieldwork), and acquaintance with the history of the city seem to qualify the researcher to decide when natives disagree about the social position of one another.

The social rankings of the informants accumulated and interlocked in such a way that it would be possible to draw a Bloomfieldian (1933:46-47) diagram of their linguistic interaction. (The intermediaries who provided introductions to the informants as well as the twenty-three informants whose speech was not part of the linguistic analysis would also be a part of such a diagram.) As with social rank, there is a pragmatic definition of speech community--a network of individuals in linguistic interaction, something that must be taken for granted in randomly sampled populations.

The changes in the socio-economic character of Charleston during the last generation marked the end of a period of near-stagnation lasting from the War Between the States until World War II. Even in 1860 Charleston had been in a forty-year period of relative decline from a post-Colonial Golden Age. For example, in 1801, South Carolina, of which Charleston was the economic (and social) center, had produced half of the nation's cotton. Twenty-five years later, three and one-half times as much South Carolina cotton constituted less than a quarter of the nation's production.

Like the first-generation colonists of Carolina, the two generations after the War Between the States were engaged in a search for a stable economic base on which to build fortunes. Rice and indigo had come and gone and the throne of King Cotton was anything but secure.[8] Yet Charleston's old guard were opposed to industrialization; moreover, there was a stigma to industrial work [recall the caste status of Up Country textile workers[9] (McDavid:1948)].

With the mobilization for World War II, the economy of Charleston became rejuvenated. Even today the level of military activity artificially stimulates or retards the entire economy. Both jobs attendant to the operation of Charleston's military installations, and those created by a corresponding growth in other economic sectors, created a demand for labor that could be met only by migration from other areas. During the eighty years before 1940 the population grew at an average rate of 385 persons per year; between 1940 and 1968 the growth was 5,000 persons per year.

In 1960 thirty-one percent of Charleston's Whites and three and one-half per cent of Charleston's Negroes were in-migrants, i.e., they had lived in some other part of South Carolina or in another state five years previously. While only nine per cent of the White migrants and two per cent of the Negro migrants were from the area immediately dominated linguistically by the Charleston focus,[10] fifty-three per cent of all migrants last lived in a state (including South Carolina) that was either Southern or South Midland linguistically.

During the last generation, then, migration to Charleston has been of a regional or sub-regional character. The migrants are largely White and appear to be skilled workers or managers and professionals; linguistically, they are at least familiar with, if not actually introducers of, South Midland and Southern speechways.[11] There has been no significant migration from abroad, so multilingualism is not an urgent issue. Unlike the situation in megalopolitan areas of the North and North Midland, there is not the problem of mass importation of nonstandard linguistic features across major dialect boundaries, and there is no complicating correlation of linguistic differences with physical differences from the dominant culture.

It is worth recalling, however, that the South Carolina Low Country, dominated linguistically by Charleston, was settled by expansion inland from the coast and dominated by planter politics. The Up Country, on the other hand, was settled predominantly by migrants who had moved southward in the Midland speech area from Pennsylvania and Virginia, and was politically a classic populist constituency. Naturally, there were and still are linguistic differences corresponding to these cultural divisions. And there are traditional mock-forms of Low Country speech.

Correlated with the changes in the socio-economic character of Charleston is the recession of several phonological traits of traditional Charleston speech, including the loss of a contrast between /ɛ/ and /ɪ/ before (historical) /r/; maintenance of a contrast between /ɛ/ and /ɪ/ before nasals; monophthongal or ingliding allophones of /e/ and /o/; and allophones of /aɪ/ and /aʊ/ with centralized first elements (before voiceless consonants).[12] These traits are traditionally associated with Charleston and the South Carolina Low Country, but they are in competition with (and receding before), respectively, a contrast between /ɛ/ and /ɪ/ before /r/ (or its allophones); lack of a contrast between /ɛ/ and /ɪ/ before nasals; upgliding allophones of /e/ and /o/; and allophones of /aɪ/ and /aʊ/ with low (and fronted) first elements. The latter are all rather generalized characteristics of the South and/or South Midland speech areas.

Sylvester Primer observed the lack of contrast in such sets as fear: fair and beer:bear, [fɛə] and [bɛə]. The records of the Linguistic Atlas of the United States and Canada, as summarized in The Pronunciation of English in the Atlantic States (PEAS) (Kurath and McDavid:1961), indicate that while a contrast was well-established in the interior of South Carolina, high vowels were generally lacking before /r/ in the Lower South (coastal South Carolina and Georgia). Where found on the coast, the contrast was most likely to be in the speech of cultivated informants (LAUSC Type III, cf. Kurath et al.:1939).[13] Where a contrast was found, informants preserving postvocalic /r/ had the high vowel [i], e.g. fear [fiɚ]; informants lacking postvocalic /r/ had the high vowel /ɪ/, e.g. fear [fɪə].

Primer did not mention any loss of contrast in sets like pen:pin. The PEAS summary of the LAUSC records notes that /ɛ/ in pen typified cultivated speech. Southern folk speech (LAUSC Type I), on the other hand, almost universally showed /ɪ/ in pen, except along the South Carolina coast. In popular or common speech (LAUSC Type II), /ɪ/ in pen was predominant in the South, but not as widespread as in folk speech, particularly in metropolitan areas. Thus /ɪ/ in pen would not likely be native to Charlestonians, though typical of Southern and South Midland migrants to Charleston.

Raymond K. O'Cain

The 1969 follow-up survey of Charleston found that a number of informants exhibited distinct preferences for the innovative forms. Table 1 shows, in percentages, the preferences for high vowels (whether /ɪ/ or /i/) before /r/ (whether [ə] or [ɚ])[14] of members of the upper, middle, and lower White classes (UW, MW, and LW) and the upper and lower Negro classes (UN, LN), and of speakers seventy years of age or older, of speakers sixty to sixty-nine years of age, of speakers fifty to fifty-nine years of age, etc.[15] The percentages are derived from a fraction having the number of high vowel responses as numerator and the total number of responses (high and mid vowels) as denominator. The figures in Line A were compiled from the responses to the test words clear (adjective), clear (verb), ear, beard, fear, (last) year, and (new) year. Similarly, Line B shows the preferences for /ɪ/ in lend, (goat) pen, (fountain) pen, men, again, (...eight, nine) ten, ten (twenty, thirty...).

	UW	MW	LW	UN	LN	70	60	50	40	30	20	10
A.	28	61	61	78	59	21	31	39	57	44	78	81
B.	7	45	57	31	60	6	11	17	29	60	68	56

Table 1

Figure 1 shows the number and social distribution of the idiolects in which A (high vowel in ear, etc.) is (a) fully innovated or (b), underlined, fully conservative. Figure 2 shows the number and social distribution of the idiolects in which B (/ɪ/ in pen, etc.) is (a) fully innovated or (b), underlined, fully conservative. Figure 3 shows the number and social distribution of the idiolects in which (a) both A and B are fully innovated or (b), underlined, both A and B are fully conservative. Figure 4 shows the number and social distribution of the idiolects in which innovation in B is taking place faster than innovation in A (regardless of whether either is fully innovative or fully conservative).

	70	60	50	40	30	20	10
UW				1	1		1
MW	1	2	1	1	1	7	5
LW		1	2		1/1	3	2
UN				2		1	
LN							

Figure 1. A categorical.

	70	60	50	40	30	20	10
UW	1	1		1			1
MW		1	1			1/3	2
LW		2	1		3	4	1
UN		1	1	1	1		
LN						1	

Figure 2. B categorical.

	70	60	50	40	30	20	10
UW							1
MW						2	2
LW		1			1	3	1
UN							
LN							

Figure 3. A and B categorical.

	70	60	50	40	30	20	10
UW					1		
MW	1	3	1	1	1		
LW		2	1	1	3	3	1
UN					1		
LN		1				1	2

Figure 4. B spreading faster than A.

The PEAS summary of the LAUSC evidence indicates that innovation in A began among cultivated informants; thus the change is not only local, but respectable as well. There has been little tendency in the UW to generalize the change, however, for there is a noticeable conservatism among younger speakers of that class.

The much greater preference (Table 1) for innovation in A among other classes does not indicate the generalization of a change initiated in the UW. Notice that the older members of the MW and LW are distinctly conservative, suggesting that class lines were sufficiently rigid to inhibit rapid (within a generation) spread from the UW. Innovation in A, then, is an independent development among yonnger speakers in the MW and LW, those natives who learned English at the time when Charleston was much less uniform linguistically than when their parents learned English.

The UN, xenophilic by Charleston standards, appear also to have initiated the change in A independently. The UN have a long tradition of formal instruction, both inside and outside the city, by outsiders.[16] And if A could not easily spread among socially proximate Whites, it hardly seems plausible that it could so quickly spread to Negroes from Whites in a short time. If innovation in A had spread from the MW and/or LW to the UN, it seems that B likewise would have spread, but the UN show little inclination to innovate in B.[17] Notice that the only idiolects fully conservative in B as well as fully innovative in A occupy the cells UN40 and UW10.

The distribution of innovative and conservative idiolects of the MW and LW for feature B is similar to that for A, but B has no innovative tendencies in the UW that would suggest spread from that source. The statement in PEAS confirms the lack of a local or respectable origin for innovation in B. As Table 1 suggests, Figure 2 represents a less advanced pattern of innovation than Figure 1, and B is a change that began later and/or spread more slowly than A.

Inspection of the younger cells of the MW and LW in Figures 1 and 2 and of Table 1 suggests that the MW is more innovative in A, whereas the LW is more innovative in B. Figure 2 is especially revealing in this respect, for the cell (MW20) containing the oldest fully innovative idiolect in the MW also contains a fully conservative idiolect, whereas the cells LW10-30 are occupied only by idiolects fully innovative for B. Figure 4 is confirming that the distribution of idiolects, where B is spreading faster than A, is defective in the younger cells of the MW while occupied by the younger cells in the LW. The wide distribution of idiolects in which B runs ahead of A suggests that though B began later, it is spreading faster than A, a pattern than also sets off the LN from the UN.

It is also of interest to note that the only idiolect both fully innovative in B and fully conservative in A is in the cell LW30. Incidental observation reveals this pattern common in the South Carolina Low Country at a remove from the immediate coastal regions. Thus the changes are taking place in the order B, then A, in the inland Low Country,[18] as well as among the LW and LN of Charleston; the order A, then B, prevails among the UW, MW, and UN in Charleston. It seems safe to say that ultimately all speakers in the Charleston focal area will complete innovation in both A and B, an exchange of one contrast for another. To hazard further, it appears that the MW and LW will complete the exchange first, then the LN, then the UN, and finally, the UW.

A characteristic of Charleston speech that both natives and non-natives have long recognized is the monophthongal or ingliding allophones of /e/ and /o/. A familiar jocular shibboleth is "We'll have a late date at eight" [wil hæv ə leᵊt deᵊt ‡t eᵊt]. Sometimes [eᵊ] is exaggerated to [ɛᵊ] as in "State Paper" [stɛᵊt pɛᵊpə].[19]

Primer's statement that "one first notices a slight shade of difference in the pronunciation of certain vowels" is too vague to be of value. PEAS shows monophthongal (in final position) and ingliding (before consonants) /e/ and /o/ rather widely distributed in the Low Country of South Carolina and along the coasts of Georgia and Florida. On the basis of trends he observed in the usage of Charlestonians, McDavid (1949) suggested that upgliding /e/ and /o/, [e‡] and [oᵘ], would replace the traditional pronunciations, probably initiated by migration from inland.

Table 2 shows in percentages the class and age group preferences for upglided allophones of /e/ in the test words eighteen, eighty, eighth, eight, April, train, plane, cake, vase, and radio in line C. Line D of Table 2 shows the preferences for upglided allophones of /o/ in the test words radio, nose, throat, goat, coat, oak, okra, boat, road, and grocery.

	UW	MW	LW	UN	LN	70	60	50	40	30	20	10
C.	38	59	66	85	63	0	27	37	74	60	83	71
D.	38	52	59	63	43	5	16	24	57	51	76	64

Table 2

Figure 5 shows the number and social distribution of idiolects in which (a) C[20] has been completely innovated, and (b), underlined, C is still uninitiated. Figure 6 shows the number and social distribution of idiolects in which (a) D has been completely innovated, and (b), underlined, D is still uninitiated. Figure 7 shows the number and social distribution of idiolects in which both C and D are (a) completely innovative, and (b), underlined, completely uninitiated. Figure 8 shows the number and social distribution of idiolects in which D is spreading at a rate faster than C, regardless if either is categorical.

	70	60	50	40	30	20	10
UW	1		1				
MW	1	1				3	1
LW		2	1	2		5	1
UN				1			1
LN				1		1	

Figure 5. C categorical

	70	60	50	40	30	20	10
UW	1	1			1		
MW		2	1			2	1
LW		1	2	1		3	1
UN				1			
LN							2

Figure 6. D categorical.

	70	60	50	40	30	20	10
UW	1						
MW						2	1
LW		1				2	1
UN				1			
LN							

Figure 7. C and D categorical.

	70	60	50	40	30	20	10
UW				1		1	
MW	1	1	1			1	2
LW		1	1	1	2	1	1
UN							
LN							

Figure 8. D spreading faster than C.

Figures 5-7 show a distinct complementation in the distribution of the categorically innovative and the categorically conservative idiolects (cf. Figures 1-3). Not only do no two cells contain both types of idiolects, but rarely are adjacent cells occupied by both types of idiolects There is a greater likelihood that an idiolect will show divided usage in C and D than in A and B, for though fewer are categorically innovative fewer are categorically conservative.

Figure 8 (cf. Figure 4) shows that the idiolects in which the normally slower change (cf. Table 2) runs ahead are rather uniformly distributed throughout the MW and LW, and conspicuously absent among Negroes. It can be expected, then, that the distribution of D will come to resemble that of C, and that eventually both will be categorically innovative. It ought not be surprising if C and D are both completed at about the same time, for there is no disturbance of a set of contrasts in equilibrium as in the case of A and B.

Since there is more divided usage within idiolects for C and D than for A and B, there are no striking discrepancies or overlaps in the distributions of the idiolectal types. And since there is no disturbance of an equilibrium of two contrasts, what discrepancies there are in the distribution of the idiolectal types seem less likely to be diagnostic. Table 2 appears to be more suggestive of the loci of initiation of innovation, probably the same as for A and B: the UW; nearly simultaneously in the MW and LW (but independently of the UW), perhaps spreading upward socially; spreading downward socially among Negroes.

Though the distributional patterns of conservatism and innovation in C and D point with less certainty to the origins of innovation, comparison with the patterns for A and B does lead towards conclusions about the relative rate of innovation in the two sets. Recall that A was an innovation already in progress a generation ago, whereas innovation in C and D was described by McDavid (1948) as an incipient change. (No commentary was made on B, suggesting that it was considered stable and perhaps unlikely to show innovation soon.)

Comparison of Figure 1 with Figure 5 (and presumably Figure 6 will very shortly show a distribution like Figure 5) for the LW shows that the "leading wave" of innovation has carried the innovation to older speakers in C than in A; likewise, the "trailing wave" of conservatism covers younger speakers for A than for C (and D). The same pattern is apparent in the comparison of Figures 2 and 5. As Tables 1 and 2 suggest, C is overtaking A (as will D), a change that began earlier; and C is maintaining a lead over B (as will D), a change that was most likely initiated later, but certainly no earlier.

The rate of initiation of linguistic change is but one dimension of rate. The rate of generalization after the initiation is another,[21] and the two are not the same for the sets A and B and C and D. Whereas the rate of initiation of C (and D) is faster, the lesser number of categorically innovative idiolects in a social class (cf. Figures 1-3 vs. Figures 5-7) points to the conclusion that the "amplitude" of the innovative "wave" in C and D is smaller than for A and B. Once the latter have been initiated, they appear to be generalized more quickly by a speaker.

Still a third traditional characteristic of Charleston speech is the centralized beginnings of the diphthongs /aɪ/ and /aʊ/. Long recognized by both natives and non-natives, this trait also has a jocular shibboleth: "about the house," with /aʊ/ generally rendered as /u/ [əbut ðə hus].

Primer, again, does not treat this feature. PEAS shows that before voiceless consonants /aɪ/ and /aʊ/ regularly have a centralized first element like [ɐ] or [ʌ] in the coastal regions of South Carolina, Georgia, and Florida.

Line E of Table 3 shows in percentages the modern preferences for an uncentralized first element in /aɪ/ in ice, twice, rice, and right. Line F similarly shows modern preferences for an uncentralized first element in /aʊ/ in out, without, mouth, and house.[22]

	UW	MW	LW	UN	LN	70	60	50	40	30	20	10
E.	23	49	47	49	52	14	17	17	33	35	73	63
F.	3	40	41	56	56	0	6	0	38	28	51	74

Table 3

Figure 9 shows the number and social distribution of idiolects in which E^{23} is (a) fully innovated or (b), underlined, completely unintiated. Figure 10 shows the number and social distribution of idiolects in which F is (a) fully innovated or (b), underlined, not yet initiated. Figure 11 shows the number and social distribution of idiolects in which E and F are both (a) completely innovated or (b), underlined, still uninitiated. Figure 12 shows the number and social distribution of idiolects in which F is spreading faster than E.

	70	60	50	40	30	20	10
UW	1	1	1		1	1	
MW	–	2	1	1	1/1	1/4	2/2
LW		2	2		2/1	3	1
UN				2		1	1
LN				1			1

Figure 9.   E categorical.

	70	60	50	40	30	20	10
UW	1	1	1		1	2	1
MW	1	5	2	2	1/1	3/3	2
LW		2	3	2	2/1	1/4	3
UN			1	1	1	1	1
LN			1	1			2

Figure 10.   F   categorical.

	70	60	50	40	30	20	10
UW	1	1	1		1	1	
MW	–	2	1	1	1/1	1/1	1
LW		2	2		1	3	1
UN				1		1	1
LN				1			

Figure 11.   E and F categorical.

	70	60	50	40	30	20	10
UW							
MW				1		2	2
LW				2	1		2
UN		1		3			
LN							3

Figure 12.   F spreading faster than E.

Innovations in E and F show a less advanced pattern than those already considered. The statement of Kurath and McDavid that centralized first elements of /aɪ/ and /aʊ/ (before voiceless consonants) appeared to be spreading geographically and socially reinforces the conclusion that these innovations were among the last to be initiated, or perhaps the most resistant to innovation. From another perspective, it can be concluded that E and F are relatively late innovations since categorically innovative idiolects, with one exception, LN40, are confined to cells 10, 20, and 30. Further evidence of the recency of innovations in E and F are the wide distribution of categorically conservative idiolects and the lesser absolute preferences (Table 3) for innovative forms.

E and F, like other innovations, show the strongest innovative tendencies in the younger speakers of the MW and LW, and the UW are notably conservative. The overlapping distribution of conservative and innovative idiolects in the MW and LW, and the relatively fewer idiolects displaying divided usage point to innovations that spread rather slowly from speaker to speaker, but which are rather quickly generalized once initiated. Negro speakers are set off from Whites in this regard, for the higher absolute preferences, the greater proportion of idiolects with mixed usage, and the complementation in the distribution of categorical idiolects point to a pattern of innovation more like that for C and D, in which innovations are easily initiated but slowly generalized by speakers.

It was seen previously that in paired innovations one is regularly more advanced than the other. Setting aside idiolects in which both features were categorical or in which both were equally innovated (but not completed), about half again as often as B, A was more likely to be nearer completion, and about three times as often, C was nearer completion than B. E and F resemble A and B in their relative progress. But the distribution of the idiolects in which F is in advance of E is much less regular than for that of D in advance of C or B in advance of A (cf. Figures 4, 8, 12). For B and D, the even distribution of the "anomalous" idiolects coincides with the social classes that are most innovative.[24] At a later stage in E and F the distribution of idiolects more advanced in F may regularize, i.e., Figure 12 might resemble Figures 4 and 8. And with no balance of contrasts to be upset, the proportions may change.

It is also true that E and F are less symmetrical in other ways. The innovations in /aɨ/ and /aʉ/ are part of a complicated realignment of allophones. Kurath and McDavid found /aɨ/ and /aʉ/ to have [ɐ] as a first element before voiceless consonants (with no apparent distribution elsewhere), and low-central [ɑ] as a first element in other environments. In addition, "scattered" instances of a low-back [ɒ] beginning of /aɨ/ were observed.

In the 1969 survey, /aɨ/ was found to have the low-back beginning very rarely before voiced consonants or finally; just as rare were low-central beginnings of /aʉ/ in the same environment. There was a low-front [a˂~a~a˃]beginning in /aɨ/ about sixty per cent of the time (with the low-front element socially distributed much like the innovations heretofore examined), and /aʉ/ began with a closer low-front [æ~æ˅~æ̬˃~a̭˂] about thirty per cent of the time. With younger speakers in the MW and LW still leading the way, monophthongization of /aɨ/ has appeared in all social classes in Charleston, though Kurath and McDavid found it rare along the South Carolina coast.

Before voiceless consonants, /aɨ/ has generalized a less centralized first element [a˄~ɐ˅] in idiolects where centralization appears. Where there is no centralization, the first element is uniformly [a~a˃]. Monophthongization of /aɨ/ before a voiceless consonant, never found in the South Carolina Low Country by Kurath and McDavid, and not predominant in the Up Country, was found in three speakers in the MW and in three speakers in the LW. All were from the youngest age groups, and none gave more than one example.

Before voiceless consonants, /aʉ/ was found to have first elements with not only the same range as in other environments, but also [a˂~a~a˃~a˄~a̭˃~

e$~ev~e?]; just over ten per cent of the time, a more strongly centralized
[e<~e~e?] was found, about two-thirds elicited from the UW or older (40
or over) informants in the MW and LW.[25]

Given the evidently strong linguistic influence of a recently established in-migrant group introducing or reinforcing competing speechways,
it would seem reasonable to find those features for which Charleston is
most highly differentiated under greatest pressure for innovation. Yet
the conservatism in E and F belies this generalization, even though E and
F are the subjects of overt commentary,[26] and furthermore, were already
in flux. Not in flux, and not the subject of overt commentary, B shows
appreciably more innovation, even though conservatism in B is closely
restricted to the Charleston area.[27] In contrast, the feature relatively
more diffused geographically, and thus more likely to appear (in their
conservative forms) in the speech of the in-migrant group, namely A, C,
and D, are distinctly innovative, perhaps reinforced by overt commentary.
And recall that A was already in flux in Charleston by the time of the
migration.

Using the evidence of LAMSAS as a baseline, it has been possible to
interpret the findings of an intensive follow-up survey of a highly
stratified linguistic focus during a period of transition. Charleston
speech is certainly less homogeneous than it was a generation ago--and
probably less homogeneous than it will be a generation hence. For the
time between at least, there will be an appreciable social significance
in the distribution of the realizations of the several characteristics
treated herein.

SOURCES CITED

Allen, Harold B. Linguistic Atlas of the Upper Midwest, Volume I.
Minneapolis: University of Minnesota, 1973.

Atwood, E. Bagby. A Survey of Verb Forms in the Eastern United States.
Ann Arbor: University of Michigan, 1953.

Bloomfield, Leonard. Language. New York: Holt, Rinehart, and Winston,
1933.

Herzog, Marvin I. The Yiddish Language in Northern Poland: Its Geography
and History, Publication 37 of the Indiana University Research Center
in Anthropology, Folklore, and Linguistics. Bloomington: Indiana
University, 1965.

Kurath, Hans. A Word Geography of the Eastern United States. Ann Arbor:
University of Michigan, 1949.

_____ et al. Handbook of the Linguistic Geography of New England.
Providence: Brown University, 1939. (2nd ed. New York: AMS Press, 1973)

_____ and Raven I. McDavid, Jr. The Pronunciation of English in the
Atlantic States. Ann Arbor: University of Michigan, 1961.

Labov, William. Sociolinguistic Patterns. Philadelphia: University of
Pennsylvania, 1972.

McDavid, Raven I., Jr. "Postvocalic /-r/ in South Carolina: A Social
Analysis," American Speech, 23 (1948), 194-203.

_____. "The Position of the Charleston Dialect." Publication of
the American Dialect Society, 23 (1955), 35-49.

O'Cain, Raymond K. "A Social Dialect Survey of Charleston, South
Carolina." Dissertation University of Chicago 1972.

Primer, Sylvester. "Charleston Provincialisms," Transactions of the
Modern Language Association, 3 (1887), 84-99.

Raymond K. O'Cain

_____. "The Huguenot Element in Charleston's Pronunciation,"
Publications of the Modern Language Association, 4 (1889), 214-44.
Wang, William S-Y. "Competing Changes as a Cause of Residue," Language,
45 (1969), 9-25.

NOTES

*The earlier SAMLA-ADS version of this paper was called "A Diachronic
View of Some Charleston Idiolects." Read at the SAMLA-ADS Meeting,
Atlanta, Georgia, November 1973.

[1]Charleston is also represented in the forthcoming Dictionary of
American Regional English by two field records. Executed by the author,
these interviews served as a preliminary investigation, but they were
not systematically incorporated into any of the present analysis.

[2]The Linguistic Atlas of the United States and Canada, a series of
autonomous regional surveys of American English. Only the first of
these, the Linguistic Atlas of New England (Kurath et al.:1939-43) has
been fully published. Three summary volumes are available for the
Atlantic Seaboard: Kurath (1949), Atwood (1953), and Kurath and McDavid
(1961). Volume I of the Linguistic Atlas of the Upper Midwest (Allen:
1973) presents the lexical evidence from the Upper Midwest. LAMSAS, the
largest of the surveys, is being prepared for publication.

[3]O'Cain (1972) is the source for the data and the historical background in this paper.

[4]The interviews for the Dictionary of American Regional English carried
out in other parts of South Carolina also served in this respect.

[5]Some of the native informants could trace the history of their families
in Charleston back well in excess of two centuries (and these were not
necessarily members of the upper class). Others were first-generation
Charlestonians, sometimes the children of immigrants from abroad, more
often the children of Americans.

[6]The geographical area of the survey was restricted to the peninsular
city of Charleston and the highly urbanized areas adjacent to the city.
City limits are unreliable since Charleston has not extended its
corporate limits appreciably in some years, and much of the urbanized
area is either unincorporated or separately incorporated. The precedent
of Levine and Crockett ["Speech Variation in a Piedmont Community:
Postvocalic r." Sociological Inquiry, 36 (1966), 204-26.] has been
adapted in restricting the survey to the "functional community, i.e.,
the set of people who look upon themselves, and are regarded by others
as community residents."

[7]The first Negro elected to the South Carolina General Assembly in this
century was a member of this elite.

147

[8]But only in 1955 was cotton displaced as the number one money crop. Low prices after World War I and the boll weevil infestations of the 1920's pushed South Carolina into a depression several years in advance of the Wall Street Crash.

[9]The resentment towards outside capital dates to the Revolution. Even older is the disparagement of work. As the landed gentry became preeminent, effort expended in pursuit of a livelihood was stigmatized. Both these factors, as well as a century-long out-migration, contributed to the depletion of a strong middle class in Charleston. Artisans and merchants who could afford land became planters; others left the state.

[10]There is also an undetermined number of commuters, some from as far as eighty miles away, who increase the Low Country influences on Charleston speechways to the extent such features are present in their speech. Doubtless, many of these commuters are not Low Country natives.

[11]Charleston naturally shares many features of South Midland and Southern speech. It is the competing forms that are of interest.

[12]Not considered is postvocalic /r/, in which there is widespread innovation of constricted [ɚ] replacing unconstricted [ə].

[13]All the Upper White informants would qualify as LAUSC Type III, as would a number of informants from the Middle White and Upper Negro Classe

[14]/ɪ/ is much more likely than /i/ to appear before [ɚ] in the speech of the informants for the 1969 survey. /ɪ/ also remains predominant before [ə]. Likewise /e/ is a distinctly recessive alternate for /ɛ/ in A and B, though it appears in all social classes.

[15]Displayed are the numbers of informants in each group:

	70	60	50	40	30	20	10	
UW	1	1	1	1	1	2	1	8
MW	1	5	2	3	3	9	6	29
LW	0	2	3	5	4	7	3	24
UN	0	1	1	4	1	1	2	10
LN	0	0	1	1	0	1	3	6
	2	9	8	14	9	20	15	77

[16]Most of the informants in the UW and UN have at least some private schooling in their background. The MW and LW attend public or parochial schools almost exclusively, and the LN attend only public schools. Racial integration of the schools, though underway in 1969, has hardly had time to have linguistic consequences.

[17]This observation holds true for the UW as well.

[18]Those who have heard the delivery of my reports on the speech of Charleston are thanked for suffering my generally unsuccessful attempts to differentiate such sets as pen:pin and beer:bear.

[19]A number of informants reported, though less frequently, that /ε/ in beer, etc. is a trait that both Charlestonians and outsiders recognize as distinctive of the city (and the South Carolina Low Country). Though there is no standard shibboleth, beer comes as close as any word--hardly surprising to those who are familiar with Charleston's disdain for prohibition.

[20]C is upgliding /e/ [e‡]. D is upgliding /o/ [o$^{\upsilon}$].

[21]Compare Wang (1969:14-15).

[22]Compare the phonetic environments found by Labov on Martha's Vineyard to favor centralization. Following /t,s; p,f; d,v,z; k,θ,ð; ∅; l,r; m/, in decreasing order favor centralization. Preceding /∅,h,l,r, w,m,n/ favor centralization. Stress increases the degree of centralization for speakers who regularly centralize.

Given are the numbers of Charleston informants having centralization in the various test words, all uttered under full stress: ice, 39; twice, 44; rice, 41; right, 45; out, 47; without, 44; mouth, 45; house, 52.

[23]E is uncentralized forms of /aɨ/; F is uncentralized forms of /aʉ/.

[24]The disturbance of a pattern of symmetry in structurally parallel elements seems to be diagnostic of relatively intense activity in the processes of linguistic change. On Martha's Vineyard centralization in /aɨ/ is normally stronger than in /aʉ/. But those speakers striving to assert their identity by centralization exhibit indices of centralization greater for /aʉ/ than for /aɨ/ (Labov 1972:22-40, esp. Tables 1.2-5; 165-71; 178-80).

[25]Further testimony to the unsettled nature of /aɨ/ and /aʉ/ can be obtained by closer inspection of the phonetic quality of the first element in each in the environments specified. The various first elements of the two diphthongs were divided into groups phonetically similar in the degree of centralization. For /aɨ/ there were six groups (with 1,2,2,2,2, and 5 members) and for /aʉ/ there were five groups (with 3, 3,4,4, and 5 members). Those informants who categorically used any group in any environment were tabulated:

/aɨ/ before		/aʉ/ before	
C_{vl}	elsewhere	C_{vl}	elsewhere
30	34	31	28

Sixteen informants were categorical (whether in one group or two) for both environments for /aɨ/ and twelve were likewise categorical for /aʉ/; only three informants were categorical in both environments for both diphthongs.

[26]This overt commentary comes in response to questions like, "Have people noticed from your speech that you are from Charleston? Do you recognize the traditional Charleston accent?" Spontaneous comments were offered from time to time in the elicitation of various words. In response to "How far up and down the coast and how far inland do people seem to talk like Charlestonians?" informants occasionally characterized the area as a narrow coastal strip, but more generally they stressed the

Raymond K. O'Cain

uniqueness of Charleston speech. Expressions of pride in or affinity for old-fashioned Charleston speech were frequent, especially among speakers who more or less regularly used one or more of the conservative norms. Even among innovative speakers, the majority reported that they enjoyed hearing conservative speech. Perhaps a fifth of the informants were neutral in their attitudes, but only three or four--all in the NW and LW in their twenties or thirties--expressed aversion or hostility towards traditional speechways.

South Carolinians in the interior of the state are also keenly aware of the cultural separateness of Charleston. In light of the long-standing antipathy (somewhat muted nowadays) between the Low Country and the Up Country, it is hardly surprising that the attitudes of Up Countrymen towards Charleston are somewhat less favorable.

[27]With respect to South Carolina and the geographical and social origins of the recent migrants to Charleston, of course.

B may have special status among the innovations considered herein if it is indeed the case that, as Labov (1972:300) states, "One of the universal constraints on change...[is] that in contact situations, mergers expand at the expense of distinctions (Herzog, 1965:211)." But recall that there is also a contrast spreading in Charleston at the expense of a merger--in beer:bear, etc.

[28]The restoration of postvocalic /r/, the loss of which spread from Charleston (McDavid:1948) over the Low Country in general and into cultivated speech in the Up Country, resembles the more innovative traits in its distribution. It is not often the subject of overt commentary.

150

SOME METHODOLOGICAL PROBLEMS IN RECENT INVESTIGATIONS
OF THE Ø COPULA AND INVARIANT BE*

Howard G. Dunlap

In the past several years, sociolinguistic discussions of American English have focused upon a few selected features of phonology, morphology, and syntax in the speech of Northern urban dwellers of African ancestry. These linguistic forms have been designated as elements of "Black English," and much speculation has been indulged in regarding the possible origins of certain dominant forms among black speakers in this country. This paper is not concerned with such speculation about origins. It is impossible, however, to ignore the fact that a number of writers dealing synchronically with what they call Black English have identified their subject as a social dialect which differs not only radically but consistently from standard English and as a dialect which is restricted in its use exclusively to blacks. J. L. Dillard states, for instance:

Syntax, the focus of more modern linguistics, is the area in which the analysis of Black English is most revealing.[1] Superficially similar Standard English forms are really very different in their underlying structures.[2]

John Fickett concurs, saying:

In the case of Black English, the quest for meaning has been impeded by the resemblance of forms to English forms and the beforehand decision that Black English is a dialect of English.[3]

And even William Labov, with less than his usual caution, asserts:

There is one feature of the NNE [Negro nonstandard English] verb system which seems to be unique to the NNE system, and is not shared by any WNS [white nonstandard] dialect or by SE [Standard English], and that is the use of the invariant verb be with a meaning of 'habitual' or 'general'.[4]

Perhaps the most extreme extension of this view of the uniqueness of black speech is found in Susan Houston's study of "Child Black English." Stating that "dialects are regional; genera are racial; registers are situational; and species are social,"[5] Houston says:

The term 'Black English' seems to us clearly expressive of the intended distinction, since one may also speak of 'White English' as the complementary genus. It is possible to speak of BE [Black English] as a unified genus of language distinct from WE [White English] because there are a number of linguistic characteristics on all levels of language which appear exclusively in the speech of black children (and adults).[6]

Houston continues, however:

161

It is not possible to state at this time what the distinguishing
characteristics of Black English are, on any level, largely
because there is not sufficient data on either Black or White
English to make any meaningful comparisons except in the most
general terms. As will be shown subsequently, this writer feels
that the differences between BE and WE lie preponderantly in
the realm of phonology, in fact overwhelmingly so, and that
syntactic differences between the two genera have been greatly
overemphasized in many previous works.[7]
In setting up Black English and White English as distinct genera (which
are "racial"), Houston states in effect that because of race no black
person could ever speak totally like a white person, no white person
could ever speak totally like a black person:
    Bidialectism does not seem to exist. As a matter of fact, one
    might go so far as to say that it does not exist by definition:
    we have stated that occasional overlap in ranges of BE and WE is
    not significant, since they do subsume different ranges and are
    different genera of English.[8]
Houston's definition of genera as "racial" is of course untenable.
    In contrast to the kind of research represented by Houston, Joy Miller
and Juanita Williamson demonstrate persuasively at the grammatical level
that race is not the factor which separates so-called Black English from
White English.[9] Williamson's citations for the use of invariant be call
into question Labov's statement that this usage is "unique to the NNE
system, and is not shared by any WNS dialect." Terms such as "Black
English," "White English," "Negro Nonstandard English," etc.,[10] are
nowhere adequately defined and are misnomers, for the dialect differences
that they seem to cover are in fact differences of region, of education,
of social class, and of caste, rather than of race.
    Absolute statements, then, regarding Black English grammar and phonology
(as well as White English grammar and phonology) are suspect, especially
when such statements are made by native Northern linguists. Any reliable
description of related dialects which are in contact with one another will
require the use of qualifiers such as "frequently," "usually," "often,"
and "occasionally," or an explicit indication of the frequencies of
occurrence.
    Now having cautioned against the danger of absolute statements which
attempt to establish "Black English" as a variety of language distinctive
or totally apart from "White English," I will indicate some of the
problems apparent in recent sociolinguistic research by considering
data collected in 96 interviews with native Atlanta fifth-grade speakers
(half black, half white) in the Atlanta, Georgia public schools. The
six schools at which the interviews were taped represent upper-middle
class, lower-middle class, and lower class neighborhoods, with one
black and one white school at each socio-economic level. Altogether,
more than 350,000 words of the free conversation of these children were
taped. The analysis of this corpus provides the basis for the following
remarks.
    No aspect of the speech of relatively uneducated blacks has received
more attention in recent years than has their characteristic use of the
verb be, especially the omission of the copula in the present tense
("My daddy Ø a janitor"; "He Ø not at home right now") and the use of
the so-called "invariant be" for repeated occurrence ("When I get home
from school each day, my mama be at work").

The most extensive work that has been done on the use of the verb be
in the speech of blacks is that of Labov in A Study of the Non-standard
English of Negro and Puerto Rican Speakers in New York City and Shuy,
Wolfram, et. al., in several works emanating from the Detroit Survey. It
is in his New York study that Labov formulated his theory of the inherent
variability of the English copula:
    ...wherever SE can contract, NNE can delete is and are, and vice-
    versa; wherever SE cannot contract, NNE cannot delete is and are,
    and vice-versa.[11]
Labov has defined contraction as "the removal of an initial schwa before
a lone consonant as in am, is, are."[12] This definition presents problems
for the analysis of the fifth grade native-Atlanta speech. If the three
parallel utterances "I am here," "he is here," "You are here" are produced in a normal conversational manner (or in what Labov calls "allegro
speech"), the parallel results in the speech of the informants for this
study are usually "I'm [am] here," "He's [hiz] here," and "You're
[juə~juɚ] here." Yet according to Labov's definition of contraction
and according to his ordered rules,[13] only the first two of these are
contractions. The third, with the vocalization of [r], is not a contraction, but an altered full form. Labov's contracted form [jur] is
not typical of the speech, black or white, of the Atlanta fifth graders
who were interviewed. Because for most of these speakers the full form
of are is [ɑ.~ɑə], without [r] and therefore without the possibility of
contraction in Labov's sense, the term contraction was replaced by the
term reduced form in the analysis of data for the Atlanta study.
The use of the term contraction in Labov's sense of the word has
caused data in Labov's A Study of the Non-standard English of Negro and
Puerto Rican Speakers in New York City and in Wolfram's Description of
Detroit Negro Speech to be interpreted differently from the interpretation
that was given similar data in the Atlanta study. Wolfram states:
    In most cases, the frequency of zero realization of are is twice
    as great as the frequency for is....there are 7 of the working-
    class informants who have categorical absence of are contraction.
    ...one can conclude that zero realization of is is considerably
    more socially stigmatized than the zero realization of are. One
    important reason for the predominance of are zero realization over
    is can be attributed to the phonological pattern of post-vocalic
    r absence.[14]
Earlier, in his discussion of phonological variables, Wolfram states that
"In most cases in which constriction [i.e., of [r]; HGD] is absent, a
central vowel, either [ə] or [ɨ], is present...."[15] Despite the presence
of this central vowel, Wolfram apparently considers an utterance such
as [ðeə + hæpɪ] to be an instance of zero realization of are; he cannot
count this as contraction because it does not represent "the removal of
an initial schwa before a lone consonant." And he obviously does not
count it as a full form since he cites the high frequency of zero realization of are. Wolfram does not provide phonetic transcriptions for his
examples of contraction of are and zero realization of are. Labov, on
the other hand, considers [ðeə], [deə], or [wiə] as representing variant
full forms of are[16] and adds that--for Negro nonstandard English and for
Southern white speech--there is no middle ground between this variant
full form and deletion: "Contraction of are is therefore equivalent
to deletion."[17] Labov comments, "We can understand how white Southerners
can delete are, since they have the r-vocalization rule which deletes

post vocalic schwa...."[18] Since contraction of they are in Labov's and Wolfram's sense of the term would have to resemble [ðer~der], it is not remarkable that Wolfram finds a "predominance of are zero realization over is" in uneducated Negro speech; he would probably find a similar degree of zero realization of are in the speech of cultivated native whites from the Old Confederate States. But this is not a tenable position for Wolfram. Cultivated Southern speakers (of both races) regard medial deletion of the copula as non-standard, and therefore do not delete it. The mid-central vowel of [ðeə] and [wiə] does not represent the contracted form of are (in all varieties of Southern speech). Clearly Labov's and Wolfram's category of contraction is not a useful one for analyzing the data collected from the Atlanta informants.

A second departure from Labov's and Wolfram's classifications seems necessary for the treatment of the forms [ɪs], [ðæs], [dæs], and [hwʌs]. According to Labov's ordered rules, the forms [ɪs] and [ðæs] are not contracted forms parallel to [ɪts] and [ðæts] in which the [t] has been assimilated to the [s]; rather, they represent deletion of the verb:[19]

The contradiction lies in the assumption that the [s] of [ɪs] is derived from is, as indicated by the practice in dialect literature of writing i's. It now seems clear that this [s] is the assibilated [t] of it--the verb is has entirely disappeared, leaving only this footprint on the preceding pronoun.

Labov gives generative rules for the phonology of Negro Nonstandard English and concludes that [ɪs] represents deletion of the verb:[20]

ɪt##ɪz
ɪt##əz   vowel reduction
ɪt## z   contraction
ɪs##z   assibilation
We have already seen that deletion must be categorical after sibilants, so it follows that the result is
ɪs##   deletion
The generative rules do not allow for the generation of the standard contraction it's. Despite Labov's concern with the inherent variability of the English copula, he apparently regards the deletion of the copula in [ɪs, ðæs, dæs, hwʌs] as instances of inherent variability.

Although this Atlanta material does show that the final voiceless stop of it, that, and what is frequently lost through assimilation, the data does not support Labov in his finding that this assimilation (which Labov regards as deletion) is almost categorical among LB speakers (See Table 1) Even among LB informants, where the greatest degree of assimilation occurs, [ɪts] outnumbers [ɪs], nor is [ðæts] totally replaced by [ðæs] and [dæs].

INCIDENCE OF STANDARD vs. ASSIMILATED FORMS OF IT'S, THAT'S, AND WHAT'S

	UMW	LMW	LW	UMB	LMB	LB
it's as [ɪts]	256	163	162	18	133	162
it's as [ɪs]		1	3	6	20	104
that's as [ðæts]	108	56	51	46	35	44
that's as [ðæs]	1	1	17	2	45	41
that's as [dæs]					14	50
what's as [hwʌts]						1
what's as [hwʌs]						1

Table 1

It is suggested here that Labov's classification of [ɪs] and [ðæs] as deleted forms parallel to [Ø], as in "It my daddy" and "That my daddy," does violence to the native speaker's intuitive feeling about his language. The Atlanta data has been tabulated, therefore, with [ɪs], [ðæs], and [dæs] as instances of the reduced verb form parallel to [ɪts~ðæts~dæts], rather than as instances of deletion, as Labov and Wolfram count them.

A third departure from the procedures found in most of the recent literature on the speech of lower class Blacks concerns the treatment of the so-called "invariant be." Ralph W. Fasold says:

The meaning of Black English BE, as we shall show, involves repeated but not continuous occurrence. At any moment the predication may be valid, but there are gaps between instances of the event described.[21]

Fasold and Wolfram in a later publication enlarge upon this definition:

The use of invariant be in Negro dialect has two explanations: deleted will or would and distributive be....with a meaning something like "object or event distributed intermittently in time."[22]

And Fasold elsewhere writes:

It is also interesting to note that the time adverbs now and right now are most frequent with the present tense concord BE forms [am, are, is: HGD], but never co-occur with non-concord BE....A small number of exceptions is to be expected when- ever a large amount of real language data is examined, but it is instructive in this case to examine these four exceptions more closely....These exceptions are deviant because they seem to refer to a single event in the past.[23]

Yet Beryl Bailey cites examples such as "He be there now," "He be there soon," and "He be there yesterday" to illustrate the point that the element of time is optional in the verb when time is expressed adverbially or contextually in a nonstandard dialect. It is easy enough for Fasold and Wolfram to say that whatever does not fit one's definition is "deviant," but a definition however neat which is too limited to account for the facts of observed phenomena is not a useful one. The data from the Atlanta study provide numerous instances that call into question the accuracy of Fasold's and Wolfram's limited defini- tions of invariant be. Fasold's statement that "the time adverbs now and right now...never co-occur with non-concord BE...." is not accurate. The Atlanta corpus shows that one child said:

I don't know how old he be; I don't know how old he is now.

And certainly the "right now" of the present moment is implied in the following example:

It don't be night; it be day out there.

This was said as the child's father sleepily resisted being awakened on Christmas morning and the child insisted it was time to get up. It seems then inaccurate to say that invariant be "involves repeated but not continuous occurrence," for both the examples above and those following indicate either a continuous state or a one-time occurrence:

They [baby ants] be like little grains of rice.
No, it just be they Ø gonna have a prom.
She say that the television be broken.
It be like our school room, the living room is.
The stream be way down to the sewage [sewer].

And the frequency with which invariant be is used to indicate past events,
as is evident in the following sentences, makes the adjective "deviant"
seem questionable for this usage:
    It be there when we moved over there.
    And then she come to our house, and my mama be gone.
    It was one time when she be cold, cause my dad [now dead] he would
    always keep my mother warm when she be cold in the wintertime.
Thus, the invariant be form is used not only for repetitive action and
for future or conditional occurrences with will or would omitted as Fasold
states, but also for the present moment and for a past occurrence.
    The chief point that should be emphasized from this data is not just
that invariant be has wider use than has formerly been acknowledged, but
that its use is nowhere categorically required--at least not in the dialec
of the children interviewed for the Atlanta study.
    Many of the LB informants provide similar utterances which show that
invariant be alternates both with regular present tense forms and with ∅
copula. Each group of sentences below represents a single informant:
    He is divorced.
    He's spoiled.
    I don't think she ∅ married, but she got a son.
    I be scared of ghost men.

    When it's time for a operation....
    When we ∅ out of school....
    When it be real cold....

    When I'm at home....
    If the lady ∅ at home....
    When it be down there....

    I don't know how old he be; I don't know how old he is now.
    Sometime the lunch is not good.
    They ∅ not a real nice class.
    My father sometimes don't be home.

    All children in our class ∅ nice.
    Them people be so slow.
It has become conventional to treat the ∅ copula as deletion of the
remnants of contraction,[24] but the three following examples of connected
discourse indicate that ∅ is also a substitute for an underlying be
rather than for a finite form:
    Sometime different teachers be in charge. Sometimes my teacher
    be in charge. When she ∅ in charge, we go at 11:30.

    They got wood covering the door and it look like they ∅ close
    [i.e., not open for business], but they don't be close.

    ...another place where it ∅ quiet and don't be no fighting.
It is also conventionally said that the negative of ∅ is "∅ not." If
that were uniformly true, the two preceding examples should have been:
    They got wood covering the door and it look like they ∅ close,
    but they ∅ not close.

    ...another place where it ∅ quiet and ∅ not no fighting.
    It should be evident that the linguistic situation among lower class
black speakers of English is not nearly so neat as some investigators
have reported. It is true the invariant be was not used by any of the
white informants in this study, but appears among all classes of black
informants (see Table 2).

INCIDENCE OF INVARIANT BE

	Number of Informants	No. having Inv. be	Total Forms of Simple Present Tense of BE	Total Inv. be	% of Inv. be
UMB	3	2	160	2	1
LMB	13	8	574	29	5
LB	32	28	1026	138	13
	48	38	1760	169	10 Av.

Table 2

Judging solely on the basis of the conversation recorded from the 96 native fifth-grade Atlanta informants, it might be said (as Labov has said) that the use of invariant be is the one grammatical marker which distinguishes the speech of blacks from that of whites. It is evidence such as this which has led to the "creole substratum" hypothesis, but this evidence can be used equally well to point to the culmination of the development of the American caste system rather than to African origins. Attestation of invariant be only among black informants may indicate the "generalized substandard Afro-american koine" which McDavid predicted might "arise in the future if the fault-lines in our society continue to widen."[25] But as has been pointed out already, invariant be is by no means a requirement as a simple present tense or non-tense form in the speech of the black children interviewed for this study.

The Atlanta data provide more than 60 clear-cut instances from the LB corpus in which a finite form or Ø actually appears, but in which invariant be would have been expected according to Labov, Fasold, Wolfram, et. al. Invariant be appears in the speech of the black children interviewed (seldom among UMB's, more frequently among LMB's, and most often among LB's) not as an inevitable grammatical construction in any particular context, but as an alternate form accounting for only 10 per cent of the 1760 instances of simple present tense of BE, whereas the Ø copula accounts for 14 per cent and standard forms account for 76 per cent.

The important task ahead is to resist making exclusive statements which are unsupported by large quantities of facts from observed data. To quote Labov with approbation, the important task is "to involve variation as a systematic fact," not to "dispose of it and eliminate it in the final analysis."[26]

NOTES

*The earlier SAMLA-ADS version of this paper was called "A Synchronic View of Some Atlanta Idiolects." Read at the SAMLA-ADS Meeting, Atlanta, Georgia, November 1973.

[1] J. L. Dillard, Black English (New York: Random House, 1972), p. 40.

[2] Ibid., p. 44.

[3] Joan G. Fickett, "Tense and Aspect in Black English," Journal of English Linguistics, 6 (March, 1972), 17.

[4]William Labov, A Study of the Non-Standard English of Negro and Puerto Rican Speakers in New York City (Bethesda, Md.: ERIC Document Reproduction Service, 1968), p. 228.

[5]Susan Houston, "Child Black English in Northern Florida" (Atlanta: Southeastern Education Laboratory, 1969), p. 34.

[6]Ibid., p. 9.

[7]Ibid., p. 10.

[8]Ibid., p. 33.

[9]Juanita V. Williamson, "Selected Features of Speech: Black and White," CLA Journal, 13 (June, 1970), 420-23, and Joy L. Miller, "Be - Finite and Absence: Features of Speech - Black and White," Orbis, 21 (1972), 22-27.

[10]See Lee Pederson, "Black Speech, White Speech, and the Al Smith Syndrome," Studies in Linguistics in Honor of Raven I. McDavid, Jr., ed. Lawrence M. Davis, (University: University of Alabama Press, 1972), p. 124, and Raven I. McDavid, Jr., "Dialectology: Where Linguistics Meets the People," Emory University Quarterly, 23 (1967), 216-17.

[11]Labov, op. cit., p. 185.

[12]Ibid., p. 188.

[13]Ibid., p. 208.

[14]Walter A. Wolfram, A Sociolinguistic Description of Detroit Negro Speech (Washington: Center for Applied Linguistics, 1969), pp. 173-74.

[15]Ibid., p. 109.

[16]Labov, op. cit., p. 74.

[17]Ibid., p. 220.

[18]Ibid.

[19]William Labov, "Contraction, Deletion, and Inherent Variability of the English Copula," U.S. Office of Education, Washington, D.C., 1968, p. 15.

[20]Ibid.

[21]Ralph W. Fasold, "Tense and the Form BE in Black English," Language, 45 (1969), 764.

[22]Ralph W. Fasold and Walt Wolfram, "Some Linguistic Features of Negro Dialect," in Teaching Standard English in the Inner City, ed. Ralph W. Fasold and Roger W. Shuy (Washington, D.C.: Center for Applied Linguistics 1970), pp. 66-67.

[23]Fasold, op. cit., p. 768.

[24]Labov, A Study of the Non-Standard English of Negro and Puerto Rican Speakers in New York City, pp. 206-14.

[25]Raven I. McDavid, Jr., "American Social Dialects," College English, 26 (1965), 258.

[26]Labov, A Study of the Non-Standard English of Negro and Puerto Rican Speakers in New York City, p. 9.

SUBJECT CONCORD OF BE IN EARLY BLACK ENGLISH*

Jeutonne Brewer

In spite of recent interest in black English, relatively little is
known about its earlier history. William A. Stewart and J. L. Dillard
have proposed that black English spoken in this country developed from
an earlier plantation creole that was related to pidgins and creoles
spoken in areas such as Africa, the Caribbean, South America, and
coastal South Carolina and Georgia. Stewart (1967) noted grammatical
similarities (for example, the absence of be and the possessive suffix
-s) between literary attestations of early black English and West
African Pidgin English, Surinam Pidgin, and Gullah. J. L. Dillard
(1971) agreed with Stewart's claim of an earlier creole period and
related the absence of the copula in present-day black English in
Washington, D.C., to that earlier system. Although Labov's (1968,
1969) studies of linguistic variation in present-day black English
did not provide supporting evidence for the creole hypothesis, he noted
(1969:719, fn. 5) that forms which do not occur frequently enough to
be considered part of the regular linguistic patterns in present-day
black English could be significant in reconstructing its history. These
studies of black English linguistic theory have not only helped to
generate interest in the study of black English but have also indicated
how much research remains to be done. Intriguing questions remain
unanswered or at best only partially answered.

If earlier pidgin and creole periods are part of black English
linguistic history, to what extent does this distinctive history account
for structural differences in present-day black English? Recent descriptive work has tended to support the claim that present-day black English
and standard English are so similar that they have the same underlying
structure (Labov, et al. 1968). Did the two grammatical systems have
different underlying structures at an earlier time? If so, what was
the form of that earlier black English grammar? In Black English
(1972), Dillard attempted to show the development of the dialect during
earlier pidgin, creole, and decreolization stages; but his work, which
is intended for a general audience, is more suggestive than definitive
in regard to the questions raised above.

Keith Whinnom (1971) has pointed out that a decreolized language can
become a dialectal variant of a standard language; that is, languages with
significantly different underlying structures can become very similar to
each other. If black English had an earlier creole period, then it could
have been restructured, that is, decreolized into a dialectal variant of
standard English.[1] Since the data used for restructuring would have been
external and skewed, one would expect attempts at restructuring to be
only partially successful. This partial success should be reflected in
parts of black English grammar that differ from standard English.

Elizabeth Traugott (1972: 187-94) has noted additional problems in the study of the history of black English. She pointed out that some structures in black English are similar both to creoles and to earlier British-based dialects in this country, and she has stressed how difficult it is to determine whether these resemblances are the result of creole influence, of seventeenth- and eighteenth-century English influence, or of the speakers' efforts to approximate standard English as they restructured black English. Of course, some resemblances could be the result of multiple influences. However, we do not yet have extensive historical evidence to indicate how other systems may have influenced blac English or how it may have influenced other dialects of English.

Adequate historical analysis depends on descriptions of a language syste at different points in time. To determine what changes have occurred in the history of black English syntax, we need descriptions of earlier periods of black English as well as other dialects to compare with studies of the current language. The extensive work that is being done on present-day black English is chiefly sociolinguistic, that is, it analyzes linguistic variation within a speech community in relation to social variables and to different styles of speaking. No comparable studies of early black English are available, nor is there any study of variation in that earlier period. Thus it is difficult to discover exactly what changes have taken place historically and to establish the relationship of black English to other dialects of English during earlier periods.

Although a single study cannot provide answers to all the questions raised in the preceding paragraphs, it can answer part of the need for historical information about black English. This study focuses on the subject concord of be in an earlier period, and its findings are compared with those of the recent study of present-day black English by Labov and his colleagues (1968). The evidence indicates that concord of be in the earlier period of black English differs from that reported by recent synchronic studies.

The present study is based on interviews with ex-slaves, collected in the 1930s as part of the Federal Writers' Project of the Work Projects Administration (WPA).[2] The material, gathered some seventy years after emancipation, has several advantages for a study of black English: it covers a time span extending back to the middle of the nineteenth century; it covers a wide geographical area; it includes a range of social levels. The quantity of data available in the 2300 narratives (Yetman 1967: 552) makes them a valuable source for early black English. These narratives concerning personal experiences during slavery were collected in seventeen states from an estimated 2 percent of the ex-slave population of the nation (Yetman 1967: 535, fn. 2).

To determine to what extent the findings presented here are comparable with those of recent synchronic studies, it is first necessary to comment briefly on some ways the two sources differ. The narratives were written down in longhand as they were spoken; recent synchronic studies have analyzed tape recordings of interviews. The WPA informants are not available for re-checking written data against actual speech, whereas informants in recent studies are still accessible. The narratives contain basically one careful style of speech; recent studies have collected and compared samples of a variety of speech styles. Labov (1968) listed four speech styles in the New York study--group or casual, single or careful, reading, and reciting word lists. The narratives record the speech of older, mainly rural blacks, whereas most socio-linguistic work has been with young, urban blacks.

It is also possible that the published narratives were edited to some extent, thus reducing their value as evidence. The correspondence of the Washington WPA office, however, directed the interviewers to record the narrative in the words of the ex-slaves.[3] Thus Henry G. Alsberg, director of the Federal Writers' Project, advised WPA interviewers that "all stories should be as nearly word-for-word as is possible."[4] The recent publication of the WPA interviewers' typescript copies of the narratives prepared for the Washington office (Rawick 1972, 1:xvii) also helps reduce the severity of the problem. Moreover, the narratives were collected by a number of different interviewers in different areas of a state. For example, the ten Mississippi narratives included in this study were collected by eight interviewers in seven different localities. Similarities are thus more likely to reflect grammatical structures used by the ex-slaves than the bias of a single interviewer.

It seems likely that linguistic elements used during the time of slavery were still in use at the time the narratives were collected. One would expect elements of the pre-Civil War linguistic system still to occur in the narratives, unless there had been a complete linguistic change from the black English of slavery to standard English grammar within seventy years.[5] The continuation of the prewar life-style in the South and the scarcity of schools there make the latter suggestion seem unlikely.

In The Shadow of the Plantation (1934: xi-xii, xx), Charles S. Johnson pointed out that the plantation system of the early 1930s remained "essentially what it was before the Civil War. With emancipation the Negro field hand on the plantation suddenly became the Negro tenant farmer. However, actual change was not great."

Data from twenty-two narratives were analyzed for this study, twelve from Texas and ten from Mississippi. Each narrator was born and lived his life in the state in which the narrative was recorded. The oldest narrator was 101, the youngest 75. Nine of the Texas narrators were male, three female; six of the Mississippi narrators were male, four female.

The narratives show significant differences between the use of be in early black English, in present-day black English, and in standard English. Discussion of these differences is divided into three parts: a general survey of the subject concord of be in early and present-day black English, a detailed examination of the occurrence of be forms with various personal-pronoun subjects in the narratives, and an analysis of the social variables that account, at least in part, for apparent dialectal differences between the Texas and Mississippi narrators.

Subject Concord of Be

Early black English did not differentiate am, is, and are in the same way standard English and present-day black English do. Unlike the standard dialect, in early black use these forms regularly did not agree with the person and number of their subjects. Consequently, statements about agreement and nonagreement in the following discussion refer to the concord expected in standard use.

This situation contrasts with the findings of Labov's (1968) New York study. He concluded that "person-number agreement exists in NNE [Negro nonstandard English] for only one verb, be₁, which differentiates am, is, and are in the same way the SE [standard English] does" (p. 250). Thus the present tense conjugation of be in present-day black English

stands as an exception to a general rule of lack of agreement.[6] On the
basis of this research, Labov also concluded that, although is and are
can be deleted without a trace in present-day black English, am with
the first person singular pronoun cannot be deleted. The regular occurrence of am reinforces his claim of the existence of underlying is and
are in present-day black English grammar.

In early black English, however, person-number disagreement was the
rule rather than the exception. For example, full forms of is occurred
eighteen of twenty-three times (78 percent) with pronoun subjects other
than third person singular he, she, or it. This high percentage of
person-number disagreement contrasts with the findings reported by Labov
for present-day black English. For example, in table 3.18 of the New
York study (p. 222) of present-day black English, Labov notes the high
degree of regularity (or the low percentage of person-number disagreement)
of is in appropriate third-person singular contexts. For all groups
studied, is occurred with subjects other than third-person singular
pronouns only 5.3 percent of the time. Although the number of is
occurrences on which I have based my comments in this section is small,
the analysis of forms of be occurring with pronoun subjects in the next
section will further substantiate the claim made here.

The lack of be concord with personal-pronoun subjects is partly accounted
for by the fact that the form are was not part of the early black English
lexicon. Are occurred only once in the data:[7]
1. And he would say, "Them are your slaves. You whip them." [Tex. 29:96]
This lone example of are was used by a narrator whose dialect differs from
the dialects of the other narrators in more closely approximating standard
English.[8] It should be noted, however, that the narrator was quoting a
statement made by her former master.

The absence of are following plural pronoun subjects could support
Labov's analysis that are is deleted without a trace. Or it is possible
that, if are is not part of the early black English grammar, then there
are only two forms of present tense be--am and is. If one of these forms
occurs regularly with singular pronoun subjects and the other with plural
pronoun subjects, then the question of which form occurs in place of
are would be readily apparent. The grammar would have been regularized
to use one form with singular subjects, the other with plural subjects.
However, the situation is not a matter of simple regularization. Other
forms of be, such as am, is, and 's,[9] as well as zero, occur with plural
pronoun subjects where one expects are.

Before analyzing the data, I will summarize the characteristics of early
black English that have been presented in this section: person-number
disagreement is typical, the form are is not part of the lexicon, and
other forms of be (am, is, and 's) occur with plural pronoun subjects.
Each of these characteristics indicates significant points of difference
between the use of be in early black English, in present-day black
English, and in standard English.

Be with Pronoun Subjects
This section analyzes four early black English forms, am, is, 's
and zero, and the personal pronoun subjects with which they occur. It
will show that, although the forms am and is occurred in early black
English, their distribution differed from that of standard English. This
different distribution is the substance of the claim that subject concord
of be was not a feature of early black English. But even more significant

Jeutonne Brewer

is the fact that the distribution suggests a far more basic difference between the grammars of black English and standard English.

Am with Pronoun Subjects. The use of am in early black English grammar was quite different from its standard English use with I. Furthermore, its distribution is linguistically significant because it suggests a dialectal split between the narrators from Texas and Mississippi.

Am occurred nineteen times with personal-pronoun subjects in the narratives included in this study. In only three of the twenty-two narratives did am occur with the pronoun I. The only two examples of am in the Mississippi narratives both occurred with the pronoun I; sentence 3 is a line from a song:

   2. I'm old an' can hardly git about. [Miss 11:71]
   3. 'Cause I'm a Captin in de army. [Miss 24: 159]

In the Texas narratives a quite different picture emerges. Only one Texas narrator used am with I, and she used it with no other pronoun:

   4. I am taken for a Mexkin very often. [Tex 29:100]
   5. I'm gettin' a little pension, but it ain't near enough to keep us. [Tex 29:105]

In five other narratives (Tex 1, 5, 14, 16, and 18) am was consistently used with pronoun subjects other than I, that is, with he, him, we, us, and they. Twelve of the seventeen am forms in the Texas narratives had he, him, or it as subject. In other words, the majority of the am forms used by the Texas narrators occurred in those contexts where one expects is. Am also occurred once after each of the plural pronoun subjects we, us, and they:

   6. And he am good like my first massa, he never whipped me. [Tex 5:16]
   7. Dey brung massa in and I's jus' as white as he am den. [Tex 16:50]
   8. Him am kind to everybody, and all de folks' likes him. [Tex 5:14]
   9. Dey calls me Paul Barnes, but my name ain't Paul, it am Joe. [Tex 14:45]
   10. At dinner, when the field hands come, it am the say way. [Tex 1:2]
   11. I's sho' glad when I's sold, but it am short gladness. [Tex 5:15]
   12. We'uns am not use' to sich and some runs off. [Tex 5:15]
   13. But lots of time when us sposed to mind de calves, us am out eatin watermillions in de bresh. [Tex 18:55]

The use of objective pronouns as subjects was rare in the narratives but did occasionally occur, as the use of him and us in sentences 8 and 13 illustrates.

Am was used in a past context in sentence 7, the past indicated by the past tense marking of brung. A past meaning is also implied by the larger context in which sentences 6, 10, 11, and 14 occurred. For example, this sentence immediately preceded sentence 11 in the text of the narrative: "But dat Delbridge,he sold me to Massa House, in Blanco County." The third-person singular -s, which appears with like in sentence 8 and with run in sentence 12, seems to indicate the present. However, these sentences occurred in a past context in the same narrative as sentences 6, 11, and 14. Seven of the seventeen occurrences of am were used by this narrator (Tex 5). This suggests the possibility of what Dillard (1971) has called optional tense marking. Once the tense is marked for a context, then additional tense marking may be unnecessary.

Of the nineteen occurrences of am in all the narratives, fifteen (78.9 percent) were used with pronoun subjects other than I. These nonstandard uses of am were in the Texas narratives. Am occurred seventeen times in six of the twelve Texas narratives; in five of these narratives am was consistently used fifteen times with pronoun subjects

165

other than I. Thus am did not agree with pronoun subjects 88.2 percent of the time in the Texas narratives.

Am with Noun Phrase Subjects. Although this paper is concerned with be forms occurring with pronoun subjects, it is of interest to note that am was used with both singular and plural noun phrases by the Texas narrators.

Am occurred twenty-two times with noun phrase subjects, sixteen times with singular and six times with plural subjects. Of the twelve Texas narrators, each of the five who used am with third-person singular pronoun also used am with singular noun phrases (Tex 1, 5, 14, 15, 16).

15. Massa tell his neighbor, "My nigger am comin' to you place." [Tex 1:
16. My name am Andy J. Anderson. [Tex 5:14]
17. Den surrender am 'nounced and massa tells us we's free. [Tex 5:16]
18. The truth am, I can't 'member like I used to. [Tex 14:46]
19. Jus' like to de fat beef, massa am good to us. [Tex 15:47]
20. And people says now dat Aunt Harriet am de bes' cook in Madison-ville. [Tex 16:49]
21. When de weather am too cold, dey sometimes give us pants. [Tex 18:56
22. De quarters am built from logs like dey's all in dem days. [Tex 5:15
23. Massa live in de big box house and de quarters am in a row in de back. [Tex 14:45]
24. Back in de old days de white men am hones'. [Tex 15:48]
25. Charcoal and onions and honey for de li'l baby am good. [Tex 16:50]

Am was used with a past meaning in sentence 24. It occurs in identity contexts in sentences 16 and 20, and it seems to have an habitual meaning in sentences 19 and 21.

Is with Pronoun Subjects. In both the Mississippi and the Texas narra-tives, the majority of full forms of is occurred with pronoun subjects other than he, she, or it. Is occurred a total of twenty-three times with pronoun subjects, five times in the Texas narratives and eighteen times in the Mississippi narratives. It was used five times with a third-person singular pronoun subject and eighteen times with other pronoun subjects, four times after I, once after we, three times after you, and ten times after they.

Is occurred in four Texas narratives (Tex 1, 5, 18, 29). Two of the narrators used is with the pronoun subjects I, we, and you:
26. You's free as I is. [Tex 18:57]
27. Don't you think Massa Dave ain't comin' round to see we is fed. [Tex 1:2]
28. Listen, white folks, you is gwine start a graveyard. [Tex 1:3]

Is occurred eighteen times in eight Mississippi narratives (Miss 3, 6, 8, 9, 11, 12, 13, 14); three narrators (Miss 11, 12, 14) each used is once with a third-person singular pronoun subject. Seven narrators (Miss 3, 6, 8, 9, 12, 13, 14) used is with I, you, and they; for example:
29. Us was better fed den dan I is now. [Miss 6:36]
30. Well den hol' yo' head high so folks can see you is quality. [Miss 13:83]
31. You know what kinda white folks dey is. [Miss 8:55]
32. I's old and dey is forgot me, I guess. [Miss 3:21]
33. Co'se dey is worked on it several time since den. [Miss 12:73]

The majority of the full forms of is occurred with pronoun subjects other than the third person singular. In the Mississippi narratives is occurred with third-person pronoun subjects only three times; fifteen of eighteen times (83.3 percent) is had other subjects, being used three times after I twice after you, and ten times after they. In the Texas narratives is occurred with third-person singular pronoun subjects twice; three times (60 percent) is occurred with other pronoun subjects, once each after I, we, and you. Thus in all the narratives is occurred 78.3 percent of the time with pronoun subjects other than the third person singular.

's with Pronoun Subjects. The be form that occurred most frequently after pronoun subjects in the data was 's. The Texas and the Mississippi narrators used the form with almost equal frequency, fifty-three uses by the former and fifty-one by the latter. The form 's occurred seventy-six times after the subject I, nineteen times after he, she, or it, once after we, four times after you, and four times after they.

34. I'se thankful I ain't got no mem'ries 'bout slav'ry times an' dat I an' my folks is done well. [Miss 12:72]

35. I'se retired now 'cause dey say I too old to work any longer. [Miss 12:72]

36. But lots of times she's so tired she go to bed without eatin' nothin' herself. [Tex 18:54]

37. De Niggers today is de same as dey always was, 'cepting' dey's gittin' more money to spen'. [Miss 7:47]

38. Dey's all big 'nough to work in de field. [Tex 18:54]

Nonstandard 's also occurred in sentences presented in the discussions of am and is: with I in sentences 7, 11, and 32, with we in sentence 17, with you in sentence 26, and with they in sentence 22. Of the 104 occurrences of 's, 85 (81.7 percent) did not agree with their pronoun subjects.

Both groups of narrators used 's after all pronoun subjects, with one exception. The Mississippi narrators did not use 's after the first-person plural pronoun we. But the lack is evidently a gap in the data, since the pronoun we was not used by any Mississippi narrator. The pronoun we also occurs infrequently in the Texas data; the narrators from that state used we only five times with the four be forms discussed in this paper.

's and the Past Tense. The frequency of 's is possibly the result of its use as a contracted form of is, as it may have been used in the local dialects of the white population. It is also possible, however, that 's was learned or analyzed by the narrators as a form of be distinct from is. Sentences 34-38 above present a problem in analyzing 's as a contracted form of is. Sentences 34, 35, and 37 are obviously present contexts, but the larger contexts of sentences 36 and 38 have past reference despite the 's in them. These sentences are not exceptions, as the following show:

39. I 'members when I's jus' walkin' round good pa come in from the field at night and taken me out of bed and dress me and feed me and then play with me for hours. [Tex 1:2]

40. I's born in 1843. [Tex 5:14]

41. I's most scared to death when de war end. [Tex 16:50]

42. But I's not realize what I's in for till after I's started, but I couldn't turn back. [Tex 5:16]

The past is clearly indicated by past tense marking on other verbs in sentences 7, 39, and 42.

It can be claimed that 's is a contracted form of both is and was, with only the context indicating which form occurs in the underlying sentence. That is, you's free in sentence 26 has an underlying you is free, and I's born in sentence 40 has an underlying I was born, with both is and was freely contracted after pronoun subjects. This is the most obvious solution. However, the following sentences indicate that the solution would not account for all cases of 's:

43. I's cook big skillet plumb full corn at de time and us all have plenty meat. [Tex 16:49]

44. I's boil red oak bark and make tea for fever. [Tex 16:50]

Here the 's seems to serve as a past tense marker. These examples, both from the same narrator, can be explained by analyzing I's as an allomorph of I and allowing the main verb to appear with no past marking. However, this analysis raises additional questions: Are the occurrences of I's in sentences like ·7 and 39-42 contracted forms of was or is, or allomorphs of I with no be form in the sentences? Or is 's a past tense marker of some kind in early black English?

To claim that 's with pronoun subjects is allomorphic is at best an ad hoc solution. It also seems unlikely that the present tense be form which occurs most frequently in the data is an allomorphic variant of zero. It also seems doubtful that 's is a separate past tense marker. It occurs in both present and past contexts, the past meaning often indicated by marking on other verbs in the same sentence or in the larger context.

It has been suggested by R. Whitney Tucker (1966:77) that the present tense I's, a contraction of I is, was a characteristic "plantation darky form," while the past tense I's was related to the Southern dialect form, a contraction of I was. Labov (1969:755), on the other hand, has pointed out that there seems to be no general process to delete initial w in English. Because Tucker's comment on the matter is impressionistic rather than definitive, while Labov's comment is based on a detailed descriptive analysis of black English, it seems more likely that 's is a contracted form of is in early black English. It may be an example of tense neutralization, that is, optional tense marking.

Be for Standard English have. The form 's also occurred where one would expect auxiliary have:

45. I's had 'speriences durin' dat time. [Tex 5:14]

46. For de first couple hours de pain am awful. I's never forgot it. [Tex 5:15]

47. I's been here eighty years. [Tex 1:3]

48. I'se hear'd dat a heap o' cullud people never had nothin' good t' eat. [Miss 6:38]

49. I'se been married three times. [Miss 7:48]

50. I's lived a long life an' will soon be a hun'ed. [Miss 8:55]

51. Fac' is I'se worked right 'roun' white folks mos' all my days. [Miss 9:58]

It is a question whether this perfective 's is related to has rather than is.

A preliminary analysis of perfectives in early black English shows that none of the narrators used full forms of auxiliary have or has. There were seven examples of -a, which could be considered reduced forms of have, following modals. Six of the seven examples of I'd a, could a, and would a were used by one Mississippi narrator (Miss 6), and one was used by a Texas narrator (Tex 18). The absence of full forms of perfective have and has in the data and the frequency of 's and is perfectives suggest that is functioned as a perfective in place of standard English have/has. The Mississippi narrator who used -a most frequently also used 's seven times. It is possible that could a and would a

were single morphemes rather than modals followed by a reduced form
of have.

→ Absence of be with Pronoun Subjects. Both the Texas and Mississippi
narratives include sentences having pronoun subjects without be where
standard English requires it. Be was absent thirty-eight times after
pronoun subjects--four times after I, twenty times after he, she, and
it, nine times after we or us, twice after you, and three times after they:

52. One time he whippin' me and I busts de button off my shirt what
he holdin on to. [Tex 18:56]

53. Dat Bandy Joe he say he a spirit and human both. [Tex 18:57]

54. You free now. [Tex 24:74]

55. But how us gwine a-take lan' what's already been took? [Miss 6:42]

56. Dat man Duncan, he say us gwina hol' fun'al rites over dat dog.
[Miss 7:46]

57. I didn't git nothin' when us freed. [Tex 15:47]

58. I know when peace 'clared dey all shoutin'. [Tex 15:47]

Sentence 35 also contains an example of the absence of be after the
pronoun I.

Three Mississippi narrators used the zero form of be a total of seven
times after pronoun subjects, twice after I, twice after he, and three
times after us. It has already been noted that the subject pronoun we
did not occur in the Mississippi narratives. The zero form of be
occurred after pronoun subjects I and us in one narrative (Miss 6),
after us in another narrative (Miss 7), and after I and he in a third
narrative (Miss 12).

In eight Texas narratives the zero form occurred after all subject
pronouns and after us used as a subject pronoun--twice after I, eighteen
times after he, she, or it, once after we, five times after us, twice
after you, and three times after they.

Is the absence of be in early black English the result of contraction
and deletion processes like those proposed by Labov (1969) for present-
day black English? Labov has stated that deletion, the removal of a lone
consonant left after contraction, is categorical when the consonant is a
continuant following a pronoun subject. If we assume that the absence
of be is the result of the deletion of the lone consonant /s/, then only
occurrences of zero after third-person singular pronoun subjects indicate
agreement. Other occurrences indicate disagreement. On this assumption,
it is apparent that the zero form of be frequently lacks subject concord.

The zero form of be occurred with pronoun subjects other than the
third-person five of seven times (71.4 percent) in the Mississippi data
and thirteen of thirty-one times (41.9 percent) in the Texas data. For
all narratives zero occurred with nonstandard pronoun subjects eighteen
of thirty-eight times (47.4 percent).

Summary. It has been shown that the lack of standard subject-verb
concord of be was a characteristic of early black English in the WPA
slave narratives. This lack of concord has been demonstrated for four
forms of be--am, is, 's, and zero. Every form of be used by the
narrators fails to agree with pronoun subjects a significant percentage
of the time, with the exception of am in the Mississippi narratives.

The distribution of be forms after pronoun subjects also suggests a
deeper question to be investigated. For example, in the Texas narratives
am occurred with all pronoun subjects except you. In five Texas narratives (Tex 1, 5, 14, 16, 18) am and at least one other be form--is, 's,
zero--occurred after third-person singular subjects. One narrator

(Tex 5) also used am and 's after the subjects we and they. Another narrator (Tex 9) used only one of the forms discussed in this paper, am, after a third-person singular subject. It was noted earlier that one Texas narrator (Tex 29) approximated standard English, her use of are indicating standardization. However, this narrator also used both am and 's after the pronoun subject I.

The distribution of forms of be after pronoun subjects may indicate a meaning difference; that is, it is possible that different forms of be in early black English had separate syntactic or semantic functions, at least in the Texas narratives. If this is the case, it would provide a grammatical explanation for the lack of subject concord of be; the function of the be forms superseded subject-verb agreement.

In order to determine whether be forms had separate syntactic or semantic functions or were randomly distributed in the narrators' attempts to approximate standard English, an analysis of the frequency with which present tense forms of be occur in certain environments, such as locatives, noun phrases, predicate adjectives, and the future intentional gonna/gwine, is needed.

Social Variables

The use of am by the Texas narrators with pronoun subjects other than I indicates a dialectal difference between the Texas and the Mississippi narrators. This situation is somewhat surprising because present-day black English is generally considered to be nongeographical. Except for some interference from local dialects, black English in such widely separated areas as New York, Detroit, and Los Angeles has been described in recent sociolinguistic studies as consistently similar. Yet in this study there seems to be a distinct difference between two groups of narrators from different geographical areas.

Recent sociolinguistic studies have also shown that linguistic variation is related to social variables such as age, sex, and education. This section therefore presents social variables that could account for the major linguistic difference between the Texas and the Mississippi narrators: age, sex, education, place of residence, and occupation. Of these variables, only a narrator's occupation during slavery proved to be significant.

Age. Because all the narrators were adults of 75 years or older, age was unlikely to be a significant social factor. However, the 26-year span between the oldest and the youngest narrators suggested the possibility that there could be some linguistic variation related to the age of the narrator. For example, the youngest narrator (Tex 29) was the one who most closely approximated standard English; the oldest Texas narrator (Tex 5), at age 94, was one of the most divergent linguistically, using am with non-first-person subjects more than any other narrator. Similarly divergent, however, was another Texas narrator (Tex 1) who was only 80 years old, close to the youngest in age. The oldest narrators in the study were from Mississippi (Miss 6, 8), being 100 and 101 respectively. Both used am only after the pronoun subject I, and neither used the am, is/'s variation. The age of the narrators, therefore, did not provide a clue to their linguistic difference.

Sex. Analysis of the variable of sex was also inconclusive. Of the twelve Texas narrators, nine were male, three female. Five male narrators (Tex 1, 5, 9, 14, 18) used am after pronoun subjects other than I. One male (Tex 15) used am after noun phrase subjects but not

170

after pronoun subjects. One female (Tex 16) used <u>am</u> with pronoun
subjects other than <u>I</u>; another (Tex 26) did not use <u>am</u> at all. The use
of <u>am</u> by a third female (Tex 29) has already been discussed. There were
too few females to indicate any trend on the basis of the sex variable.

    <u>Education</u>. Since there was only scanty information in the narratives,
it was not possible to ascertain with any accuracy the educational
backgrounds of thirteen of the twenty-two narrators.

→<u>Place of Residence</u>. <u>William A. Stewart (1967) noted that between field
slaves and house slaves there was a social cleavage related to linguistic
differences, the field slaves speaking a plantation creole and the house
slaves speaking a more standard form of English</u>. This claim actually
includes two social distinctions, occupation and place of residence
during slavery. Information in the WPA narratives indicates that some
slaves lived in the slave quarters but worked as house or personal
servants in the master's house, while other slaves both lived and worked
there. Therefore, I coded the data in the narratives in terms of two
separate variables.

    The place of residence was coded into two categories, the slave quarters
and the master's house, or the big house, as the narrators often referred
to it. <u>Where the slave lived during slavery should be significant</u>. The
slave who lived in the slave quarters would receive continual linguistic
reinforcement from his family and friends. The slave who lived in the
master's house would be likely to be more aware of standard English.
Stewart's comments on social distinctions stressed the importance of the
slave's proximity to the master and his family.

    Most of the Texas narrators had lived in the slave quarters. Of eight
who did so, two (Tex 3, 26) did not use <u>am</u> at all. Three narrators
(Tex 15, 24, 29) did not state where they lived during slavery; one of
them (Tex 15) used <u>am</u> with noun phrase subjects but not with pronoun
subjects. Of the ten Mississippi narrators, five (Miss 3, 6, 11, 12, 13)
had lived in the slave quarters, two (Miss 8, 24) had lived in the big
house, and three (Miss 7, 9, 14) did not state where they lived during
slavery. Of the two Mississippi narrators who used <u>am</u> with <u>I</u>, one
(Miss 11) lived in the slave quarters and the other (Miss 24) lived in
the big house. Although place of residence seems to have had some
influence, the analysis of the narrators' use of <u>am</u> in relation to this
variable was inconclusive.

    <u>Occupation</u>. Stewart's comments on the social cleavage between field
slaves and house slaves indicate that the occupation of the slave during
slavery should be a significant social variable. From information in
the narratives, I found it possible to set up an occupation scale of
seven categories: field worker, stocktender, nurse, overseer, skilled
laborer (for example, carpenter), cook, and house (or personal) servant.
These categories reflect jobs that the narrators deemed important,
whether referring to themselves or to the other slaves. Of these
categories the first two (field slave, stocktender) seem to correspond
most closely to Stewart's field slave category. The three middle
categories (nurse, overseer, skilled laborer) are intermediate categories that are more difficult to classify according to Stewart's
dichotomy.

    The variation of <u>am</u> is explainable by the narrator's occupation during
slavery, in spite of the relatively small number of <u>am</u> occurrences. Of
the seven Texas narrators who used <u>am</u> without concord, two (Tex 5, 18)
worked as field slaves, one (Tex 16) was a cook, and two (Tex 9, 15)

were house servants. It was not possible to ascertain the occupation of
two narrators (Tex 1, 14). In spite of the spread of the narrators along
the occupational scale, there is some order to the seeming diversity. Th
narrators were ranked in order of the decreasing frequency of lack of
subject concord with am; pronoun and noun-phrase subjects with non-
agreeing am were counted together for the purpose of the ranking.

Thirty-seven of the thirty-nine occurrences of am in the Texas narrativ
lacked concord. Two narratives (Tex 5, 18) accounted for twenty-six
(66.7 percent) of them; one of the narrators (Tex 5) worked in the field,
and the other (Tex 18) worked as a stocktender. The former showed lack
of concord of am eighteen times, the latter eight times.

Five narratives accounted for the other examples of am without subject
concord; none of these narrators used am more than three times. Two were
house or personal servants (Tex 9, 15), one of them was a cook (Tex 16).
The occupation of two (Tex 1, 14) was not ascertainable.

One narrator (Tex 29) used am twice but only after I, and four narrator
(Tex 3, 21, 24, 26) did not use am at all. Two (Tex 3, 26) were house or
personal servants, and one (Tex 21) a nurse who lived in the master's
house. The occupation of two narrators (Tex 24, 29) was not ascertainabl

As the preceding three paragraphs show, there are really three groups
of narrators. In the first there was a significant lack of subject
concord of am; in the second a small lack, 7 percent or less, and in
the third none at all. At extreme ends of the occupational scale are
the members of the first and third groups, field slaves and house slaves
respectively. The middle group also contains domestic or house servants.
Perhaps we could tentatively call them the linguistically aspiring group
of house or personal servants, or the group showing the greatest
linguistic insecurity. It may be that they were in the process of
eliminating the lack of subject concord of am from their linguistic
systems but had not yet been successful when the narratives were collecte
It would be interesting to know how long the house servants in the second
and third groups had worked at their jobs during slavery.

Conclusion

The analysis of the data presented in this paper indicates that the
use of be with personal-pronoun subjects in early black English differed
from the pattern of both standard English and present-day black English
as presented in recent sociolinguistic studies. Differences include the
high percentage of person-number disagreement of be forms with pronoun
subjects. Lack of subject concord of be was a characteristic of early
black English.

The evidence has not been presented as a counterargument to the claim
of an underlying be in early black English. If there were earlier pidgir
creole stages of black English without underlying be, as claimed by
Dillard and Stewart, the black English recorded in the WPA narratives
represents a stage of the decreolization process in which black English
was assimilating be forms. However, their functions may have differed
significantly from those of standard English.

Although analysis of the variation of am in relation to the social
variable of occupation during slavery is revealing in some ways, the
functions of what may be contrastive forms of be in early black English
require further investigation. This research could have significance
for the question of pidgin-creole stages in early black English.

Jeutonne Brewer

Sources Cited

Bloomfield, Leonard. Language. London: Allen & Unwin, 1969. Originally
  published in 1933.
Dillard, J. L. "The Creolist and the Study of Negro Non-Standard Dialects
  in the Continental United States." In Pidginization and Creolization of
  Languages, edited by Dell Hymes, pp. 393-408. Cambridge: Cambridge
  Univ. Press, 1971.
_____. Black English. New York: Random, 1972.
Labov, William. "Contraction, Deletion and Inherent Variability of the
  English Copula." Language, 45 (1969), 715-62.
_____; Cohen, Paul; Robins, Clarence; and Lewis, John. A Study of the
  Non-Standard English of Negro and Puerto Rican Speakers in New York
  City. Cooperative Research Project no. 3288. Vol. 1. New York: Columbia
  University, 1968.
Mangione, Jerre. The Dream and the Deal. New York: Little, 1972.
Rawick, George, ed. The American Slave: A Composite Autobiography. Vol.
  1, From Sundown to Sunup. Vol. 4, Texas Narratives. Vol. 7, Oklahoma
  and Mississippi Narratives. Westport, Conn.: Greenwood, 1972.
Stewart, William A. "Sociolinguistic Factors in the History of American
  Negro Dialect." Florida FL Reporter, 5 (Spring 1967), reprint, 1-4.
Traugott, Elizabeth Closs. A History of English Syntax. New York:
  Holt, 1972.
Tucker, R. Whitney. "Contraction of 'Was.'" American Speech, 41
  (1966), 76-77.
Whinnom, Keith. "Linguistic Hybridization and the 'Special Case' of
  Pidgins and Creoles." In Pidginization and Creolization of Languages,
  edited by Dell Hymes, pp. 91-116. Cambridge: Cambridge Univ. Press,
  1971.
Yetman, Norman K. "The Background of the Slave Narrative Collection."
  American Quarterly, 19 (1967), 534-53.

NOTES

*The earlier SAMLA-ADS version of this paper was called "Grammatical
Features and Their Social Correlates: A Study of Black Dialect in
Slave Narrative." Read at the SAMLA-ADS Meeting, Jacksonville, Florida,
November 1972.

[1]The idea that black English has undergone decreolization is not new.
Leonard Bloomfield (1933:474) suggested that black English was in the
last stage of such a process.

[2]The research presented here is part of a more comprehensive study of
the verb system of early black English based on the data contained in the
WPA slave narratives. The research was assisted by a grant from the
Ford Foundation.

[3]It seems that the Washington WPA office had a strict editing policy
for the material to be published as part of one of its projects, the
State Guides. However, there seems to have been a different policy for

173

Jeutonne Brewer

the slave narratives. Professor Mangione (personal communication, 7 February 1974) stated that his general comments on editing did not necessarily apply to the slave narratives. A letter from files of the Mississippi WPA ex-slave studies (National Archives, Record Group 69) indicates that this was the case. Burnette Yarbrough, the supervisor of workers' assignments, wrote the following comments to the state director, Eri Douglas (19 July 1937): "All of these [ten autobiographies are in the same phraseology as recorded by the field workers. No revision has been attempted other than a partially standardized form of spelling. The same word has not always been spelled the same way in each autobiography, however. Consistent spelling throughout one manuscript has been attempted so far as it seemed feasible. Example: if one Negro used de for the, we have allowed this throughout the entire manuscript. If another Negro uses th' for the, th' has been used throughout. Note that one Negro says niver for never, while another uses neber. We have tried to avoid too consistent spelling lest we destroy the personality of the story....I have made no revision of form as I did not want to risk a stilted, formal, or unnatural narrative. Too, am I not correct in my supposition that Washington wants them this way?" The attitude and official position of Washington was stated in the directions accompanying the questionnaire (see footnote 4).

[4]This point is reiterated several times in the memorandum that accompanied the standard questionnaire prepared by John A. Lomax. The memorandum and the questionnaire are reprinted by Rawick (1972, 1: 173-78).

[5]Black English--also referred to as Afro-American English, black vernacular English, Negro nonstandard English, Negro nonstandard, black dialect, and Negro dialect--is a sociolinguistic term used to designate a form of English spoken almost exclusively by blacks. In the midst of this terminological maze, it is possible to state that black English is characteristic of a particular segment of the black population, the lower socioeconomic group; blacks, particularly those of upper socioeconomic groups, also speak other varieties of English.
The term standard English designates the variety of English accepted by the education system of this country. In reality, it should be called edited American English as it refers to a national written standard rather than a spoken standard.

[6]There is no third-person singular marker for regular verbs in black English; therefore, forms such as has, does, and says are not part of the black English lexicon, although they are part of standard English. In the case of the past tense of be, the form was occurs for all persons; were is not part of the black English lexicon. (Labov et al. 1968: 246-50).

[7]Sample sentences used in this paper have been presented exactly as they appear in the typescript copies of the narratives. The numbers in brackets indicate the narrative number and the page number in the volume in which the sentence occurs. For example, Tex 14:45 indicates the fourteenth narrative in the Texas volume (i.e., volume 4), page 45. The narratives were listed only by name in the volumes; therefore, I numbered the narratives consecutively in each volume for easy reference.

I then determined which narrators were born in and had lived their lives in the state in which the narratives were collected; only those narratives are included in this study. They are Texas narratives 1, 3, 5, 9, 14, 15, 16, 18, 21, 24, 26, add 29 and Mississippi narratives 3, 6, 7, 8, 9, 11, 12, 13, 14, and 24.

[8]This narrative includes the only examples of were as well as the only example of are. However, the narrator's dialect is not entirely standard. She used I's in place of I am two times, and she used was thirteen times and were fourteen times with plural pronoun subjects (we was~we were, you was, they was~they were, and them was).

[9]Because I have used written narratives as a data base, I have not assumed a priori that 's is a contraction of is but rather have listed 's separately for analysis.

BLACK ENGLISH AND BLACK ATTITUDES*

David L. Shores

   Among the issues current in social dialectology and education, none
has aroused more interest and generated sharper differences than the
topic of Black English. In view of the amount of time and energy
expended on the speech of Blacks, it may seem that the addition of
another paper to the already voluminous pile calls for an apology, if
not this, at least some justification. When I think of the almost
countless papers, workshops, institutes, and in-service discussions
that center about the speech of Blacks, the resultant conflicting
viewpoints and conclusions, and the fact that I do not offer here a
reconcilement of the precedent conflicting views, I do hesitate about
adding still another paper. Nevertheless, I have chosen to do so. I
merely want to share an idea or an experience or two that may possibly
be of use to those concerned.

                                    I
   This paper is an informal attempt to supply a partial answer to the
question of the range of feeling in the Black community on the topic
of Black English. It is informal in that it is more observational than
statistical and a partial answer in that it deals with the attitudes of
only Black educators in predominantly Black colleges. In a word, it
is more expository than scholarly. The plan of the paper is to consider
1) the controversy about the relationship of the speech of Blacks to
that of Whites, 2) the presence of certain "distinctive" features in the
speaking and writing of Black college students, and 3) the attitudes of
Black college educators about these and other relevant matters. For this
paper, I draw from my involvement as associate director and instructor
in three USOE summer institutes and eleven two-day regional conferences
for college English instructors in predominantly Black colleges, all of
which have been organized and operated by Norfolk State College in
Norfolk, Virginia. We have touched over sixty of the over eighty
traditionally Black colleges and hundreds of Black educators, including
English and reading instructors, departmental chairmen, academic deans,
college presidents--all of whom, at one time or another, have engaged in
the discussions of the language problems of Black students and have
expressed their views, and all, I might add, with commitment and
responsibility. What I have to say then is derived from this experience.

                                   II
   My primary question requires that I first deal with the controversy of
Black English as a distinct dialect as it has appeared in scholarly
discussion. As you know, there has been in the last ten to fifteen years
considerable discussion among linguists and educators and others about

whether it is possible to characterize certain "distinctive" nonstandard features of American English as Black English. Though one paper lists about forty linguistic features of Black speech,[1] most treat from six to twelve, the most frequently mentioned of which are the uninflected plural (five girl), the uninflected possessive (the boy hat), the uninflected third person singular (he think), the uninflected past tense and past participle (he play, he has play), the absence of the copula (he here), the uninflected be (It be), overinflection (I knows), final consonant reduction (firs), the existential it (it is a man there), and question inversion (I want to know can he go).

Even though these and other features consistently show up in the studies of Black speech, some people, both lay and professional, deny the existence of typological differences between the speech of Blacks and Whites. In an issue of the NAACP magazine Crisis, an editorial states emphatically that "Black English is more regional than racial and more Southern than Black." Joe Black, the former pitcher of the Cleveland Indians and now a vice-president of the Greyhound Corporation writes "There is no Black language."[2] Many other educated Blacks view the concept of Black English as a "cruel hoax," just another attempt at stereotyping Blacks. Still others consider it just bad grammar and the result of carelessness. Those associated with the Linguistic Atlas, notably Hans Kurath and Raven McDavid, and Frederic G. Cassidy of the Dictionary of American Regional English project prefer to speak of statistical differences rather than inherent, structural differences. Their views can be summarized in Juanita Williamson's work, the result of twenty years of observation in the South, which concludes that "...the speech of the Negro does not differ materially from that of Whites of the same economic and educational level of the area in which he has lived the greater part of his life,"[3] and that the so-called distinctive features of Black English are "neither Black nor White just American."[4] This group has constantly implored linguists to study the regional evidence in the Atlas materials and the closely related projects If they do, they say, they will find that all the "forty" features can also be documented from American White speech. This represents one side of the issue. The other side is more varied.

William Labov, who says that he did make some use of the Atlas data, makes what he considers to be a careful statement about the speech of Blacks.

> Many features of pronunciation, grammar, and lexicon are
> closely associated with Negro speakers--so closely as to
> identify the great majority of Negro people in northern
> cities by their speech alone.[5]

Ralph W. Fasold and Walt Wolfram have written:

> ...not all Negroes speak Negro dialect (Black English). There
> are many Negroes whose speech is indistinguishable from others
> of the same region and social class, and there are many whose
> speech can be identified as Negro only by a few slight
> differences in pronunciation and vocal quality.[6]

They add that "Negro dialect shares many features with other kinds of English,"[7] but that "Its distinctiveness...lies in the fact that it has a number of pronunciation and grammatical features which are not shared by other dialects."[8] Whether people think that the arguments and current research justify using terms like Black English, Black dialect, Negro dialect, Nonstandard Negro English, or ghetto English even, they say,

isn't really relevant. The fact of the matter is, they argue, that
there is a kind of English closely associated with Blacks, which appears
to be more deviant from Standard English than that of most uneducated
Whites.

Orlando Taylor, one of the few Blacks doing research in the field,
thinks that there are problems in both viewpoints. Though White linguists
seem to be very careful to limit Black English to lowerclass Blacks,
Taylor maintains "...a substantial core of Black English is known and
used (particularly in communicating black to black) by most, and probably
all, classes of blacks."[9] Taylor, as we would expect then, speaks of
Black Standard English, which he characterizes as having "primarily a
standard syntax, plus a few black syntactic elements."[10] "The remainder
of Black Standard English," he says, "may include varying degrees of
black vowel patterns, ethnically marked suprasegmental features and
black lexical items."[11] In another paper, Taylor writes that "...identi-
fiable African features can be found at virtually all levels of language
in the overwhelming majority of contemporary black Americans."[12] Taylor
will acknowledge numerous overlapping linguistic features in the speech
of Blacks and Whites but states that "there is unquestionably a core
black culture and linguistic behavior"[13] and contends "...that every
black person in America, except those born and raised in virtually all
white areas, has some knowledge of that language."[14] We must not take
these observations, however, to mean that Taylor would accept the commonly
listed features as distinctive features of Black speech. It is interesting
to note that Richard Long prefers "Black Vernacular English" as a rubric
to indicate a difference between the speech of lowerclass and middleclass
Blacks.[15]

Thus, we see that it is perfectly possible for some groups to maintain
that there exists such a dialect as Black English and for others to
deny it, both apparently committed and responsible people with good reason
and some evidence. Both groups appear to have a basis for truth in their
arguments. Yet each line of argument is faced with certain difficulties,
which appear fatal to the claims of the other. Thus the claim of those
that there exists a kind of speech they call "Black English" appears to
break down when those of contrary belief find that the "distinctive"
features are found in the speech of others,[16] an awkward fact that
apparently gnaws at the very notion of dialectal distinctiveness. In the
same way, the advocate of the belief that the speech of Blacks is
nothing more than Southern regional English is met with the fact that
Blacks and Whites can identify each other and each group a great majority
of the time by speech alone.[17]

III

There may be considerable doubt among some of the disputants about the
"reality" of Black English and its relationship to the speech of Whites,
about whether Black English is a matter of incidence (frequency of occurrence) or typology (definitive structural differences), but there is no
doubt among those who assign, annotate, and grade papers of Black
college students that certain nonstandard features of speech, which some
linguists have designated as the benchmarks of Black English, appear with
high frequency in the speech of their students and are passed on into
their writing. The listing below shows a variety of examples and
frequencies of occurrence of these nonstandard features in fifty-six
freshman English papers, which averaged about three hundred words:

David L. Shores

<u>Uninflected Plural</u>: <u>46</u> occurrences in <u>30</u> papers
  many literary work
  The cause of many human death
  one of the most prized possession
  one of the main reason
  their protest are not
  the next three paragraph
  all of these thing
  there are several way
  one of his famous speech
  all country
  these special force
  two most important element
  the way word develop
  the Black boys and girl
  all my Black brother
  all your Black sister
  both race are
  a group of animal
  different group are
  the animal are
  two are natural being
  several year younger

<u>Uninflected Possessive</u>: <u>31</u> occurrences in <u>17</u> papers
  a person health
  Waller conclusion
  on today campuses
  our nation defense
  the old student body ideas
  America wars
  the White women hair
  the White women hands
  Clever statement
  the Black man stake
  the Black man color
  someone else feeling
  someone problems
  people farms
  it life
  a young girl who life
  the first stranger physical appearance
  many a man heart

<u>Uninflected Third Person Singular</u>: <u>121</u> occurrences in <u>36</u> papers
  If group one want
  this country want
  China need to try
  James Baldwin have
  John recollect
  Not only do John tell
  It also describe
  what he think
  one person act
  a person continue to do so
  that he know

180

he don't care
it don't
one tend to look
this often tend
when he do return
the red man live in
everybody want
he have
that look alike
any cause that suit
what the Negro realize
everything I see have
which also destroy
Good writing give
hatred grow
he never look up
of how he feel
Cleaver like
what Cleaver think
this to me mean
her husband make the money
she want
Cleaver try to think
cutting classes have
the book which tell about

Word Final Consonant Reduction: 66 occurrences in 40 papers
  Uninflected Past Participle: 39 occurrences in 20 papers

the United States have cause
a novel base on
Gabriel's sins are mention
I have notice
that are need
I have mention
all the things has happen
he can be satisfy
he has express
he has been accuse
that were close
that is concern
they have love
they are tire
he have confuse
he had touch
it has travel
they want things govern
many are deny
they are influence

Uninflected Past Tense: 8 occurrences in 7 papers

I mention Kent State
I omit Jackson State
John's aunt regret coming to North
If they pull out
the White man establish
they way he wish things would be

181

David L. Shores

she listen to what people say
his manner arouse suspicion
<u>Others</u>: <u>19</u> occurrences in <u>13</u> papers
the firs
for the firs time
his mine
a big different
had though
feeling of self-confident
mathematic
physic
the Black man haven
had alway
<u>Overinflection</u>: <u>49</u> occurrences in <u>27</u> papers
to killed
will never really solved
will then decided
theses problems
happends
alcoholic drinks tends
they damages
the poets tells
we knows
the birds sings
a meetings
as time pasted
Jobs do not tends
the people needs
she begins
man doesn't understands
the Black mens
as he dids
this desire does goes
We all wants
I thinks
four or five people does
a mice
a Black women
an ugly White women
<u>The Uninflected Be</u>: <u>6</u> occurrences in <u>2</u> papers
Alcoholic drinks be strong
You be gambling
they be doing something
it be their
<u>Absence of Copula</u>: <u>5</u> occurrences in <u>4</u> papers
if it night
the Black women not going to let
he a Black bitch
what he mean he was in
<u>Double Negation</u>: <u>3</u> occurrences in <u>3</u> papers
Others don't believe in nothing
a Negro lady wasn't no more
God didn't make no two people alike

182

David L. Shores

Question Inversion: 2 occurrences in 2 papers
  I wonder will she use them now
Existential It: 2 occurrences in 2 papers
  It is a differents
  It isn't no way
Double Subject: 1 occurrence in 1 paper
  the poem it convey
Of the total 98 papers examined, 50, or 51 percent, did not contain any
of the above features. Forty-eight, or 49 percent, as the listing shows,
did contain one or more nonstandard features. Let me make clear that I
do not introduce this data to prove the existence of a dialect that we
may want to call "Black English." I introduce it here to show that many
Black college students have many nonstandard linguistic features in their
writing, features that cannot be dismissed merely as informal functional
varieties of English as many teachers have a tendency to do. Though not
the result of a random sample, what is shown here, I think, would be
indicative of a larger sample gathered by strict statistical procedures.

IV

And finally, this brings us to the attitudes of Black college educators
toward the existence of Black English and the "dialectal" features in
the language of their students. Perhaps it goes without saying that all
these matters are surrounded by tension and suspicion. And there are
other matters, of course, the always tenacious and prevailing attitudes
of racism, white supremacy, separatism, and breathless White liberalism,
all of which, as we know, are intricately interwoven into the fabric of
our society--and at times tend to come to the surface to cause us to lose
sight of what we are about. This hurts, but it may be unavoidable--
because language matters are people matters, because languages of people
are linked to identities of people, and because language is not only a
means of communication but also an expressive system of culture, making
it both a personal and public matter, touching a person and his community
in a tender way. But despite these sensitive attitudinal complications,
the relevant linguistic and pedagogical matters must be confronted for
the sake of the students involved and because serious scholars and others,
both Black and White, have discovered that we need to know how the Black
community feels about these matters. What is summarized below should
not be taken as unified community opinion. It is what I see as the general
feeling of a good number of Black educators.

First, the attitude of Black educators toward the existence of Black
English. As a rule, they refuse to accept Black English as a separate
dialect independent of American White English. They do not deny that there
is a kind of speech that can be closely associated with Blacks, for many
of them say that they, a great majority of the time, can recognize Blacks
and Whites by speech alone, but they do not feel that it is so radically
different that it needs to be crystallized and set off as a distinct
dialect with the rubric of "Black English" or some other ethnic label.
They, moreover, find it insulting, if not errant nonsense, to characterize the rich variety of language style in the Black community as a
separate kind of speech strictly on the basis of forty stigmatizing
forms, or for that matter, several phonological and grammatical variables.
They prefer, for the most part, to think of the so-called "distinctive"
features as bad and careless grammar, or usage problems, and to set
these up as "dialectal features," they say, is foolish tolerance,

regardless of how systematic and well-ordered they are. What bothers them even more is that people in the Black English business give the impression that these features are in the speech of all Blacks and that all Blacks, regardless of age, region, and social class, speak alike. Furthermore, they view with suspicion, some with resentment, as they should, the whole enterprising nature (and I use the word advisedly, for Blacks have recognized that Black English is a booming business) of the investigation of Black speech. They are especially put off by the linguists who say that it was they who have studied, described, and have struggled to get Black English accepted as a legitimate language. Their response to this seems to be "Mmmm, yes, we know; but for what reason and to what end?" They say that they don't need to be told about the uniqueness and advantages of Black expression. In short, they don't buy "Black English," and as they got tired of being Moynihaned, they are now tired of being Black Englished.

Next, the attitude of Black educators toward the presence of "dialectal" features in the speaking and writing of their students. Black educators generally view these features as usage problems and bad English, not dialectal, and the result of carelessness and poor proofreading. My reading of teachers' evaluations of student papers reveals that they, as a rule, consider the features no different from the typical spelling and usage problems. They frequently, in marginal and terminal notes, admonished their students to proofread their papers more closely. On one occasion, two departmental chairmen told me that the English departments at their campuses had been indicted by their presidents because they were not teaching the students "good English," which meant that they were not eradicating these "bad" features of speech. On another occasion, an instructor remarked that these dialectal features in students' speaking and writing should be ignored because they were so expressive and deeply-ingrained patterns. Her remark was greeted by groans, and one departmental chairman replied: "I'm glad you don't work for me," a retort that drew applause. These features then, according to Black educators, are features to be abolished, not ignored or tolerated, regardless of how pervasive and deeply internalized linguists say they are.

Closely related to the attitude toward the presence of these language features is the attitude toward the target language of instruction and the suggested pedagogical approaches, which can be, for practical purposes, reduced to three: eradication, tolerance of dialectal variation, and bi-dialectalism. The attitude of Black educators toward eradication, as has already been indicated, is generally one of approval. The second, as you would expect, is somewhat offensive to them, and they consider it paternalism, even as camouflage for bitter racism. They will of course listen to the linguistic argument that all dialects are "good" and structured systems. They acknowledge, moreover, that linguists discern qualities in nonstandard speech, or deviant dialects, that elude most people. But they like to stress that all varieties are not _equal_ in reaching out. They find that the public does not place the same value judgments upon speech that linguists do and that the public as a whole is much harsher. They are quick to say to those who advocate the tolerance of linguistic differences that academic, social, and financial rewards tend to elude those who cannot use English as practiced by most of the decision makers of public affairs. Men who reach the top, they say, of our banks, industries, armies and navies, professions, pulpits, and schools and colleges are men who, as a general rule, have a control

of Standard English. The last, bi-dialectalism, the rage of some
linguists a few years ago, though not condemned, is viewed also with suspicion. The teaching of Standard English, which bi-dialectalism advocates,
they accept, for it is, as mentioned above, a useful social economic
tool without which, they believe, the opportunities of many of their
students would be greatly limited, even though some say that the King's
English would not necessarily make Blacks more socially acceptable and
employable. The other prong of bi-dialectalism, respect for and preservation of the home dialect, they do not consider a problem. They are
not convinced that a person who learns Standard English will be in any
danger of being turned out of his community. A person who learns Standard
English, they believe, will never have to shift completely back to his
home or native dialect even though he preserves his home dialect; he will
just have to avoid linguistic airs and acting uppity. They consider the
best policy as that of trying to eliminate nonstandard features from the
speaking and writing of their students, insofar as that is possible. Even
though they doubt that the classroom will have little influence on making
standard speakers and writers out of nonstandard ones. They believe that
if their students can be convinced that Standard English will make a
difference in their lives, they will learn it, with or without linguists
and teachers. This of course shows that they acknowledge that motivation and identity have a lot to do with the acquisition of Standard English.

V

In this paper, I have tried to describe some linguistic and attitudinal
aspects about the existence of Black English. I know of no study that
can be taken as a permanent solution to the linguistic problem of the
speech of Blacks as a distinct dialect independent of the speech of Whites.
Still a confusion of many voices exists. The relevant questions seem to
be: Are there distinctive linguistic characteristics of Black speech that
set it off as a separate independent dialect? Can we speak of two
different dialects if we find the same linguistic features in both? Does
the presence of distinctive features of the speech of Blacks in the speech
of Whites invalidate the idea of Black English as a separate dialect?
We all know that no language is ever completely uniform. Slight
observations reveal that there is variation in phonology, lexicon,
morphology, syntax, and in paralinguistic phenomena, which are elusive
to define. We all know, furthermore, as we go about our workaday affairs,
we encounter varieties of speech that we feel are noticeably different
from any of the varieties of what we view as Standard English even though
we are hard put to it to define Standard English. It may be that we
cannot stop arguing about the existence of Black English as a separate
dialect until we can come up with a technical, operational formulation
of dialect. Otherwise, on the basis of a statistical preponderance of
recurrent features, it seems to me that it makes just as much sense to
talk about Black dialects as it does Midland or Tidewater Virginia
dialects.

Even at the risk of ending on a negative note, I must say that I know
of no solution to the attitudinal problem either. Very often these
attitudes of Blacks, which are manifested also in their general rejection
of dialect readers and the praise of Black speech by Black separatists
and some linguists, are frequently described as caused by feelings of
inferiority and Black self-hate. I find this hard to accept. Such a
sharp dismissal of the feelings of people reveals that facts are not
always accompanied by understanding and that wisdom does not always flow

David L. Shores

from the minds of the mighty. I am not saying that the Black attitudes
are completely defensible. Whether defensible or not, in a sense, it
doesn't make any difference. The fact of the matter is that they are
clearly understandable. And linguists must come to understand that.
Raven McDavid once remarked that dialectology is where linguistics meets
people. Some linguists obviously have not thought of it quite that way.

NOTES

*Read at the SAMLA-ADS Meeting, Jacksonville, Florida, November 1972.
This version has been changed to include examples.

[1]Ralph W. Fasold and Walter A. Wolfram, "Some Linguistic Features of
Negro Dialect," in Teaching Standard English in the Inner City, ed. by
Ralph W. Fasold and Roger W. Shuy (Washington, D.C.: Center for Applied
Linguistics, 1970), pp. 41-86. Also in Contemporary English: Change
and Variation, ed. by David L. Shores (Philadelphia: J. B. Lippincott,
1972), pp. 53-85.

[2]These two quotes were taken from clipped news items of two different
magazines a colleague passed on to me. As yet, I haven't been able
to find the relevant bibliographical data.

[3]Juanita Williamson, "A Phonological and Morphological Study of the
Speech of the Negro of Memphis, Tennessee," Dissertation University of
Michigan 1961, p. 1. (Published in PADS, Number 50, November 1968)

[4]Juanita Williamson, "A Look at Black English," Crisis, 78 (August
1971), 173.

[5]William Labov, "Some Sources of Reading Problems for Negro Speakers
of Nonstandard English," in New Directions in Elementary English, ed.
Alexander Frazier (Champaign, Illinois: NCTE, 1967), p. 14.

[6]Fasold and Wolfram, p. 41.

[7]Ibid.

[8]Ibid.

[9]Orlando Taylor, "Response to Social Dialects and the Field of Speech,"
Sociolinguistics: A Cross-disciplinary Perspective, ed. Roger Shuy
(Washington, D.C.: Center for Applied Linguistics, 1971), p. 14.

[10]Ibid., p. 15.

[11]Ibid.

[12]Orlando Taylor, "Some Sociolinguistic Concepts of Black Language,"
Today's Speech, 19 (Spring, 1971), 22.

David L. Shores

¹³Ibid.

¹⁴Ibid.

¹⁵Paper read at Institute for College English Instructors. Norfolk State College, Norfolk, Virginia, May 12, 1972.

¹⁶Juanita Williamson, "Selected Features of Speech: Black and White," CLA Journal, 13 (June, 1970), 420-23. Also, see footnote 5.

¹⁷Roger W. Shuy, "Subjective Judgments in Sociolinguistic Analysis," in Monograph Series on Languages and Linguistics, No. 22, ed. James E. Alatis (Washington, D.C.: Georgetown University Press, 1970), pp. 175-85.

THE SOCIAL STRATIFICATION OF /aɪ/
AMONG WHITE SPEAKERS IN TUSCALOOSA, ALABAMA*

L. Ben Crane

The purpose of this study is to explore the relationship of the pronunciation of /aɪ/ to social class and age in the speech of whites in
Tuscaloosa, Alabama. The speech of blacks is not included because a
separate study is required to do justice to black English. Also, much
work already has been done with black speech, while few (if any) attempts
have been made to show social stratification of speech sounds other than
/r/ among white speakers in the South.

The social rank of an individual is defined for this study as the sum
of his ratings on linear scales for education, income and occupation.
Therefore, a social class is a group of individuals sharing similar social
ranks. The social classes (strata) have a built-in ordering in that each
stratum represents a range of values on a linear scale. This ordering of
strata, from the lowest valued stratum to the highest, is basic to the
present study, and stratification will be said to occur only if the
linguistic values of /aɪ/ exhibit the same direction of ordering as the
social classes or age groups within social classes.

Particular pronunciations of /aɪ/ are associated with particular social
classes and age groups in social classes; however, the appearance of a
particular pronunciation alone in the speech of an individual is not
sufficient evidence to determine his social class. Conversely, the fact
that an individual is a member of a given social class does not necessarily
mean that he will have a particular pronunciation of /aɪ/ in his speech;
yet, there is the likelihood of the appearance of a particular pronunciation in the speech of a member of a given social class.

Broadcast standard pronunciation is used in this study to refer to the
pronunciation of /aɪ/ as it is generally spoken by national radio and
television announcers. This is a pronunciation closely related to what
linguists in this country have called "general American" and which is as
free as possible of all regional variations. This pronunciation is
adopted in this paper as the standard against which the different
pronunciations used by the various social classes and age groups in
Tuscaloosa can be measured.

Another distinction of terms that needs to be made is the difference
between apparent time and real time. A consideration of age stratification
in apparent time deals with distinct age groups at a fixed point in time,
while a consideration of age stratification in real time consists of
dealing with a fixed group of informants at several distinct points in
time. All of the figures and tables regarding age stratification in the
present study deal with apparent time.

A total of fifty-six informants were originally interviewed and tape-
recorded for this study. Since Tuscaloosa's population is relatively

stable and largely native born, the decision was made to interview only
natives of Tuscaloosa and its surrounding metropolitan area. In most
cases the informants were at least third generation Tuscaloosa residents.
In certain areas of the country, no doubt, this would ignore a large
segment of the current population, but this "natives only" requirement
for Tuscaloosa seems to insure a more accurate picture of the speech
than any attempt to include non-native speakers.

Since the size of the sample necessarily had to be restricted, a
purposive sampling procedure was employed to insure a complete cross-
section of age and social status of white informants from Tuscaloosa.
Informants were selected to represent various religious backgrounds,
neighborhoods within the city, and occupations.

At the outset, it was decided to study /aɪ/ in Tuscaloosa only in
informal speech. Therefore, the linguistic interviews were devised to
elicit as natural responses as possible. No particular responses were
being sought, and informants were encouraged to talk freely on any subjects they chose. At no point in the interview was any material offered
for the interviewee to read. Since it was believed that such an intru-
sion into the natural, conversation-like quality of the interview would
have caused certain restraints and would have reminded the person being
interviewed of the artificiality of the situation, it was decided to
sacrifice the opportunity of studying the comparison of language in a
formal versus informal basis for the sake of natural, conversational
language.

The interviews were conducted between July 1971, and September 1972.
Where possible, interviews were conducted with representatives of three
generations within a family.

Originally, informants were classified in this study into three
categories: upper class, middle class, and lower class. Since the
middle class includes informants from a wide range of income, occupation, and educational backgrounds, the middle class is later redivided
into upper middle class and working class. This subdivision makes possibl
finer distinctions in the analysis of /aɪ/.

A division of the informants according to age is an important means of
studying sound change in progress, as well as, perhaps, providing a means
of studying trends of sound change within a social group or among social
groups. Rather than superimposing figures for age divisions given in
previous sociolinguistic studies, the age divisions were made in what
seemed a most natural pattern for this study. The ages of all the
informants in this study were listed in descending order from 86, the
age of the oldest informant, to 8, the age of the youngest informant.
A quick look at this age sampling showed a natural grouping into three
age categories. Because of the natural groupings into three clusters,
the decision was made to set the upper boundary of the youngest age group
at 22. The second age group is the largest and includes people from
23 to 61 years of age. The lower limit for the third age group was
set at 62.

The variable /aɪ/, heard in the pronunciation of <u>fine</u>, <u>light</u>, <u>rise</u>,
and <u>wide</u>, has a number of variants in Tuscaloosa. The frequent use of
several of these variants and at least three measurably different sounds
seems to demand a ternary system for studying /aɪ/. What is being
measured with this variable is the amount of differentiation between
the first and second element of the diphthong. This is referred to by
Labov in <u>The Social Stratification of New York City</u> as "nucleus-glide

differentiation." Since in Tuscaloosa, the first element of the
diphthong /aɪ/ is nearly always [a] or [a᷂], one really need account
within the ternary system only for the variation of the second element.
In this study of /aɪ/, an X indicates a pronunciation of /aɪ/ whose
second element approximates /I/. A Q indicates a sound whose second
element may extend only as high and as fronted as [ɛˆ]. A √ indicates
a sound consisting of a single element; again, usually [a] or [a᷂].

Certain environments affect the pronunciation of /aɪ/. Therefore,
the variable /aɪ/ is divided into three environments:
a. word-finally and preceding voiced sounds
b. preceding voiceless fricatives
c. preceding voiceless stops
The sample of words containing /aɪ/ before voiceless fricatives was
too small to be studied independently and as a result had to be excluded
from this study; however, the limited number of cases that were observed
seem to pattern more like "word-finally and preceding voiced sounds"
than like those cases preceding stops.

In the discussion of the variant pronunciations for /aɪ/, two types
of stratification will be distinguished: gradient and sharp stratification. These terms are based on those of Wolfram[1] and Labov[2] and are
redefined for the purposes of this study. Gradient stratification is said
to occur when the largest difference between the percentages of occurrences of variant pronunciations for any two consecutive groups is less
than or equal to twice the smallest difference between the values for
any two consecutive groups. Sharp stratification is said to occur when
the largest difference between the percentages of occurrences of
variant pronunciations for any two consecutive groups is greater than
twice the smallest difference between the values for any two consecutive groups. However, if the largest difference between percentages of
occurrences of variant pronunciations for any two consecutive groups is
less than 10 per cent, the stratification is considered gradient.

The percentages of the variant pronunciations of /aɪ/ by class in all
environments are shown in Figure 1. Sharp stratification is observed in
the X column for all age groups, with the 62+UC and 23+UC producing
broadcast standard /aɪ/ most frequently. The lower class produces
virtually no broadcast standard /aɪ/, with its norm between little off-
glide and no off-glide. The middle class has a norm somewhat like that
of the lower class while the upper class, in particular the 62+ and 23+
groups, displays no norm.

Figure 2 gives the percentages for the variant pronunciations by age
for /aɪ/ in all environments. While no apparent overall pattern appears,
gradient stratification is observed within the middle class. This
stratification by age within the middle class must be regarded cautiously
in light of the percentages recorded for the upper and lower classes.

In order to obtain a clearer picture of the stratification of /aɪ/ by
class, Figure 1 now is divided into Figure 3 (/aɪ/ word-finally and
preceding voiced consonants) and Figure 4 (/aɪ/ preceding voiceless
stops). One notes in Figure 3 that word-finally and preceding voiced
consonants, stratification of /aɪ/ by class is maintained in the X
column. Again, the greatest amount of nucleus-glide differentiation
occurs most frequently among the 62+UC and 23+UC groups. The latter
group's broadcast standard pronunciation in 42 per cent of the occurrences represents the greatest amount of broadcast standard pronunciation
of /aɪ/ for all groups in all environments. The lower class shows not

L. Ben Crane

FIGURE 1

% of /aɪ/ by class in all environments

S.E.C.*	X	Q	✔
62+UC	32	49	19
62+MC	7	44	49
62+LC	0	56	44
23+UC	33	37	30
23+MC	10	48	42
23+LC	2	39	59
22-UC	18	64	18
22-MC	13	51	36
22-LC	0	47	53

*Socio-Economic Class

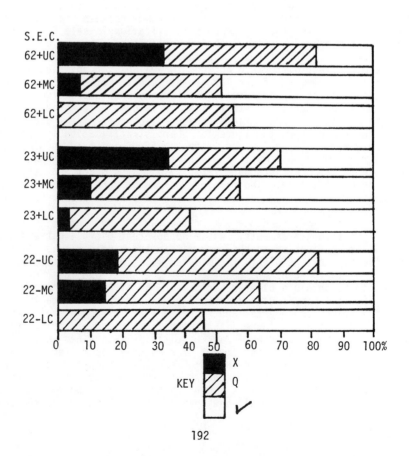

L. Ben Crane

FIGURE 2

% of /aɪ/ by age in all environments

S.E.C.*	X	Q	✓
62+UC	32	49	19
23+UC	33	37	30
22-UC	18	64	18
62+MC	7	44	49
23+MC	10	48	42
22-MC	13	51	36
62+LC	0	56	44
23+LC	2	39	59
22-LC	0	47	53

*Socio-Economic Class

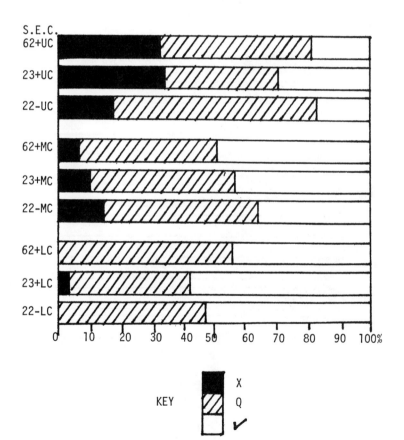

L. Ben Crane

FIGURE 3

% of /aɪ/ by class preceding voiced consonants
and word finally

S.E.C.*	X	Q	✔
62+UC	32	43	25
62+MC	5	44	51
62+LC	0	62	38
23+UC	42	26	32
23+MC	3	46	51
23+LC	0	41	59
22-UC	8	64	28
22-MC	4	48	48
22-LC	0	52	48

*Socio-Economic Class

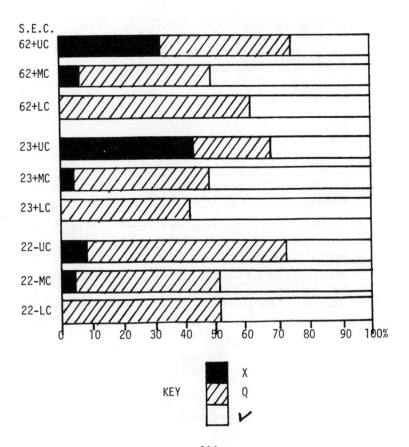

194

one occurrence of broadcast standard pronunciation of /aɪ/ word-finally
or preceding voiced consonants.

The percentages of broadcast standard /aɪ/ production before voiceless
stops, as shown in Figure 4, are larger than the corresponding percentages in Figure 3, except for the 23+UC group. Whereas class stratification appears in the X column for the 62+ and 22- age groups, the same
is not true for the middle age group, where stratification is blocked
by the unusually low X percentage for the 23+UC. The ✓ column is of
considerable importance in Figure 4, revealing no monophthongs present
before voiceless stops in the UC speech and exhibiting gradient stratification by class within all age groups.

Through a comparison of Figures 3 and 4, it can be seen that in
Tuscaloosa the percentages of broadcast standard production of /aɪ/ are
greater before voiceless stops than word-finally and preceding voiced
consonants. The environmental effect on /aɪ/ in Tuscaloosa, then, seems
to be the opposite of that shown by Labov for New York City. In
Tuscaloosa, the nucleus-glide differentiation is greater before voiceless
stops, while in New York City, nucleus-glide differentiation is greater
word-finally and preceding voiced sounds. However, it must be kept in
mind that in New York City the environmental effect is primarily on the
first element of the diphthong, while in Tuscaloosa, it is on the
second.

Figures 5 and 6 give the environmental breakdown of /aɪ/ by age. The
percentages of variant pronunciations of /aɪ/ word-finally and before
voiced consonants appear to be almost totally random as seen in Figure 5.
However, Figure 6, which gives the percentages of variant pronunciations
of /aɪ/ before voiceless stops, presents some significant findings.
A tremendous difference between the X column percentages in Figures 5
and 6 is revealed for the 22-UC and the 22-MC groups. These two groups
have broadcast standard /aɪ/ before voiceless stops in approximately one-
third of the occurrences. The figures for the 22- group are essentially
like those for the 62+ group. The Q representation (partial-glide) is
seen to be the norm for all groups except the 62+MC, and even there, the
largest figure (44 percent) is in the Q column. Therefore, the ternary
system is shown to be of value in the analysis of /aɪ/.

To investigate possible differences that might be shown were the
large middle class divided into working class and upper middle class,
a reanalysis of the data was made. Although charts and graphs were made
to correspond to each of the environments of /aɪ/ discussed earlier, only
one, Figure 7, is included in this paper because it is representative
of the sort of results yielded by all the reanalyzed data. Figure 7
is an analysis of the percentages of /aɪ/ preceding voiced consonants
and word-finally for four social classes. Class stratification is
exhibited in the X column for the middle age group only. It is interesting
that Figure 3, which shows percentages of /aɪ/ preceding voiced consonants
and word finally for three social classes, exhibits a class stratification
for all age groups. The working class is a key factor in this breakdown of stratification in the analysis of variant pronunciations of /aɪ/
for four social classes. In the 22- group, the working class has sur-
passed the upper class in broadcast standard /aɪ/ production. However,
the small figures for the upper class may be of more significance than
the "large" figures for the working class speakers.

This study of /aɪ/ among white speakers in Tuscaloosa, Alabama, in
no way purports to be all-inclusive, and yet, the most important features

L. Ben Crane

FIGURE 4

% of /aɪ/ by class preceding voiceless stops

S.E.C.*	X	0	✔
62+UC	37	63	0
62+MC	33	44	23
62+LC	0	59	41
23+UC	14	86	0
23+MC	27	53	20
23+LC	8	60	32
22-UC	37	63	0
22-MC	32	62	6
22-LC	0	92	8

*Socio-Economic Class

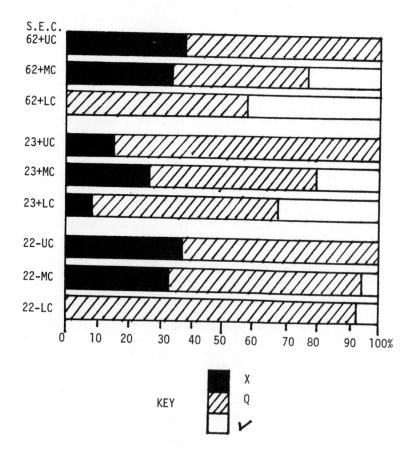

196

L. Ben Crane

FIGURE 5

% of /aɪ/ by age preceding voice consonants
and word finally

S.E.C.*	X	Q	✓
62+UC	32	43	25
23+UC	42	26	32
22-UC	8	64	28
62+MC	5	44	51
23+MC	3	46	51
22-MC	4	48	48
62+LC	0	62	38
23+LC	0	41	59
22-LC	0	52	48

*Socio-Economic Class

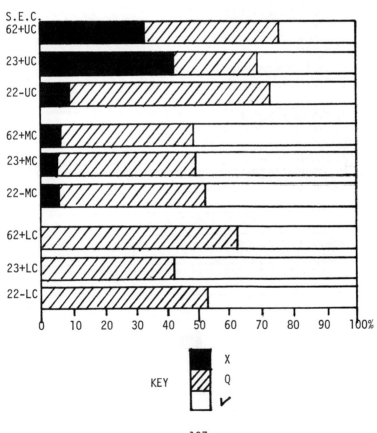

L. Ben Crane

FIGURE 6

% of /aɪ/ by age preceding voiceless stops

S.E.C.*	X	Q	✓
62+UC	37	63	0
23+UC	14	86	0
22-UC	37	63	0
62+MC	33	44	23
23+MC	27	53	20
22-MC	32	62	6
62+LC	0	59	41
23+LC	8	60	32
22-LC	0	92	8

*Socio-Economic Class

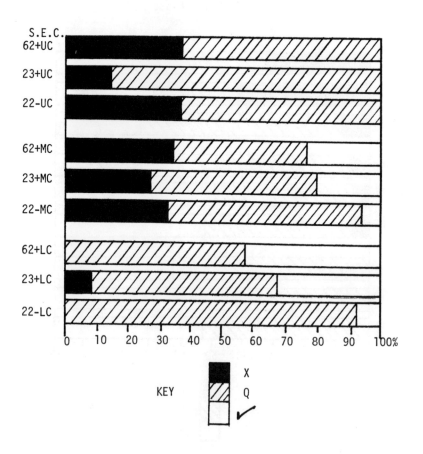

L. Ben Crane

FIGURE 7

% of /aɪ/ voiced consonants and word finally by class

S.E.C.*	X	Q	✓
62+UC	32	43	25
62+UMC	14	77	9
62+WC	0	50	50
62+LC	0	62	38
23+UC	42	26	32
23+UMC	4	45	51
23+WC	3	9	88
23+LC	0	41	59
22-UC	8	64	28
22-UMC	0	41	59
22-WC	12	68	20
22-LC	0	52	48

*Socio-Economic Class

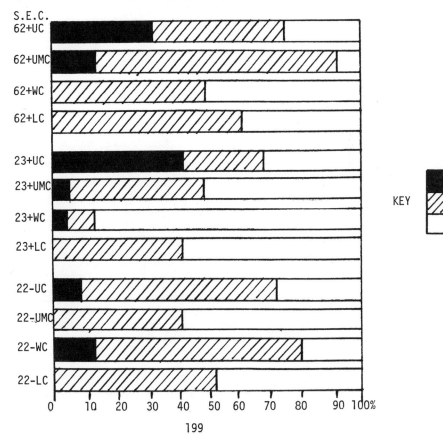

199

of /aɪ/ production have been covered. No attempt has been made to draw sociological conclusions; however, the wide gap exhibited by the older speakers in the upper and lower classes seems to have narrowed considerably between the upper and lower classes in the youngest age group. Perhaps before too many years, linguists may record the effects on language of the "levelling of society," which sociologists say is taking place right now.

NOTES

*Read at the SAMLA-ADS Meeting, Washington, D.C., November 1974.

[1]Walter Wolfram, A Sociolinguistic Description of Detroit Negro Speech (Washington, D.C.: Center for Applied Linguistics, 1969), p. 120.

[2]William L. Labov, The Social Stratification of English in New York City (Washington, D.C.: Center for Applied Linguistics, 1966), p. 235.

RESEARCH NEEDS IN TENNESSEE ENGLISH*

Bethany K. Dumas

Early in 1974, prior to my joining the faculty at The University of
Tennessee in Knoxville, I read a paper before interested persons from
the Department of English and the College of Education at The University
of Tennessee entitled "Some Observations on the Study of Tennessee
Speech." In that paper I suggested the need for continuing the study
of the spoken language of native Tennesseans, summarized briefly the
state of dialect studies in Tennessee, and outlined a proposal for a
state-wide dialect survey of Tennessee speech. At that time I also
reviewed some of the many reasons for continuing the study of Tennessee
speech. The speech of native Tennesseans is obviously of intrinsic
interest to all who live within the state. Evidence of that interest is
overwhelming and sometimes comes from unexpected quarters. On a recent
flight from Knoxville to Nashville, I conversed with a truckdriver for
a national oil company. When he found out that I was a dialectologist,
his first response was to ask if that was something like being an English
teacher. I hedged sufficiently to keep him from lapsing into the fearful
silence which often follows the discovery that an English teacher has
crept in among the honest citizenry, after which he told me a story from
"up in East Tennessee," the punch line of which involved a regional
pronunciation of the word spelled o-n-i-o-n-s. In the dialect of the
protagonist of the story, the word came out as /Iŋɘnz/. After my
travelling companion had told the story, he wanted to know if I had
heard the pronunciation elsewhere. I had not, but have since heard a
colleague from West Tennessee, near Memphis, say that his father used
to pronounce the word that way occasionally specifically in order to
annoy his mother. Clearly, whatever its boundaries, that pronunciation
is and probably was stigmatized. From such anecdotal information comes
useful insight into the kinds of questions which will be productive in
studying the language patterns of the area.
Additional reasons for studying Tennessee speech have been given by
dialectologists as well as by people in other disciplines. Raven I.
McDavid, Jr., articulated the rationale for the first detailed survey,
the Linguistic Atlas of the Gulf States (LAGS), when he suggested, in
a paper entitled "What Happens in Tennessee?", that a detailed survey
would be necessary to discover what happens to the patterns of distribution of linguistic features that have already been regionally identified
along the Atlantic Seaboard, what the folk vocabulary of Tennessee is
like, to what extent collapsing of historical phonemic differences has
taken place, and what the grammatical situation is.[1] More generally,
J. Kenneth Moreland, a cultural anthropologist with a deep interest in
the South, has suggested that time is crucial for the study of dialects

in the South. Several years ago he urged that needed research be started
quickly:

The South might be characterized as a formerly distinctive
region that is fast losing its distinctiveness. It has been
different from other American regions in its caste-like
system of race relations, its agriculturally-based economy
and its relatively slow industrialization, its fundamentalist
religion, and its feelings of separateness from the rest of
the nation. All of these characteristics are probably being
altered as cultural traits and patterns throughout America
become similar.[2]

Since that time, I have learned that collecting in Tennessee for the LA
project is virtually complete. This is important for other studies, beca
it means that traditional Atlas data has now been gathered for the study
the speech patterns of adult natives of Tennessee. What now seems most
needed in Tennessee is the gathering of additional kinds of information
for the study of the language patterns of adult natives of Tennessee and
gathering of sociodialectal data which will yield sound and relevant peda
gogical information. This can best be done by including in a survey an
examination of the language of children, partly for immediate pedagogical
usefulness, partly so that researchers can gain insight into the processe
of obscolescence and replacement in the syntactic and phonological system
(and possibly also the lexicon) of three or four generations of native
speakers of Tennessee English. Such an investigation must be based upon
careful examination of existing data and should take into account the
expectation that all records for the LAGS project will be ready for editi
by July 1, 1977.[3]

Additionally, such a survey ought to result in the collection of the
kinds of data which will enable us to study the relationship between spee
and writing in the dialects of native Tennesseans. We know--and those of
us who teach freshman English anywhere are usually reminded of the fact
daily--that written skills are not dependent on oral ones. In terms of
contemporary grammatical theory orthographic rules do not apply to the
output of phonological rules. No matter how we understand the semantic
or conceptual structures underlying language, we know that transformational rules are applied to them to rearrange, delete, or add constituent
and to supply various non-lexical morphemes. Then the lexicon provides
morphemes with true lexical meaning. The resulting syntactic surface
structure contains in linear form all the morphemes of a sentence and
specifies their relationship to each other. Such grammatical morphemes
as PAST, PERFECT, PRESENT, PLURAL, etc., do not have phonological representations when they are generated by transformational rules. The rules
for replacing abstract formatives such as PLURAL with a specified
phonological shape vary among English dialects. It is crucial that both
phonological rules and orthographic rules operate on the same syntactic
surface structures or map underlying phonological representations into
pronunciation and spelled forms. Orthographic rules do not operate on
the output of the phonological rules. (For a more detailed examination
of these phenomena and their relevance for English teachers, see Gary N.
Underwood, "Bidialectal Freshman Handbooks--The Next Flimflam." Paper
read at the Conference on College Composition and Communication, Anaheim,
California, April 5, 1974.) For these reasons I propose to collect
samples of written English from at least some of the informants interviewed. This is why I now find it appropriate to speak of Tennessee
English or Tennessee language, rather than Tennessee speech.

The first stage of the investigation is bibliographical and has been going on since September 1974, for students enrolled in English 4430 at The University of Tennessee during the Fall quarter of 1974 participated in a group project in which they compiled a bibliography of works about Tennessee English. Beginning with James B. McMillan's indispensable Annotated Bibliography of Southern American English (Coral Gables, Florida: University of Miami Press, 1971), these students surveyed the literature about Tennessee dialects. One of the students, Jonathan Lighter, contributed to the project a list of all the works in his slang collection which concern Tennessee language use.[4] As the bibliographical stage of the investigation continues, I am preparing annotations of all existing works.

There are two large collections of data which will also be useful in planning the survey, that of the LAGS project, of course, directed by Lee Pedersen of Emory University (for additional information, see Pedersen, "The Linguistic Atlas of the Gulf States: An Interim Report," American Speech, 44 (1973), 279-86 and Pedersen, et al., A Manual for Dialect Research in the Southern States (Atlanta: Georgia State University, 1972) and that of the Dictionary of American Regional English (DARE), directed by Frederic G. Cassidy of the University of Wisconsin at Madison. Records from both these projects will be examined in the planning stages of the projected survey. As a matter of fact, Professor Cassidy has already provided copies of the tapes that were collected for the project in Tennessee, a total of 49 from the 22 communities studied in the state. Additionally, there are available the published results of the postal survey of the Interior South, undertaken by Gordon R. Wood of Southern Illinois University. Finally, there are the records collected by the late Harold Orton and his students when he was at the University of Tennessee. All these are being considered for immediate and long-range usefulness.

Once the basic bibliography is compiled and other materials have been examined, work will begin on the construction and testing of a questionnaire. Since all records have been collected in Tennessee for the LAGS project, it will not be necessary to collect those items which have been target items in the Linguistic Atlas projects. Instead, it will be possible to concentrate on phonological, orthographic, and syntactic systems of informants. It will probably not be productive to collect vocabulary items at this point--though of course it will not be desirable to ignore the possbiility of eventually collecting specialized lexical information that is not elicited by the LAGS questionnaire.

At this time I think that the best way to achieve the desired ends of this projected study is to make use of research methods similar to those developed for the Arkansas Language Survey (ALS), begun by Gary N. Underwood at the University of Arkansas in Fayetteville in 1970. My work as Associate Director and Principal Investigator of the ALS, together with my earlier work in Newton County, Arkansas,[5] enables me, I feel, to make reasonable projections about the usefulness of its research design in Tennessee. The research design for the survey there was drawn up after existing data had been examined--the recordings of Arkansawyers interviewed for the DARE project, pilot interviews conducted in conjunction with dialectology courses taught at the University of Arkansas, and published observations on Arkansas dialects--and in accord with the following principles:
1. Neither vocabulary items nor incidental pronunciations are

integral features of a dialect and, therefore, are not dialect differen-
tiators.

2. Large-scale dialect surveys ought to incorporate wherever possible
the innovations and improvements in methodology and theory provided by
investigators of urban dialects, such as Labov[6] and Shuy, Wolfram, and
Riley[7].

3. The arguments set forth by critics of American linguistic geography
(Pickford, Bailey, and Dillard, and Underwood)[8] should be given serious
consideration as future surveys are planned.

Since one of the goals was to draw a sample that would provide a cross-
section of native-born Arkansawyers, one that would provide both social
and geographic distribution of participants, a random sample of the
entire state population was initially considered: this plan was abandoned when it was realized that it was not feasible for a variety of
reasons. Instead, the state was initially divided into geographic-
cultural regions. Then for each region certain population characteristics
were determined, using the 1970 census data. These included: (1) per
capita income, (2) percentage of urban population, (3) percentage of
non-white population, and (4) the average number of inhabitants per
county. For each region a sample county was selected by choosing the
county in each region having population characteristics that most closely
matched those of the region as a whole. Then a sampling procedure that
was a modification of the one used in the Detroit Dialect Study (Shuy,
Wolfram, and Riley) was developed. The sample was drawn initially from
school rosters, and twelve persons were interviewed in each county, a
school-child, a parent, and an older relative from each of four families.

Another problem was how to determine the social stratification of the
sample. Several methods were considered; finally, it was decided to
retain the subjective classification of speakers with the following
designations being used:

1. Lower Class: Grade school education or less; laborers, share-
croppers, tenant farmers, unemployed, welfare recipients, etc., struggling
existence.

2. Working Class: Perhaps some high school; blue collar workers,
small farmers, more comfortable living conditions.

3. Lower Middle Class: High school graduates; small businesses,
craftsmen, white collar workers, semi-professionals, medium-sized farmers;
pillars of the community, children in college, luxuries.

4. Upper Middle Class: College graduates; professionals, managers or
owners of medium-sized businesses; large farmers or ranchers; people with
high incomes and considerable social status in their communities.

5. Upper Class: Graduates of prestigious universities; high-level
officers, managers, or owners of large businesses; the social elite.[9]

For the sake of brevity, I shall not try to describe in detail the
format and content of the interview. The goal was to design an efficient,
productive questionnaire to be completed in about two hours. The resulting
questionnaire has as its model transformational grammar and is divided into
four large sections, each designed to elicit responses in a different
style:

I. Conversation	25 minutes
II. Elicited Responses	40 minutes
III. Reading	15 minutes
IV. Subjective Responses	40 minutes

204

Bethany K. Dumas

It is anticipated that a similar research design will be developed for use in Tennessee, with the proviso that it may be most efficient to treat the three major geographic-cultural regions in the state--East Tennessee, Middle Tennessee, and West Tennessee--more as discrete areas than as parts of a larger unit. Professor McDavid has summarized the reasons why this is true:

> Tennessee is a state of peculiar shape and size. It is barely
> 112 miles across at the widest point; yet by highway it is some
> 500 miles from east to west, from Mountain City to Memphis. It
> is cut into three traditional domains--East, Middle, and West
> Tennessee--by the Cumberland Plateau and the red hills between
> the Tennessee and the Mississippi. The major rivers, the
> Tennessee and the Cumberland, rising in the Appalachians, swing
> southwest and then northwest, to enter the Ohio not far upstream
> from the confluence of the Ohio and the Mississippi. Even in the
> heyday of rail travel, it was very difficult to go by train from
> east to west within the state; the only such route from Knox-
> ville to Nashville was the late Tennessee Central -sometimes
> affectionately called the "Tennessee Creeper"--with a slow
> schedule and beautiful scenery along most of its right of way.
> Clingman's Dome, in the Great Smoky Range along the North
> Carolina line, reaches 6642 feet above sea level, while Memphis
> on the Mississippi is but 182. From colonial days on, East
> Tennessee has been strikingly different in outlook from the
> central and western parts of the state. The eastern counties
> never joined the Confederacy, and consistently voted Republican--
> at least in national elections--long before that action became
> respectable elsewhere in the South. The cotton country of West
> Tennessee was also often at odds with the tobacco and dairying
> interests of the Nashville Basin.[10]

If this is done, there will be slightly different specific aims in each of the three areas. But at this time it appears likely that the following set of general aims (similar to those of the ALS) will be of interest in the entire state:

1. To test the hypothesis that Tennessee is divided linguistically into two major dialect areas and to shed light on the exact location of the geographic boundary if it exists.

2. To gain insight into the processes of obsolescence and replacement in the syntactic and phonological systems (and possibly the lexicon) of three or four generations of native speakers of Tennessee English.

3. To determine the linguistic correlates of social stratification of Tennessee English, specifically to identify the most important identifying correlates of dialect differentiation and to examine the extent to which there exists in Tennessee a distinct variety of English which may be identified as Black English.

4. To determine the importance of style shifting as an explanation of linguistic variation in Tennessee.

5. To test hypotheses concerning the linguistic insecurity or negative self-evaluation of Tennessee speakers.

6. To provide a body of information about Tennessee English which can be used as background knowledge for later intensive studies in the urban centers and possibly also in the relic areas of the state.

7. To provide accurate and relevant linguistic data upon which pedagogical applications can be based for evaluating and possibly modifying language arts instruction in Tennessee schools.

205

8. The gathering of data which will yield information about the
relationship between speech and writing.[11]
[For the general aims of the ALS see Underwood (1972), pp. 5-6.]
The final aim represents an innovation, as noted above, and will follow
a precedent set by Jacob Ornstein and Z. Anthony Kruszewski, co-director
of the Cross-Cultural Southwest Ethnic Study Center at the University of
Texas at El Paso. For the Sociolinguistic Studies in Southwest Bilingualism project, their researchers took a stratified random sample of
the full-time, unmarried, undergraduate population. Additionally, a
ten percent sub-sample was taken of the larger sample, limited to
bilingual Chicanos, whose speech and written language (in both English
and Spanish in both cases) are being studied extensively.[12] In doing
this, I shall be working in accord with the principle articulated in
the closing paragraphs of Hans Kurath's Studies in Area Linguistics:

  Many of the problems with which research in social dialectology is faced are also encountered by the student of bilingual communities, such as the correlation between the
  several languages with social groups, the conditions that
  prompt the choice of the medium of communication on the part
  of bilingual speakers, and differences from one medium to
  the other.

  Since the lines are more sharply drawn between languages
  than between dialects, the student of bilingual areas has
  certain advantages in dealing with such problems. For this
  reason it seems highly probable that the social dialectologist can improve his techniques and interpretations by
  keeping in touch with research now underway in the field
  of bilingualism.[13]

In view of the work that remains to be done before the final format of
the projected survey can be decided upon, it is obviously impossible to
make detailed projections about exactly when and how the aims of the sur
vey I have described will be carried out. However, the bibliographical
stage of the survey is nearly complete, and the next stage of the investigation, the construction and testing of a questionnaire, will begin
during the Winter quarter of 1976 when, with the support of the Department of English, a course in "Dialectology: Field Methods" will be
offered to qualified students at the University of Tennessee. A Spring
quarter seminar will provide opportunity for analysis and revision.
Thus it is expected that by the end of the 1975-76 academic year an
appropriate questionnaire will have been developed. It is also expected
that decisions about interviewing sites in East Tennessee will have
been made, and that at least a few interviews will have been conducted.
Once these immediate goals are accomplished, long-range projections can
be made. It is hoped that data from the entire survey can be computer-
ready by September 1, 1979.

NOTES

*The earlier SAMLA-ADS version of this paper was called "Suggestions
for Investigating Tennessee English: A Sociolinguistic Approach to

Dialect Study." Read at the SAMLA-ADS Meeting, Washington, D.C., November 1974.

[1]Raven I. McDavid, Jr., "What Happens in Tennessee?" in Dialectology: Problems and Perspectives, ed. Lorraine Hall Burghardt (Knoxville: University of Tennessee Press, 1971), pp. 119-29.

[2]Kenneth J. Moreland, "Anthropology and the Study of Culture, Society, and Community," in Perspectives on the South: Agenda for Research, ed. Edgar T. Thompson (Durham, North Carolina: Duke University Press, 1967), p. 140.

[3]Letter to author. Atlanta, Georgia, August 6, 1974.

[4]Lighter is working on a dictionary of American slang. See, as a sample of his work, "The Slang of the American Expeditionary Forces in Europe, 1917-1919: An Historical Glossary," American Speech, 47 (Spring-Summer, 1972), 5-142.

[5]Bethany K. Dumas, "A Study of the Dialect of Newton County, Arkansas," Dissertation University of Arkansas 1971.

[6]William Labov, The Social Stratification of English in New York City (Washington, D.C.: Center for Applied Linguistics, 1966).

[7]Roger W. Shuy, Walter A. Wolfram, and William K. Riley, Field Techniques in an Urban Language Study (Washington, D.C.: Center for Applied Linguistics, 1968).

[8]Glenna Ruth Pickford, "American Linguistic Geography: A Sociological Appraisal," Word 12 (1956), 211-33; Charles-James N. Bailey, "Is There a 'Midland' Dialect of American English?" Paper read at the Summer Meeting of the Linguistic Society of America, July 1968 (ERIC ED 021 240); J. L. Dillard, "The DARE-ing Old Men on Their Flying Isoglosses or, Dialectology and Dialect Geography," The Florida FL Reporter, 7:2 (1969), 8-10, 22 and "How to Tell the Bandits From the Good Guys or, What Dialect to Teach?" The Florida FL Reporter, 7:1 (1969), 84-85, 162; Gary N. Underwood, "Problems in the Study of Arkansas Dialects," Orbis, 22 (1973), 64-71.

[9]See Gary N. Underwood, "The Research Methods of the Arkansas Language Survey." Paper read at the International Conference on Methods in Dialectology, University of Prince Edward Island, Charlottetown, Prince Edward Island, Canada, July 25, 1972 (ERIC ED 074 823). (To appear in American Speech.)

[10]McDavid, p. 123.

[11]For the general aims of the ALS, see Underwood (1972), pp. 5-6.

[12]For a detailed description of the sampling procedure, see Bonnie S. Brooks, Gary D. Brooks, Paul W. Goodman, Jacob Ornstein, Sociolinguistic Background Questionnaire: A Measurement Instrument for the Study of Bilingualism, Revised, (El Paso: Cross-Cultural Southwest Ethnic Study

Center, The University of Texas at El Paso, 1972; Ornstein, "Toward an Inventory of Interdisciplinary Tasks in Research on U.S. Southwest Bilingualism/Biculturalism," in Bilingualism in the Southwest, ed. Edgar T. Turner (Tucson: The University of Arizona Press, 1973), pp. 321-39; "Toward a Classification of Southwest Spanish Nonstandard Variants," Linguistics, 93 (December 1973), 70-87; "Mexican-American Sociolinguistics: A Well-kept Scholarly and Public Secret," in Sociolinguistics in the Southwest--A Symposium, eds. Bates Hoffer and Jacob Ornstein (San Antonio, Texas: Trinity University, 1974), 91-121;"The Sociolinguistics Studies on Southwest Bilingualism (SSSB)--A Status Report," in Southwest Area Linguistics, ed. Garland Bills (San Diego: Institute for Cultural Pluralism, University of California, 1974), 11-34; and Jacob Ornstein and Bethany K. Dumas, "A Broad-gauge Pattern for Investigating Mexican-American Spanish-English Bilinguals: A Sociolinguistic Approach," paper read at the Rocky Mountain Modern Language Association, El Paso, Texas, October 18, 1974 (To appear in Papers in Southwest English I: Research Techniques and Prospects, ed. Betty Lou DuBois (San Antonio, Texas: Trinity University).

[13](Bloomington: Indiana University Press, 1972), p. 184.

III. LANGUAGE VARIATION AND USE

ON DEFINING STANDARD AMERICAN ENGLISH*

Edward A. Stephenson

The thesis of this paper is that there is such an entity as Standard American English. As recently as a few years ago, that statement would have been so noncontroversial that there would have been no point in making it. Any argument then would have been only about what forms this standard takes--an argument between purists (including many pedagogues) on the one hand, with their absolutist views of correctness handed down from such eighteenth-century grammarians as Robert Lowth and Lindley Murray and repeated in schoolbook after schoolbook from then on, and, on the other hand, linguists aware of the history and diversity of English and, more particularly, knowledgeable about twentieth-century scholarly studies of English usage (some of which will be briefly reviewed below). The attack from the Right Wing, if I may use that metaphor for the purist position, still goes on virtually unabated; witness, for example, the ignorant fury of the purist assault on Webster's Third during the 1960s. But nowadays, it seems, from a new Left Wing comes a radically different attack, a questioning of the very notion of Standard American English itself--an interesting change from attackers who believe in an absolute standard to attackers who believe in no standard. Evidence that I am not creating a straw man comes from Professor Donald Barnett, Director of Freshmen English at my university, who tells me that many of his young charges--some thirty or more teachers of composition, most of whom are candidates for a Ph.D. in English--object to being required to teach standard spelling, standard grammar, standard lexical usage, and the like, and to take these matters into consideration in grading papers. Perhaps this excess of democratic generosity stems at least in part from a belief that Standard English is impossible to define and consequently can be disregarded.
  Much of the following will be familiar doctrine to many linguists. Except for the expanded definition of good usage to be offered near the end of this paper, little that is really new will be presented here. But my intended audience also includes such wielders of power as the composition teachers mentioned above, as well as some of our younger linguists who are rather vague about anything that happened in linguistics prior to 1957. The latter group assuredly does not include Professor Walter Meyers, whose Handbook of Contemporary English[1] contains a very sensible and well-informed "Glossary of Usage" that draws upon several of the studies to which I will refer. Furthermore, his admirable article on usage items[2] is the latest of the scholarly investigations that I will cite in support of my position.
  Admittedly, Standard English is difficult to define, is constantly changing, and is relative not only to time but to situation and place as

211

well. Some of the difficulties of definition will be discussed below.
For a change occurring right now in my part of the country, see my recent
article on "Linguistic Predictions and the Waning of Southern [ju] in Tune
Duke, News."[3] Also consider the following examples of chronological
variation. King Alfred the Great, in his standard Old English, used the
neuter pronoun hit; this form is still with us but is nonstandard today.
Thomas Gray, using standard eighteenth-century English, entitled his
most famous poem "Elegy Wrote in a Country Churchyard"; editors today
silently change the second word of the title to "Written." Examples of
situational variation could be nearly endless; let us merely compare
one difference between written and spoken English. Although I would
write "Whom did you see?"--and I believe that the canons of Standard
Written English, at least of the formal variety, would require whom in
that sentence--I would never (or hardly ever) say whom as the first word
in a sentence. And I would defend "Who did you see?" as Standard Spoken
English. To turn to geographical variation, what is a biscuit? That
depends on your origins. If you are an Englishman, your biscuit is what
I call a cracker; and despite the un-American title of the National
Biscuit Company (which now masquerades under the name Nabisco), when I
have ham and grits and biscuits for breakfast, there are no crackers on
the table. I have to admit, however, that since the day when I married
a Yankee woman from Boston, I have gotten that particular breakfast
very seldom. (Incidentally, according to Meyers's "Glossary of Usage"
I have just used gotten in a nonstandard way, if I rightly understand
his discussion; but that use is natural to me.) Mention of the Yankee
woman should lead me into a brief consideration of our "cute little
regional dialects," as J. L. Dillard has contemptuously called them,[4]
and so it will. But first a statement of principles, further clarifying
my position, will be in order.

Human languages tend to have, perhaps always have, both vertical and
horizontal dimensions. One oversimplified but useful schema that we
might draw for certain aspects of American English would have vertical
lines separating the regional dialects and horizontal lines separating
the social dialects. To any scholar who respects the pursuit of truth,
both regional and social dialects are fully deserving of study. Hence,
intemperate attacks on area linguistics are unworthy of a serious
scholar. American dialectology originated in the study of regional
dialects (though be it remembered that from the beginning of the Linguistic Atlas investigations there were those three types of informants,
of varying educational and social backgrounds). Nowadays in dialectology
we are witnessing a greatly increased emphasis on the study of social
dialects, and that is good--though perhaps not so new as generally suppose
What is new is the focus on racially oriented studies.[5]

My schema, with its horizontal lines intersecting vertical lines,
implies that there are both standard and nonstandard levels of regional
dialects--producing one kind of diversity in Standard American English.
An interesting example can be adduced from my own immediate family, in
the pronunciation of the word part (and others of similar structure).
My mother, who is a native speaker of what Cabell Greet long ago termed
"Plantation Southern," says [pɔːt]; my Bostonian wife says [paːt]; my
two daughters says [pɑrt]. And I would not dare contend that any of
them use a nonstandard pronunciation. I can illustrate a nonstandard
Southern pronunciation, however, from my boyhood, when I used to pronounce
throw and through as [θo] and [θu], dropping the prevocalic [r] in these

Edward A. Stephenson

environments. On the standard level, examples of grammatical variation are hard to find, but I did discover one some years ago when I was teaching at the University of Virginia. I had an office-mate, a native of California, who chided me for saying "I would like for you to meet me in the lounge" and explained that the grammatical way to express the thought was to omit the for. But my southern dialect calls for the retention of both the for and the to in the infinitive-clause complementizer after like and a few other verbs; my friend's dialect evidently deletes the for in such cases. Each of us was right--according to the rules of his own dialect. On the nonstandard level, a good deal of grammatical variation exists, as is well known. Nevertheless, too few English teachers (and teachers in general) are aware of the extent to which the nonstandard variants are regionally distributed. Atwood's survey of verb forms is very instructive in this regard. The "double modal" might could ('might be able to'), for instance, is distinctively a Southern and Southern Mountain form, though also current in the German area of Pennsylvania.[6] It is hardly to be found in New York and New England. On the other hand, the form hadn't ought ('ought not') is a Northern usage prevalent in New England, New York, northern Pennsylvania, and most of New Jersey.[7] It seldom occurs in the South except in a pocket of eastern North Carolina.

In Standard American English another kind of diversity arises from the existence of different styles or "functional varieties," as Kenyon called them.[8] Martin Joos in The Five Clocks has elaborated Kenyon's formal and informal varieties into at least four styles--frozen, formal, consultative, and casual--though perhaps we should draw a discreet curtain over the fifth style, intimate, which is generally used between only two persons, normally of opposite sex.[9]

Since there are so many kinds of Standard American English, I will now limit the subject and be concerned from here on with the problem of defining Standard Written English (even though not all of the studies and statements cited below deal exclusively with written English). This limitation at least has the advantage of avoiding the problems presented by pronunciation variants; furthermore, the minimal amount of geographical variation (mostly in lexical items) in Standard American Written English may be disregarded without much oversimplification.

I should also add that I have no pedagogical ax to grind. I think it desirable that all children be given the opportunity to learn Standard English, to the extent that it is not their native dialect; but I do not know what the schools can best do to promote this desirable goal. In the long run, no doubt James Sledd is right in the view implied throughout his famous article on bi-dialectalism: the only way to do away with the language of the slums is to do away with the slums.[10] However, Sledd's somewhat overwrought attack on the white businessman, whom he regards as a sort of linguistic dictator, seems to me a mistaken emphasis; in my opinion the high-school English teacher has a great deal more to do with the shaping of linguistic attitudes. In any event, the opponents of the notion of Standard English should take no comfort from this article: not only does Sledd tacitly show his commitment to the idea of Standard English by writing in Standard English; he also alludes to the fact of its existence in a number of passages, including his statement (p. 1313) that "for all the talk about revolutionary advances in linguistics, neither the structural nor the generative grammarians have yet produced a satisfactory basic description of even standard English."

213

Edward A. Stephenson

Let us consider a preliminary definition of Standard English, by
Frederic Cassidy:
> The language of cultivation, being that normally used by the
> leading part of the community, and that most widely understood
> within the English-speaking world, has high prestige and is
> considered to be of the 'upper' level. This is Standard
> English.[11]

For a linguist to apply a definition of this kind, he must make social
judgments to determine such things as the identity of "the leading part o
the community." It may be protested that the making of such judgments
goes beyond a purely objective description of a variety of language. But
surely it is legitimate to investigate the social correlates of language
use--and thus to move from the field of pure linguistics into the field
of sociolinguistics.

A more serious complaint is that even the best of lexicographers sometimes disagree in classifying certain usages as standard or nonstandard
(and in appending such labels as cant, slang, vulgate, illiterate, and
the like to usages considered nonstandard by some). This charge can be
quickly verified. Take, for instance, three reputable, fairly recent,
and widely used desk dictionaries: Webster's New World Dictionary
(College Edition), Funk & Wagnalls Standard College Dictionary, and the
Random House Dictionary (College Edition). Then compare their treatment
of the words corny ('old-fashioned, lacking in subtlety, trite'),
egghead ('an intellectual'), frisk ('search a person for concealed
weapons, etc.'), gripe ('complain, grumble'), shyster ('a pettifogging
lawyer'), snide ('sly and malicious'). In not a single instance do all
three dictionaries agree in their labeling.[12] And no two of them agree
in their treatment of bonehead ('a stupid person, blockhead'): Webster's
New World classifies it as slang; the Standard College Dictionary labels
it informal and the Random House Dictionary appends no restrictive label
at all, thus certifying the word for formal use.[13]

Since these contradictions must be attributed to subjective elements
in the editorial judgments involved, it will be instructive to review
the history of some attempts, in the past four decades, to achieve a
degree of objectivity in trying to determine what Standard English really
is.

Sterling A. Leonard's Current English Usage (1932) reports a survey of
opinion about 230 expressions about which there might be some question.
Leonard used a "jury" system by polling 229 members of the prestige group
in the English-speaking community--including linguistic experts, members
of the NCTE and MLA, well-known authors and editors, and leading business-
men. These "jurors" were asked to rank each item on a scale ranging
from "Literary English" to "illiterate speech." Leonard then summarized
the resulting opinions for each of the 230 expressions as either
established or disputable or illiterate, depending on the degree of
approval accorded by the "jurors." An example of an item rated as
established is "None of them are here."[14]

In 1938 A. H. Marckwardt and Fred Walcott published their Facts About
Current English Usage, which was a critique of Leonard's survey. They
investigated the same 230 expressions but in a different way. The
status of about half of the expressions of Leonard's list was left in
doubt, since the classification disputable refers only to opinion and
cannot properly describe a level of usage. To resolve these doubtful
cases, Marckwardt and Walcott turned to important new compilations of

Edward A. Stephenson

linguistic fact, in particular the 1933 Supplement to the OED and the second edition of Webster's New International Dictionary (1934). The results were surprising: Leonard's "jurors" were seen to be much more conservative than the recognized authorities, and 87 percent of the "disputable" items were found to be in cultivated use, according to the authorities. For example, the following was reclassified as in cultivated literary use: "Everyone was here, but they all went home early."

In 1940 Charles C. Fries, in his American English Grammar, tackled a couple of the basic problems: How can one define the elite group whose usages we may call Standard English? And even when the group has been defined, how can one obtain an adequate sampling of its language? Fries acquired access to a large number of handwritten, holograph letters in the files of the U.S. government. For his purposes certain information about the writers of the letters was required, and eventually some 3000 suitable letters were assembled. Fries arranged the letters in three "social or class" groups according to the information concerning the writers. In Group I he placed letters from college graduates of recognized standing in their communities; these letter-writers "included college professors, physicians, lawyers, judges, clergymen," and others. In Group II Fries placed letters from substantial citizens (but not professional workers) who had finished from one year of high school to one year of college. The letters placed in Group III were from unskilled workers with an eighth-grade schooling or less. Calling the language used by Group I "Standard English," that used by Group II "Popular or Common English," and that used by Group III "Vulgar English," Fries then proceeded inductively to ascertain what linguistic forms were characteristic of Standard English, Popular English, and Vulgar English--as he had defined these levels. For the present purpose I am more interested in Fries's method than in his findings, which are not very startling. One example, however, of various discoveries that handbook writers would do well to heed is the following: the Standard English letters almost universally failed to observe the school-grammar rule requiring the genitive form of a noun before a gerund. Only one such genitive occurred, whereas sentences like the following were very common: "There is no necessity for her son being with her."

The role of the copy-editor looms large in a work published in 1956 by J. N. Hook and E. G. Mathews, Modern American Grammar and Usage. These scholars based their generalizations about current usage on the writings in their "Bibliography A," a list of fifty selections of about one thousand words each in fifty different books, magazines, and newspapers-- all published in the United States within the previous decade. "Bibliography A" includes a PMLA article by Cleanth Brooks, articles from the Saturday Review and the Atlantic Monthly, and editorials from the New York Times and the Christian Science Monitor, among others. Hook and Mathews give hundreds of documented quotations from these sources. One of their conclusions is that the adverbial use of due to (often condemned in handbooks) "is now widely employed and is regarded as reprehensible only by the purists" (p. 340). Meyers's "Glossary" in his Handbook of Contemporary English is more conservative than Hook and Mathews on this point and cites the prescriptive American Heritage Dictionary on the supposed unacceptability of adverbial due to.

The last book in this scholarly tradition to be mentioned here is Margaret Bryant's Current American Usage (1962), sponsored by the Committee on Current English Usage of the NCTE. Based on a great number

of individual studies, this book is one of the most reliable of works
of its kind. It is a dictionary of usage, with the items arranged in
alphabetical order. Each entry is divided into three parts, with a
summary of the evidence as the first part. For instance, on the question of feel bad versus feel badly, the summary notes that "usage is
almost evenly divided between feel bad and feel badly" (p. 35), with
feel badly the more common in spoken English but feel bad predominant
in formal written English. The second part of the entry, called data,
discusses the point and gives citations--in this instance from Ernest
Hemingway, Ernie Pyle, and Walter Lippman. The final part, called
other evidence, gives bibliographical references to scholarly treatments of the point in books and journals.

Let it not be inferred that such linguistic studies tend to claim that
"anything goes" in language. As well as the established items cited
above, the foregoing studies also identify a number of nonstandard
usages. The Leonard report, for example, classifies as uncultivated or
illiterate the use of complected, as in "A light complected girl passed."
Fries found that the plural pronoun youse (or yous) occurred in only the
letters of his Group III, as in "I am writing youse this letter...."
Hook and Mathews failed to discover any instance of the verb enthuse
in their corpus of reputable writings. Bryant cites as nonstandard the
use of considerable as an intensifier, as in "considerable more"; another
nonstandard form she lists is drug as the preterit of the verb drag.

An important potential source of information about Standard American
English of the written variety should be mentioned here: the Brown
University Corpus, which consists of approximately one million words of
edited American English prose published in 1961, in five hundred samples
of about two thousand words each, obtained mostly from holdings in the
Brown University Library.[15] The corpus is stored on computer tape and
is accessible for various kinds of print-out programs. Walter Meyers's
1972 article "A Study of Usage Items" (mentioned earlier) is based on
this corpus. Of the twenty-nine items Meyers investigated, two are of
sufficient interest to cite here. The Greek loanword phenomenon has
of course a foreign type of plural, phenomena. Has it also a new
Anglicized plural phenomenons? In Standard English, apparently not.
In the Brown Corpus, Meyers reports (p. 158), the plural phenomena
occurs twenty-six times, almost as often as the singular phenomenon
(thirty-five times); but phenomenons does not occur at all. Another
example may illustrate a limitation characteristic of all corpus-based
studies--namely, that with the passage of time the corpus may come to
be out of date. Meyers found (p. 169) only one occurrence of the sentence adverbial hopefully ('it is to be hoped'): "Hopefully the
perennial battle of Rule 22 then would be fought to a settlement once and
for all." But that was in the year 1961. Unless my impression is grossly
in error, hopefully in this sense has come up in the world a good deal
in the past ten years and is now widely used by well-educated writers.
It is my guess that a survey of usage since 1970 would show that such a
use of this adverbial has become Standard English.[16]

Some types of American English are more prestigious than other types;
this is a fact, if not a simple fact. The prestige of a more favored
type derives from the prestige of those who speak or write it. Usage
determines the standard--not anyone's self-appointed authority. All of
the foregoing studies were based at least implicitly on belief in some
version of the Doctrine of Usage--which I define more explicitly than

216

Edward A. Stephenson

is usual, as follows:
   What is socially acceptable in language is determined by the
   usage of the best educated and most prominent members of the speech
   community--especially those members whose prominence (whether literary, intellectual, social, artistic, political, or economic) is
   such that they acquire the status of models considered worthy of
   emulation by substantial numbers of other language users less
   privileged.
Although what is considered to be the prestige dialect will vary somewhat from one speech community to another, the linguistic studies cited
above were concerned with the national speech community. To the extent
that they display converging results, we may believe with some confidence
that Standard American English has, in part, been identified, at least
for the time being. The task of identification is difficult, but good
scholarship has pointed out some of the approaches that the task can
take. And perhaps new approaches can be devised. Because of the volatile
nature of language, investigation of its usage levels must be carried out
again and again. But that requirement should not be regarded with despair,
but rather as an opportunity for our young scholars to do something really
worthwhile.[17]

NOTES

*Read at the SAMLA-ADS Meeting, Washington, D.C., November 1974.

[1]Walter E. Meyers, Handbook of Contemporary English (New York: Harcourt, 1973).

[2]"A Study of Usage Items," College Composition and Communication, 23 (1972), 155-69.

[3]American Speech, 45 (1970), 297-300.

[4]J. L. Dillard, "How to Tell the Bandits from the Good Guys, or What Dialect to Teach," in David L. Shores, ed., Contemporary English: Change and Variation (Philadelphia: Lippincott, 1972), p. 289.

[5]For example, Juanita V. Williamson, "A Phonological and Morphological Study of the Speech of the Negro of Memphis, Tennessee," Publication of the American Dialect Society, 50 (1968), pp. 1-54.

[6]E. Bagby Atwood, A Survey of Verb Forms in the Eastern United States (Ann Arbor: Univ. of Michigan Press, 1953), p. 35 and Fig. 28.

[7]Atwood, p. 33 and Fig. 26. This locution is not so definitely non-standard in New England, where it is used by "one third of the cultured informants" (p. 33).

[8]John S. Kenyon, "Cultural Levels and Functional Varieties of English," College English, 10 (October 1948), 31-36. Also reprinted in Shores, Contemporary English.

Edward A. Stephenson

[9]Martin Joos, The Five Clocks (New York: Harcourt, 1961), p. 11.

[10]"Bi-Dialectalism: The Linguistics of White Supremacy," English Journal, 58 (1969), 1307-15, 1329.

[11]Funk & Wagnalls Standard College Dictionary (1963), p. xxiii.

[12]For several of these examples I am indebted to Austin C. Dobbins, "The Language of the Cultivated," College English, 18 (October 1956), 46-47, although he compares other dictionaries.

[13]In this instance, however, the differences in labeling may reflect an actual change in the status of the word. These dictionaries were published in 1953, 1963, and 1968, respectively.

[14]The "jury" approach has generally (and rightly, I think) been regarded by competent scholars as one of the least reliable ways to discover the truth about usage. A juror who has made no scholarly study of the language--even though he may be able to use it effectively--can assert only his prejudices, which may be at variance with the facts. Hence it is disheartening to see the American Heritage Dictionary (1969) revive the obsolete jury system, with its Usage Panel of approximately one hundred members. Even Morris Bishop, in his article on usage in the front matter of this dictionary, revealingly says of the Usage Panel members that "many of them revealed, on particular questions, an attitude more reminiscent of Dr. Johnson than of the modern linguistic view: they tend to feel that the English language is going to hell if 'we' don't do something to stop it, and they tend to feel that their own usage preferences are clearly right" (p. xxiii). For a devastating review of the AHD, see Patrick Kilburn, "The Gentlemen's Guide to Linguistic Etiquette," Union College Symposium, 9 (Spring 1971), 2-6; also reprinted in Shores, Contemporary English, pp. 178-87.

[15]For a description of the corpus, with some examples and suggestions for possible uses of it, see W. Nelson Francis, "A Standard Corpus of Edited Present-Day American English," College English, 26 (January 1965), 267-73.

[16]I find some support for my guess in the fact that 44 percent of the Usage Panel of the AHD judged hopefully to be acceptable in the sense discussed.

[17]With my encouragement, several of my former students at the University of Georgia have produced commendable brief studies of current usage: Louise Hanes, "1. Less and Fewer" and "2. Blond and Blonde," American Speech, 44 (Fall 1969), 234-37; Ann Alexander Warren, "Quite an Indefinite Word," American Speech, 44 (Winter 1969), 308-10; and C. Dale Whitman, "1. Like as a Conjunction" and "2. Some as an Adverbial," forthcoming in American Speech.

CAN (AND SHOULD) STANDARD AMERICAN ENGLISH BE DEFINED?*

Walter E. Meyers

In a way, any attempt to define Standard American English is redundant, because the folk already know what it is: it is that kind of English which they do not speak. Patty Keene knows this, even though she is only a minor character in Breakfast of Champions, a novel by Kurt Vonnegut, Jr. Patty, as her creator tells us,

> was used to apologizing for her use of language. She had been encouraged to do a lot of that in school. Most white poople in Midland City were insecure when they spoke, so they kept their sentences short and their words simple, in order to keep embarrassing mistakes to a minimum....
>
> This was because their English teachers would wince and cover their ears and give them flunking grades and so on whenever they failed to speak like English aristocrats before the First World War.[1]

But though this description may satisfy Patty, the question today is, presumably, whether we can define Standard American English to our own satisfaction.

Definitions of a standard dialect are not hard to find, of course, and courtesy, if nothing else, demands that we examine those first. A freshman handbook used by thousands says "Standard English is the language used by educated people, the language that commands respect and esteem, that provides social and professional status."[2] This example is so familiar to all here in both content and wording that its value as a representative will not be challenged. The echoes of similar definitions resound through the shelves of handbooks, books on usage and composition, books on socio-linguistics, and so on. But one of the terms cries for closer examination--who are "educated people?" I consult a doctor with medical degrees from Duke University and Johns Hopkins; he numbers a state governor among his patients; he even comes from "good family," being related to a university professor so eminent that even Time magazine has noticed him. Yet, when this doctor wrote me a prescription for hypodermic needles, he misspelled gauge. (I would be happy to document this error, but the druggist, perhaps suspecting my intentions, refused to let me retain the original prescription blank.) Clearly nothing in our language is so standardized as spelling, but as we can see, it's not a reliable index of what we would all want to call education. Two further handbooks show the additional difficulties we run into when deciding who "educated people" are.

The first shows that some animals are indeed more equal than others: it defines an "illiterate usage" as "one which occurs in the speech of uneducated persons but not in the writing of educated professionals...."[3]

You are therefore safe unless you happen to be in the wrong profession, since the same source goes on to say, "The more deliberate inventions of advertising copywriters ('our whisper-weight wool dress, to be accessoriz[e] [sic] casually') have little chance of being widely used or accepted and can be considered illiteracies."[4]

Advertising writers can take heart though--they are not alone in the outer darkness; they are joined by well-educated conformists. As another handbook says:

Some speakers show a strong desire to conform. They may even
know that there are guidelines for choices between who-whom,
I-me, and badly-badly, but lack confidence or experience to
apply them correctly. It is highly unlikely that an uneducated
speaker would fall into the unnaturalness and incorrectness of
sentences like Whom do you think you are? They gave the present to him and I, and I felt badly about the error. Ungrammatical uses of this kind represent an "educated nonstandard"
English.[5]

The more works we consult, the more the speakers of standard English dwindle. Wolfram and Fasold phrase their definition this way:

In every society, there are people who are in a position to
use their judgments about what is good and bad in language
in making decisions affecting other people. The most
obvious such people in our society are school teachers and
employers responsible for placing people in public-contact
positions....our use of the term "Standard American English"
will refer to the informal standard language of teachers
and employers of people who fill public-contact positions,
and of other speakers whose speech resembles the speech of
these two groups.[6]

The definition continues with a dazzling non sequitur: "Standard American English, then, will be the real spoken language of the educated middle class."[7] If you are willing to believe that personnel directors are educated and public-school teachers make enough money to be considered middle-class, you might think the definition has some validity.

In any event, the intersection of the sets of speakers honored in these works gives us the following composite definition of Standard American English: "the language of confident, experienced, non-conformist teachers and personnel directors when they are not writing advertising copy."

Perhaps the search for a definition is premature; let us turn to the more important question, the one presumed by our search: should we define Standard American English? For some, the definition of standard English becomes a means to a very clearly visualized end. William Labov closed of paper by discussing those children "who need the ability to use Standard English, [but] do not learn this form of the language."[8] In a discussion that followed, Labov was asked to enumerate "the five indices of Standard English in New York City" that had been the subject matter of his study. These, remember, are part of the language that children need to be able to use. They are:

1. The use of r in post-vocalic and pre-consonantal position
   (guard, horse, but not including work and shirt--which
   are special cases).

Thanks to Labov's special cases, the Chancellor of my university, who hab tually says [wɔɪk] and [šɔɪt], can continue to believe that he speaks

Standard English.
2. The vowel of bad, ask, dance, had, cash.
3. The stressed vowel in awful, coffee, and office.
4. The use of (θ) in thing and thin.
5. The use of (ð) in then and the. [9]
Do New Yorkers really need to pronounce bad as [bæd] rather than [bɛəd]? After all, the Senate Rules Committee was concerned not with how Nelson Rockefeller pronounced cash but with how he distributed it.

William Labov is further quoted as mentioning "that one of the most important social contrasts in American English is found in the /ɑ/~/ɔ/ collapse." He estimated that people in about half the geographic area of the U.S. have no contrast between 'hock' and 'hawk' or between 'cot' and 'caught.' I am not entirely sure what this means--what, for example, is an "important social contrast"?--but on one reading it seems to state that those who lack the contrast, like me, don't quite speak standard English.

"Should we define Standard American English" would be answered positively by other writers for other reasons, four of which we have time to mention. The first might be called the "propriety" or "Amy Vanderbilt" theory. I think we all agree that different styles of speech are appropriate on different occasions, but too often the theory confuses dialect with diction and makes statements about syntax that would be hard to defend. Recent political events have perhaps given this approach a new respectability: as one writer put it several years ago, "The vocabulary, idiom, and grammatical patterns appropriate in the locker room would be out of place...in the President's office."[11] To that I say "Amen"--but perhaps for other reasons.

Wolfram and Fasold provide us with a second reason for defining and using a standard, one we might call the "psychological theory"; according to it,

a standard language...may serve a unifying function by linking an individual speaker with a larger community. Whereas the unifying function may unite individual speakers, what is identified as the separatist function opposes the standard language to other languages or varieties as a separate entity, thus potentially serving as a symbol of national identity.[12]

The authors are quite confident of the power of these functions to homogenize the language: "Language standardization seems to be inevitable in American society, as it is in most of the countries of the world...."[13] Or, with even more assurance, "we must realistically concede that the establishment of prescriptive norms for 'correct' speech is an inevitable by-product of the awareness of behavioral norms of all types."[14] Two problems come to mind with this theory: if language standardization, like Marxism, marches to the tune of historical inevitability, why do prescriptivists find it so difficult to help it along? Why do they even find it necessary? The second problem is the counter-example provided by countries like Switzerland, that seem to lack a desire for a single language, let alone a single dialect. Woodstock should have taught us that a nation is not a state but a state of mind, and we may well doubt whether a black Harlem cabbie, a white Richmond lawyer, and a Chicano farmer all find their idea of national identity fulfilled in just the same way.

Next there is the "power and prestige" theory. According to this, the rich and influential have matters their own way in language, too, and they won't smile on you if you don't talk like they do. Standard English, according to one analyst, consists of "the speech habits of one linguistic group--the group, not surprisingly, containing nearly all the most powerful members of society."[15] If this is indeed the case, one wonders why the speech of the middle class need be bothered with at all--we should be out there interviewing the Vanderbilts, the Mellons, and the Hunts if we want to find standard English. Yet wealth and power do not seem to be infallible guides to good English: no President since I became politically aware--not Eisenhower nor Kennedy nor Johnson nor Nixon--has had his speech escape unscathed from those who like to comment on other people's English.

Finally, there is what we might call the "better tool" theory. This notion commits one to the belief that "the sort of standard English appropriate for formal and some informal writing...is necessary for the serious business of the world, and any student hoping to exert influence on affairs must command it....a carpenter cuts a board with a saw... because it works better than a breadknife. Standard English is necessary because it works better for serious purposes."[16] Surely the authors are here talking about vocabulary, and if so, their theory cannot be seriously maintained. The fallacy lies in an inability to decide whether standard English is a matter of pronunciation or vocabulary or both. On the one hand, some proponents of the theory want to maintain that a speaker is using the standard if he calls a piece of furniture a [čer] but using a dialect if he calls it a [čir]. But if this distinction is true, then it is pronunciation that determines which brand you speak, and one can be using dialect while saying "Turn on the electrostatic precipitator," just as surely as when saying "Turn on the spigot."

The most degenerate form of the theory becomes factually false in statements like this: "The written language of metropolitan areas has an advantage in its wider range of sentence patterns and its very much larger vocabulary, as compared with the dialects spoken in the provinces or backwoods."[17] Of course, no city dweller uses a single sentence pattern that the loneliest mountaineer does not also use. As a final comment on the question of the size of rural and urban vocabularies, I cannot resist quoting the poem "I Called Them Trees," by Gerald Barrax:

> The last time
>   I went to the library
> I looked at the flowers
> surrounding the statue of Steven Collins
> Foster and the old darkie ringing
>   the banjo at his feet
>   :flowers planted
> in four triangular beds
> alternating red and white.
> But I saw they were all the same kind.
> There were others
>   in front of the building
> In long wide rectangular rows
> bordered by round clusters of pastel green
> and white that were too deep, too dark
>   red, maroon, for easy images
>   :I called
> them all flowers.
> And the stunted trees I
> wished I had known, bending over the green

```
terrace above the flowers
     like women whose faces
I couldn't see washing
their hair in deep green pools, I called
trees.  If I had told you would you
     have known them?
                         There were
flowers for me.  There
were trees.  There were kinds
of birds and something blue
that crouched
                    in the green day waiting
for evening.
If I had told you would
you have known?
So I sat
        on a bench among flowers
and trees facing
the traffic surveying all
I knew of impalas, cougars, falcons
     barracudas, mustangs, wild
                              cats,
marlins, watching cars
go by.  I named them
all.[18]
```

In conclusion, we might well ask what pressing need there is to define a presently non-existing dialect, a dialect, moreover, that would certainly raise more problems than it solved. A standard dialect is sometimes a useful fiction, to be sure, just as a purely synchronic state of a language is a useful fiction, but that utility hardly argues for the establishment of a standard that, as Johnson said of an Academy, "every man would have been willing, and many would have been proud to disobey."

To end on a positive note, let me introduce my own definition of Standard American English: "those parts of phonology, syntax, and vocabulary that all dialects hold in common."

NOTES

*Read at the SAMLA-ADS Meeting, Washington, D.C., November 1974.

[1]Kurt Vonnegut, Jr., Breakfast of Champions (n.p.: Delacorte Press, 1973), p. 142.

[2]Robert M. Gorrell and Charlton Laird, Modern English Handbook, 5th ed. (Englewood Cliffs, N.J.: Prentice-Hall, 1972), p. 598.

[3]Langdon Elsbree and Frederick Bracher, Heath's College Handbook of Composition, 8th ed. (Lexington, Mass.: Heath, 1972), p. 277.

Walter E. Meyers

[4]Elsbree, _Heath's_, p. 278.

[5]William F. Irmscher, _The Holt Guide to English_ (New York: Holt, Rinehart, 1972), p. 377.

[6]Walt Wolfram and Ralph W. Fasold, _The Study of Social Dialects in American English_ (Englewood Cliffs, N.J.: Prentice-Hall, 1974), p. 21.

[7]Ibid.

[8]William Labov, "Stages in the Acquisition of Standard English," reprinted in _Social Dialects and Language Learning_, Roger W. Shuy, ed. (Champaign, Ill.: NCTE, 1964), p. 497.

[9]Ibid., pp. 498-99.

[10]Ibid., p. 499.

[11]Elsbree, _Heath's_, p. 271.

[12]Wolfram, _Social Dialects_, p. 22.

[13]Ibid.

[14]Ibid., p. 23

[15]Frederick Crews, _The Random House Handbook_ (New York: Random House, 1974), p. 173.

[16]Gorrell, _Handbook_, p. 600.

[17]Elsbree, _Heath's_, pp. 348-49.

[18]Gerald Barrax, "I Called Them Trees," reprinted from _Another Kind of Rain_ by permission of the University of Pittsburgh Press, 1970, pp. 40-41. Copyright 1970.

IS SOUTHERN ENGLISH GOOD ENGLISH?*

Jane Appleby

Years ago, during my first week in Wisconsin, I was asked by a fellow teacher, "Do you mean they let you teach English?" The speaker was a Canadian with what I thought a very peculiar accent. Soon after that, a woman working on a degree in speech asked me with all the kindness and gentleness of which she was capable whether I would let her teach me how to talk right. If I had had her zeal and patience and kindness, I might very well have made the offer first, for I thought her speech highly unsatisfactory. Who should teach whom? What is the standard pronunciation in American English? Should one of the objects of education be to make everybody sound like everybody else? And were this desirable, would it be possible? And if possible, by what method? And, completing the circle, how will everybody talk?

One of the dividends of the recent surge of interest in dialectology has been the growing awareness that America has several dialect areas and that differences from area to area are the result of so many factors that their very diversity makes it impossible to declare one regional speech superior to another.

It will take a long time for such conclusions to reach people like the doctor who said to me recently /mɪnɪ av ma pəyʃəns θɪŋk ah æm fram ðə ŋɔəθ bɪkɔwz æz ən ɛdʒəkeytɪd pəsən ah don av koəs hæv ə səðən æksɪnt/ (Many of my patients think I am from the North because as an educated person I don't of course have a Southern accent.) Or the teacher who said /ah hæv dɪlɪbərɪtlɪ wəkt tu gɛt rɪd av ɪnɪ treysɪz av æksɪnt æz ah θɪŋk ɔwl ɛdʒəkeytɪd pipəl ʃud du· ah prad masɛf ðæt ah hæv nat wən hwɪt av ɪnɪ treysəbəl æksɪnt ɪn mah spitʃ/ (I have deliberately worked to get rid of any traces of accent as I think all educated people should do. I pride myself that I have not one whit of any traceable accent in my speech.)

But when linguists stand outside of or above classifications which they insist should include everybody in one dialect or another, it is evident that even these "experts" have not come to terms with their facts.

In a panel discussion at the National Council of Teachers of English recently, a description of the speech sounds of the "culturally deprived" was such an accurate description of some of my own that I volunteered to illustrate what had just been described for those in the audience who had never heard such speech. Everyone laughed, and one of the speakers said, "Anyone can tell by the way you're dressed and by the fact that you're here that you're not culturally deprived." The Sartorial Standard and the Convention Criterion were not ones I had run into before, but they made about as much sense as some of the others.

225

What is substandard in one region may be standard in another. Ruth I. Golden, reporting on her work with the "disadvantaged" in the city of Detroit, said that on a battery of tests she had given, non-Detroiters made four times as many mistakes as were made by Detroiters.[1] Doesn't this prove nothing more than that a Detroit speaker set the standard? And so the test becomes simply, "Do you speak Detroit Standard?" This is not, of course, to say that what these non-Detroiters said would have been standard in another region nor that they should not have been given the opportunity to learn Received Detroit as new citizens of that city; it is rather to deplore the failure of those who are trying to help others with their speech to know exactly what it is they are doing and to recognize honestly what they are aiming at. Spoken by a well-dressed person in a secure position, many of the items on the tests would have been accepted as standard within other regions, and even in Detroit would probably have been classified as regionally variant, not socially substandard.

Of course when a person moves into another dialect region, he expects and accepts with such grace as he may reactions to the differences in his speech. He may eradicate, consciously or not, some or all of the variants; or he may enjoy and even cultivate the differences. But as the outsider coming in, he must do any necessary adjusting.

If, however, that person stays at home and speaks the standard language of his region, he by rights should be filled with consternation when someone declares his speech unacceptable. And this is exactly what is happening in some Southern schools. It is not enough that students still occasionally run into a teacher who considers a split infinitive "ungrammatical" or refuses to allow a preposition at the end of a sentence; what is much worse is that efforts are being made to "correct out" the regional characteristics in their speech.

I have the impression that the practice of at least one large speech department in the Southeast may be widely general and that in most speech classes what is called General American is used as the standard for pronunciation. But one speech teacher has said to me that it is really a matter of teaching what sounds pleasant. Asked, "Pleasant to whom?" she replied, "To educated people." When I pointed out that educated people could hold widely differing opinions, that for instance to me my pronunciation of card /kaəd/ and morning /mɔwnɪn/ is much more pleasant than hers, she very obviously felt that I therefore should not consider myself an educated person. (The day after our discussion she sent me a note recommending recent published material on "Replacing the non-standard dialect with a standard dialect." I might in turn recommend to her Joseph A. Friend's little book in which he remarks that in language "one may prefer some items to others, much as one prefers, say, chocolate ice cream to strawberry, or blondes to brunettes. But preference is not a valid reason for foisting one's personal tastes on others."[2])

Speech teachers to whom I have talked contend that they do not try to rid students of their Southern accent, only to train out that which is unintelligible, slovenly, and unpleasant. Considered as such are /keynt/ (can't); /hɛp/ (help); /spikɪn/ (speaking); /hɜɪd/ (heard); /ah/ (I); /mɪnɪ, pɪn, bɪnɪfɪt, hwɪn/ (many, pen, benefit, when). These may indeed not appeal to the taste of some people, but that they are unintelligible, even to the speech teacher, I doubt. And, as Friend says, to the person who regularly hears and says them they are not slovenl

Jane Appleby

It must undoubtedly strike some thoughtful students as peculiar that pronunciations that are "contemptibly substandard" in the Speech Department are in general use among the University faculty, sometimes even within that department.

Surely speech teachers should realize that to pronounce a sound simply because it was once in the word and is therefore represented by spelling is absurd. Even a glance at their own correct speech presumably would show them salmon, forehead, breeches, comptroller, etc. etc. And when they say /iŋlənd/(England), as I believe most of them do, don't they realize they are accepting the raised vowel before the nasal, a vowel that started even farther down?

Further, they should realize that unless one is going into drama, where an unrelenting regional dialect might be a deterrent to success, a person who knows the standard of his own region will adjust to new conditions as need arises. As linguistic advisor to the Columbia Broadcasting System, W. C. Greet recommended that a speaker aim at the better speech of any one of the five regional types. "Of one thing," he says, "we can be sure: language goes its own sweet way. The so-called purist, in giving himself a good time, may teach his students to distrust their native idiom, but aside from the splitting of their personalities, his work is fruitless. The elocutionists and the eclectic American stage have had no effect upon American speech. The wise teacher labors with a minimum of correction to help his students express themselves effectively in their native tongue. As they learn to hear themselves, they will lose enough of the manners that seem rough to strangers."[4] Bloomfield pointed out that "the only danger that threatens the native speaker of a standard language is artificiality: if he is snobbish, priggish, or timid, he may fill his speech (at least when he is on his good behavior) with spelling-pronunciations and grotesque 'correct' forms. The speaker to whom the standard language is native, will hardly ever find good reason for replacing a form that is native to him."[5] And Baugh agrees that "good English is the usage--sometimes the divided usage--of cultivated people in that part of the English-speaking world in which one happens to be."[6]

William A. Stewart of the Center for Applied Linguistics warns that there is a danger of transforming the students into language snobs.[7] The reverse seems much more likely, for as Bloomfield recognized, "Almost all people, including even most native speakers of a standard language, know that someone else's type of language has a higher prestige....Diffidence as to one's speech is an almost universal trait."[8]

The artificial, inconsistent, dogmatic imposition of speech sounds brought in from another regional dialect or concocted by the stirring together of ideas of pleasantness and correctness and universality may aggravate his natural diffidence.

Surely, if the speech teachers stopped to think, they would realize that even if they could accomplish their mission, they would be creating an Orwellian nightmare. Who wants to live in a world where everyone talks just alike? (But in an age when even the studied non-conformist revolts against convention only to erect a new uniformity as the object of his idolatry, we should perhaps not be surprised at the evangelistic zeal in its behalf.)

In some speech classes, words in written phonetics drills are checked as incorrect if they do not conform to "General American." One student learned quickly what was expected of her on quizzes and could transcribe

a paragraph that would get her an excellent grade, though she frequently
had to use spelling or conjectured pronunciations as her guide. But
oral exercises were another matter, for though it is fairly easy to write
a certain symbol if you know the paper-grader wants you to do so, it is
another thing altogether to work into one's speech the sound which the
symbol represents. One day in utter frustration, she burst into my
office with "What's wrong with my bicycle?" (/hwats rɔwŋ wɪθ ma
basɪkəl/) After a careful examination of the vehicle, I told her it
seemed /mahtɪfahn/ (mighty fine) to me.

NOTES

*The earlier SAMLA-ADS version of this paper was called "What's Wrong
with my Bicycle?" Read at the SAMLA-ADS Meeting, Atlanta, Georgia,
November 1968.

[1]"Changing Dialects by Using Tapes," in Social Dialects and Language
Learning, ed. Roger W. Shuy (Champaign, Ill., 1964), p. 64.

[2]An Introduction to English Linguistics (Cleveland, 1967), p. 96.

[3]Ibid., p. 95.

[4]"A Standard American Language?" New Republic, 95 (May 25, 1938),
pp. 69-70.

[5]Language (New York, 1933), p. 498,

[6]A History of the English Language (New York, 1935), p. 413.

[7]See Social Dialects, p. 67.

[8]Language, p. 497.

SOUTHERN STANDARDS REVISITED*

Raven I. McDavid, Jr., and Raymond K. O'Cain

The nation has made a stronger commitment than ever before to the teaching of Standard English to all who attend its schools. This commitment is of double concern to members of SAMLA and its affiliates: (1) most of those for whom new programs for the teaching of Standard English are designed speak Southern-based, or at least Southern-related, varieties of English, often, but not necessarily considered Nonstandard in the South; (2) those who have grown up speaking and continue to speak standard varieties of Southern English unashamedly are in a position to testify to the multivalence of Standard English as a cornerstone in American cultural pluralism.

The thesis of this paper is that the Atlantan, Charlestonian, or Knoxvillian has the same right to his own vowels as the Bostonian or Chicagoan, and that no program for teaching Standard English can be meaningful if it offers as a target variety a deracinated "General American," "consensus English," or "network English." It is further suggested that it is necessary to recapitulate the study of Southern standard pronunciation, so as to provide some indication of the complexity of the problem.

Perhaps surprising to some, the recognition of Southern standards is fairly old. Before the turn of the century Sylvester Primer had commented on the speech of both Charleston and Fredericksburg, Va.[1] In the 1930s appeared studies by C. M. Wise,[2] Katherine E. Wheatley,[3] and Cabell Greet.[4] More recently, a number of detailed studies, both of regions and of specific features, have drawn on the evidence in the collections of the Linguistic Atlas of the Middle and South Atlantic States (LAMSAS).

To summarize the history of these studies, and the attitudes expressed in them, is beyond the scope of this brief treatise; consequently, we confine ourselves to one subregional standard, that of the South Carolina Low-Country--Charleston and its cultural dependencies. We do this for two reasons: (1) this area has been given less attention in previous studies: e.g., Wheatley confesses ignorance; Wise mentions only that psalm is a homonym of Sam; (2) we have three generations of observations: (1) Primer in the 1880s, (2) McDavid's 1948 study of postvocalic /r/[5] and 1955 summary of the LAMSAS evidence,[6] and (3) O'Cain's dissertation nearly a generation later.[7]

It would be unrealistic, of course, to expect that these observers would treat identical phenomena. Their efforts span in excess of three-quarters of a century, and each operated from a different perspective. The studies of Primer, Wheatley, Wise, and--to a lesser degree--Greet, are anything but systematic. Greet and Wise were experienced modern phoneticians, and, correspondingly, commented on more details than

Primer or Wheatley. Primer offered historical, and even social, perspective; Greet's judgments were refined by his experience with the recorded archives at Columbia. Kurath and McDavid[8] worked with the evidence from the LAMSAS field records, almost all by McDavid and Guy S. Lowman, Jr. O'Cain set up a distillation of the observations of Primer and Kurath and McDavid for his independent field study.

   The table classifies all the phenomena treated by at least four studies in terms of the three categories treated in Kurath and McDavid: (1) differences in the phonemic system; (2) differences in the phonetic quality of the phonemes; and (3) differences in the incidence of the phonemes.

Primer, Wise, Wheatley, Greet, Kurath & McDavid, O'Cain
(/:neutral; +:prestigious; -:stigmatized; ∅:not treated)

Differences in the Phonetic System

	Pr	Wi	Wh	Gr	KM	OC
/ɪn/ = /ɛn/	∅	-	-	/	/	/
/hw/ >/w/	/	/	∅	/	/	/
/c,ɟ/	/	-	∅	/	/	/
/or/ ≠ /ɔr/	/	+	+	/	/	/

Differences in the Phonetic Quality of the Phonemes

	Pr	Wi	Wh	Gr	KM	OC
[ʉ, ʊ]	∅	/	∅	/	/	/
[3ɫ] in bird	∅	-	-	/*	/	∅
[3] in bird	∅	/	-	/	/	∅
/aɫ/ - central onset	∅	-	∅	/	/	/
/aɫ/ - monophthongal	∅	-	∅	/	/	/
[æʊ] in house	∅	-	/	/	/	/
[ʌᵛ]	∅	/	/	-	/	∅†
loss of /r/	/	/	/	/	/	/

Differences in the Incidence of the Phonemes

	Pr	Wi	Wh	Gr	KM	OC
/e/ in again	/	-	/	+	/	/
/æ/ in palm, pa	/	/	∅	/	/	/
/n/ ~/ŋ/	∅	/	/	/	/	∅

*Gr considers it old-fashioned.
†Phonemicizing as /ʌ/ makes [ʌᵛ] unrecoverable at present.

   All observers agree--explicitly or implicitly--that in general all dialects of American English share the same phonemic system. Differences noted in the South are minor: the lack of contrast between /ɪ/ and /ɛ/ before nasals; the loss of the initial cluster /hw/; palatal stops /c, ɟ/ as in car, garden; a contrast between close /o/ and open /ɔ/ before postvocalic /r/ or its reflexes. Of these, Wise and Wheatley consider the first substandard, the fourth prestigious; Wise considers the third substandard, Greet considers it a talisman of old-fashioned elegance.

Raven I. McDavid, Jr., and Raymond K. O'Cain

Differences in the phonetic quality of the phonemes were reported in greater numbers: a high-central articulation of /u/ and /ʊ/; an up-gliding diphthong, or constriction of /ɜ/, in first, worm, nurse; a centralized beginning of the diphthong /ai/; monophthongal /ai/ (sometimes falling together with /ɑ/; [æ] as the first element of /au/; a lowered /ʌ/ in cut; loss of /r/ in bear, board, etc. Except for the first (noted by only four observers) and the last, each of these features is considered as not standard by one or more observers who have commented on Southern speech.

Although the greatest number of observations deals with the incidence of phonemes, the observers differ so much in their inventories that a consensus is difficult to establish--testimony to the diversity and complexity of Standard English in general and Southern Standard in particular. Only three features are generally discussed: /e/ in again; /æ/ in palm, pa, etc.; /n/ in laughing, etc. (The reverse phenomenon, /ŋ/ in chicken, mountain is rarely discussed.)

An interpretation of the summary must take into account not only the interests and biases of the observers, but the passage of time as well. Eighty-one years passed between Primer's article and O'Cain's fieldwork; a quarter-century between McDavid's fieldwork for LAMSAS and the latter. Let us see what has been happening in Charleston.

(1) Homonymy of pen and pin was not a part of traditional Charleston speech; but it has appeared during the last generation.

(2) The palatal stops are rare except in the speech of professional Charlestonians.

(3) The contrast between /or/ and /ɔr/ is less consistent than it used to be, especially among younger speakers.

(4) The fronted /u/ and /ʊ/, [ʉ] and [ʊ], which once set off the uplands from the coastal plain, has appeared in Charleston.

(5) Constricted /ɜ/, as in first, is increasingly common.

(6) The centralized beginning of /ai/, a Low-Country feature, is less common than it used to be; a monophthongal /ai/, especially before a voiced consonant or finally--characteristic of the Up-Country--is becoming established.

(7) Contrary to the prediction of Kurath and McDavid, [æu] has obtained a lodgment among younger white Charlestonians, though it is rare before voiceless consonants, where it competes with the more prestigious centralization.

(8) Postvocalic /r/ has advanced at a rate that surpasses almost every innovation in Charleston speech. Only aristocrats and older whites of other classes consistently approach fully /r/-less speech.

(9) /e/ in again is still common, but far from universal; it competes with /ɪ/.

(10) While only professional Charlestonians maintain /æ/ in psalm, palm, it is common in almost every social group in pa, ma or grandpa, grandma.

(11) Participial /n/ is still extremely common, especially in informal speech; /ŋ/ in chicken, mountain is virtually unknown.

Having discussed these phenomena, we can attempt some explanations:

(1) The LAMSAS records--1933-48--show that speech patterns in South Carolina were very complicated; the Low-Country was by no means as uniform in its speech as the more frequently studied Virginia Piedmont.

(2) Profound social changes have swept across the South since 1933. As Pederson has pointed out, several generally simultaneous cross-currents

231

Raven I. McDavid, Jr., and Raymond K. O'Cain

of migration have occurred.[9] Negroes have moved from Low-Country farms and towns to cities in the inland South, the Northeast, or occasionally the Middle West; Up-Country Whites have moved to the coast to flesh out the depleted labor supply. The standard of living, though still low, is beginning to approach the national norm--in income, education, and aspirations.

Inland speech patterns and hyper-forms are competing with the Charleston tradition of leisurely elegance. We need not look to the media for explanations--only to the different distribution of social advantages; that military service and military bases have been among the agencies of distribution is but an economic fact.

At all events, the definition of Standard English in the Low-Country, and elsewhere, promises to remain a complicated problem that will demand our best efforts.

NOTES

*Read at the SAMLA-ADS Meeting, Washington, D.C., November 1974.

[1]Sylvester Primer, "Charleston Provincialisms," American Journal of Philology, 9 (1888), 198-213 and "The Pronunciation of Fredericksburg, Virginia," Publications of the Modern Language Association, 5 (1890), 185-99.

[2]Claude M. Wise, "Southern American Dialect," American Speech, 8 (1933), 37-45.

[3]Katherine E. Wheatley, "Southern Standards," American Speech, 9 (1934), 36-45.

[4]William Cabell Greet, "Southern Speech" in Culture in the South, ed. W. T. Couch (Chapel Hill, N.C.: University of North Carolina Press, 1934).

[5]Raven I. McDavid, Jr., "Postvocalic /r/ in South Carolina: A Social Analysis," American Speech, 23 (1948), 194-203.

[6]_____, "The Position of the Charleston Dialect," Publication of the American Dialect Society, 23 (1955), 35-49.

[7]Raymond K. O'Cain, "A Social Dialect Survey of Charleston, South Carolina," (Dissertation University of Chicago 1972).

[8]Hans Kurath and Raven I. McDavid, Jr., The Pronunciation of English in the Atlantic States (Ann Arbor, Mich.: University of Michigan Press, 1961).

[9]Lee Pederson, "Black Speech, White Speech, and the Al Smith Syndrome," in Studies in Linguistics in Honor of Raven I. McDavid, Jr., ed.Lawrence M. Davis (University, Ala.: University of Alabama Press, 1972).

232

FRENCH-ENGLISH LITERARY DIALECT IN THE GRANDISSIMES*

William Evans

By the time George Washington Cable wrote The Grandissimes, in 1879, use of the French language in Louisiana was in decline. Like the French speech of England five hundred years before, it could still be heard and would continue to be heard, but its day of dominance was over. Unlike the French of medieval England, of course, this New-World French had been the native language of the European settlers of the area and had become firmly entrenched in the homes of simple and sophisticated alike. And even during the forty-odd years of Spanish rule in the latter eighteenth century, when Spanish was the official language, French actually prevailed--not only in the home, but also on most levels of communication.[1] It was only with the official arrival of the Americans in 1803--the period in which The Grandissimes is set--that the commanding position of French began to be seriously threatened. Nine years later, when the southern tip of the Louisiana Purchase became a state, the handwriting was clearly on the wall. Although laws were to be written and cases tried in both French and English for decades,[2] and although judicial announcements were to be published in French in the New Orleans papers for more than a hundred years afterwards,[3] it was obvious by 1812 that the intruding Americans had the authority and the numbers to make their language ultimately the dominant one. And it is equally obvious from contemporary documents, such as C. C. Robin's Voyage to Louisiana,[4] and from the pages of Cable's novel that the Creoles[5] of the period were not about to give up their linguistic heritage without a bitter struggle. It is significant, for example, that one of Cable's most outspoken Creoles in the novel, Agricola Fusilier, maintained that he knew "men in this city [New Orleans] who would rather eat a dog than speak English."[6] And even Cable's most captivating feminine character, the Creole Aurore de Grapion Nancanou, took a letter written to her in English and "held it out...as if she was lifting something alive by the back of the neck."[7]

It was out of this tangle of passionate hatred of the new and strange and American, and passionate attachment to the old and familiar and French, that Cable wove his novel of contrasts and clashes between Creole and American and between Creole and Creole in the earliest days of American rule in Louisiana. And the same minute attention that he gave to the people and to the times, he gave also to their language--as reflected, however, in the speech of their descendants seventy-five years later.[8] Cable's close study of the speech of the Creoles of his day--especially their colorful blend of French and English--is suggested by his informal, but informative, comments on French-English phonology in his historical volume The Creoles of Louisiana. His observations here are somewhat impressionistic, to be sure, and are not always marked by a

clear distinction between sound and symbol. The Creole, according to
Cable, "makes a languorous z of all s's and soft c's except initials"
and he "flattens long i, as if it were coming through cane-crushers."[9]
But Cable is often perceptive underneath it all, and most of his comments
in this discussion are graphically reflected in the pages of The
Grandissimes.

PHONOLOGY

The major phonological characteristics of the literary dialect of The
Grandissimes, from the point of view of a speaker of standard English,
include alteration of consonants, variation in vowels, and some apparent
change in prosodic patterns. The consonant alterations usually involve
final consonants, which are either lost or modified in various ways. The
dental stops /t/ and /d/, for example, tend to disappear in final
clusters (innocent/innocen', and/an'). In the final unstressed syllables
of words like impossible and people, the liquid /l/ tends to be lost and,
from the English viewpoint, the syllable as well--though for the French
speaker this would presumably be simplification of a consonant cluster
(impossible/impossibe, people/peope). Preconsonantal and final /r/
tends to disappear also, not only in final unstressed syllables, but in
both stressed and unstressed syllables, whatever their position (for/
fo', father /fatheh, retards/retahds, merchant/mehchant). There are a
few initial losses: the initial fricative /h/, in both words and
syllables, often tends to disappear (head/'ead, behind /be'ine) but, on
the other hand, is frequently added in words beginning with vowels
(ask/hask). And in the initial sequence /hw/ that occurs historically
in words like what and where, the first element /h/ also tends to disappear (what/w'at, where/w'ere). However, the fricatives /f/ and /s/
and stops /p/, /t/, and /k/ in final position after vowels are not lost,
but tend to become voiced (if/iv, yes/yez, shop/shob, not/nod, knock/
knog). Replacement of the velar nasal /ŋ/ by the dental nasal /n/ is
frequent in final position (crying/cryne, anything/annyt'in'). Sometimes prevocalic /r/ presumably becomes more characteristically French,
as indicated by an orthographic h (recollect/rhecollect, preserved/
prheserved, cherishing/cherhishing). The dental fricatives /θ/ and
/ð/ usually appear as the corresponding stops /t/ and /d/ (month/mont',
something/somet'ing, think/t'ink; with/wid, other/odder, those/doze).

Variations in vowels are also relatively frequent in the novel, but
they are confined largely to front vowels. The high-front and mid-
front tense vowels /i/ and /e/ often change--again from the English
point of view--to the corresponding lax vowels /ɪ/ and /ɛ/. Instead
of please and fever, for instance, we find pliz and fivver; and instead
of slave and make, we find slev and mek. Occasionally the reverse
occurs: the vowels /ɪ/ and /ɛ/ appear as /i/ and /e/. Hence, we may
find ees and tale instead of is and tell, but not often. Somewhat more
frequently, the vowel /ɛ/ will appear as /æ/, but usually before nasal
consonants (send/sand, enter/hanter). Finally, the vowel /ai/ often
occurs presumably as /ɑ/ (I/ah, cry/crah, write/wrat). Apparently this
is what Cable was referring to in his descripiion of "long i" flattened
as if it were coming through cane-crushers.

Cable's representation of the prosodic aspects of his French-English
dialect is somewhat limited--partly, of course, because of the limitations of English spelling. But he is able to suggest certain variations
in stress--and sometimes in transition as well. On occasion, he uses
the fairly obvious convention of italics, sometimes in conjunction with

respelling: <u>certainly</u> emerges once, for example, as <u>certainlee</u>, with the last syllable italicized and respelled, presumably to indicate final stress. More often, however, he avoids italics and settles primarily on respelling, sometimes with a hyphen, to indicate an unusual stress. Primary stress seems often to be on the first syllable of a word that historically has it elsewhere. <u>Refer</u> and <u>relation</u>, for example, tend to appear as <u>riffer</u> and <u>rillation</u>, presumably /ˈrɪfər/ and /ˈrɪleʃən/. <u>Because</u> is spelled <u>bic-ause</u>, presumably /ˈbɪkəz/, in similar fashion, except that a hyphen appears instead of a repeated consonant; with this device, Cable is able to suggest even more clearly the alteration of syllable boundaries that is presumably also reflected in <u>riffer</u> and <u>rillation</u>.

GRAMMAR

Besides the loss, replacement, and occasional addition of consonants and the changes in front vowels and in stress and transition patterns, Cable's French-English in <u>The Grandissimes</u> is also characterized by grammatical variations that set it off from conventional English. Notable among these are inflectional losses in verbs and nouns and syntactic differences involving determiners, pronouns, adjectives, and larger grammatical units. The present/past/past-participle distinction in irregular verbs is often lost, typically in favor of the present form ("who <u>struck</u> him"/"oo <u>strigue</u> 'im," he got his head <u>struck</u>"/ "'e godd his 'ead <u>strigue</u>"). The preterit and past participle dental suffix of regular verbs tends to disappear ("he <u>betrayed</u>"/"he <u>betray</u>'," "I am <u>amazed</u>"/"I am <u>amaze</u>'"); the same is true of the third-person singular present indicative suffix <u>s</u> of all verbs ("he <u>says</u>"/"he <u>say</u>'"). And in like fashion, the noun occurs without the customary plural <u>-s</u> ("the <u>weeds</u>"/"de <u>weed</u>'").

Determiners vary significantly--both the definite article and the indefinite article. What would presumably be <u>the</u> in conventional English often becomes <u>that</u> or <u>those</u> in French-English ("You was in <u>dad</u> shob," "to hass all <u>doze</u> question'"). And what would normally be <u>a</u> or <u>an</u> sometimes becomes <u>one</u> ("Ah cannod be one Toussaint l'Ouverture"). Notable too is the use of an emphatic pronoun, usually a repeated first-person singular form in the objective case ("I would say dad, <u>me</u>, fo' time' a day"). The descriptive adjective is sometimes converted to a substantive in instances where the English adjective is not convertible ("Clotilde is sudge a <u>foolish</u>").

But one of the most striking syntactical variations is the tendency toward a declarative form in questions, both <u>yes/no</u> and <u>wh-</u> questions. The <u>yes/no</u> questions are syntactically indistinguishable from English echo questions, in which the interrogative meaning is conveyed by intonation rather than syntactic change ("You want a clerk?" "You was in dad shob of 'Sieur Frowenfel'?"). But they are noticeable in being usual for <u>yes/no</u> questions in the dialect, whereas they are only occasional in English. The <u>wh-</u> questions, on the other hand, are distinctly unconventional syntactically, since for them the lack of subject-verb inversion or of the auxiliary <u>do</u> is not a grammatical option in English ("W'ere you was, <u>cheri</u>?" "Wad 'e said?" "W'ere you lef' you' hat?").

SOURCES OF THE DIALECT

Most of the grammatical variations in Cable's French-English, like the phonological ones, are understandable in view of the differences between

the two languages: a speaker of French learning English with relatively
little systematic instruction might be expected to say innocen' rather
than innocent, fivver rather than fever, or "he say'" instead of "he
says," and the like.[10] And a speaker of French in southern Louisiana
would be susceptible to such tendencies as the loss of r, a characteristi
that is widespread, though not universal, in the English of this area and
of much of the rest of the South.[11] Hence, French and English would
appear to be the major contributing elements in the dialect, and French-
English would seem to be an appropriate name for it.

Some of the characteristics of this French-English, however, such as
those reflected in innocen' and "he say'," also occur in other dialects
spoken in southern Louisiana--in some varieties of black English, for
example. Hence, there are other psosible sources for some aspects of
Cable's literary dialect. The Creole historian Charles Gayarre suggested
as much when he insisted that Cable made his Creoles speak in what was,
according to Gayarre, the "broken, mutilated africanized English of the
black man."[12] And it is also possible that there was some influence from
what might be termed the "black French" of Louisiana--more often called
the "patois negre," the "gombo dialect," or, rather ambiguously, the
"Creole dialect." For example, preconsonantal r is also characteristical
absent in this patois, as well as in much black English. Influence from
black English or the patois would be difficult to demonstrate, however.[13]
The Creoles of Louisiana were as fiercely proud of their linguistic heritage as they were of other aspects of their cultural tradition. French
continued to be their principal language, even down to Cable's time. It
would seem natural that this prestige speech--along with standard souther
English--should exert the strongest impact on their acquisition of anothe
tongue, particularly a tongue to talk to the Americans with. Furthermore
a number of the most frequently recurring characteristics of Cable's
dialect occur also in other literary representations of French-English,
far removed from nineteenth-century New Orleans in place or time, or
both. Much of the phonological and inflectional simplification already
discussed is also found, for example, in the literary dialect of the poet
William Drummond, writing in Quebec at the turn of the century, and in
that of the playwrights George Farquhar and Thomas Shadwell, writing in
England two centuries earlier.[14] In both instances, the influence of
black English and the patois negre would have been unlikely. Thus, while
these dialects may have had a reinforcing influence on some aspects of
the speech represented by Cable, it would seem reasonable to infer that
the principal sources were the French of Louisiana Creoles and the Englis
of the Americans with whom they had the most frequent contacts--in other
words, relatively conventional French and English.

ACCURACY OF THE DIALECT

The charge has been made by some of Cable's critics that the speech he
attributes to reputable Creoles--whether essentially French-English or
not--is inappropriate and misleading socially. One critic felt, for
example, that the dialect in The Grandissimes was an "artistic mistake"
by which "accomplished women and cultured cavaliers" are made to talk "ir
a jargon unreal and impossible beyond conception in people of their
class." He concluded that "no such lingo ever existed except in Mr.
Cable's imagination, or as picked up in the French Market of New Orleans,
among the most degraded of dagoes."[15] As already suggested, however, mos
of the characteristic variations in Cable's "lingo" are plausible for

speakers of French in general, whatever their class. Furthermore, Cable typically distinguishes between French-English-speaking characters with different kinds of education and different degrees of proficiency in English. There are also a number of letters by contemporaries, some of them Creoles, who were perceptive and in a position to know, affirming that Cable's dialect is appropriate to his characters.[16] Finally, Cable has a chronological advantage in representing French-English speakers of three-quarters of a century earlier. However cultivated some of the Creoles may have been in their English in Cable's day--and there is evidence to suggest that some, like the highly educated historian Alcee Fortier, were not so cultivated as they liked to think![17]--the probability is that the Creoles of 1803, with less exposure to English, would have been much less polished in the language, particularly in view of the antipathy that many of them had toward anything associated with les Americains. In short, it seems likely that in The Grandissimes Cable represented the French-English dialect of a number of southern Louisiana Creoles, largely those of culture and accomplishment, in a reasonable, realistic manner.

LITERARY EFFECTIVENESS

The problem of how far to go in the direction of realistic detail, in fact, seems to have been a bothersome one during the writing of The Grandissimes and afterwards, if we are to judge from the comments of Cable's editors and critics and from the changes he made in the dialect in a subsequent revision.[18] The minute research that served him so well in gathering historical background for his fiction sometimes became a doubtful virtue in his handling of dialect. About literary artistry, Cable could say very dispassionately in the late 1890's, "It is probably always best that dialect should be sketched rather than photographed."[19] But even his staunchest advocates would probably admit that twenty years earlier he was sometimes using the camera too much and the crayon too little. At any rate, in The Grandissimes there is a great deal of difference in the density of the dialect in the speech of various characters, ranging from what one might call full-scale presentation in Aurore and Clotilde de Grapion Nancanou to the barely minimal touches in the white Honore Grandissime, half-brother of the quadroon Honore.[20]

Quite apart from the exotic charm that many critics and other readers have found in the speech of the two Nancanou women, mother and daughter, the abundance of dialect in their conversation is understandable in terms of much of the emphasis in the story. Among other things, The Grandissimes is a novel of ideas--advocating understanding, tolerance, and freedom for nationalities, races, and individuals. Although Aurore and Clotilde are far from expendable in the story as a whole, they are not the primary exponents of these ideas. Much of their dialogue is clearly less essential to plot and theme than that of the protagonists, the white Honore Grandissime and an American nondialect speaker, Joseph Frowenfeld. Thus a reader is not likely to lose the thread of the story or the essence of Cable's thought even if he misses an occasional dialect word or sentence by Aurore or Clotilde. Furthermore, a substantial part of their dialogue is given in conventional English--Cable's way of representing their French speech and of making it clear that in keeping with their class and education they were quite capable and cultivated speakers of their native tongue.[21] Hence, a significant portion of their dialogue would present no problem to a reader.

In their French-English dialect speech Aurore and Clotilde are virtual
indistinguishable, both of them exhibiting most of the features of sound
and grammar already mentioned, and others in addition. The following
selection is approximately representative:
[Aurore] asked in English, which was equivalent to whispering:
"W'ere you was, cherie?"
"'Sieur Frowenfel'--"...
"'E godd his 'ead strigue, 'Tis all knog in be'ine! 'E come in blidding
"in w'ere?" cried Aurora.[22]
"In 'is shob."
"You was in dad shob of 'Sieur Frowenfel'?"
"I wend ad 'is shob to pay doze rend."
"How--you wend ad 'is shob to pay--"
Clotilde produced the bracelet. The two looked at each other in silence
for a moment, while Aurora took in without further explanation Clotilde's
project and its failure.
"An' 'Sieur Frowenfel'--dey kill 'im? Ah! ma chere, fo' wad you mague
me to hass all doze question?"
Clotilde gave a brief account of the matter, omitting only her conver-
sation with Frowenfeld.
"Mais, oo strigue 'im?" demanded Aurora, impatiently.
"Addunno!" replied the other. "Bud I does know 'e is hinnocen'!"
A small scouting-party of tears reappeared on the edge of her eyes.
"Innocen' from wad?"
Aurora betrayed a twinkle of amusement.
"Hen'ryt'in', iv you pliz!" exclaimed Clotilde, with most uncalled for
warmth.
"An' you crah bic-ause 'e is nod guiltie?"...

"Mais, anny'ow, tell me fo' wad you cryne?"
Clotilde gazed aside for a moment and then confronted her questioner
consentingly.
I tole 'im I knowed 'e war h-innocen'."
"Eh, bien, dad was h-only de poli-i-idenez. Wad 'e said?"
"'E said I din knowed 'im 'tall."
"An' you," exclaimed Aurora, "it is nod pozzyble dad you--"
"I tole 'im I know 'im bett'n 'e know annyt'in' 'boud id!"
The speaker dropped her face into her mother's lap.
"Ha, ha!" laughed Aurora, "an' wad of dad? I would say dad, me, fo'
time' a day."[23]
Brief though it is, the passage reveals many of the common characterist
in the language of the two women. Their speech is not alike in every
particular in this brief selection, of course, but their French-English
dialect elsewhere in the novel demonstrates that their language is repre-
sented as being of the same kind. While this dialectal closeness in
two characters might be a defect in another novel, it seems to be
defensible here--like the quantity and the density of their dialect
speech. For Aurore and Clotilde are presented as hardly separable in
appearance, in character, and in function. Joseph Frowenfeld says of the
"I can hardly understand that you are not sisters."[24] Though Clotilde
is perhaps shier than her mother, and certainly less loquacious, they are
both coy, coquettish, and yet charming--both irrepressible, unpredictable
and yet irresistible. And both have essentially the same role--to
attract and captivate one of the two protagonists in the novel. In the

ultimate marriages of Clotilde and Aurore--women as like in essence as
in dialect--to the American Frowenfeld and the Creole Honore Grandissime,
respectively--men very different in cultural background--Cable seems to
be embodying his optimistic desire for greater harmony in Louisiana
between the French and the Americans, and between feuding factions within
the French community itself.

Just as Clotilde is a natural reflection of Aurore, so the quadroon
Honore Grandissime is a natural foil for the Creole Honore, who stands at
the opposite end--the minimal end--of the dialect continuum. Although
the quadroon has had virtually the same education as his white half-
brother, his French-English dialect resembles that of Aurore and Clotilde,
as his first remarks in the novel suggest:

One day...the landlord [the quadroon]...noticed in Joseph's hand a
sprig of basil, and spoke of it.
"You ligue?"
The tenant did not understand.
"You--find--dad--nize?"
Frowenfeld...expressed a liking for its odor.
"I sand you," said the landlord.[25]

The quadroon's speech, like Aurore's, is marked by the same conversion of
dental fricative /ð/ to the corresponding stop /d/, the change of /ɛ/ to
/æ/, and the voicing of final stops like /t/ and /k/. His relatively
dense French-English dialect presumably reflects less contact with the
English-speaking Americans than his brother has had; he is characterized,
in fact, as a shy, retiring individual. But his dialect speech is also
recognizably different from Aurore's, sometimes in obvious ways, sometimes more subtly. This contrast is clearly indicated, for example, by
the fact that in the conversation already quoted between Aurore and
Clotilde, and in their speech generally, the pronoun I retains its conventional spelling. But in the speech of the quadroon, I often appears
as ah. In fact, ah is the only form he uses in one of his encounters
with Joseph Frowenfeld, where the pronoun occurs half a dozen times:
"Ah lag to teg you apar'," "Ah was elevade in Pariz," "Ah wand you
mague me one ouangan," "Ah ham nod whide, m'sieu'," "Ah ham de holdez
son of Numa Grandissime," "Ah can nod spig Engliss."[26] In more subtle
fashion, his speech also reflects the loss of preconsonantal /r/ and the
loss of dental stops in final clusters, but much less frequently than in
the speech of Aurore; and Aurore's tendency to stress words like because
and refuse on the first syllable does not appear. On the other hand,
the quadroon has a greater tendency (from the English speaker's point of
view) to omit auxiliaries like will ("I sand you") and pronoun complements
like it ("You ligue?").

In contrast to the withdrawn, introverted quadroon, the Creole Honore
is a merchant with extensive business and social contacts among the
Americans, as well as the Creoles. The comparative lack of variation
from conventional English in his dialogue is quite natural and understandable. For the most part, his speech is unmarked, except for the
relatively consistent absence of preconsonantal /r/ and the presence,
presumably, of a characteristically French /r/ in other positions:

My-de'-seh, rhecollect that to us the Grhandissime name is a
trheasu'e. And what has prheserved it so long? Cherishing the unity
of ow family; that has done it; that is how my fatheh did it. Just
or-h unjust, good o' bad, needful o' not, done elsewhere-h o' not,
I do not say; but it is a Crheole trhait.[27]

William Evans

On rare occasions we find a few additional dialect characteristics,
notably in one passage in which the Creole is talking with intense feeli
about the color problem in Louisiana. There are at most a dozen example
reflecting things other than the peculiarities of /r/--most of them
phonological, and most of them involving loss of final consonants (mos'
and thousan', for example). But this minor linguistic lapse is striking
appropriate and effective and is underlined by Cable's comment, "He was
so deep in earnest that he took no care of his English."[28] In the parti
revision of The Grandissimes in 1883, dialect characteristics are
systematically removed from the Creole's speech. An occasional my-de'-s
is retained, but, except for the variations in the emotional passage
mentioned, practically everything else has been normalized:

My-de'-seh, recollect that to us the Grandissime name is a treasure.
And what has preserved it so long? Cherishing the unity of our family;
that has done it; that is how my father did it. Just or unjust, good
or bad, needful or not, done elsewhere or not, I do not say; but it
is a Creole trait.[29]

Cable's motive seems clear enough. Although, for the most part, only
the representation of the consonant /r/ was unconventional in the
original edition, this difference would account for a sizable number of
alterations of standard spelling in a paragraph or a page of dialogue--
as the first quotation from the Creole suggests-and would have given a
reader the impression of much more variation in speech than was actually
represented.[30] Since the Creole Honore is one of the two principal
spokesmen for the author in the novel, Cable presumably felt that his
character would have more dignity and that his ideas would be clearer an
carry more weight in a closer approximation to conventional English.
And, for most readers, he was probably right.

CONCLUSION

In The Grandissimes, then, Cable presents a French-English dialect tha
is probably a reasonably accurate reflection of the occasional speech of
some southern Louisiana Creoles of the nineteenth century. It was a
dialect, as Cable apparently realized, that could sometimes be vulnerabl
to criticism on various grounds. To unsympathetic readers like Charles
Gayarre, the English of some of the Creole characters was not only
"broken"; it was "mutilated." Nevertheless it was an English, a French-
flavored English, that could be useful and effective in linking like
characters together, in differentiating contrasting characters, and in
distinguishing different moods in a given character. And it formed a
significant part of Cable's attempt to preserve something of a unique
and valuable, but declining, culture and to make the world aware of it.

NOTES

*The earlier SAMLA-ADS version of this paper was called "French-Englis
Literary Dialect in George Washington Cable's Novel The Grandissimes."
Read at the SAMLA-ADS Meeting, Atlanta, Georgia, November 1971.

[1]Edwin A. Davis, Louisiana: The Pelican State, 3d ed. (Baton Rouge:
Louisiana State Univ. Press, 1964), p. 104.

[2]Davis, p. 131.

[3]Reginald F. Trotter, Jr., "An Index of the Comptes Rendus of l'Athenee Louisianais and a General History of the Organization," Thesis Tulane 1952, pp. 4-16, 18-19, and 31-32. Announcements of judicial proceedings were regularly published by the French newspapers of the state until prohibited by the Legislature in 1868. This privilege was restored to the French press of New Orleans a decade later, but finally withdrawn in 1916.

[4]Voyages dans l'Interieur de la Louisiane (Paris: F. Buisson, 1807), trans. and abridged by Stuart O. Landry as Voyage to Louisiana (New Orleans: Pelican Publishing Co., 1966). Landry's translation includes a lengthy memorandum (pp. 163ff) written by Robin, at the request of a number of French-speaking Louisianians, on the importance of retaining French as the language of the territory.

[5]Creoles here refers to the white descendants of the colonists who came directly (or occasionally by way of the Caribbean) to Louisiana from France--and, to some extent, from Spain--at various periods beginning at the end of the seventeenth century; the Creoles were people of prestige and spoke a dialect that was very closely akin to cultivated continental French (William A. Read, Louisiana French, rev. ed., Baton Rouge: Louisiana State Univ. Press, 1963, p. xvii; August W. Rubrecht, "Regional Phonological Variants in Louisiana Speech," Dissertation University of Florida 1971, pp. 11ff.). Their attempt at English speech is sometimes referred to as Creole also (as noted, for example, by Arlin Turner in his edition of some of Cable's stories and articles, Creoles and Cajuns: Stories of Old Louisiana, Garden City, N.Y.: Doubleday, 1959, p. 8). But French-English is a less ambiguous term and probably fairly accurate as a description, as will be demonstrated later.

[6]The Grandissimes: A Story of Creole Life (New York: Scribner's, 1880), p. 60. All subsequent references will be to this edition, except where otherwise indicated. The novel first appeared in serial form in Scribner's Monthly, beginning in the fall of 1879. The task of finding and examining manuscripts and editions of the book and other materials about it was made much easier because of the generous help of many people--among them, Connie Griffiths, who, as Director of Special Collections at the Howard Tilton Memorial Library of Tulane University, made available the excellent resources of the Cable Collection; Ray Browne and Larry Landrum, who, as curators, provided access to the increasingly valuable collection of Cable materials at Bowling Green State University; and Evangeline Lynch, who opened up the riches of the Louisiana Room at the Louisiana State University Library.

[7]The Grandissimes, p. 83.

[8]It seems clear, as Kjell Ekstrom points out, that Cable "made no attempt to reconstruct the English of the Creoles of the early nineteenth century but took the artistic liberty of putting into their mouths the English of contemporary Creoles" (George Washington Cable:

William Evans

A <u>Study</u> <u>of</u> <u>His</u> <u>Early</u> <u>Life</u> <u>and</u> <u>Work</u>, University of Upsala Essays and Studies on American Language and Literature, Upsala: A. B. Lundequistska Bokhandeln, 1950, p. 177).

[9]<u>The</u> <u>Creoles</u> <u>of</u> <u>Louisiana</u> (New York: Scribner's, 1884), pp. 317-18. This "long i" would be rather difficult to pin down with any precision solely on the basis of Cable's description. However, in his actual respellings for this and other sounds in <u>The</u> <u>Grandissimes</u>, it is usually fairly clear what he intends. His respellings are those of a relatively acute, though not scientifically trained, observer of languages, particularly English and French. In my comments on pronunciation, the phonemic system is essentially that of Hans Kurath as set forth, for example, in his <u>Phonology</u> <u>and</u> <u>Prosody</u> <u>of</u> <u>Modern</u> <u>English</u> (Heidelberg: Carl Winter, 1964).

[10]Specifically, the influence of the French phonemic system can easily account for the occurrence of <u>innocen'</u> and <u>fivver</u> in terms of the historical loss of many final consonants in French and the lack of a French phonemic contrast corresponding to that between the English /i/ and /ɪ/. Similarly, the occurrence of "he <u>say'</u>" can be readily accounted for by the lack of a third-person singular <u>-s</u> in French and, in fact, by the frequent absence in spoken French of any third-person singular and plural contrast, except with certain kinds of liaison. In like fashion, most of Cable's other variations in sound and grammar can be reasonably interpreted as a reflection of the attempt of speakers of French to communicate in English. Extremely useful in this sort of interpretation are discussions such as Claude M. Wise's chapter on French in North American in his <u>Applied</u> <u>Phonetics</u> (Englewood Cliffs, N.J.: Prentice-Hall, 1957), pp. 325-63. For a few of the characteristics of Cable's French-English, such as the apparent shift of stress to the first syllable of words like <u>refer</u>, exact explanation is rather elusive. One would expect a shift in the opposite direction, where appropriate. Yet a possible parallel presents itself in the phenomenon of emphatic stress on various syllables in French as discussed, for example, by Pierre Delattre in "Comparing the Prosodic Features of English, German, Spanish and French," <u>International</u> <u>Review</u> <u>of</u> <u>Applied</u> <u>Linguistics</u>, 1 (1963), 199-205. Or the shift might perhaps be a kind of hypercorrection the French speakers having noted the tendency toward initial stress in English in general and in similar words like <u>differ</u> and <u>suffer</u> in particular.

[11]It seems quite evident that this loss of /r/ in Cable's dialect can be explained, not with respect to any French interference, but in terms of the particular variety of English that the French speakers were exposed to. Rubrecht ("Regional Variants," pp. 159-62 and 217ff.) provides some of the most recent evidence of the extent to which the loss of /r/ has penetrated southern Louisiana. Occasionally, on the other hand, one of Cable's variations--such as that in the vowel sound /ai/--apears to reflect both French and Louisiana English equally. Something approximating the /ɑ/ phoneme might be anticipated, both because of the lack of a diphthongal sound /ai/ in French, and because of the variety of articulations of /ai/, including monophthongal ones in southern Louisiana (as noted also by Rubrecht, pp. 176-79).

William Evans

[12]Ekstrom, George Washington Cable, p. 176, n. 11. Needless to say, this hardly represents Cable's view of the matter.

[13]In addition to the absence of /r/, of /t/ in final clusters, and of the -s verb inflection, much black English resembles Cable's French-English in other characteristics. These can be observed in the useful and illuminating discussion by Louise A. DeVere, "Black English: Problematic but Systematic," South Atlantic Bulletin, 36, no. 3 (May, 1971), 38-46. But resemblance is not necessarily influence. The patois negre has another feature, in addition to the lack of preconsonantal and final /r/, that is somewhat reminiscent of Cable's dialect-- the absence of the copula (James F. Broussard, Louisiana Creole Dialect, Baton Rouge: Louisiana State Univ. Press, 1942, pp. 2 and 14-15). Since much black English is also marked by this absence and since it is not characteristic of conventional French, there is perhaps a more tangible possibility of influence on Cable's dialect in this respect than in most others. Although the lack of the copula seems, on occasion, to be part of the French-English speech of some of Cable's characters, the trait is not found at all in the speech of the quadroon Honore Grandissime, where it might be expected. Furthermore, about two-thirds of the examples in Cable's dialect occur with a present participle in what would be called a present progressive form in conventional English ("I goin' rad now"). It is not inconceivable that a French speaker might omit the copula in his attempt to reproduce a common English construction that he has often heard. In fact, in such sequences as "You lookin' verrie well" or even "You de bez man" (without a participle), the lack of the copula can be quite plausibly interpreted simply as loss of final or preconsonantal /r/. Finally, as Juanita V. Williamson has pointed out, the lack of a copula in Southern speech is not confined to black English ("Selected Features of Speech Black and White," CLA Journal, 13, no. 4, June 1970, 421, 424-25).

[14]The French-English dialect of William Henry Drummond, an integral part of his Collected Poems (Toronto: McClelland and Stewart, 1926), does not appear to have been investigated in much detail. But the dialect efforts of Farquhar, Shadwell, and some other Restoration playwrights have been illuminated by Brother William F. Gruber, Jr. ("The Broken English of French Characters of Restoration Comedies: A Linguistic Analysis," Thesis Louisiana State University 1971).

[15]"The Writing of George Washington Cable," The Critic (2 January 1893), n. pag.

[16]Ekstrom, George Washington Cable, pp. 177-80.

[17]Ekstrom, p. 179.

[18]For example, Irwin Russell, an editorial assistant at Scribner's and a writer of dialect himself, frequently questioned the probability of some of Cable's carefully recorded linguistic details. Most reviewers of the first edition of the book had some difficulty with the dialect, some finding it tedious in its total effect. And the changes that Cable made in the dialect in the revision of 1883 were mostly in the

direction of simplicity (Arlin Turner, George W. Cable: A Biography, Durham, N.C.: Duke Univ. Press, 1956, pp. 96-101.)

[19]"Editor's Symposium," Current Literature, 22, no. 3 (September 1897), 193.

[20]There is also a middle ground, exemplified by a few dialect-speaking characters in the novel in addition to the quadroon Honore, notably a clerk with the unlikely name of Raoul Innerarity, whose speech, though decidedly dialectal, also differs from that of Aurore and Clotilde in a number of ways.

[21]This is one effective rejoinder to those contemporaries who felt that cultivated Creoles were being misrepresented as low life in Cable's writings.

[22]Early in the book, Cable converts Aurore to Aurora, remarking that "it sounds so much pleasanter to anglicize her name" (p. 88). The conversation as a whole needs some explanation. Through a misunderstanding, Frowenfeld had been hit on the head by a servant; and Clotilde witnessed the ensuing confusion because she had gone to his shop--a pharmacy and sometimes pawnshop--to raise money on a bracelet in order to pay the rent that the women owed to the quadroon Honore Grandissime, who also happened to be Frowenfeld's landlord. Only partly concealed behind Clotilde's words is her growing affection for Frowenfeld. The situation is made even more complex by the fact that Clotilde, unknown to him, had helped to nurse Frowenfeld back to health after a nearly fatal bout with yellow fever in his earliest months in New Orleans.

[23]The Grandissimes, pp. 276-78.

[24]The Grandissimes, p. 117. Frowenfeld had been told of the actual relationship of the two women earlier in the story by the Creole Honore Grandissime (p. 70).

[25]The Grandissimes, p. 53.

[26]The Grandissimes, pp. 134-37. The first statement is an amusing example of Cable's occasional bilingual humor, but at the same time an expression that is quite appropriate to the dialect and understandable in the speaker. Presumably the quadroon's request reflects the French idiom prendre quelqu'un a part and means, as Frowenfeld recognizes, 'to take someone aside.' The ouangan referred to in the third statement is the quadroon's term for some sort of magical love potion or 'poudre d'amour,' as he later calls it (p. 140).

[27]The Grandissimes, p. 289.

[28]The Grandissimes, p. 201. This realistic intensification of dialect under emotional stress occurs also in the speech of the quadroon at one point (pp. 256-57) where he is speaking heatedly of Agricola Fusilier, the one person in the world for whom he has a passionate hatred. On this occasion, some words that otherwise have the conventional English high and mid-front lax vowels /ɪ/ and /ɛ/ in his speech appear with the corresponding tense vowels /i/ and /e/ (didn't/deen, dead/dade).

William Evans

[29]The Grandissimes: A Story of Creole Life (New York: Scribner's,
1888), p. 289. The 1883 edition was not available to me, but all subsequent reprintings have retained the dialect changes made in that year
(Louis D. Rubin, George Washington Cable: The Life and Times of a
Southern Heretic, New York: Western, 1969, p. 282).

[30]The inadequacy of the English spelling system for representing dialect
variations in pronunciation--combined with the probable inability of the
Creole readers, like most readers, to sufficiently distinguish between
spoken and written language--doubtless goes a long way to account for
the violent reactions of such readers as Charles Gayarre to Cable's
French-English dialect.

EYE DIALECT AS A LITERARY DEVICE IN THE WORKS OF SIDNEY LANIER*

Paul H. Bowdre , Jr.

When William Faulkner has a black servant say to Colonel Thomas Sutpen, "Hyer I am, Kernel," using the nonstandard spelling kernel for colonel, he is using Eye Dialect. The same may be said about Tennessee Williams when he has Baby Doll talk about wearing "clo'se skintight" and uses the spelling clo'se for clothes. Stephen Crane is using Eye Dialect when he spells says with sez and Sinclair Lewis is also using it when he spells listen with lissen. These nonstandard spellings do not represent nonstandard pronunciations--they appeal only to the eye, not to the ear. They actually indicate a standard pronunciation of the word involved, and yet they convey to the reader the impression that there is something peculiar about the speech of the person using these nonstandard spellings. The reader is reading Eye Dialect, a useful literary device frequently used by many American novelists, poets, and dramatists in their attempts to give the impression of nonstandard speech.

The term Eye Dialect was apparently a coinage of George Philip Krapp, and was first used in his chapter on literary dialects in The English Language in America (published originally in 1925). The term appears in the following passage:

Of the dialect material employed in American literature, several clear kinds may be distinguished. First and most extensive in use is the class dialect which distinguishes between popular and cultivated or standard speech. This calls for no detailed discussion. The impression of popular speech is easily produced by a sprinkling of such forms as aint for isn't, done for did, them for those, and similar grammatical improprieties. This impression is often assisted by what may be termed "Eye Dialect," in which the convention violated is one of the eye, not of the ear. Thus a dialect writer often spells a word like front as frunt, face as fase, or picture as pictsher, not because he intends to indicate here a genuine difference of pronunciation, but the spelling is merely a friendly nudge to the reader, a knowing look which establishes a sympathetic sense of superiority with the humble speaker of the dialect.[1]

Actually, relatively little has been written about Eye Dialect and an examination of many of the standard works on language indicate that they neglect the subject entirely. Those who mention the term at all usually confine themselves to a definition and a few examples of Eye Dialect spellings. Raven I. McDavid, Jr., has defined Eye Dialect as "a crude but common device often utilized to convey the illusion of substandard pronunciation...a quasi-phonetic respelling of common words."[2] H. A. Gleason, Jr., stresses that "Eye Dialect is not...to be considered as an

247

actual portrayal of folk or regional speech so much as a stylized literary device to signal that folk speech is intended."[3]

At first glance it would appear that Eye Dialect is all around us in such quasi-phonetic spellings as Duz for the well known "washday product," Gleem for Gleam as in "Gleem Toothpaste" or Stix for sticks in "Fish Stix." But these advertising trade names are not properly in Eye Dialect since they are not intended to represent the speech of anyone. Nor do the quasi-phonetic spellings used in James Russell Lowell's The Biglow Papers represent speech in most cases. They are usually found in letters written by Ezekiel or Hosea Biglow and simply indicate these two gentlemen can't spell. Leaving out such cases from consideration as Eye Dialect, there are still a surprising number of examples of the use of quasi-phonetic spellings to represent actual speech in the works of American writers. It is these examples which may be properly called Eye Dialect.

Eye Dialect is found in the works of frontier humorists like George Washington Harris (who created the dialect character, Sut Lovingood), David Ross Locke (who is responsible for Petroleum V. Nasby) and many others; it is often seen in the works of local colorists such as Edward Eggleston, James Whitcomb Riley, and Joel Chandler Harris; Stephen Crane uses it in Maggie, A Girl of the Streets and The Red Badge of Courage; twentieth century novelists who use it include Lewis, Steinbeck, and Faulkner; and it is even found in certain plays of Eugene O'Neill, Tennessee Williams, and Arthur Miller.

As a literary device, Eye Dialect has been used to produce a variety of effects. The frontier humorists usually use it to help convey the lack of education of their comic characters. James Whitcomb Riley often uses it when he wants to be "folksy," which is rather often. Sinclair Lewis, on one occasion, uses Eye Dialect to indicate that the speaker is intoxicated, while Tennessee Williams uses it to help give the impression that the speaker is from the South. There are no more subtle uses of Eye Dialect, however, than those found in the few dialect poems of Sidney Lanier, and in his prose work, Tiger Lilies. It is to Lanier's use of Eye Dialect that the remainder of this paper is devoted.

Lanier has used nonstandard spellings in only a few short poems and in a small portion of his novel, Tiger Lilies, yet it is not difficult to find Eye Dialect spellings within this relatively small body of dialect writing. He has represented the speech of both poor whites and Negroes. There is an interesting comment in the introduction to the first volume of The Centennial Edition of the Works of Sidney Lanier:

Though the modern attitude favors the use of idiom and speech tune rather than dialectal misspelling—feeling a false exaggeration in the phonetic representation of illiterate speech which implies that educated speech conforms to standard spelling—Lanier was more meticulous and accurate than most of his contemporaries in recording the actual language of the Negro, as well as of the Cracker.[4]

This evaluation of Lanier as being "meticulous and accurate" in "recording the actual language" seems, at first glance, contradictory in view of his rather extensive use of Eye Dialect. However, at least part of his use of Eye Dialect is clever and purposeful. He appears to make certain conscious uses of it in a number of instances when he wishes to gain a special effect.

Paul H. Bowdre, Jr.

One of his most striking Eye Dialect spellings is the use of cum for come. It is present in what is probably Lanier's best-known dialect-poem, "Thars More in the Man Than Thar Is in the Land." The poem concerns a "cracker" who sells his farm, leaves to seek his fortune in Texas, and returns emptyhanded five years later. The stanza is as follows:
    And that was Jones, standin' out at the fence,
    And he hadn't no waggin, nor mule, nor tents,
    Fur he had left Texas afoot and cum
    To Georgy to see if he couldn't get sum
    Employment, and he was a lookin' as hum-
    ble as if he had never owned any land.
The spelling of come as cum in the third line and some as sum in the fourth are examples of an unusual use of Eye Dialect. It seems probable that Lanier changed the spelling in order that cum, sum and hum might be "perfect rimes"--that is, that the vowels and final consonants might be identical in appearance as well as in sound. Cum appears again in the sixth stanza of another dialect-poem, "Jones' Private Argument," and also in the third stanza of "Them Ku Klux," but in four other dialect-poems it is absent, with come being given its standard spelling.

A clever use of Eye Dialect to form "perfect rimes" occurs in "Them Ku Klux." The lines are as follows:
    "I'll read you," says I, "but whur air my spex?
    I thought that I laid em right thar, jest nex
    to that newspaper: Nancy wher air my spex?"
Spex is Eye Dialect for specs, a shortened form of spectacles, which is good colloquial usage. Nex, though at first glance it does not appear to be Eye Dialect, actually is, since in the usual pronunciation of next to only one t is pronounced. By changing the spelling of specs and by leaving the t out of next, Lanier is able to make a "perfect rime." The effectiveness of the device can be seen by comparison of the similarity in appearance of spex and nex and the lack of similarity of specs and next.

Sidney Lanier wrote only seven dialect-poems in all. Five of them--"That's More in the Man Than Thar Is in the Land," "Jones' Private Argument," "Civil Rights," "Them Ku Klux" and "9 from 8"--are attempts to represent cracker dialect; the remaining two (which he wrote in collaboration with his brother Clifford Lanier) are attempts at Negro dialect. These two--"The Power of Prayer" and "Uncle Jim's Baptist Revival Hymn" are quite sparing in their use of Eye Dialect, particularly considering that roughly fifty per cent of the words in these poems have nonstandard spellings. The word enough is spelled enuff in a line from "The Power of Prayer,"which reads "De Debble's comin' round dat ben, he's comin' shuh enuff." Lanier is only one of many writers who have felt an urge to respell enough and have come up with an Eye Dialect form. Probably he was only using a traditional Eye Dialect spelling. This poem also uses the common Eye Dialect spelling vittles for victuals. A more unusual Eye Dialect spelling in the same poem is sence for sense.

To mention some other Eye Dialect spellings in the five cracker dialect-poems--and there are quite a few of them in these poems--one may find the following in "9 from 8": nuthin' for nothing, forrad for forehead, workin' for working, giv for give, and sum for some. In "Thars More in the Man Than Thar Is in the Land" there is found the common Eye Dialect spelling wimen for women. "Civil Rights" has bin for been though the

Paul H. Bowdre, Jr.

same word is given its standard spelling five lines earlier in the poem. It appears that Lanier changes the spelling to bin so that it will look like agin (again) as well as rime with it. In "Jones' Private Argument" the word tare in the line, "But tare up every I O U" is an Eye Dialect spelling for tear.

Turning to Lanier's prose, the novel Tiger Lilies makes considerable use of Eye Dialect in conveying the speech of mountaineers and Negroes. Cain Smallin, a mountaineer of the Great Smokies, comes to the rescue of his friends during a fight and makes the following statement: "I was a right smart time a-comin', but when I did come, I cum, by the livin'! Phe-e-e-w!"[5] The italics of cum are Lanier's and this use of Eye Dialect is one not encountered in any of the other authors mentioned. The spellings come and cum are in the same sentence, but cum is obviously used here as a more emphatic form of the word. There is no indication of any pronunciation difference represented in the two spellings, except that the Eye Dialect here seems akin to the use of the exclamation point.

Another curious use of Eye Dialect occurs in Tiger Lilies with the spelling of coffee as kauphy. Lanier explains his use of kauphy in the following passage:

...we, genuine coffee being invisible as any spirit during
the war, made hideous images of it and paid our devotion
to these morn, noon, and night. We made decoctions of
pease, of potatoes, of peanuts, of meal, of corn, of okra
...and called them kauphy.[6]

There is nothing in the nonstandard spelling of coffee used here to indicate any change from the standard pronunciation. The grapheme combination au represents the vowel of the first syllable of coffee as accurately as does the grapheme o, which is used in the standard spelling. It represents this same vowel in fault, laud, Paul, and haul. The grapheme combination phy represents in such words as physics, trophy, and philosophy the same sounds as those in the second syllable of coffee. Thus kauphy is a suitable spelling to represent the standard pronunciation. The value of the nonstandard form lies in its ability to emphasize to the reader the artificiality of the beverage in question. It also helps to express the contrast in the writer's attitude toward being forced to drink kauphy and being able to get a genuine cup of coffee.

In summary, it may be said that Lanier made frequent use of Eye Dialect in five of his seven dialect poems, and he also used it freely in Tiger Lilies. On most occasions Eye Dialect is mixed in with Sub-standard Dialect and Regional Dialect in his representation of the speech of mountaineers, crackers, and Negroes. There are a number of cases, however, such as those mentioned above in connection with "perfect rimes," and those connected with cum used for emphasis and kauphy used to show lack of genuineness, in which Lanier uses Eye Dialect cleverly to obtain effects that would be difficult or impossible to obtain without it.

Some critics and experts on literary dialects have objected to the use of Eye Dialect as misleading. Sumner Ives has written, "To the extent that an author relies on this purely visual dialect, he can be said to be deliberately overstating the ignorance or illiteracy of his characters."[7] Ives feels that a substantial use of Eye Dialect reflects on the craftsmanship of the writer. After all, it would appear that the writer is either unable to depict actual speech peculiarities or else he simply is taking a path involving less effort, namely the use of Eye Dialect. However, others have viewed the use of Eye Dialect in a different light.

Paul H. Bowdre, Jr.

Krapp has said, "It may be safely put down as a general rule that the more faithful a dialect is to folklore, the more completely it represents the actual speech of a group of people, the less effective it will be from a literary point of view."[8] The purpose of a literary dialect, after all, is not to arouse wonder at the author's ability as a student of speech, but to secure sympathetic attention for his characters. From this point of view, Sidney Lanier deserves commendation for his subtle use of Eye Dialect in achieving some unusual literary affects.

NOTES

*Read at the SAMLA-ADS Meeting, Greenville, South Carolina, November 1964.

[1] George Philip Krapp, The English Language in America (New York: Frederick Ungar Publishing Co., 1960), I, 228.

[2] Raven I. McDavid, Jr., "American English Dialects"in The Structure of American English by W. Nelson Francis (New York: The Ronald Press Co., 1958), p. 541.

[3] H. A. Gleason, Jr., An Introduction to Descriptive Linguistics, rev. ed. (New York: Holt, Rinehart and Winston, 1961), p. 406.

[4] The Centennial Edition of the Works of Sidney Lanier, ed. Charles R. Anderson et.al. (10 vols.: Baltimore: The Johns Hopkins Press, 1945), I, xlix.

[5] Ibid., V, 107.

[6] Ibid., p. 149.

[7] Sumner Ives, "A Theory of Literary Dialect," Tulane Studies in English, Vol. II, (1950), p. 147.

[8] George Philip Krapp, "The Psychology of Dialect Writing," The Bookman, 63 (Dec. 1926), 523.

SOME REMARKS ON THE LOGIC OF GRAPHEME MANIPULATION IN DIALECT WRITING*

C. William Foster

With few exceptions, comment on literary dialect has tended to concentrate on the difficulty presented the reader by authors who use dialect
respellings extensively in their works. Scholarly work in the last
decade has concentrated more on the relative accuracy of individual
authors in recording dialect than on the possibility of an underlying
system of any sort. It has been established, for example, that Joel
Chandler Harris put into the mouth of Uncle Remus a dialect limited to
the general area around Atlanta, which provides the setting for the
Uncle Remus tales, and similar limits have been established for the
dialect of Lowell's Hosea Biglow in New England and Charles W. Chesnutt's
Uncle Julius in North Carolina.[1] Analyses of the spelling manipulation
used by such writers as Harris and Lowell, along with those used by
lesser writers such as Chesnutt, T. N. Page, Mary Murfree, Percy Mackaye,
and Paul L. Dunbar seem to indicate that while use of the apostrophe and
use of substitution of words homophonous with dialect pronunciations
are techniques used in the works of most writers, the most common technique employed is the manipulation of graphemes. This manipulation,
furthermore, is apparently based on orderly sets and sub-sets of phoneme-
grapheme correspondences established by words of a high frequency of
occurrence in English.
   In the work of most dialect writers who are considered to be accurate
in their representations, the technique used least is that of word
substitution. Non-significant substitutions, such as <u>sez</u> for <u>says</u> or
<u>deer</u> for <u>dear</u> are generally employed more frequently by writers of "eye-
dialect," who rely for a good part of the humor of their writings on the
absurd spellings and malapropisms of their characters. The use of such
spellings is usually considered out of place in authentic dialect fiction
in that it manipulates graphemes for no reason other than what such
spellings may imply about the social status or the education of the
dialect character. But a certain amount of eye-dialect is to be found
in the work of all dialect writers; the conscientious recorder of dialect
in fiction uses word substitution, furthermore, as a means by which to
elicit pronunciations when manipulation of graphemes would be awkward or
bewildering. Such substitutions may be seen in the following examples,
taken from the works of Paul L. Dunbar, G. W. Harris, J. C. Harris, and
C. W. Chesnutt: <u>suckumstance</u> (circumstance); <u>cheer</u> (chair); <u>shut</u>
(shirt); <u>cuddle</u> (curdle); <u>lack</u> (like); and <u>rudder</u> (rather). Such substitution seems most often to be used to indicate loss of preconsonantal
/r/ when respelling or use of the apostrophe might prove unwieldy or
confusing. Although perhaps the least reputable of the devices discussed
here, these homophonous substitutions are significant, and cannot therefore be classified as eye-dialect.

A second manipulation which is based on a logical extension of the orthographic system is the dialect writer's use of the apostrophe. In all works consulted, the apostrophe is used freely and, in most cases, clearly as a grapheme indicating certain morphophonemic circumstances not normally reproduced in the writing system. It is used commonly by Chesnutt and other writers of Negro dialect to indicate "r-loss" pronunciations when the spelling cues might prove misleading, as in sta'ted (started, /stæ:t≠d/). Most dialect writers use the apostrophe freely in its common function--indicating omission of a sound by omitting a letter; but they often use the mark where word-substitution would give the desired sound, but would obfuscate the meaning. For example, where Artemus Ward or Petroleum Nasby might use witch to indicate an unaspirated pronunciation of which, more conscientious recorders of dialect would use w'ich. Such use of the apostrophe enables the writer to stay close to the conventional spelling while indicating, at the same time, dialectal pronunciation.

It must be obvious to anyone who is at all familiar with literary dialects that these techniques produce only a small part of the corpus of a literary dialect. By far the most productive technique is that of respelling, or grapheme manipulation. The author who undertakes to represent accurately the dialect of his characters must rely on the common orthographic background he shares with his readers. Since the writer is faced with the task of imparting phonetic information without recourse to a specialized phonetic alphabet, he must manipulate graphemes within the conventional spelling system, using spelling patterns which are associated with certain phonemes in the experience of his readers. His manipulation, moreover, must be based on grapheme combinations which, while they may be quite different from those normally used in representing the words in conventional spelling, should elicit the proper phonemic response on the part of the reader, yet remain recognizable. The orthographic frame should be such that visual recognition be preserved whenever possible. Since he is relying on the orthographical background shared by all literate speakers of English (albeit filtered through his own dialect), the author will substitute graphemes or combinations of graphemes from common words containing the syllabic phoneme he wishes to elicit in his representation. For example, when he wishes to indicate the /i/ phoneme in a character's pronunciation of itch, he respells the word, using the ⟨ee⟩ grapheme,[2] which represents /i/ in the conventional spelling of keep, sleep, teeth, tree, and knee, spelling the word ⟨eetch⟩ in his character's speech. In this instance, only the initial grapheme is changed, leaving the remainder of the word as conventionally spelled in order to facilitate recognition by the reader. Substituting ⟨each⟩ would have elicited the desired pronunciation, but would tend to hinder or confuse the reader.

Nelson Francis has commented at length on the fact that, although basically an alphabetic writing system, American English orthography is handicapped by having only twenty-six single graphemes for the representation of approximately thirty-six segmental phonemes; there is, moreover, no single one-to-one correlation in the system.[3]

Later studies, directed at spelling and reading problems in school children have, however, asserted that American English is phonemically-based, and both Paul Hanna and C. C. Fries asserted that American English writers and readers learn implicitly to assign appropriate graphemes to the phonemes of spoken words.[4] The approach to teaching

C. William Foster

of reading known as "phonics" keys the reader to respond to the "office"
of certain letters, and the success of this technique in elementary
reading instruction implies a correlation system of phonemes and graphemes
at some level of the language.

The assertions of Fries and the findings of the Hanna-Hanna-Hodges-
Rudorf study indicate that the writer operates in a system, the fluidity
of which allows him to manipulate graphemes to indicate dialectal pronunciation, basing his manipulation on the reader's recognition response
as well as on his ability for analogical extension. This manipulation
is possible because a large part of learning to read involves learning
to respond to certain conventional spelling patterns. Just as the habits
of pronunciation that a child develops in learning his native language
are not habits of hearing the separate sounds as isolatable items, so
the habits of reading alphabetic writing are not habits of responding
to the individual letters as representative of isolatable phones. As a
reader becomes more proficient, the "phonic" system becomes less
suitable, but the extent of correspondence between phones and graphs
provides him with a basis for what Fries calls a high-speed recognition
response.[5] This response, based on word patterns already known to the
reader, enables him to respond to certain spellings with certain sounds,
although the degree of exactness in words of infrequent occurrence may
vary. The conscientious writer of dialect, in seeking to represent
variations from "Standard" English, uses this system as a means by which
to trigger phonemic responses in the reader. He is, in effect, extending
the correspondence system, in that he is using it to form graphemic
combinations not unlike the nonsense words used to elicit spelling
patterns in Fries' study.

Another consideration springs from what might be called the artistic
burden of the dialect writer. If an author is truly concerned about the
accuracy of his representation of dialect, he must face the problem
involved in eliciting the responses necessary for a faithful representation while avoiding ambiguity or misreading. In his attempts to
respell for pronunciation while maintaining some graphic similarity to
the original printed word, the writer may have to use various graphemes
or grapheme clusters to represent the same sound on different occasions.
Ives, for example, found this to be Harris's practice in the Uncle Remus
dialect.[6] With the exception of the devilish orthographic r, dialect
writers are, as a rule, understandable, and this fact seems to indicate
that, however complicated and arbitrary the English graphic system may
be from the writer's point of view, it is relatively systematic from
the viewpoint of the reader, thus enabling writers to represent dialectal
pronunciations through spelling patterns associated, in their minds at
least, with phonemes occurring in the dialect under observation. Ideally,
the writer shares a common ground of pronunciation with the projected
reader, and he respells on the basis of the phoneme-grapheme correspondences in words common to both. In the dialect spelling Aidge for Edge,
for example, the reader usually responds with the /e/ phoneme normally
represented by the ⟨AI⟩ spelling, although this grapheme cluster may
occur in relation to other phonemes, as in aisle. Obviously, frequency
of occurrence is a primary consideration in the interpretation of
phoneme-grapheme correspondence.

In the illustrative table of phoneme-grapheme correlation I have used
four word-lists as bases for conclusions about frequency of occurrence
of phonemes and graphemes. The second, third, and fourth columns are

from one source, although each occurs as a separate word-list in that
source. The source is The Teacher's Word Book of 30,000 Words, compiled
by E. L. Thorndike and Irving Lorge.[7] I based my decision to use this
work for three of the four lists used on Fries' statement:

Thorndike's list has been almost universally considered as
the ultimate in the matter of word counting. Nearly every
subsequent study has used it as a basis for comparison and
as a model for the technique....The vast majority of
critics have praised it as the most valuable and reliable
list.[8]

Thorndike's word count was taken from almost three hundred sources,
including selections from major English and American authors. In addition
Thorndike consulted several newspapers, text-books, and magazines. From
the 30,000 words listed he drew his bases for establishing what he called
the first and the second five hundreds. The first five hundred list
contains the five hundred commonest words, and the second list the five
hundred next commonest. The Lorge magazine count included nearly a
million words from twelve issues each of the five major American magazines
spread evenly over an eleven-year period.

The most recent major study is Phoneme-Grapheme Correspondences As
Cues to Spelling Improvement, by Paul Hanna, Jean Hanna, Richard Hodges,
and Edwin Rudorf, Jr., (1966). The purpose of their study, however, was
to determine the extent of correlation between phonemes and graphemes in
as wide a sampling of American English as possible, and frequency of
occurrence was considered, if at all, only of secondary importance. This
study, because of its breadth and, in my opinion, because of the questionable validity of the computer responses in some instances, shows
considerable variation at some points from the percentages established
by the other, earlier studies. The significance of the study here is
that it shows, in its variance with the other lists, the systems of
correlation in words of higher frequency of occurrence.

Tabulation of spellings in the word-lists indicates that there is a
considerable correspondence between phonemes and graphemes in English,
and that even the so-called "irregular" spellings are not random, but
fall into subsets which are consistent within themselves. This correspondence, especially within the subsets, provides the basis for literary
dialect respelling. (See Table 1.)

Suppose one wishes to indicate a dialect pronunciation of edge as /edʒ/:
one sees that the most common grapheme representing this phoneme (/e/) is
the discontinuous ⟨A-E⟩ grapheme. The ⟨A-E⟩ spelling would seem to be,
then, the most likely choice, as indeed it is, in such dialect respellings
as rale (real), skace and skacely (scarce and scarcely), and caze (because
But the words where /e/ is substituted for /ɛ/, such as leg, egg, fresh,
and edge, the use of the ⟨A-E⟩ grapheme would be either misleading or
confusing: lage* would seem to indicate a pronunciation of /ledʒ/ by
analogy with age or rage; agge* and frashe*, where ⟨a⟩ is followed by
two consonants or by a double consonant, would suggest /æ/, and there
is little possibility of analogy; adge*, by analogy with badge or
similar words, would seem to indicate an /æ/ pronunciation. The most
likely second choice would be the simple ⟨A⟩ spelling, but this would
produce lag, agg, and frash, all misleading. The third subset, using
the complex ⟨AI⟩ grapheme, suggests the /e/ pronunciation most satisfactorily in this instance, providing a basis for analogical extension
from aid. This example also illustrates the practice, common among

PHONEME-GRAPHEME CORRELATION

Grapheme	Hanna, et al.	First 500	Second 500	Lorge	Average*
		/i/**			
EE	09.81%	39.39%	37.14%	31.70%	36.07%
EA	09.65	24.24	45.71	26.82	32.25
E	69.54	21.21	-----	19.51	20.36
		/I/			
I	68.40	76.47	84.37	83.77	81.53
Y	23.04	01.96	-----	01.43	01.69
		/e/			
A	44.57	43.33	25.53	35.00	34.61
A-E	35.14	50.00	34.04	47.50	43.18
AI	09.25	03.33	34.68	15.00	17.67
		/ɛ/			
E	90.94	75.00	70.42	79.41	74.94
EA	03.81	05.35	22.53	04.41	10.76
		/æ/			
A	96.58	94.23	100.00	98.00	97.41
		/ɑ/			
O	93.74	61.90	75.00	71.52	69.17
A	04.81	38.09	20.00	28.47	28.85
		/ɔ/***			
A	89.31	90.90	76.92	94.11	87.17
		/ɔ/			
O	40.67	46.34	64.00	21.42	43.92
A	21.51	39.02	16.00	64.28	39.76
AU	19.03	04.71	08.00	14.28	08.99
		/ʌ/			
U	85.95	34.69	57.89	38.18	43.58
O	07.94	42.85	10.52	32.72	28.69
O-E	01.84	02.04	10.52	12.72	08.42
		/o/			
O	72.51	70.00	63.33	66.66	66.66
O-E	14.30	23.33	20.00	30.00	24.44
OA	04.87	03.33	10.00	-----	06.66
		/u/			
U	54.34	18.18	50.00	11.11	26.43
OO	30.97	54.54	50.00	44.44	49.66
OU	-----	27.27	-----	38.88	33.07
		/u/			
OO	38.18	33.33	20.00	25.00	26.11
U	20.52	-----	13.33	-----	13.33
O	08.16	20.00	-----	25.00	27.50
U-E	07.50	06.66	13.33	08.33	09.44
OU	06.40	13.33	06.66	20.83	13.60
UE	03.53	06.66	-----	-----	06.66

Grapheme	Hanna, et al.	First 500	Second 500	Lorge	Average*
		/aɪ/			
I-E	37.44%	47.22%	55.88%	39.13%	47.41%
I	37.38	33.33	26.47	36.95	32.25
Y	14.23	10.81	08.82	15.21	11.61
		/au/			
OU	55.91	65.29	77.77	56.25	66.43
OW	29.31	34.31	22.22	43.75	33.42
		/ɔɪ/			
OI	61.74	66.66	60.00	75.00	67.22
OY	32.21	33.33	40.00	25.00	32.77
		/ɜ/			
E	39.77	26.66	33.33	27.77	29.25
U	25.79	13.33	40.00	16.88	23.40
I	13.21	01.20	13.33	16.88	10.13

*Average excludes the Hannas-Hodges-Rudorf study.
**International Phonetic Alphabet
***A phoneme (/ɑ/ before /r/) in dialects of "r-less" speakers. Low, back unrounded phoneme which is distinctive in pot and part as pronounced by an "r-less" speaker.

Table 1.

writers of dialect, of using different graphemes for the same sound when circumstances warrant, thus insuring as much clarity as possible. Further examples, although numerous and handy, are omitted, since they merely reiterate the information given in the correlation chart.

I do not mean to suggest that such a laborious mental drill is performed consciously by writers of dialect or by their readers. I do, however, maintain that whatever else may be said about the dialect writing which enjoyed such vogue in the late nineteenth and early twentieth centuries in America, there is considerable evidence that the dialect respellings of the authors whose aim was the accurate recording of particular dialects are based on logical extensions of the phoneme-grapheme correspondence in the more common words of American English, and on the recognition response which this correspondence makes possible.

NOTES

*Read at the SAMLA-ADS Meeting, Atlanta, Georgia, November 1969.

[1]Sumner Ives, "The Negro Dialect of the Uncle Remus Stories," Dissertation University of Texas 1951; James W. Downer, "The Dialect of the Biglow Papers," Dissertation University of Michigan 1958; C. William Foster, "The Representation of Negro Dialect in Charles W. Chesnutt's The Conjure Woman," Dissertation University of Alabama 1968.

[2]Graphemes, which are equivalent, orthographically, to phonemes, are the smallest units of writing or printing that distinguish one meaning from another. Graphemes are marked with $\langle\rangle$ in this study.

[3]W. Nelson Francis, The Structure of American English (New York: Ronald Press, 1958), pp. 447ff.

[4]Paul Hanna, Jean Hanna, Richard Hodges, and Edwin Rudorf, Jr., Phoneme-Grapheme Correspondences as Cues to Spelling Improvement (Washington, D.C.: Government Printing Office, 1966); and C. C. Fries, Linguistics and Reading (New York: Holt, Rinehart and Winston, 1962).

[5]Fries, Linguistics, p. 170.

[6]Sumner Ives, "The Phonology of the Uncle Remus Stories,"Publication of the American Dialect Society, 22 (November, 1954), p. 7.

[7]E. L. Thorndike and Irving Lorge, The Teacher's Word Book of 30,000 Words (New York: Teachers College, 1944).

[8]C. C. Fries, English Word Lists (Washington, D.C.: American Council on Education, 1940), p. 23.

DIALECT AND DICTION IN THE NOVEL*

Richard Gunter

It may seem that we readers look on passively while the novelist creates
characters before our eyes, but in fact we always take a hand in the creation. Sometimes, to be sure, the author addresses us directly, telling
us explicitly what we are to think about some character; but far more
often he merely shows the character living and being, and we make our
own deductions. The speech of a fictional character plays a crucial role
in these deductions. It works on our imagination even when we are
unaware of it. Thus dialect and diction in the novel merit the closest
study. That study leads us away from the novel out into the world of
everyday. We may then return to the novel with new understanding.[1]
    The events and characters of a novel bear a complex relationship to
the events and persons in the real world, and that relationship raises
anew many of the questions that philosophers have wrestled with for
centuries--questions about what we know and how we know it. A central
question is this: how is the novelist able to put speech in the mouth
of his creature in such a way that we readers respond as a community--
so that we all imagine that creature in much the same way? This paper
gives an answer that John Locke would approve. That is, we readers do
not construct fictional character out of a priori ideas, but out of our
experience with people and language in the everyday world. Our minds
are filled with memories of people and the way they talk, so that a
particular piece of language is associated in our memories with particular
traits of character in people we have known and heard. The novelist
assembles bits and pieces of language in a new constellation--a new
idiolect that he supplies to his creature. That idiolect summons up in
the reader's imagination a new configuration of traits--a new fictional
character. In short, both the character and his speech are rearrange-
ments of old impressions and memories. We have a community of response
to a fictional character because we share with the author, and with
each other, a community of experience with people and their language.
Thus the author can draw up a set of directions for imagining a creature
and, following those directions, we readers imagine him.
    This line of thought argues that the novel reflects the world in a
complicated way. It moves us to focus our conscious attention upon
ourselves and our fellows as we speak and act together in everyday
affairs. That attention to speech in the world reveals many of the
reasons for our reactions to speech and character in fiction. Thus it is
that we may turn again from the world to the novel with sharpened perceptions of the author's devices for manipulating our sympathies. Such
at least is the argument of this paper. In the following we shall see
some notions about life and language as they are exemplified by the

261

characters in Robert Penn Warren's novel <u>All</u> <u>the</u> <u>King's</u> <u>Men</u>. There will be some going back and forth from speech in the novel to speech in the world, for the point is to demonstrate the connection between the two. But first it is necessary to explain the notion <u>character</u> as it is used here.[2]

Every speaker of English is a character in two senses. First he has a <u>social identity</u> in that he comes from a particular region and is of a particular age, sex and condition. Thus someone may have this social identity: middle-aged man from Boston, protestant Christian, husband, father, banker and the like. Or someone may have this identity: young woman from Dubuque, unmarried, high school educated, secretary and the like. Social identity is the definition of a human as a cluster of roles and statuses.

The second part of character is <u>personality</u>, that is, the inner self with its tendencies and motives that are expressed in moods and acts. Personality cannot always be sharply distinguished from social identity, for some traits cannot be clearly assigned to the one side of character or the other. For example, if someone likes to read <u>True</u> <u>Detective</u> rather than <u>House</u> <u>Beautiful</u>, it is difficult to say whether this taste is an expression of the inner person or the other. Marxists might even suggest that personality derives entirely from social identity, but there is clearly a range of personality within each identity. Of all the unmarried secretaries in Dubuque who graduated from high school, some will be patient and some edgy; some will be dull and some bright. It seems wise, therefore, to keep these two sides of character distinct.

A person's speech tells us much about his character in both senses. It announces his part in the human comedy and it foretells what kind of player he will be--artful, malicious, stolid or whimsical. When someone speaks, he tells us who he is and what he is like. Sometimes a single sentence can carry a wealth of insight into the character of a speaker. Below are three short utterances. The reader will find that he can make several deductions about the speaker of each:
1) This china is lovely--oh, but so fragile-looking.
2) You took my cracker. Give it back.
3) Hell, I seen him run out the back door.
Thus the diversity of English mirrors the diversity of those who speak it.

In part it is the content of speech that reveals character. If someone is always talking about business conditions, for example, we can guess a great deal about him. Or if someone is always talking about housekeeping and babies and laundry, we can tell a lot about that speaker. But speakers also stand revealed by the form in which they talk about these topics, that is, by their pronunciation, vocabulary and grammar.

Everyone knows these facts, of course, at least in some unexamined way, but perhaps no one yet realizes their full importance. Dialect and diction in a country like the United States are the fundamental index to those we meet--a rich set of clues to character in all its aspects. Thus as we go our daily rounds, the speech of others acts as a sort of guide for us. The speech of a friend tells us his mood, tells us which of his roles he is playing at the moment. The speech of the stranger tells us--more surely than anything else--whether he is a candidate for our circle, and whether we might learn to like and trust him. In life we discover the characters of people through their speech; in novels we do much the same thing in imagination.

Richard Gunter

What we are constantly trying to do, both in life and in novel-reading, is to make sense of people, and the sense we make often takes the form of the stereotype. A new character is a challenge to be recognized as a type. There seem to be two processes that we go through in trying to decide who someone is.

First there is integration. We try to fit the parts of someone together in a recognizable way. We try to see his various social statuses as coherent, and try to fit together the parts of his personality so that they make a plausible bundle. Going back to our banker for a moment, suppose that we are just becoming acquainted with him, and that we have only two clues--his speech and his profession as a banker. We begin to build a hypothesis about him. Then if we discover that he is an Episcopalian, we may easily begin to see all three clues as consonant. They all tend to reinforce each other and to tighten the integration.

Second, there is the oddity that may be called interpretation. Suppose, for illustration, that our banker turns out to be a poker player. It costs us no great effort to fit this trait in with the others; indeed, once we have integrated this trait with the others, those others now begin to color the poker-playing. It is not, we see, a grubby scramble for money, but a good-natured and gentlemanly affair, though we may sense a sharp edge of competitiveness. We may regard this poker as a middle-aged man's version of ivy-league football--at bottom a modern-day form of knightly jousting. Thus a given trait in the integrated bundle takes on color from the others.

We can see the extent to which the poker is colored by the rest of our banker's identity if we now imagine that it is not a banker who likes poker but a truck driver. Suddenly the game, the reasons for it, the spirit of the play--all change subtly in our imagination. We are interpreting.

With a few traits of character as clues, we may arrive at a first hypothesis about a person, and may interpret as necessary to integrate all the traits. But it may happen that we then get further clues that cause us to abandon that first hypothesis and to adopt a second. We then interpret evidence to fit the second hypothesis. Suppose, for instance, that someone is speaking to a gathering and he says:

Boys, we just ain't got no more money.
If we have no other information about the speaker, we might conclude that he is ill-educated, that his status is low, and that he speaks his mind forthrightly on public occasions. But now suppose we learn that the speaker is a university president, speaking to his assembled deans. We will certainly reinterpret his speech--as a playful jest rather than his normal manner. We will certainly reinterpret his status. Perhaps we will also reinterpret the notion that he speaks his mind forthrightly on public occasions. Our tendency is to recognize stock characters, and we are ready to bend evidence to achieve a stereotype. If the evidence is overwhelming against a first hypothesis, we adopt a second and then reinterpret the evidence to fit.

The novelist makes use of these tendencies in two ways. First, he lets the reader have his head, so to speak, on occasions when it suits his purpose to let the reader stereotype a minor, unimportant character; but second, the novelist is constantly thwarting this tendency in the reader when his purpose is to give depth, unpredictability and interest to a major character.

263

Richard Gunter

Warren uses the stereotyping technique on many occasions in <u>All the King's Men</u>. He simply gives one or two clues to a minor character, lets him say a few lines, and then trusts the reader to supply the rest. This is Warren's technique in one scene in which Willie Stark, the governor who has risen from the backwoods to the statehouse, is paying a visit to a small town in his native hills. Willie goes to the local drugstore for a coke. He is seen and recognized. A crowd of admirers quickly gathers. In this crowd is Malachiah, with whom Willie plays the politician. Malachiah is introduced as follows:

Then the Boss spied a fellow at the far end of the soda fountain, a tall, gaunt-shanked, malarial, leather-faced side of jerked venison, wearing jean pants and a brace of mustaches hanging off the kind of face you see in photographs of General Forrest's cavalrymen, and the Boss started toward him and put out his hand.

This conversation follows:

"How you making it, Malachiah?" the Boss asked.

The adam's apple worked a couple of times, and the Boss shook the hand which was hanging out there in the air as if it didn't belong to anybody, and Old Leather-Face said, "We's grabblen."

"How's your boy?" the Boss asked.

"Ain't doen so good," Old Leather-Face allowed.

"Sick?"

"Naw," Old Leather-Face allowed, "jail."

"My God," the Boss said, "what they doing round here, putting good boys in jail?"

"He's a good boy," Old Leather-Face allowed. "Hit wuz a fahr fight, but he had a leetle bad luck."

"Huh?"

"Hit wuz fahr and squahr, but he had a leetle bad luck. He stobbed the feller and he died."

This scene occurs early in the book, and serves to set up in the reader mind a stereotyped example of the backwoods voters, Willie's constituents who have no specific major roles in the novel, but wait in the background like a great, unseen force. The reader now has Malachiah in mind to stand for that force.

This stereotype is erected with the greatest economy. We are given a swift description of Malachiah; we are given his name, with its connotations of an older, rustic America; and we are given nine short lines of his speech. But these clues are enough to allow the reader to construct a social identity for Malachiah, and that identity connotes a stock personality. It is not a very deep or demanding personality, but that is the whole point of this technique. The author does not want to interrupt the story by turning a wooden figure into a real person who would demand the reader's thought and attention. Malachiah is a pure social identity; his personality is completely submerged in that identity. That is what a stereotype is.

But when a more complex purpose is to be served, we may say that interpretation is intertwined with stereotyping. When something does not fit a conception, the reader has a strong tendency to bend that something so that it will fit. This effect is of thoroughgoing inportance in novels. For example, once it has been established that <u>All the King's Men</u> has a southernsetting, Warren does not need to take great pains to make the language obviously southern. It will <u>sound</u> southern to the reader, who now expects it to do so. (The not-so-southern speech of

264

Richard Gunter

Sadie Burke is an important exception to this generalization, but this problem must be passed over in such a short article.)

Nor does the author need to respell words constantly to indicate some character's pronunciation. The reader can be counted on to hear the speech in the intended way once he is given clues about what he is supposed to be hearing. In an earlier day authors attempted a thorough-going naturalism in the rendition of speech, as Crane did in Maggie. Such writing bristled with editorial devices intended to suggest the natural flow of ordinary talk, but usually they had quite the opposite effect. The devices demanded so much attention for themselves that they suggested heaviness and strain, which defeated their purpose and served merely to annoy the reader. Such devices were given up as tedious, uneconomical, and indeed unnecessary; for actually all the author need do is perform what might be called sample naturalism. That is, he renders a few words naturalistically, and those samples set up in the reader the expectations that cause him to perceive the rest of the speech in the intended way. For instance, in the Malachiah scene Willie is being his most folksy self, and the reader hears his speech as folksy—once he is led to expect it to sound that way. This sentence may illustrate the point:

"My God," the Boss said, "what they doing round here, putting good boys in jail?"

In this sentence the participles doing and putting are spelled in the normal way, with the -ing ending. But the reader can be counted on to hear these words with -in' rather than -ing. Warren does not need to clutter up the page with apostrophes. He can count on the reader to interpret.

So much for stereotyping. We may now turn to the novelist's main task—the creation of depth in character. There are several ways to accomplish this task through the use of dialect and diction.

One technique is that of mixed diction. The character is made to speak two distinct kinds of English. This mixture, if the stage has been properly set for it, does not sound like an ignorant person trying—and failing—to speak a kind of language that is more elevated than his normal kind; rather it suggests that he is master of both kinds of speech. By using mixed speech he shows that he is free of those social tyrannies that make some people anxious about the correctness of what they say. Mixed diction connotes irony, linguistic ability and self-confidence. We often sense these overtones when Willie speaks. Here is a speech that Willie makes when he has been threatening to dig up some dirt on his political opponents:

"Dirt's a funny thing," the Boss said. "Come to think of it, there ain't a thing but dirt on this green God's globe except what's under water, and that's dirt too. It's dirt makes the grass grow. A diamond ain't a thing in the world but a piece of dirt that got awful hot. And God-a-Mighty picked up a handful of dirt and blew on it and made you and me and George Washington and mankind blessed in faculty and apprehension. It all depends on what you do with the dirt. That right?"

On another occasion, when Willie is talking about political hacks, he singles out the sycophant Tiny Duffy with the following:

"It ain't any secret that my old schoolmate Alex was a heel. And it ain't any secret that Tiny Duffy is as sebaceous a fat-ass as ever made the spring groan in a swivel chair."

265

Willie, one of the most interesting linguistic creations in American literature, is constantly talking this way. His native dialect is redneck, but he has apparently heard more bookish speech, or has encountered it in his studies, and has learned to use it for his own purposes. He can switch with ease from redneck to bookish, or mix them. Thus his lightest thoughts may be expressed in fine-wrought classical language, but his profoundest thoughts may come out cloaked in the grammar and vocabulary of the hill-billy. And in a given sentence there may be a mixture of Milton and the backwoods. No part of Willie's speech is predictable from any other part. Our tendencies to integrate and interpret are constantly thwarted. The reader associates many things with rednecks, and thus he has expectations about how Willie will behave. Some of these expectations are, in fact, confirmed in Willie's actions and manner, but he refuses to be submerged in his social identity. His personality keeps breaking through and asserting its independence. Willie gains in depth and power through his mixed diction.

Another way to portray personality, and a generally interesting device in the novel, is the dialect encounter. This term means the meeting of two persons as that meeting is considered in its purely linguistic aspects. Extremely interesting things happen in such encounters--in life and in the novel.

There is, for example, linguistic chameleonism. This is a conscious attempt to tailor one's speech so that it meets and blends with the level of speech of one's interlocutor. Speech can be demoted or promoted; we can condescend or we can put on linguistic airs.

We in the academic community have a limited, middle-class view of this matter. We know, of course, when we ourselves are tailoring our own speech--when we are talking up or down--and we can sometimes tell when others are talking up or down to us. Our linguistic inferiors betray themselves when they commit the hyperurbanism--a naive expression that the folk manufacture when they are trying to copy elevated speech. An example comes from the writer's own experience with a family in Alabama. The mother of this family had social ambitions. Since the family had recently acquired money, she was trying to refurbish their speech to suit their new style of life. Formerly she had pronounced the present participle as in this series: fishin', talkin', runnin', huntin'. But with her new riches she now made a great point of saying fishing, talking, running and hunting. But she extended this analogical formula too far and made hyperurbanisms, as in the following:

This summer we are going to take the childring to the mountings.

Such naive speech forms are common in chameleonism. Indeed, there may be other phenomena of the sort--things that we do not discuss, since we have no names for them and perhaps not even any clear awareness of them. For example, it may be that when we attempt to talk down to others we commit the hyporusticism, though we are unable to supply examples, being unaware of what we have done. Or perhaps our linguistic betters make hyporusticisms when they are condescending to us, though we do not know enough about upper-class speech to detect them.

Willie Stark never seems to fall into these traps, though he plays the chameleon constantly. When he is talking to his constituents, he speaks their language, for he understands the political value of doing so. When he does use polished or bookish language in his speeches to the back-country, it oddly has only the effect of inviting his audience to believe that they, too, could talk that way if they chose. Willie's speech always seems right.

But chameleonism does not always take place in conversation, neither in the real world nor in the fictional. One can distinguish at least three sorts of encounter in which there is no apparent chameleonism. All three give insight into character.

In the first case the interlocutors simply discover that they are of about the same social station and of about the same linguistic personality, that is, they have about the same degree of linguistic inventiveness and playfulness. Or to state the matter the other way round, they have about the same degree of linguistic stolidity. In these cases nothing seems to happen to speech; but of course something important happens to the interlocutors--they make a discovery about each other, and that discovery may lead to ripening familiarity, increased volubility and the like.

In the second case, there may be an interlocutor who just does not commit chameleonism, for that person has only one linguistic gear. In the novel before us, Anne Stanton is such a character. She is pictured as an attractive, unaffected young woman. And her speech never changes from level to level. The effect is that she seems even more sincere. Warren has already led us to think of her as guileless, and her unvarying style of speech becomes a part of that guilelessness.

In the third case, we see an effect of the greatest dramatic importance. It may be called dialect loyalty. The speaker refuses to change his speech to meet that of his interlocutor--and may do so defiantly. Anne Stanton, we suppose, does not practice chameleonism because she feels no impulse to do so--it never occurs to her. But dialect loyalty involves will and often hostility. We see this attitude in Willie Stark in an important scene at the house of Judge Irwin. The Judge is an aristocrat, and Willie shows his contempt for that status, and for the Judge, by refusing to brush up his language. Indeed, the reader senses that Willie deliberately puts on his most rustic manner to irritate the Judge. The effect is electric in that scene, which is already filled with tension.

We can, of course, see dialect loyalty at work in the world around us, for there are deep forces in American society that compel this loyalty. Our families and fellows are willing enough to have us rise in the world, but they require that we assure them ritually from time to time that we ourselves are unaware of having risen. One of the ways we can give this assurance is, for example, by speaking the old language of childhood and youth when we go home for Christmas. In the catalogue of American sins, the greatest sin is putting on linguistic airs.

An anthropologist of this writer's acquaintance once described his leave-taking from friends at Oxford University, where he had spent a year in special study. When he was about to depart, he heard himself saying "cheerio," and impulsively remarked that he had better forget that expression before he got home to Iowa. His English friends, puzzled, asked why. The anthropologist, in haste to depart, manufactured some explanation. He later mused that it would have taken him years to make the thing clear to the puzzled English. Probably every American can understand this anecdote instantly, but few perhaps could explain it readily, for the explanation lies deep in the character of this nation, deep in American loyalties.

Dialect loyalty becomes most passionate when it is infused with political or social tension. This turbulent century has given us many an example of the disaffected region and the disaffected group who make their case against national power in the language of their own people. We hear the Georgian, the Negro, the downeaster, the city boy from the wrong side of the tracks--hear them talk defiantly in the language of their own. It is as if they sense that any concession to the standard speech of the public forum would rob them of the purity of their cause. It would represent a surrender. The novelist knows these things. In a short dialogue he can suggest the powerful currents that flow beneath the surface of American linguistic manners.

While dialect loyalty suggests the conscious will of the speaker, there are other ways in which the novelist can break through social identity to reveal the inner person, and some of these ways do not suggest self-consciousness at all. One such way is to show the character speaking under stress. Warren tells us something about Anne Stanton in this way. When she speaks out of deep earnestness, her speech comes in short little phrases, often elliptical ones. Each phrase takes up where the last ended, or repeats some part of that last. The effect is somewhat like the song of the robin--broken, repetitive, weakly musical and a little sad:

"I mean it. He's got to. To save himself." She grabbed my arm again. "For himself. As much as for everybody else. For himself."

Again in the same scene:

"Stop it," she ordered. "Stop it, and tell me. You are trying not to tell me. You are talking so you won't tell me. Now, tell me."

In the same way Warren reveals a world about Sugar Boy, Willie's devoted chauffeur. Throughout the book Sugar Boy stutters. He is always saying something about some "b-b-b-bas-tud." His impediment is so severe that he is unable to make a single sentence without difficulty--until one scene near the end of the book.

Sugar Boy had worshipped Willie. Now Willie has been murdered by Adam Stanton. In the scene in question Jack Burden toys with Sugar Boy, implying that there is an accomplice to the murder, who is still hiding behind the scenes. Jack implies that he knows that person's identity. Sugar Boy is instantly at full attention:

"Suppose," I continued, "suppose I could tell you who--suppose I could prove it--what would you do?"

Suddenly his face wasn't twitching. It was smooth as a baby's and peaceful, but peaceful in the way that intensity can sometimes momentarily make a face look peaceful and pure.

"What would you do?" I demanded.

"I'd kill the son-of-a-bitch," he said. And he had not stuttered at all.

In that one sentence, remarkable only because of what it does not contain, Sugar Boy has his only chance to take on dimension. Much can be revealed by a nugget of speech when it is uttered under stress.

Such, then, are the uses of the technique for portraying character through dialect and diction. The author puts into the mouth of his creatures various sorts of language that tell the reader who the character is and what he is like. As we read along, we do what we do in everyday life: we seek to form a hypothesis about each character as his speech reveals his social identity and his personality. We try to integrate traits. In doing so we shape and bend the evidence to fit the hypothesis. We interpret. But if some piece of evidence refuses to fit, we may form a second hypothesis--then reinterpret the evidence to fit this second picture.

We stereotype minor characters when the author permits us simply to draw on our bank of stock types, though he may occasionally shock us into a brief glimpse of the inner person, as in the case of Sugar Boy. But in the case of major characters, the author very often checks our tendencies to stereotype. He does this by showing the linguistic virtuosity of those characters, as in mixed diction or in dialect encounters or in scenes when the characters speak out of anger, sorrow or fear. At a given momentthe novelist may be manipulating our sympathies in the most subtle way, and the effect may be clear to us, though we have no explicit notion of its sources.

To makes these sources explicit, there is nothing to do but study them. It is, in fact, an extremely stimulating task to read an American novel like Babbitt or The Great Gatsby with these questions in mind: 1) Exactly what is the source of the reader's information about the characters? 2) What part of that information is purely linguistic? 3) What, in the reader's experience in the real world, gives a particular bit of language special power?

Such an examination of dialect and diction in a novel leads from the novel to the world and back again. We return from that excursion with new respect for the novelist as a master observer; we return with a keener understanding of the way he works his will upon us; and we return with the knowledge that the reader collaborates with the writer to create the fictional world.

NOTES

*Read at the SAMLA-ADS Meeting, Jacksonville, Florida, November 1968.

[1]Although this paper is short, it is much indebted to others: first to my students, who have listened patiently as these notions have developed; second, to several members of the 1968 ADS-SAMLA, who heard an earlier version of the paper and gave encouragement; third, to the many books and papers from which I have received stimulation--stimulation whose exact source I fear I may have forgotten by now, though I do feel a conscious debt to these: Raven McDavid, "The Dialects of American English," in W. Nelson Francis, The Structure of American English, Ronald Press Co. (1959), and David Abercrombie, Studies in Phonetics and Linguistics (especially the essay entitled "R. P. and Local Accent"), Oxford University Press (1965); fourth, to John Russell, who read a late draft of the paper and made many valuable comments; and finally, to Phyllis Gunter, whose good influence is present here as in all my work. All remaining shortcomings are entirely my own.

[2]This writer began by supposing that his technical terms, here given in underlining, were original--at least in the exact sense intended. (Of course hyperurbanism, which has long been current in such discussions, and such words as character and personality, were known to be exceptions.) But it turns out that some of the others, which the

writer thought to be his own coinage, also have some currency in at least some related form or sense. For example, _social identity_ turns out to be quite current in some works on anthropology and sociology. It is thus not at all easy to find new terms in social linguistics that do not already have a history of usage in something like the sense intended. The lesson seems to be that thought about this branch of study is by no means as modern as some of us had supposed.

THE VOGUISH USES OF NON*

John Algeo

Jonathan Swift, in a letter to the Tatler in 1710, observed that "certain Words invented by some pretty Fellows...are now struggling for the Vogue, and others are in Possession of it. I have done my utmost for some Years past to stop the Progress of Mob and Banter; but have been plainly born down by Numbers, and betrayed by those who have promised to assist me."[1] Swift wanted to start an annual "Index Expurgatorius" to rid the language of voguish words, but the proposed Index, like the Academy he proposed two years later, came to nothing. Words have continued to come into, and pass out of, vogue along with hemlines, hair lengths, and folk heroes. Language, as George Campbell pointed out some time ago, "is purely a species of fashion,"[2] a way of behaving that followed the conventional usage of a time and place. A vogue in language, as in other kinds of fashion, is recognizable by what Webster's Third, that notorious purveyor of permissiveness, calls its "obvious popularity and wide acceptance" (s.v. fashion). What the Dean overlooked in his concern about linguistic fashion (though it is hardly surprising that he did so) is that the vogue is a kind of Darwinian jungle, testing the fitness of a linguistic species to survive. Mob and banter, in spite of Swift's disapproval, have endured; phizz and plenipo, two other objects of his spleen, have not. The struggle for survival of linguistic species in the jungle of fashion still goes on, and the Dean has spiritual descendants among those who write letters to the editor and among those who review dictionaries, as the teapot tempest over Webster's Third a few years ago amply demonstrated. Some of us, however, are content to observe the struggle with some dispassion and to get as much sweetness and light from it as we can.

Among the items that best exemplify the power of vogue in the struggle for survival is one of the most insignificant entries in the English lexicon, the prefix non. Throughout its development in English, it has shown the effects of voguish uses--from the earlier history of the morpheme through its present vogue uses to a recent mutation that has taken place in the species, a mutation that has resulted in the evolution of two new species. Or, to use the voguish jargon favored by linguists concerned with such matters, we may say that non has undergone morphemic split. But first to the earlier history.

The prefix first appears in English in the late fourteenth century, in the Anglo-French form noun. The earliest attestation of the OED is from Chaucer's Boece (3, pr. 5, line 19 of Robinson's edition). Dame Philosophy, in the course of explaining that power does not give happiness, says: "But yit, al be it so that the remes of mankynde strecchen broode, yit moot ther nede ben moche folk over whiche that

271

every kyng ne hath no lordschipe ne comaundement. And certes uppon thilke syde that power fayleth, which that maketh folk blisful, ryght on the same syde noun-power entreth undirnethe, that maketh hem wrecches." The semantic field in which the prefix appears--one of authority, power, and kingship--is indicative of the subsequent development of the morpheme, for its earliest use seems to have been in the law courts and the statute books.

From the fourteenth century there are recorded only a handful of lexical items with non. In addition to nonpower, there is noncertain, a noun with the meaning 'uncertainty' as in Chaucer's Complaint of Venus: "in nouncerteyn we languisshe." The adjective noncertain is much later and is an independent coinage. Three other fourteenth-century forms do not appear in Chaucer; they are nonage 'legal minority,' nonresidence 'the state of a clergyman who does not reside at his benefice,' and nonsuit 'failure to prosecute a case.' All three are from the jargon of the lawcourt.

Most of the new fifteenth- and sixteenth-century constructions with non were technical legal terms. Nonability, nonappearance, nonclaim, nonperformance, nontenure, nonuser are examples. The legal fondness for non is perhaps due in part to the extreme commonness of the adverb in law-Latin, especially in the titles of writs. The fashionable influence of law-Latin continued through the seventeenth and eighteenth centuries, as attested by most of the early dictionaries, and was mocked by Wycherley's "The Plain Dealer" in the person of the litigious Widow Blackacre, who is, by her own confession, "a Relict and Executrix of known plentiful Assets and Parts, who understand myself and the Law."

During the seventeenth and eighteenth centuries the prefix gained rapidly in popularity. The OED lists only about 65 formations with non from the fifteenth and sixteenth centuries combined; it has over 160 new forms from the seventeenth century alone, and about 75 others from the eighteenth. The marked increase in the use of non during the seventeenth century coincides with the general Latinizing tendency of the period. Non made its contribution to the age of the Inkhornism. For a morpheme like non, the OED's entries are unlikely to be complete, but the proportional representation is probably accurate. Between 1500 and 1700 the popularity of non increased more than sevenfold (the OED records 31 forms in use by 1500 and 229 forms in use by 1700). Early dictionaries, because they did not aim at listing all the words of the language, even deliberately excluding the most common, are poor guides to the frequency of a lexical item. But in this case, the dictionaries of the seventeenth and eighteenth centuries tell the same story. In 1623 Henry Cockeram listed 4 items with non; in 1730 Nathan Bailey listed 41; and in 1755 Samuel Johnson gave up the good fight to list all non forms by taking the sensible step of providing a separate entry for the prefix. It was clear to Johnson, as it should have been to other lexicographers before him, that non was freely combinable with abstract nouns of action or condition (Johnson's examples include nonregardance, nonconcurrence, nonadmission, nonpayment, nonattention).3

In addition to the legal use of the prefix, the seventeenth and eighteenth centuries extended it freely to institutions like the Church, the Army, and politics. Nonconformist, nonjuror, nonelect, noncommissioned, noncompounder, noneffective are examples. Noneffective is a good illustration of what has happened with several non forms. It first occurs in the mid eighteenth century in the meaning 'pertaining to a

John Algeo

soldier or sailor who is not fit for active service.' The general, analytical meaning 'not effective, producing no effect' is not found until the later nineteenth century and is probably a new formation, unrelated to the earlier military use of the word. During the seventeenth and eighteenth centuries the prefix begins to appear commonly in scientific terminology, a use that becomes thoroughly familiar in the nineteenth century. Nondescript, nonnatural, noncondensing are examples, and Joseph Priestley in his unjustly neglected Rudiments of English Grammar cites nonconductor and nonelectric. The prefix also occurs with greater frequency in nontechnical uses during the seventeenth and eighteenth centuries: nonmember, nonsense, nonchalant, nonessential, But it was not until the nineteenth and especially the twentieth centuries that the prefix came into its own, both in its freedom to combine with stems and in the frequency with which it does so.

The increased twentieth-century use of non is easy to demonstrate. Including obsolete forms, the OED lists some 500 derivatives with non in use before 1900. That list is admittedly incomplete, but it can be compared with the 3000 derivatives in Webster's Second, which is also incomplete. Statistics of this kind, however, are meaningless and unnecessary. Those who have ears to hear can hear. Nons are all about us, some semantically transparent, others not. Thus a nonlaugher is somebody who does not laugh, but a noncamper may be somebody who does not like Batman or Andy Warhol as well as someone who does not go on camping trips. The Hon. Nancy Mitford popularized non-U (the term, not the thing; Miss Mitford was committed to the proposition that if it's me, it's U). Almost every town in the United States has at least one nondenominational church where ecumenicism does not wait upon the piety of COCU (as the Consultation on Church Union is acronymously known). Cities have housing-problems and nonhousing-problems, that is, every other conceivable difficulty. The president has made nonpolitical trips to the orient, where he has met the leaders of obscure nations, like Thailand, and of nonobscure nations, like China. Nonlethal military equipment (trucks and transport planes) is used for nontraditional military projects (helping civilians). Our friendly banker will draw up a nonmarital trust, which is not intended to benefit nonrelatives. We make social progress through nonviolence, although after Stokely Carmichael became chairman of the Student Nonviolent Coordinating Committee, the word was sometimes set off by quotation marks.

Why has the prefix become so popular in our time? Several factors seem to have been at work. In the first place, it is apparent that non has filled a need. It may serve to define a class that has no common characteristic other than the exclusion of some group. Thus nonverbal communication includes every conceivable means of interaction other than articulated speech--writing, painting, whistling, gestures, semaphore, Morse code, Braille, and so forth. There simply is no other term to designate precisely that class. Nonschool situations include home, church, Y, and back alley. When nondraft cards are burned, they may be social security, credit, library, or identification cards.

In its most strictly privative use, non denotes 'lack of.' Thus, UN debates may be exercises in nonpower. Plans are laid to reduce the rat population to nonproblem levels. We accept war news with the same non-thought as the morning cup of coffee. Words with similar meaning for non are nonproliferation, nonrecognition, nontalent, and nonuse. When non prefixes a word in adjunct use, its sense may be 'other than.' Thus

John Algeo

nonbook materials are 'materials other than books' and nonfood reasons
are 'reasons other than food.'
  Non may also contrast with other negative prefixes in that it is
unemotionally privative, whereas un-, in-, and dis- often express contrariety and an unfavorable judgment. Thus a noninspired poem may still
be critically good, whereas an uninspired poem is not. The civil law
is nonreligious, rather than irreligious. A non-American activity is
not a subject of interest to a committee on un-American activities. A
Moslem is a non-Christian, but only a Christian can be un-Christian in
behavior. A nonrealistic novel is one whose goal is other than
realistic view of the world, but an unrealistic novel is likely to be one
that aims at, and fails to achieve realism. Other examples come readily
to mind: nonmoral/immoral, nonbeliever/unbeliever, nonobedient/disobedie
  The simple, privative non is sometimes useful to avoid potential
ambiguities. Inflammable was replaced by flammable because the initial
morpheme was, or seemed to be, ambiguous ('into' versus 'not'); consequen
the only unambiguous negation of flammable is nonflammable. As a racial
term, colored (which is out of vogue for reasons other than ambiguity
nowadays) can be interpreted either specifically as 'Negro' or generally
as 'not Caucasian'; nonwhite unambiguously has the latter sense. Nonlivi
matter is unambiguous, whereas dead matter may ambiguously suggest matter
that was once alive. In all such examples, non is useful because it hel
to denote a semantic content that otherwise has no representation in the
lexicon. Other uses of non, however, are quite different.
  Often the twentieth-century affinity for non seems to be due to kindnes
or delicacy. This is, non has become a prefix for forming euphemisms.
Any writer on usage who calls something substandard is opening himself to
charges of prescriptivist heresy. Nonstandard seems both more objective
and kinder. To call a child illiterate is needlessly harsh, so he become
a nonreader without prejudice. Bel Kaufman in Up the Down Staircase
observed, "Reluctant learners...under-achievers, non-academic minded,
slow, disadvantaged, sub-paced, non-college-oriented, underprivileged,
non-linguistic, intellectually deprived, and laggers--so far, I've count
more than ten different euphemisms for 'dumb kids,'" nearly a third of
which begin with non. A sixteen-year-old does not want to be a child or
a minor; nonadult is less onerous. The government has laws relating to
noncitizens, who seem less menacing than aliens. The nonpermanent member
of the UN Security Council doubtless feel securer than they would, were
they called impermanent or temporary members. A nonsuccess is better tha
a failure. An Associated Press writer referred to Mr. Humphrey's nongain
when the candidate he was backing did not survive the Minnesota primaries
it is clear that old politicians never lose, they only make nongains. In
Japan and Korea, the military had a policy of nonfraternization, which
was in no way directed against brotherhood. Delicacy could hardly be
carried further.
  Besides the euphemistic use of non, there is a prestige use, which can
be explained by the earlier history of the prefix. The legal, quasi-
legal, and scientific uses of the morpheme endowed it with an aura of
precision and objectivity, associating it with knowledgeability and
trustworthiness. Since the prefix is invested with legal and scientific
associations, it was inevitable that advertisers would grow fond of it.
Those bodiless TV voices who bring "a word from our sponsor" have
brought a good many words beginning with non: we are urged to buy
nonabsorbent wrapping paper, nonporous coffee pots, and shampoo in

274

John Algeo

nonbreakable tubes. We read of nonpartisan politics, nonprofit organizations, and noncontributory pension plans (in which the noncontribution is
made by the employer). Many of these terms are just fancy ways of saying
what might be put more simply. Nonpublic is the same as private; non-
prejudicial is a five-syllable synonym of fair. A nonsalaried official
receives the same nothing as an unpaid worker, although it is possible
that there is an implied difference: if the nonsalaried official were
salaried, he might be expected to get more money than the unpaid worker,
were the worker paid. Consequently, there is greater prestige in being
nonsalaried than in being unpaid. Linguists, most of whom are scientists
nowadays, are particularly fond of non: nondistinctive, nonsyllabic,
nongrammatical, noninflected, nonsentence, and nonnasal abound in the
literature. If we did not know that all linguists are devoted to the
simplicity principle, we might suspect a hint of pomposity in formations
like nonfricative obstruent for 'stop.' But nothing the linguist produces can match nondirective counseling, an activity in which the
counselor quietly listens to the counselee talk without ever giving
advice, or a noninstructional activities period, which is the time school-
children spend on the playground (or as it might be more appropriately
named, the noninstructional activities area). Genuine technical use of
the prefix, as in the logician's nondescription as a term for utterances
like I apologize (also called performatives), may pass by imperceptible
degrees into fashionable pomposities like nonmatrixed, which seems to
mean no more than 'unplanned' or 'chance' when it is used to describe
the relationship between the audience and the play in some of the more
avant-garde forms of contemporary theater.
   The recent increase in the use of non is due partly to its filling a need
in the semantic system, partly to its euphemistic value, and partly to its
prestigious associations with the worlds of science and law. But the most
important fact about the current vogue for non is that the prefix has
undergone a morphemic split. There are now several homophonous prefixes.
   The basic meaning of non has been simple negation; indeed as already
noted, it sometimes contrasts with other negative prefixes that may have
a more active sense of contrariety (nonresponsible versus irresponsible).
Sometime around 1960, however, the prefix came to be used in a new way
that can be called the pejorative non to distinguish it from the other
privative non. It seems to have been first so used in the word nonbook.
   The term nonbook has been applied to a book consisting of photographs
of babies or stills from old movies with clever captions under each
picture. It has also been used to describe the sort of "gift volume"
that is of a size intended for large coffee tables rather than normal
book shelves, is flossily bound, and contains more colored illustrations
than text. The Time-Life Company publishes nonbooks. Two works by the
comedian Alan King, Anybody Who Owns His Own Home Deserves It and
Help! I'm a Prisoner in a Chinese Bakery, have both been called nonbooks,
as has William Burrough's The Soft Machine, although presumably for
different reasons. In brief, a nonbook is something that has the shape
and superficial appearance of a book, but that the critic feels to be
devoid of value, use, or worth commonly associated with books. It is a
book with commercial but not artistic value. The function of the prefix
non is to make a negative judgment on the true worth of the book, and
hence it is pejorative.
   The pejorative non is more than an extension of the old morpheme.
It is itself a new morpheme that can contrast with the privative non in

a minimal pair. For example, book combines with both of the prefixes. In contrast to the use of book with pejorative non, it may also take privative non, as in the sentence, "The library's collection includes books and non-book materials," in which nonbook refers to microfilms, newspapers, journals, maps, clippings, or indeed anything that is not a book but might be stored in a library.

Another example of the new morpheme is nonevent, which has been defined as 'an occasion that is arranged by, and has meaning only when and as reported by, the mass communications media.' These two forms, nonbook and nonevent, were the first examples of the pejorative non to be recorded; they are listed in the Britannica Book of the Year, 1962 and 1964, respectively. The Britannica records nonbook as first used in 1960, which thus may be taken as the date of the morphemic split. The new prefix, which has the sense 'possessing the superficial form, but not the values of,' has extended itself during the last dozen years to a great many words other than book and event. The eighty lexical items with pejorative non in the glossary at the end of this article are the fruit of desultory reading in a few sources over several years and include only a fraction of the citations in my files. A concerted program of reading would certainly turn up a great many more forms. Additional examples, however, are hardly needed to establish that the prefix is a new morpheme that can be freely added to a wide variety of words.[4]

Although the current vogue for this prefix seems to be no older than 1960, there were precursors. Nonsense, from its first use by Ben Jonson in 1614, has carried a pejorative meaning. Nonentity first occurs in 1600 with a privative sense, 'something that does not exist,' but by 1710 Steele had used it in the Tatler in a pejorative sense, 'a person of no consequence.' Nondescript first occurs in 1683 as a technical term in botany, referring to a species 'not hitherto described, but by 1806 it had acquired the semipejorative meaning, 'lacking distinctive character.' Apart from these three items, nonsense, nonentity, and nondescript, there are no clear examples of pejorative non before 1960. There are a few ambiguous cases that may represent nonce uses. For example, Milton in his divorce tractate discusses the theological question of whether God can give a dispensation from the divine law. Milton thinks not. He quotes one of his adversaries as arguing that God can, but by unknowable means. Milton replies, "We cannot be content with his non-solution." The non here is privative, because the problem of how God dispenses has not been resolved, but there is a pejorative overtone to the word. A much later ambiguous use is recorded in Webster' Third (1961). The entry nonman is defined privatively as 'a being that is not a man,' but the illustrative citation strongly suggests the pejorative sense: "a man who is completely dehumanized by snobbery, a non-man, a monster" (E. R. Bentley).

Since 1960, the pejorative non has become firmly established as a freely combinable prefix. There is an ironic contrast between it and the older non prefix. The privative non has been popular because it is purely negative in meaning and impartial in tone. The pejorative non, on the other hand, is used to make a highly emotional judgment; it is distinctly polemical in tone. It is ironic that an emotional, judgment-passing morpheme should develop from an impartial, colorless one. But perhaps the vogue for pejorative non is due to that ironic contrast. The non in nonbook looks like the impartial, privative morpheme. Under the guise of that apparently scientific objectivity, it sneaks in a highly personal evaluation.

There are signs that other negative or adversative prefixes may also be developing new meanings. Antihero is common as a term for the irresolute and ineffective protagonist of much recent fiction. An antimusical is a musical comedy with a serious message, such as the Broadway show Company, about a twentieth-century Everyman-playboy who discovers the virtues of the conjugal life. The term antipoetry has been applied to modern poetry in general. One writer has used the term Uncatholic to denote a person who identifies himself as a member of the Church but who questions or rejects much of the discipline required by the hierarchy. These are, however, only sporadic occurrences. They lack the frequency and the clearly isolable new meanings of non.

Non is also the most versatile of the negative prefixes. For, in addition to its privative and pejorative senses, a third meaning has developed in recent years, a meaning that can be contrasted with the other two in a three-way homonymy. Thus, a noncandidate with privative non is literally 'one who is not a candidate' and might apply, for example, to Mayor Richard Daley in the 1972 Democratic presidential primary. Noncandidate with pejorative non is 'one who is a declared candidate but whose selection is so unlikely that he can be set aside as a possible contender,' for example, the nominee of the Prohibition Party for the presidency of the United States in almost any year after 1919. Noncandidate with the third kind of non is 'one who is not a professed candidate and who may officially deny his candidacy but who is nevertheless regarded as a candidate by many newsmen, politicians, and possibly himself,' for example, Edward Kennedy in 1972 and Ronald Reagan in 1968. This third use of non, which might be defined as 'possessing the value, but not the surface characteristics or acknowledged identity of,' might be called the dissimulative non. In several ways it complements pejorative non. The latter indicates that the thing it describes possesses (in theological jargon) the accidents, but not the substance named; dissimulative non indicates that the thing possesses the substance though not the accidents. Pejorative non is unfavorably critical in its implications; dissimulative non, though it may be arch, often suggests an admiration of the thing described. Thus nonacting with dissimulative non denotes a style of acting that is so restrained and realistic as to appear not to be acting at all; the appearance, however, is deceptive, for such nonacting requires a high degree of acting skill. Nonacting with pejorative non would, on the other hand, refer to egregiously bad acting, especially overacting, and thus is the contrary of dissimulative nonacting. A dissimulative nonwatch is a fashionable and perhaps costly time piece worn somewhere other than on the wrist--thus, at first glance, appearing not to be a watch. A pejorative nonwatch would be a Mickey Mouse or a Spiro Agnew watch or some inefficient and unreliable wristwatch.

Dissimulative non has been less productive than its pejorative homonym, as the sixteen examples in the last part of the glossary suggest when compared with the eighty examples of pejorative use. It must be, however, of approximately the same age; indeed it may be slightly older. The earliest instance of dissimulative non that I have recorded is nonprofit 'profit not subject to taxation because of the privileged status of the investment that produces it,' from Jessica Mitford's 1963 American Way of Death. By 1964, however, Louis Auchincloss used nonfact 'fact whose existence is officially denied' and attributed the word to George Orwell, thus suggesting 1950, the year of Orwell's death, as a terminus ante quem for the new meaning. The word is certainly appropriate to the author of Nineteen Eighty Four, but I have been unable to locate it in his writings.

There are, thus, three distinct albeit homonymous prefixes: privative, pejorative, and dissimulative non. They form minimal lexical contrasts by occurring in different senses with the same stem. It is not possible to be sure which prefix is occurring in every instance, a problem by no means limited to non but frequent with homonyms that are of the same part of speech and have common semantic fields. The problem of identifying non in each instance of its use is further complicated by the playful and sportive inventions that the vogue for non has led to. Since as early as 1967, charitable groups have been organizing such nonevents as nonballs or nondinners that feature nonspeakers at five dollars a non-plate, to which noninvitations are sent requesting a donation with the nonacceptance. Such negative forms of fund-raising are certainly more charitable to the organizers and contributors than the more customary sort of affair. At least one experimental college (as reported by the Chronicle of Higher Education, 11 May 1970, p. 8) is selling nondegrees for twenty-five to a hundred dollars as part of a fund-drive, in what is perhaps a more honest search for money than that of the more traditional degree honoris causa. Another arch product of the vogue for non in the National Organization for Non-Parents, acronymically NON, which promotes nonparenthood according to Time (3 July 1972, p. 35) by decreeing two new holidays, Non-Mother's Day and Non-Father's Day on which nonparents are to be honored, presumably by one another, rather than by nonchildren. Finally, because one must call a halt to such cuteness, however abundant the raw material may be, there is Joseph Wood Krutch's nihilistic prediction in the American Scholar (37, Spring 1968, 210): "Now the mini-skirt is, of course, halfway to becoming a non-skirt. When it has reached its entelechy and is then designed to accompany a topless blouse, the anti-costume will be complete and just right for the non-woman reading anti-novels, looking at nonrepresentational pictures, and listening to atonal music."

The current vogue for non continues the earlier history of the form, bu has increased the rate of popularization and the range of uses. Non first became a vogue form in the seventeenth century when legal and semi-legal uses predominated. By the eighteenth century it was freely combinable, especially with nouns denoting action or condition, and had extended its use to more general areas. In the mid twentieth century, morphemic split occurred, and the three resulting morphemes enjoy a wide-ranging grammatical use: with nouns of action (nonparticipation) or of actor (nonuser), with abstract nouns (nonlinearity) or concrete (nonmetal with adjectives and adverbs of several kinds (nonalcoholic, nonbusiness, nonfabricated, nonintoxicating, noncognitively, nonlaterally), and even with verbs (nonconform), to cite examples of privative non. Pejorative a dissimulative non are used most typically with nouns denoting events, persons, or objects.

The current orthography of words with the prefix, in any of its senses, shows a good deal of variation between hyphenated and solid spellings. Despite dictionaries and publishers' style sheets, which almost uniformly show a solid spelling for words like nonbook, nonnative, and nonstandard, hyphenated forms are common. Indeed, over 70 percent of the written citations in the following list are spelled with hyphens. This violation of what is supposed to be customary practice is all the more remarkable in view of the fact that the hyphens had to survive the formidable opposition of blue-pencil-armed copyeditors to reach the printed page. It also raises questions about the practice of even those dictionaries that pride themselves on reporting actual usage and are castigated for so doing. In the matter of hyphenation at least, usage seems to have been sacrificed for consistency in the lexicographical treatment of prefixed words. The discrepancy between usage and reportage exists also for other prefixes like semi-, anti-, and sub-.

Although not one of the major shibboleths, non has received some attention from those who advise English speakers how they should use the language. The new senses of pejorative and dissimulative non have gone unnoted, but the general vogue for the prefix has caught the attention of several writers. Objections to it fall into three broad groups. First, Rudolf Flesch (ABC of Style, New York: Harper, 1964) is of the opinion that non "always makes ugly words," an opinion in which he was anticipated by A. P. Herbert (What a Word! London: Methuen, 1935, p. 44), who believes that nonchalantly is a word that "is difficult or impossible to read aloud without stuttering, coughing, and spitting." And Wilson Follett (Modern American Usage, New York: Hill and Wang, 1966, p. 356) deplores the "ugly, unarticulated compounds it produces," although what unarticulated can mean in this context is anybody's guess. Second, a common objection to non forms is that they are easily made and thus are temptations to the indolent to indulge their lazy habits (Herbert, p. 29; Follett; H. W. Fowler, Modern English Usage, 2d ed., New York: Oxford Univ. Press, 1965; Sir Ernest Gowers, Complete Plain Words, Baltimore: Penguin, 1964). The suggestion is that use of non violates the Protestant work ethic and is unworthy of the playing fields of Eton. Third, Fowler, Gowers, and Follett have observed that non forms are often unnecessary, nonessential being the same as unessential, and nonpublic as private. A fourth objection that is apparently unique to Wilson Follett is that "the twofold division with non- is likely to suggest a strictness that it does not always possess." There is some irony in an objection to dichotomizing from the most dichotomic of all usage guides.

On the whole, British objections to non have been stronger than American ones. Margaret Nicholson's adaptation of Fowler to the American market (Dictionary of American-English Usage, New York: Oxford Univ. Press, 1957) discusses only the problem of hyphenated versus solid spellings rather than the use of the prefix. (Fowler himself, it should be noted, was not much exercised about non; MEU, 1st ed., limits its discussion of the prefix to a preference for nonmoral over the Greco-Roman hybrid amoral, the condemnation cited above from MEU, 2d ed., being Gower's addition.) Indeed, so unconcerned have Americans been that Roy H. Copperud (American Usage: The Consensus, New York: Van Nostrand, 1970) can dismiss objections to non's ugliness as "quixotic." If it were not for the watchful eyes of Wilson Follett and his co-workers, the American use of non would be almost without censure, thus confirming the worst suspicions of the Mother Country about colonial degeneracy. As it is, however, we are well looked after, for Follett objects to non on all three grounds mentioned above, as well as from his own special distaste for misleading dichotomies.[5]

Although the most often cited objections to non forms are that they are cacophonous, indolent, and unnecessary, the real complaint may be that many are relatively new and still have about them an air of the faddish vogue. Time alone will tell whether the vogue will continue and the new morphemes will maintain their identities or even further poly-furcate. The one certainty is that change will go on. Since the English history of non begins with Chaucer, it is fitting that he should have the last word. Speaking in the person of the Squire, Chaucer says, "Men loven of propre kynde newefangelnesse," a proposition whose truth is well illustrated by the history of non.

GLOSSARY

Pejorative non

nonaction 1968 Jan 20 Hollis Alpert Saturday Review 33 "Toward the end [of the film], Mailer imperiously halts the nonaction and incoherently barks directly to the audience."

nonanswer 1968 Mar 11 Duane Bradford Gainesville (Fla) Sun 8 "They were nonanswers--words calculated solely as a physical response to solv the immediate need for some kind of a response generated in a news con-ference." 1971 Dec 6 "Dear Abby" Atlanta Constitution 2B "The letter signed 'Resigned' interested me, but your very clever non-answer interested me even more."

nonarchitecture 1968 Joseph Wood Krutch American Scholar 37:210 "I might go on to discuss the proposed Kennedy Memorial as a fine example of non-architecture."

nonart 1967 Apr 28 Barbara W Tuchman Gainesville (Fla) Sun 5 "Non-art, as its practioners describe it, the blob school, the all-black canvasse the paper cut-outs and Campbell soup tins and plastic hamburgers and pieces of old carpet." 1968 Brigid Brophy Fifty Works of English Literature We Could Do Without 5 (with ref to Beowulf) "boring as a story...a fine example of primitive non-art."

nonauthor 1964 Louis Auchincloss Tales of Manhattan 55 "Stohl was what he termed a 'non-author' and his novel a 'non-book.'"

nonbook 1: Bound printed matter 1966 Apr 8 Time (with ref to William S. Burroughs The Soft Machine) "A hallucinatory little non-book of babble." 1967 Mar 3 Time 102 (with ref to Marshall McLuhan The Medium is the Massage) "The authors of this eye-stopping, mind-wrenching whazis have created the utlimate in non-books." 1968 Dec 20 Time 88 (with ref to Revolution for the Hell of It) "The author of this dis-jointed but somehow engaging nonbook is in reality Abbie Hoffman." 1970 Feb 8 Karl E. Meyer Gainesville (Fla) Sun 12B "'Son of the Instant Button Book' (a non-book with blank buttons and decals)." Apr 18 Curtis G. Benjamin Saturday Review 19 "Certain lofty-minded literary publishers and commentators...like to describe many kinds of nonliterary works as 'non-books.'" Aug, Harley C. Shands Language Sciences 11:12 "The book in which Wittgenstein presents the work of his mature years is a 'non-book.' It has many of the qualities of free-associational material." 1972 June 26 Time 20 (with ref to the hoax autobiography of Howard Hughes) "Presumably Irving still intends to pay for his folly by writing a book about how the threesome did their nonbook." 2: Libretto 1969 Feb 6 Clive Barnes Gainesville (Fla) Sun 7C (with ref to Hair) "Gerome Ragni and James Rado, who wrote the non book and the sweet lyrics, have not dropped out."

noncampaign 1972 Nov 9 Hal Gulliver Atlanta Constitution 4A "This painfu' Presidential election time, the year of the non-campaign."

noncase 1972 July 3 letter to editor Time 3 "Thank God for the acquittal

of Angela Davis and the jury...who were able to see and think above
the prosecution's shallow non-case."
noncommunicating 1967 May 21 Art Buchwald Gainesville (Fla) Sun 4B
"Weiss contends that business organizations are turning out so many
communications that they are not communicating with anybody....Weiss
is correct in stating that there is too much non-communicating going
on."
noncommunication 1969 Oct 10 Time 43 (headline) "Briefings: A Ritual
of Noncommunication."
nonconclusion 1969 Mar 22 Granville Hicks Saturday Review 54 "Nog is
a non-novel about a non-hero who goes through a number of non-
experiences, arriving at a non-conclusion: 'I'm not asleep or awake.'"
noncountry 1970 Sep 24 C. L. Sulzberger Gainesville (Fla) Sun 6A
"Jordan was and remains a non-country, created out of sandscape by
Britain to pay off a dynastic debt."
noncourse 1969 Jan 19 Rich Oppel Gainesville (Fla) Sun 4A "Kibler said
he opposes moves to establish autonomous 'black studies' colleges on
campus on the grounds that they would be 'noncourses not derived by
academic methodology.'"
noncrime 1966 July 8 Time 65 "She was arrested, along with her mentally
ill grandson, and grilled for two hours for the non-crime of 'Investigation, suspected of Assault and Shooting.'"
nondance 1969 Mar 22 Walter Terry Saturday Review 71 "It was a pleasure
for us who are in constant attendance at dance events to see a
questing, adventuresome choreographer who is unwilling to abjure
movement--oh, yes, some of today's choreographers are of the non-dance
persuasion."
nondiscipline 1970 May 18 college teacher's conversation "Well, we've
got history and then all those other nondisciplines [social sciences]
follow along."
nondrama 1968 Jan 20 Hollis Alpert Saturday Review 33 "The ninety
minutes to which it [the movie title Wild 90] refers are not wild.
They are noisy, and most of the noise is made by Mailer, who, as
principal player in a turgid nondrama--presumably a turgid nonfiction
nondrama--barks sometimes like a dog and sometimes like a seal."
nonemergency 1967 May 27 Saturday Review 6 (with ref to a plane trip on
which several passengers prayed aloud) "She didn't have anything or
anyone to appeal to in this non-emergency."
nonending 1969 Feb 21 Time 87 "Marvin likes to claim credit for the
non-ending of the film [Hell in the Pacific]. The non-meaning goes
with it."
nonestate 1967 Mar 31 Time 23 "Ruby made out three separate wills,
dividing his non-estate (mostly personal effects) among sisters,
nephews and a friendly prison guard."
nonethic 1967 Oct 15 sermon by university chaplain "These people
espouse a nihilistic nonethic....They are followers of Hugh Hefner
and Timothy Leary."
nonevent 1967 Apr 11 Londoner on CBS-TV interview (with ref to Billy
Graham's London Crusade) "I thought it was a nonevent." July 7
Time 41 "Far too many p.r. men still think their chief function is
to stage lunches, cocktail parties, junkets, cruises, screenings,
no-news press conferences, and other non-events." 1970 Dec 12 New
Yorker 44 "Bill Doll, the eminent press agent...a genial, low-key
persuader who can turn the tawdriest non-event into a major

celebration." 1972 May 31 news reporter NBC radio (with ref to the fact that Nixon did not meet the Cardinal Primate of the Polish Church during a visit to Poland) "There was one notable nonevent." Dec 2 Saturday Review 22 "All agree that this [a press interview with Miss America] is a nonevent."

nonexperience See nonconclusion

nonexpose 1971 Feb 15 Time 52 (with ref to an article suggesting, without proving, improper financial dealings) "The best that could be said for the Connally nonexpose was that it cleared the air."

nonface 1969 Feb 15 John Ciardi Saturday Review 14 (with ref to the blank facial expression of a go-go dancer) "And when I stole a look at the animals on either side of me, I saw the same non-face."

nonfact 1971 Jan 23 New Yorker 92 "Books of nonfiction (many of which, like 'The Sensuous Woman,' are also books of nonfact)."

nonfood 1970 June 13 William Hines Gainesville (Fla) Sun "The non-foods usually offered at a cocktail buffet probably intensify the next morning's suffering."

nongovernment 1970 July 24 Columbus (Ohio) Dispatch "The danger facing Italy today is that it could be overtaken again by desperation and turn from its present comical non-government to the grim no-government of a dictatorship."

nongovernor 1968 Feb 20 Gainesville (Fla) Sun 6 "It is a bogus package conceived by a limp Legislature misled by a non-Governor with a non-program determined to make Florida a non-state."

nonhappening 1968 Feb 13 Jack Gould Gainesville (Fla) Sun "The [TV] medium's extraordinary ability to suggest that a true happening resides in a non-happening may eventually be self-defeating."

nonhero 1964 O.F. Snelling 007 James Bond 13 "Sensational fiction is full of slightly caddish protagonists, non-heroes." 1966 Sep 5 Gainesville (Fla) Sun (dateline NY) "Not one youngster polled named President Johnson, who instead was termed a 'nonhero.'" 1967 (title of book by George R. Maret) Richard Strauss: The Life of a Non-hero. 1968 June 8 Richard Plant Saturday Review 52 "The nonhero watches himself carry out self-destructive deeds, then watches himself watching, and analyzes the analysis." 1969 Apr 25 Time 113 "The non-hero is another of those nobodies who do nothing."

nonhistory 1966 Nov 11 Time 34 "The Ramparts-Jones non-history is riddled with factual errors and perverse conclusions." 1970 Thomas Pyles English: Introduction to Language 335 (with ref to a folk etymology tracing booze to a distiller name Booz) "Thus is linguistic nonhistory made."

nonhomily 1968 Mar 1 Time 41 "Many clergymen have applauded Steinberg's non-homilies."

noninterview 1967 Jan 20 Bob Thomas Gainesville (Fla) Sun "Reporters have been inclined to view Paul Newman in negative terms, as an 'antistar' who portrays 'nonheroes,' lives an unglamorous personal life and gives 'noninterviews.'"

nonissue 1972 Nov 1 Atlanta Constitution 6B "But most admitted that their votes were probably subtly influenced 'perhaps subconsciously,' one man said, by the non-issues." Nov 20 Time 28 "'Unfortunately for the country, there were a lot of non-issues in this campaign,' Kennedy told Time on Election Night."

nonlanguage 1968 Mar 30 Robert M. Utley letter to editor Saturday Review 63 "Let us recall, too, while assigning credits for 'nonlanguage,' that the official names of units of the National Park System are fixed by the U.S. Congress." 1970 Jan 10 college teacher's conversation "The nonlanguage of sociologists and educators."

nonleader 1969 Aug 9 Saturday Review 10 "The honeymoon was over for Richard Nixon. Marianne Means called him an 'unhurried nonleader.'"

nonliving 1972 Feb 14 Time 60 "He is the adjunct of his possessions, the stereo set, transistor and white antiseptic machine for nonliving he calls his 'home unit.'"

nonmeaning See nonending

nonminded 1966 Aug 20 William F. Buckley Tampa Tribune "The sheer nothingness to which Republicanism, under the Tribune's leadership and that of other like-minded, or non-minded men, had been reduced."

nonmoney 1970 Sep 26 conversation overheard "This new nonsilver silver, this nonmoney."

nonmovement 1972 July 22 Saturday Review 40 (headline for an article dealing with the lack of organization in the free school movement) "The Free School Nonmovement."

nonmovie 1967 Sep 15 Time 101 "Man is likely to blur Warhol's image as the Zanuck of the non-movie."

nonmusic 1966 Aug 18 William F. Buckley Gainesville (Fla) Sun 6 "A bed sheet upon which one of the Beatles had slept in San Francisco while there to commit non-music....No doubt poor Mr. Lennon wishes at this point that he had never opened his mouth except to emit music, or rather non-music."

nonname 1972 May 30 Athens (Ga) Banner-Herald 4 "Neither blacks nor whites, students nor parents like the new names. Clarke Central was a non-name, a title without any character whatsoever....this non-name was created from ashes designed to please everyone but actually pleasing no one."

nonnation 1966 Mar 11 Time "More new non-nations are waiting impatiently in the wings; Bechuanaland, Basutoland, British Guiana and Mauritius are all due to become independent this year....Libya was written off as a hopeless non-nation--until oil was found floating beneath the deserts."

nonnetwork 1973 May 8 Atlanta Constitution 16-A (CDN news service) "Inexorably, the Nixon administration is turning public television into either a government propaganda arm or a bland, faceless non-network."

nonnewsconference 1967 Sep 10 TV reporter (with ref to a chaotic press conference called by a South Vietnamese presidential candidate) "Here is where the newsconference, or nonnewsconference, came off."

nonnovel 1967 Feb 11 Granville Hicks Saturday Review 31 "A fictional non-novel is a book that is represented as being a novel but has as a major purpose the dissemination of presumably useful knowledge." See also nonconclusion.

nonpainting 1968 Joseph Wood Krutch American Scholar 37:210 "I might go on to discuss...the work of a recently deceased painter as non-painting. He...gradually abandoned all colors, used only blacks of varying intensity."

nonpeople 1972 June 17 letter to the editor Saturday Review 28 "Women are beginning to realize that this kind of pornography is a symptom of hatred of women and an inability to see us as anything but nonpeople."

nonperson 1967 June 9 Time 118 "The machine will either turn him into a collectivized, automatic non-person or blow him back to the jungle."

John Algeo

July 21 <u>Time</u> 46 "The nation's 8,000,000 welfare recipients have tended
to become what Supreme Court Justice Abe Fortas calls 'constitutional
nonpersons.'" 1968 Aug 12 Max Lerner <u>Gainesville</u> (Fla) <u>Sun</u> 6 "And
now Agnew, a nonentity and non-person who squeezed in as governor in
Maryland." 1969 Apr 5 Robert Sommer <u>Saturday</u> <u>Review</u> 67 "'Hippies'
complain that 'squares' do not look at one another but treat each
other as non-persons." 1971 Sep 14 <u>Atlanta</u> <u>Constitution</u> 4A "Nikita
Khrushchev, who died Saturday of a heart attack at 77, was a nonperson
in the Soviet Union." 1972 Mar 9 <u>Atlanta</u> <u>Constitution</u> "'As far as the
politics of 1972 is concerned,' says the campaign manager for one of
the leading Democratic candidates, 'Lyndon Johnson is a non-person.'"
nonplanning 1966 Nov 27 letter to editor <u>Gainesville</u> (Fla) <u>Sun</u> "The
    Plan Board of Gainesville is once again engaged in non-planning on a
    large scale."
nonplay 1968 Feb 13 Jack Gould <u>Gainesville</u> (Fla) <u>Sun</u> "After all, he
    did induce NBC to part with $112,000 for the non-play of the year."
    1971 Sep 20 Time 41 "<u>Mass</u> is a jumble of literal and symbolic meanings,
    a contrived happening with pretentious overtones, a non-play about a
    non-Mass."
nonpoem 1968 June 14 Time 94 "Vesta tempts Enderby into writing non-
    poems for her journal under the signature of Faith Fortitude."
nonpolitician 1973 Apr 26 E.B. Furgurson <u>Atlanta</u> <u>Constitution</u> 4A
    (dateline Washington) "That [the atmosphere that gave rise to the
    Watergate affair] is not 'just politics,' and it never was. At least,
    not until this group of nonpoliticians came to town."
nonproblem 1968 Sep 3 member of a univ seminar (with ref to an ad hoc
    solution to a problem in grammatical notation posed by another member)
    "How's that for weasling out of it? A nonsolution for a nonproblem."
nonprogram 1967 Sep 13 <u>Gainesville</u> (Fla) <u>Sun</u> 4 "The Republican legislatc
    whose negativism...made Kirk's nonprogram possible."
nonreply 1972 Jan 23 <u>Family</u> <u>Weekly</u> 6 "While carrying on an animated
    conversation, Mrs. Nixon can deftly emit 'nonreplies,' uttering words
    but vouchsafing nothing."
nonromance 1968 June 14 <u>Time</u> 91 "The actors ricochet helplessly through
    a nonromance between a girl who is some kind of nut and an orthopedic
    surgeon who seems to be going the same route."
nonscript 1970 Apr 9 <u>Gainesville</u> (Fla) <u>Sun</u> 3D "'Cowboy's' Non-Script
    Writer [headline]...much of the 'Midnight Cowboy' dialog was improvised
nonshow 1969 Feb 16 Jack Gould <u>Gainesville</u> (Fla) <u>Sun</u> "A re-run of
    'Dracula' would look good after the nonshow had been foisted on their
    unsuspecting audiences."
nonsolution 1968 May 5 <u>Gainesville</u> (Fla) <u>Sun</u> (headline to an article
    by Robert M. Hutchins on the danger of specialization in a university)
    "Specialization, the Non-Solution."
nonstate See nongovernor
nonstatement 1969 Sep 30 Univ of Fla <u>Alligator</u> 7 "The semantics boys
    call that a Positive Inferential Non-statement, i.e. a group of words
    that chase each other around in a circle."
nonstory 1: News report 1967 Mar 19 James Reston <u>Gainesville</u> (Fla)
    <u>Sun</u> "The Atlanta Journal carried three Kennedy stories on its front
    page: the family's return to JFK's grave site; RFK urging more money
    for the poverty program, and the latest non-story out of New Orleans
    on the Kennedy assassination 'plot.'" 1970 Jan 8 James Reston <u>Gaines-</u>
    <u>ville</u> (Fla) <u>Sun</u> "It [the Chappaquiddick inquiry] is a non-story, held

284

behind closed doors, to repeat old tales, which few people quite believe anyway." 2: Plot 1967 July 28 Time 84 "A new 'art form' wherein pages of prose by two different writers are split down the middle, pasted together, and their sentences merged to form one great non-story."

nonstudent 1970 Sep, W.D. Schaefer Bulletin of the Assoc of Depts of English 26:25 "Frankly, I am tired of being told that as chairman of an English department I have a non-subject being taught by non-teachers to non-students."

nonstyle 1972 Nov 17 Atlanta Constitution 14B "Earl Carlson, set designer for All in the Family, said the CBS staff decided on the style or rather 'nonstyle' that they wanted for Archie's chair."

nonsubject See nonstudent

nonsupper 1968 Apr 15 conversation (with ref to a meal of left-overs) "You say you're ready for your nonsupper?"

nonsystem 1972 Jan 30 Athens (Ga) Banner-Herald 2 (with ref to federal rules for posting retail prices) "The Consumer Federation of America has named Price Commission Chairman C. Jackson Grayson as America's 1972 'Blackout Award' winner for...'extraordinary achievements in sowing confusion and contradiction in a nonsystem.'"

nonteacher See nonstudent

nontheology 1966 Apr 8 Time 82 (with ref to death-of-God theologians) "Satirizing the basic premise of their new non-theology, the Methodist student magazine motive recently ran an obituary of God in newspaper style."

nonthinking 1972 June 21 Atlanta Constitution 4A "The other part of the non-thinking currently going on about the [presidential primary] race is to say that one or the other of them [Wallace and McGovern] is pragmatic enough to make whatever sacrifices are necessary."

nonthought 1966 Dec 6 William F. Buckley Gainesville (Fla) Sun "It is a nonsequitur, one of those typical acts of non-thought that distinguish high liberal Republicans."

nontitle 1971 Sep 25 Malcolm Cowley Saturday Review 26 "It is a non-book, so to speak, non-written by Andy Warhol, and it is called a, simply the lower-case first letter of the alphabet, which I suppose might pass for a non-title."

nonword 1961 Oct 27 Life 4 (title of an editorial review of W3) "A Non-Word Deluge." 1970 Jan 8 letter to editor Gainesville (Fla) Sun "The School Board's petition to the Supreme Court contained an error, the non-word 'predominately,' which was used twice in place of the correct word, 'predominantly.'...the non-word is used with some frequency here in the South."

nonworker 1967 June 2 Time 28 "Under socialism, there is little difference between the wages of skilled and unskilled workers, and almost no difference in pay between the worker who sweats over his machine and the non-worker who would rather flirt with shop girls, chat with colleagues, or take innumerable breaks for coffee, tea, snacks--or rest."

nonwriter 1961 Martin Joos The Five Clocks 42 "The writer is a rewriter, or he is no proper writer at all--like Thomas Wolfe. Nonwriters have their function too." Idem 50 "Nonwriters, like Thomas Wolfe, who simply fill the text with salt tears." 1967 Thomas Pyles College English 28:452 "Equally magisterial is Miss Dorothy Parker, who has declared that 'anyone who, as does [Henry] Miller, follows 'none' with a plural verb...should assuredly not be called a writer.' The usage in question is first recorded in the ninth century in the writings of Alfred the

John Algeo

Great.   More recent occurrences cited by the OED...are from the
writings of such non-writers as Dryden, Goldsmith, Burke, and Southey.
nonwritten See nontitle

Dissimulative non

nonacting 1968 Houghton Mifflin Sampler (brochure) "If Willy Loman is
a non-hero to Miller's critics, the play itself calls for much non-
acting--or, as the authors of Responses to Drama put it, 'kitchenistic
acting.'"
nonbuilding 1972 Jan 9 Atlanta Journal and Constitution Mag 17 (with
ref to an underground structure) "'This is a non-building, exteriorly
speaking,' Portman says. 'We've buried it, so that it becomes more
than a building. We've created at the same time a big green open space
for the city.'"
noncampaign 1967 Nov 26 Russell Baker Gainesville (Fla) Sun "My press
secretary will distribute a non-campaign kit containing my biography,
photographs, a summary of my political achievement, vital statistics
such as height and weight and anecdotes suitable for garnishing human-
interest stories." 1972 May 12 David Fry Tonight Show NBC "Tonight
we visit...Ted Kennedy at his noncampaign headquarters."
noncandidacy 1968 Jan 16 Richard Wilson Gainesville (Fla) Sun "All this
randomly built superstructure of his non-candidacy could, of course,
come tumbling down over some irrelevancy or misstep."
noncandidate 1967 Sep 22 Time 22 (heading) "The Non-Candidates." Dec 9
Saturday Review 12 "The political implications of two non-candidates
announcing and denouncing each other are profound." 1968 May 29 Art
Buchwald Gainesville (Fla) Sun 2A "Gov. Ronald Reagan, the only leading
noncandidate in the race for the Republican presidential nomination."
noncrime 1972 Jan 12 Ironsides TV program (with ref to crimes that are
not reported or are denied by the victims) "If you don't have a victim,
you don't have a crime. Apparently we are in the midst of a noncrime
wave."
noneclipse 1970 Mar, Univ of Fla Publications Newsletter (with ref to
a dense cloud-cover that obscured any view of a solar eclipse at the
town of Perry, which had advertised itself as the "Eclipse Capital of
the World") "Note for photographers--at the non-eclipse at Perry on
March 7, 20 scientists from Japan put on their own little trade show
of Nikon equipment."
nonfact 1964 Louis Auchincloss Tales of Manhattan 227 "Word had gone ou
from the chief that the episode was to be buried, and buried it would
be. It would become, in the phrase of George Orwell, a 'non-fact.'"
nonfamily 1967 July 7 Time (picture caption) "The grass is usually
greener in a hippie house. Sans Souci Temple, near downtown Los
Angeles, accomodates a happy non-family of 24 people, including these
adults and child--none of them related to one another."
nonhero 1972 Aug 31 Atlanta Constitution 4A "'These non-heroes of the
war,' he [Bert Westbrook] goes on, 'have become moral refugees at
home. Alienation and discontent sharply contrast the new veterans wit
their older counterparts from previous wars. Many who spent themselve
in Vietnam have come to realize that their sacrifice is not justified
by contemporary thinking.'"
nonmagazine 1972 Feb 12 Saturday Review 15 (ad) "What's a non-magazine?
It's a magazine that appears between hard, book-like covers, every
other month, six times a year. It's sold only by subscription. It

286

accepts no advertising. It devotes every one of its 108 pages to the best in short stories, articles, interviews, poetry, painting, and photography. In a word, it's Audience."
nonprofit 1963 Jessica Mitford American Way of Death 160 "The amount of nonprofit that could be realized through such a tax-free Comemoral is only hinted at." (Comemoral = commemoration + memorial.) 1967 Dec 22 Time 64 "Paying Taxes on Nonprofits [heading] Magazines published by tax-free organizations may not make profits, but some of those that take advertising certainly make money."
nonschool 1973 Apr Sat Rev of Ed 57 "The 'nonschool' [Heliotrope, a free university] was founded in San Francisco four years ago...to offer interesting, immediate education to anyone who wanted it."
nonsuit 1972 Mar 1 Athens (Ga) Banner-Herald (ad suppl; ref to a combination of trousers and sleeveless "tunic vest") "Sears easy-care non-suits."
nonwar 1967 May 25 C.L. Sulzberger Gainesville (Fla) Sun 4 "The world has been so obsessed with the fighting non-war in Vietnam that it has tended to ignore the non-fighting war in Palestine."
nonwatch 1966 Aug 11 Gainesville (Fla) Sun "Time was when a watch was worn on the wrist. No more. In this era of the non-book and the non-hero, thanks to teen-agers we have the non-watch watch." Oct 28 Idem "The nonwatch watch--pendant watches, charm watches, brooch and pin time pieces--use[d] on a variety of anatomical locations other than the wrist."

NOTES

*Read at the SAMLA-ADS Meeting, Charlotte, North Carolina, November 1966.

[1] Herbert Davis, ed., Prose Works of Jonathan Swift, 2 (Oxford: Blackwell, 1957), 176.

[2] The Philosophy of Rhetoric (1776), bk. 2, chap. 1. The sentiment is much older, being for example in Horace, De arte poetica, 70: "Multa renascentur, quae jam cecidere, cadentque/Quae nunc sunt in honore, vocabula, si volet usus/Quem penes arbitrium est et jus et norma loquendi"; in B. Jonson's translation: "Much phrase that now is dead, shall be reviv'd;/ And much shall dye, that now is nobly liv'd,/ If Custome please; at whose disposing will/ The power, and rule of speaking resteth still."

[3] On the lexicographical treatment of words whose uses are predictable from their parts, including some with the non prefix, see Philip B. Gove, "Self-Explanatory Words," American Speech, 41 (1966), 182-98.

[4] The new sense and wide use of non have been noted by Clarence Barnhart, "Of Matters Lexicographical: Keeping a Record of the New English, 1963-1972," American Speech, 45 (1970), 105.

[5]I am indebted to Thomas Pyles for calling my attention to several matters, including the spelling problem and the British reactions to non. See also Vigilans [pseud.], Chamber of Horrors (London: Deutsch, 1952), pp. 91-92, not available to me.

SOME ASPECTS OF "NATURE" IN COSMETICS ADVERTISEMENTS*

Boyd H. Davis

Connotations are slippery; over a period of time they may grow, melt, shift, even nudge one another aside. Changes in connotations are related to changes in a culture; however, the relationship is frequently neither simpler nor uncomplicated. An examination of changes in one category of cosmetics advertisements appearing monthly in Ebony over thirty years illustrates some of the complexities in investigating a possible parallel between language change and social forces.

The wording changes in advertisements from 1945-1975 for hair and skin products parallel a heightened consciousness of Blackness as one of the Afro-American cultural changes over the same period. And these wording changes involve a semantic shift connected with the notion natural, which again is related to social and cultural changes. But the parallel can be only roughly charted, as we will see later.

Three general tendencies may be noted for hair and skin cosmetics advertisements: a few have changed only minimally; other advertisements have disappeared or have been replaced by some for new products developed by the home company; a number have undergone a complete change.

Among cosmetic hair preparations, advertisements for hair dyes generally show the fewest changes in wording: Eau Denna, for example, has advertised itself for over two decades as an eradicator of gray hair which "will not turn the hair reddish." The efforts of manufacturers to teach what they have evidently felt to be new consumer attitudes have occasioned wording changes in the advertisements for Lustrasilk cream, Murray's Hair Pomade for men, Perma-Strate, and a selection from the Posner line of cosmetics.

Lustrasilk's advertisements have consistently employed a soft approach (as opposed to the overtly romantic connotations often employed by many facial products) to suggest the improvement in attractiveness of the user and the resulting enhanced self-concept. In 1957-59 (vols. 13, 14), Lustrasilk's captions claimed that it "straightens super-curly hair," and promised that "you'll love" its results. One caption during this period advocated what it called "The 'natural' look"; the accompanying picture showed a hair style very different from the Afro Natural popular a decade later. By the mid-sixties, Lustrasilk advertisements had abandoned their explicit claim to "straightening" to concentrate on "hair that swings," with "hairbeat," "rhythm," "spring," "swing," and "pulse" (see vols. 22-24, 1965-69).

Copy for Murray's Hair-Glo and Pomade and Murray's Superior Hair Dressing Pomade was directed specifically to men, beginning with romantic suggestions: "hearts you win" (vol. 5, 1949-50). The wording changed to blend business with romance and changed again to include the new look of the Afro Natural. The advertisement in volume 22 (1966-67) claimed that Murray's "trains kinky, wiry, hard-to-manage hair." Two years late in volume 24, "Murray's Brings You That Natural Look...The day of the 'patent-leather' look is gone. The new look is natural-like, soft and caressable." By volume 25, in 1970, Murray's offered a product designed exclusively for the "natural" hair style.

Perma-Strate was endorsed by Black celebrities in the early fifties; the ads also featured before-and-after back views, with the after being straight hair (see vol. 5, 1949-50, for examples). Endorsements continued in the late fifties, but the pictures began to give way to claims that Perma-Strate "removes all the undesirable kink" (vol. 13, no. 1), stressing "natural-looking straight hair" (see vols. 13-14, 1957-59). "Natural-looking straight hair" was still the target throughout much of the sixties. By volume 24 (1968-69), the emphasis had shifted to "when hair must be straightened before it can be styled," although the phrase "Natural-looking straight hair" was still in use. And the Posner company, makers of an enormous range of hair pressing oils and pomades, stressed the water-repellent characteristics of their creams throughout the early and mid-sixties; 1968 saw the introduction of products designe for the "Afro natural" (see vol. 24).

The claims of facial products like Nadinola, Dr. Palmer's Skin Whitene and Black and White Bleaching Cream show similar changes. In the late forties and early fifties, Nadinola Bleaching Cream and Nadinola De Luxe promised to "lighten and brighten dark skin" because "Men can't resist light, lovely skin" (vol. 5, 1949-50). The late fifties found Nadinola advertisements beginning, "Don't let dull, dark skin rob you of romance" (vol. 14, no. 6, 1958). But emphasis began to be placed on skin problem by 1966, Nadinola De Luxe advertised itself as a cream for oily skin, while Nadinola Cream presented its claims for dry skin. Similarly, the captions for Dr. Fred Palmer's Skin Whitener, which promised "lighter, clearer, younger-looking skin" in the late fifties and early sixties (vols. 13-21) became concerned with skin problems and by 1969 (vol. 24) were focused on Cleopatra, the African beauty. The advertisements in volume 25 (1970) noted that Dr. Palmer's had added lemon freshness and the product was to be used to tone in blotches.

Advertisements for Black and White Bleaching Cream were frequently overt in their references to physical attractiveness and desire. In 1950 (vol. 5), the captions advocated use of the product for "When he caresses your face" and "For those breathless moments." In 1957-59 (vols. 13-14), the advertisements stated that "He'll march up to the altar" because the user would "Be lovely, Be loved with lighter brighter skin." By 1968 (vol. 24), Black and White advertised itself as a medication against pimples.

A closer look at the contexts surrounding straight -- curly and light-- dark reveals some interesting context restrictions, which co-vary with the changing senses of natural, either overtly or by implication. Up until the sixties, advertisements for hair products were directed primarily towards the consumer's acquiring straight hair, and the word straight almost always occurred in the context "natural-looking." One could infer from most advertisements up until the sixties that beautiful hair should be "long," "shiny," and "straight," and should look as if it had always been that way. Curly had two senses: curly hair that had been straightened and then curled was positive, since it was then "naturally smooth, soft, natural-looking," to judge from advertisements

Boyd H. Davis

through volume 21 for Curl-Free, Magic in A Jar, Perma-Strate and
Murray's. The other sense of curly was negative in its early contexts:
"dry," "brittle," "kinky," "fuzzy," "unattractive," "un-manageable,"
"lifeless," "short," and "hopeless." By volumes 13 and 14 (1957-59),
curly hair was merely "stiff," "unruly," "too curly," "super-curly,"
"hard to manage," in constant danger of "reverting" or of "going back."
During 1957-66, volumes 13-21, straighteners began advertising themselves
as "relaxers" of "hard to manage" or "excessively curly" hair; hair
pomades and pressing oils began advertising their benefits as conditioners,
which would provide hair that "looks naturally smooth" (see, e.g., the
Curl Free advertisements, vol. 22). By volume 24 (1968-69), many of the
advertisements were in some way slanted "for men who wear it like it
is" or for "sisters" who "are different from brothers." An interesting
aspect of this new trend could be seen in ads for newly developed products, such as Afrosheen, which used Swahili words to appeal to "a
beautiful people," and Magnificent, which presented "natural" products;
older companies speedily promoted their own, not necessarily new, products
along these lines. Articles and advertisements in the early seventies
expanded to include hairstyles such as corn-rowing. In general, the
number of advertisements for hair care products was reduced, while advertisements for wigs increased. The most recent advertisements (1974-75)
show a variety of styles, and are glossy and glamorous.
The words "light" and "lighter" almost always co-occur with at least
one adjective; in volumes 1-12, the favorite adjectives were, in order,
brighter, clearer, softer. The words fairer, younger, and smoother
were the next most preferred. By volumes 12-13 (1956-58), the adjective
golden had become popular: Golden Peacock, for example, advertised
"you'll love my Golden Palomino Skin." These words remained in constant
use until volume 13 (1962-63), when emphasis began to dwell on softer,
smoother and clearer. Interestingly, the word natural was hardly ever
used except by implication that the use of a product would reveal lovely
soft light skin; Beatty's claimed this to be "natural" (vol. 5, 1949-50).
Late in volume 21 and throughout volume 22 (1966-68), advertisements
shifted their wording to a second, newly positive sense of "darkness,"
an emphasis which has remained.
Up to and intermittently throughout volume 21 (1965-66), "dark"
generally co-occurred with rough, dull, coarse, oily ("ugly shine"); the
word black occurred only in hair coloring ads. In volume 22 (1966-67),
Godefroy's Larieuse, a hair dye, used the phrase "Beautiful Black.
Exciting natural hair color. Beautiful dark shades to accent your natural
beauty." And Posner's Olive Tan makeups advertised themselves as being
for the "deep-toned," the "darker than fair." Ads for facial products in
volumes 22-24 (1966-69) shifted their emphasis from bleaching to medicinal
or healing purposes. The shift may be demonstrated by changes of wording
in Nadinola advertisements. In 1949-50 (vol. 5), Nadinola referred to
the "dull, dark skin" which "robbed" one of romance; in 1962-63 (vol. 18),
the user would be "lighter, brighter, clearer"; by 1966-67 (vol. 22),
Nadinola was to be used for "difficult" skin. And in 1968-69 (vol. 24),
Nadinola's new advertisement began: "Black is beautiful. Naturally
beautiful....Nadinola brings out the natural beauty of your complexion."
In the next two years, almost every pressing cream or pomade consistently
advertised itself as a conditioner, and several companies introduced
products specifically for the Afro "natural."

291

Boyd H. Davis

Several articles in Ebony discussed aspects of beauty. Skin whiteners were analyzed in 1950 (vol. 5, no. 3, 15-18), and an editorial in volume 14 (1958-59, no. 6, p. 128) noted that "a few--a very few--are seeking to glorify the naturalness of their hair." An article in volume 24 (1968-69), "The Natural Look--Is It Here to Stay?" noted a connection between militance and hair style, especially the Afro, "as recently as three years ago."

In thirty years of Ebony, we may distinguish at least four senses associated with curly--straight and dark--light and natural. The first sense has no cultural values. In the second, curly is negative and straight contains positive values; similarly, dark is negative and light positive. By the late fifties and early sixties, a third, ambivalent sense develops. Straight is still positive in value, but the frequent phrase "natural-looking straight" may indicate that natural-looking is not necessarily natural. That curly which had first been straightened and then curled develops positive values even more strongly during this period. Light now included "golden" and dark's contexts change with advertisements beginning to focus on healing. Natural is beginning to shift away from a hypothetical and desired natural (sense 2) to a "natural-looking"; by 1970, natural had acquired a fourth sense which could be termed "retrospective," in those advertisements promoting African prototypes. By 1970, straight and light have ambivalent values, dark and curly have as their fourth sense, increased positive value.

The relationship of these changes certainly seems to be keyed to cultural changes, but we must not be too sweeping in our claims. First, the data, whose wording changes, are not spoken, but written, and written in a hybrid Advertising English, with the structure of "school-value" written English and euphemistic vocabulary. Second, the data appear in advertisements in Ebony, a magazine with over a million in circulation, which is not, necessarily, an index to Afro-American cultural change. Waltrand M. Kassarjian in a 1973 article observed that Ebony "can hardly be considered representative of the Negro population as a whole."[1] Roland E. Wolseley noted in 1971 that Ebony "still speaks primarily to the middle-class black family who wants to be socially and financially successful."[2] Wolseley also said that Ebony had become "more outspoken" with the rise in militancy,[3] and warned that the climate of black opinion "is both confused and rapidly changing."[4]

The cosmetics advertisements in Ebony cannot be compared other than generally with advertisements in its counterparts. The counterparts are hard to determine. In format, Ebony most resembles Life or Look,[5] which did not have the volume of cosmetics advertising that Ebony carried. Heavier advertising for cosmetics appeared in women's magazines, such as Woman's Home Companion, but was sponsored by companies whose names in the advertising copy differed.[6]

While these factors must be taken into consideration, they do not negate the relationship between language change and social forces. Instead, these factors remind us that whether we are charting a shift in meaning today or two hundred years ago, the context of our data may not always be straightforward, and our interpretation must therefore be cautious. Those forces contributing to the shifts of meaning for nature as seen in Ebony's advertisements are still on-going. Lovejoy, the eminent historian of ideas, charted the multiplicity of connotations of nature in the eighteenth century.[7] In our own time, we are seeing a replay of the shifting connotations of nature, taking place within the context of the multiple social changes of Afro-American culture.[8]

292

Boyd H. Davis

NOTES

*The earlier SAMLA-ADS version of this paper was called "Some Economic Determinants of Cosmetic Terminology." Read at the SAMLA-ADS Meeting, Jacksonville, Florida, November 1972.

[1]Waltrand M. Kassarjian, "Blacks as Communicators and Interpreters of Mass Communication," Journalism Quarterly, 50 (1973), 287.

[2]Roland E. Wolseley, The Black Press, USA (Ames, Iowa: University of Iowa Press, 1971), p. 65. Cf. Wolseley's The Changing Magazine, Trends in Readership and Management (New York: Hastings House, 1973), pp. 104-07.

[3]Wolseley, Black Press, p. 119.

[4]Wolseley, Black Press, p. 133.

[5]Dave Berkman, "Advertising in 'Ebony' and 'Life': Negro Aspirations versus Reality," Journalism Quarterly, 40 (1963), 53-64.

[6]See Wolseley's discussion of the differences in advertising copy, volume and slant in The Black Press, USA, pp. 246-50.

[7]Paul M. Hirsch, "An Analysis of Ebony: The Magazine and Its Readers," Journalism Quarterly 45:261-65.

[8]Cosmetic products whose advertisements were examined include: Afrosheen, Allyn's Products, Beauty Star, Black Heritage, Black Strand, Black and White, Bleach and Glow, Charlene's, Clairol, Corn Silk, Curl Free, Dixie Peach, Duke Products, Dusharme, Easy Do, Eau Denna, Ebonaire, Epic, Esoterica, Esther's, eXelenta, Fleur de Gloire, Formula Nicole, Glossine, Glover's, Godefroy's Larieuse, Golden Peacock, Hair Magic, Hair-Strate, Helene Curtis, Jeris, K & K, Key Vel, Kombo, Kongolene, Kotalko, Lady Lennox, Libra, Long Aid Products, Lucky Heart Products, Lustrasilk, Magic in a Jar, Magnificent, Markhide, Medalo, Mel-O-Lox, Mercolized Wax, Mr./Miss Natural, Morganoil, Mova, Murray's Products, My Knight, Nadinola Products, Nelson's, Nestle, Night Dreams, Noxema, Nu-Nile, Overton, Olive Tan, Dr. Palmer's Products, PermaStrate, Posner's Products (Bergamot,etc.), Queen Bergamot, Raveen Products, Revlon, (Flori) Roberts, Royal Crown Products, Salene, Shampoo-Straight, Silky Strate, Straiteen, So-Mild, Strand, Style Craft, Sulfur-8, Super Groom, Tarex, Tintz, Tuxedo Club, Ultra Sheen, Ultra Wave, (Mme. C. J.) Walker's Products.

IF LADIES WEREN'T PRESENT, I'D TELL YOU WHAT I REALLY THINK

Connie C. Eble

The title of this paper is a cliché which most adult women in America
have often heard. It shows the male as the protector--shielding his
female listener from a violation of her sense of feminine delicacy and
at the same time sparing himself the effort of articulating in precise,
inoffensive, standard English.
The common use of such clichés acknowledges that the double standard
by which society differentially judges male and female behavior extends
also to language. Linguistic behavior ranges over a continuum from
behavior which is characteristically male to behavior which is characteristically female, with a neutral zone somewhere in the middle.
Terms of hostility and abuse such as curses and obscenities are generally
associated with masculinity, whereas euphemistic and superlative terms
are associated with femininity; neutral terms are associated with neither
sex. It is when females verge into characteristically male behavior (such
as the use of obscenities) and when males trespass into characteristically
female behavior (such as the indiscriminate use of adjectives like
precious, adorable, divine) that appropriateness is violated. The absence
of such female features does not make a woman's use of language masculine;
nor does the absence of typically male usage render a man's language
effeminate.
In this paper I will discuss two areas of language use in our culture
in which different standards of appropriateness apply to the two sexes,
expressions of abuse and subject matter.
Probably the most obvious sex-linked feature in American English usage
is the absence of swear words and obscenities in the speech of well-
mannered women.[1] Men have a language style, characterized by the presence
of this very feature, which is not for "mixed company." Jokes and vocabulary which are permissible, even expected, among men are indications
of coarseness and indiscretion when used by women of comparable social
status.
Several months ago International Telephone and Telegraph lobbyist
Dita Beard rose to national prominence because of her alleged involvement
in an ITT pay-off to the Republican Party. During the many weeks in which
Dita Beard was in the news, the main fact that the American public learned
about her personally was that her use of the English language was not
feminine. A New York Times story entitled "Hard-Talking Lobbyist"[2]
described her as "hard-talking, strong-minded, and fiercely independent,"
in that order. The story elaborated first on her language, quoting her
colleagues who said, "She's one of the boys; talks like a man in a poker
game," and "She has the vocabulary of a drill instructor in the Marines."
After other testimonials to Dita Beard's linguistic prowess, the Times

Connie C. Eble

account concluded with this story.

...Once at a Republican dinner meeting there to plan
fund-raising strategy, a party official, disagreeing
with a proposal stood up and used a profanity. Noticing
Mrs. Beard, the only woman in the audience, he apologized
for his language to 'the lady present.'
Mrs. Beard replied, 'I don't see any ladies present.'

Dita Beard, by her own admission, has chosen to adopt a form of linguistic behavior generally not deemed appropriate for a female, and for
that reason--because she violates social expectations--her language is
newsworthy.

Another instance of feminine linguistic impropriety which received the
attention of the American press took place in distant New Zealand.[3]

Germaine Greer, the feminist writer, received a summons to
appear in court on a charge that she used an indecent word
in an address before a mass meeting at the Town Hall. She
greeted the summons with the same word that authorities found
objectionable--an eight letter barnyard epithet. Further
undeterred, she repeated the word at another public meeting
and called on people in the audience to repeat it after her.
They did, in a mass shout.

More recently novelist Erica Jong, scheduled to speak at a Smithsonian
Institution monthly lecture series, was twice requested to "keep her talk
clean." Instead, she cancelled her appearance at the Smithsonian and
spoke at nearby Mt. Vernon College, "delivering a speech that would have
made the Smithsonian dinosaurs rattle with fright."[4]

All three of these incidents show women displaying linguistic behavior
traditionally prohibited to their sex. Such behavior is still different
and daring enough to receive national press coverage.

Sexual distinctions in language use overlap with various combinations
of other distinctions such as age, geographic region, socio-economic
class, ethnic identification, occupation, and specific social situation.
In general, the use of abusive terms is associated with males rather than
with females; with blue-collar workers on the job rather than with
professionals on the job; with parties and night clubs rather than with
formal or quasi-formal public or religious gatherings.

Although trained in school to avoid abusive language, male lowerclass workers of all occupations normally swear both on and off the job.[5]
Swearing is an expected characteristic of the conversation of factory
and construction workers and men in the armed forces. Abusive terms of
sexual and excretory reference also are common in the speech of blue-
collar workers. In a survey of on-the-job vocabulary of some 3000
midwesterners, psychologist Paul Cameron found that "dirty" words constituted almost one-fourth of the vocabulary of factory and construction
workers.[6] Sociologist Jessie Bernard explains the function of such use
of taboo words:

It is often just the sheer pleasure of word play that is
reflected in the all-male sex talk of blue-collar workers.
They enjoy the free use of words taboo in the presence of
women. Under these circumstances blasphemy and the four-
letter words are fun. They underscore the sex camaraderie
which men, liberated from the inhibitions of the presence
of women, enjoy. Sometimes the talk is just the telling
of off-color stories. Sex is funny, amusing, a joke; but

Connie C. Eble

again, in this sense, forbidden in the presence of women.
Again, half the fun in this kind of talk is the understanding which the sharing of such jokes implies: the
male world against the restrictions of the female world.[7]
Elsie Parsons in 1913 also noticed the assertion of male dominance in
the use of profanity: "Profanity, originally merely an appeal to the
gods, belongs exclusively, they [men] feel, to themselves, a prerogative
they safeguard by not even availing themselves of it before a woman..."[8]
If facility in cursing and obscenity is indeed a demonstration of
machismo, it is not surprising that it be forbidden to the ear or tongue
of the "weaker sex." Two etiquette books for men, Service Etiquette and
Esquire's Guide to Modern Etiquette, warn against cursing and profanity
in mixed company, although Esquire's adds, "...if you must, do it like
a man."[9] The proscription of abusive language for women is apparently
so unthinkable that it isn't even mentioned in the standard etiquette
manuals directed at a female audience.
Although many males disregard the traditional advice of the etiquette
books and use profanity in the presence of females, their willingness to
flout the prohibition is often mitigated by prefaced apologies like
excuse/pardon me, if the ladies will forgive me, pardon my language,
pardon my English, or pardon my French.
Whether or not actual linguistic behavior reflects the double standard
of the etiquette books and clichés is problematic. Empirical data
about verbal obscenity have been scarce until recently and largely the
by-product of research on other types of behavior. Paul Cameron points
out that the standard word frequency list used by social scientists
contains almost no profanity and is based on written English.[10] Various
experiments have shown significant and contradictory differences between
male and female recall and cued production of abusive language; but the
experimenters have been quick to caution that such factors as the medium
of communication (oral vs. written), the sex and authority of the
examiner, the familiarity of the taboo words, and the age of the subjects
must be controlled and investigated more thoroughly.[11] A "comprehensive
research project concerned with the use, function, and personal-
cultural-linguistic significance of obscene language within English and
in a variety of other languages" has been undertaken by Russell Foote
and Jack Woodward of the University of Wyoming. A preliminary report
stated that

females tended to produce more obscenities in written form and
were closer to matching males in this mode, while males tended
to be more productive orally and nearly doubled the output of
females when called upon to speak obscenities. These tendencies
suggest that while performance of the Ss overall did not differ
as a function of production mode (because of the general absence
of social inhibitions in the experimental setting), females
nevertheless brought sufficient self-generated inhibitions
(perhaps as a function of sex role) so that they retained some
tendencies to inhibit their expression of obscenity through
the more blatant oral expressive mode.[12]

The prohibitions against abusive language are breaking down. A growing
number of men and women are using publicly vocabulary that was previously
restricted to all-male contexts. It is not surprising that the female
is adopting the linguistic behavior of the male; it is human nature for
the people on the bottom to imitate the people on the top, and not vice-

297

versa. The change has brought mixed reactions. The Cosmo Girl's Guide to the New Etiquette justifies the new behavior: "The new uninhibited frankness has its place. Indeed, there is something vulgar and unpleasant about coy, simpering circumlocution to avoid plain Anglo-Saxon English or straight anatomic nouns!"[13] Male chauvinist Wallace Reyburn is annoyed, particularly with feminists, for "their peppering of their texts with four-letter words..., an attempt to copy men, to show that they are on equal footing with them."[14] Reyburn resents women infringing on the male-dominated area of four-letter words and fears that women will debase their use and effectiveness.

A second area in which the double standard applies is subject matter. The social condition of male superiority assigns important business to men and trivial business to women. Men, who are involved in the serious business of society, are expected to be straightforward and blunt in their language, whereas women, who busy themselves with the incidentals of life, are expected to cultivate a verbal style embellished with euphemisms and pleasantries.

Nowhere is the double standard as applied to subject matter more glaring than in the custom of sexual separation at dinner parties in our nation's capital. As reports the New York Times, women are

...permitted to eat dinner with the men, but afterwards,
when it's time for serious conversation, they're invited
upstairs to have coffee and chatter in the hostess' bed-
room while the men gather in the library a l'anglaise....
According to a number of men, who in this age of women's
lib were wary of being quoted directly,...the segregation
results from the women's inability to engage in intelligent
discussion.[15]

Women's dissatisfaction with banishment from the scene of serious conversation made the news in the spring of 1972 when the wives of two prominent Washingtonians walked out on a dinner party given by columnist Joe Alsop.

More than a century and a half ago the English educator Hannah More voiced her opposition to the same after-dinner tradition.

It is a disadvantage, even to those women who keep the best
company, that it is unhappily almost established into a
system, by the other sex, to postpone everything like
instructive discourse till the ladies are withdrawn; their
retreat serving as a kind of signal for the exercise of the
intellect. And in the few cases in which it happens that
any important discussion takes place in their presence,
they are for the most part considered as having little
interest in serious subjects. Strong truths, whenever
such happen to be addressed to them, are either diluted with
flattery, or kept back in part, or softened to their taste;
of if the ladies express a wish for information on any point,
they are put off with a compliment, instead of a reason; and
are considered as beings who are not expected to see and judge
of things as they really exist.[16]

Emily Post's Etiquette (12th ed. revised, 1969) still devotes almost a page to proper leave-taking by the gentlemen after dinner, but Amy Vanderbilt's Etiquette (1972) offers the choice of English or continental style, with preference for the continental fashion as "pleasanter."

The main subject traditionally forbidden to women in our society is
sex. In 1913 Elsie Parsons complained, "Men have what might almost be
called a secret language of sex, whereas women have no words, secret
or otherwise, to describe some of the simplest sex characters and
expressions."[17]
Two world wars and Freudian psychology later Alfred Kinsey and
associates observed that, "Males are much more inclined, and females
less inclined, to discuss sexual matters with other persons."[18] The
difference between male and female willingness to express intimate
feelings about sex showed up particularly in writing. The Kinsey report
states, "Among the hundreds and probably thousands of unpublished,
amateur documents which we have seen during the past fifteen years, we
have been able to find only three manuscripts written by females which
contain erotic elements of the sort ordinarily found in documents
written by males."[19]
Studies have shown that sex is a favorite topic among men, common to
the conversations of all occupations and social classes.[20] In industry
sex is a common subject in all groups from executives and managers to
manual workers, although the content and vocabulary of discussions vary
from group to group. Middle class males generally do not discuss personal
sexual experiences, while manual workers speak freely of sexual affairs
with their wives or other women.[21]
Females do talk about sex, but it has been observed that among female
white-collar workers "...crude sex jokes and personal experience are kept
at a minimum."[22] In general, female conversations involving sex have
as their main concern questions of affection and love.[23] Perhaps that
is why Anne Sexton's poem "Menstruation at Forty" in her 1967 Pulitzer
Prize collection Live or Die embarrassed and offended so many women.
The reticence and sometimes inability of women to discuss matters of
sex and reproduction can cause problems. A social worker in rural North
Carolina complained to a newspaper interviewer that, "The greatest
difficulty she faces is in getting people to realize that family planning
will help them. 'The feeling in this area is that it is something you
keep quiet, hush-hush, and don't talk about.'"[24]
This attitude is not confined to low-income women in the rural South.
Psychiatrist Theodore Reik remarks, "We psychoanalysts are often surprised and sometimes puzzled by the indirect and often too delicate way
in which women patients speak of sexual matters in their analytic
sessions."[25] To combat this attitude some psychiatrists and psychologists
are now using in therapy sexually frank novels like Erica Jong's Fear
of Flying to encourage female patients to talk about their sexual problems.[26]
Free-lance writer Ethel Strainchamps complains that even in this age
of sexual freedom and frankness it is difficult for a woman to get a
serious article published if the subject is sex.
A few years ago I got together some usage data I had compiled
as a reader for a dictionary and wrote a report on the effect
that the loosening of the obscenity laws was having on family
newspapers and magazines. Before I started writing the piece,
a Harper's editor told me he was interested, but he returned
it with the excuse that the magazine had run a piece on pornography a few months before. Then I sent it to Playboy, and
they said it was too scholarly. I sent it to American
Scholar, and they said it was too journalistic. I sent it to
Yale Review, admitting the previous rejections and offering

Connie C. Eble

to alter the piece if the information in it seemed to make
it worth the trouble. I got a letter back from Editor-in-
Chief Paul Pickrel. It began, 'At last you have found an
honest editor.' He said that none of the excuses I had been
given had anything to do with the reason the piece had not
been published and that the criticisms were not valid. The
real trouble, he said, 'is that you are a woman writing on
a subject which, according to contemporary mores, women do
not write on.'[26]
In this paper I have discussed just one facet of the difference between
the language of men and women, i.e., the different measures of appropriate
ness as applied to the use of abusive language and subject matter. This
linguistic double standard is merely an extension of the double standard
used to judge other types of behavior. When the differential measure
of appropriateness in the other types of behavior disappears, so will
the linguistic one.

NOTES

*Read at the SAMLA-ADS Meeting, Jacksonville, Florida, November 1972.

[1] Standards that apply to women also apply to public officials, as
evidenced by the objections to President Truman's "salty" language a
generation ago and more recent dismay over the deleted expletives of
President Nixon.

[2] "Hard Talking Lobbyist: Dita Davis Beard," New York Times, March 6,
1972, p. 16.

[3] New York Times, March 9, 1972, p. 31.

[4] "People," Time, January 20, 1975, pp. 44-45.

[5] Delbert C. Miller and William H. Form, Industrial Sociology, 2d ed.
(New York: Harper and Row Publishers, Inc., 1964), p. 264.

[6] "X-Rated Expletives," Time, May 20, 1974, p. 73.

[7] Jessie Bernard, The Sex Game: Communication Between the Sexes (Englewood
Cliffs, N.J.: Prentice-Hall, 1968; reprint ed., New York: Atheneum,
1972), pp. 277-78. I am indebted to this book for directing me to
the references in notes 5, 18, and 23.

[8] Elsie Clews Parsons, The Old-Fashioned Woman (New York: G. P. Putnam's
Sons, 1913), p. 152.

[9] The Editors of Esquire Magazine and Ron Butler, Esquire's Guide to
Modern Etiquette (Philadelphia: J. B. Lippincott and Co., 1969), p. 86.

Connie C. Eble

[10]Paul Cameron, "Frequency and Kinds of Words in Various Social Settings, or What the Hell's Going On?" Pacific Sociological Review, 12 (Fall, 1969), p. 101.

[11]See George S. Grosser and Anthony A. Walsh, "Sex Differences in the Differential Recall of Taboo and Neutral Words," Journal of Psychology, 63 (May, 1966), 219-27; Marilyn E. Miller and Normal Solkoff, "Effects of Mode of Response and Sex of Experimenter Upon Recognition Thresholds of Taboo Words," Perceptual and Motor Skills, 20 (April, 1965), 573-78.

[12]Russell Foote and Jack Woodward, "A Preliminary Investigation of Obscene Language," The Journal of Psychology, 83 (March, 1973), 274-75.

[13]Jeanette Sarkisian Wagner, ed., The Cosmo Girl's Guide to the New Etiquette (New York: Cosmopolitan Books, 1971), p. 42.

[14]Wallace Reyburn, The Inferior Sex (Englewood Cliffs, N.J.: Prentice-Hall, Inc., 1972), pp. 196-97.

[15]"Shall We Join the Ladies? A Custom is Challenged," New York Times, April 2, 1972, p. 50.

[16]Hannah More, Strictures on the Modern System of Female Education, 2 vols. (New York: George Long, 1813), pp. 22-23.

[17]Parsons, Old-Fashioned Woman, p. 156.

[18]Alfred C. Kinsey, et al., Sexual Behavior in the Human Female (Philadelphia: W. B. Saunders Co., 1953), p. 675.

[19]Ibid., p. 672.

[20]Bernard, Sex Game, p. 151.

[21]Miller and Form, Industrial Sociology, pp. 268-69.

[22]Ibid., p. 268.

[23]J. H. Gagnon, "Sexuality and Sexual Learning in the Child," Psychiatry, 28 (August, 1965), p. 214.

[24]Debi Potter, "Warrenton Woman Brings 'Good News,'" Durham Morning Herald, September 22, 1972.

[25]Theodore Reik, "Men and Women Speak Different Languages," Psycho-analysis, 2 (1954), 3-15.

[27]Ethel Strainchamps, "Our Sexist Language," Woman in Sexist Society, ed. by Vivian Gornick and Barbara K. Moran (New York: Signet Books, 1971), p. 359.

PARADIGMATIC WOMAN: THE PROSTITUTE*

Julia P. Stanley

I must request your patience at the outset by asking you to read and consider three diverse and apparently unrelated quotations from Mindswap (New York: Dell, 1966), a science fiction novel by Robert Sheckley. By examining the features of the semantic set comprised of our terms for prostitutes and demonstrating how the important features of this lexical set make explicit the definition of woman that our culture projects to us, I intend to show you how these quotations are related. Indeed, each of them is dependent on the other.

Analogy assures us that this is like that; it forms a bridge between the accepted known and the unacceptable unknown. It attaches the one to the other, imbuing the intolerable un- known with a desirable familiarity. (p. 10)

All of us live by the employment of countless untested assumptions, the truth or falsehood of which we can deter- mine only through the hazard of our lives. Since most of us value our lives more than the truth, we leave such tests for the fanatics. (p. 18)

"It is droll to realize," the saddlebum said, "that Custom has decreed this lady's mask, proclaiming that those who sell pleasure must portray enjoyment. It is a hard demand, my friends, and not imposed upon any other occupa- tion. For note, the fishwife is allowed to hate herring, the vegetable seller may be allergic to turnips, and even the newspaper boy is permitted his illiteracy. Not even the blessed saints are required to enjoy their holy martyrdoms. Only the humble sellers of pleasure are required, like Tantalus, to be forever expectant of an untouchable feast."

"Yer friend's a great little kidder, ain't he?" the terma- gant said, "but I like you best, baby, 'cause you make me go all mush inside."

From the virago's neck there hung a pendant upon which was strung in miniature a skull, a piano, an arrow, a baby's shoe, and a yellowed tooth.

"What are those?" Marvin asked.

"Symbols," she said.

"Of what?"

"Come on upstairs, and I'll show you, sweety-ass."

"And thus," the saddlebum intoned, "we perceive the true unmediated confrontation of the aroused feminine nature, 'gainst which our masculine fancies seem mere baby's toys."

303

   "C'mon!" the harpy cried, wriggling her gross body in a counter-
feit of passion all the more frightening because it was real.
"Upstairs to bed!" she shouted, pressing against Marvin with a
breast the size and consistency of an empty Mongolian saddlebag.
"I'll really show ya somepin!" she cried, entwining his thews
with a heavy white leg, somewhat grimy and heavily varicosed.
"When ya git loved by me," she howled, "you'll damned well know
you been loved!" And she ground lasciviously against him with
her pudenda, which was as heavily armored as the forehead of a
Tyrannosaurus. (pp. 79-80)
What has the function of analogy as a bridge to the unknown to do with
structuring our lives on the basis of untested assumptions? And what
connection do these have with Sheckley's description of Marvin's encounter
with a prostitute? If you will glance once more at the long, descriptive
passage, you will notice that it is a representation of the stereotyped
aging prostitute, including, significantly, three of the terms that
Germaine Greer cites as the names most insultingly applied to women,
termagant, virago, and harpy.¹ In addition, we are told that in this
encounter we see "the true unmediated confrontation of the aroused
feminine nature, 'gainst which our masculine fancies seem mere baby's
toys." And the woman that Sheckley chooses to represent the "aroused
feminine nature" has a "gross body"; her breasts are "the size and
consistency of an empty Mongolian saddlebag"; Marvin has "thews,"
while the woman has "a heavy white leg, somewhat grimy and heavily
varicosed"; and in case you haven't had enough, she grinds against
Marvin "lasciviously," with a "pudenda,...as heavily armored as the
forehead of a Tyrannosaurus." And poor Marvin is frightened of the
"harpy" because her passion is real.
   Sheckley certainly invites us to be repulsed by such a "grotesque" scene.
The "virago" has committed three of the unpardonable sins of women: she
is old, she is ugly, and she is aggressive. And the analogies that
Sheckley uses to represent the unknown for us provide only a glimpse into
the metaphorical possibilities for describing women. Asked to entertain
the images of "a Mongolian saddlebag" and "the forehead of a Tyrannosaurus," the term pudenda is surprisingly sterile and medical. I'm
willing to wager, on the basis of my own reading experience, that
Sheckley's description is representative of the treatment of prostitutes
in popular literature. As interesting as the use of the stereotype is
Marvin's fear of her passion, and, perhaps, her aggressive presentation
of herself.
   But we're concerned here with analogies and stereotyping. Where do we
get our stereotypes? How do we arrive at our neat pigeon-holings of
other human beings? We take all of our untested assumptions about this,
all of our beliefs about reality, our opinions, value judgments, and
biases, and, by analogy, we transfer these assumptions and beliefs to
that, about which we know little or nothing. In this way, we bring the
unknown within the bounds of our own reality, which enables us to pretend
to ourselves and others that we know all there is to know about the
unknown. The stereotype allows us to categorize people as we think they
are, on the basis of our fantasies and expectations of them. The truth
or falsity of these stereotypes is irrelevant, as is usually the case
with fantasy worlds; the mere act of naming is sufficient in itself, and
we are perpetually naming, defining the boundaries and terms of our own
existence and that of others. The names we give things affect, for all

Julia P. Stanley

time, our attitude toward them. Naming embodies our judgments as
inherent features of the objects to which we attend. As Ruth Herschberger
has commented, we lose our insight because we are always holding up a
screen of language between ourselves and the world.[2] Further, she points
out that "one of the time-honored functions of language is to push
reality into more pleasing shapes."[3] One might also say that one of the
functions of our use of language is pushing people into shapes that conform to the linguistic straitjackets we have prepared for us. Even the
most cursory examination of the terms applied to prostitutes will reveal
that these terms directly reflect men's fantasies about the relationship
of men to women and the underlying conflict that directs and maintains
those fantasies.

In the most general terms, the conflict inherent in men's attitudes
toward women has to do with our culture and its history; the conflict is
a part of our inheritance, as are the stereotypes that are signs of the
conflict. Much of the hostility and derision expressed by women as well
as men toward the Feminist Movement is based on the cultural metaphors
that structure our reality and provide us with interpretations of the
events going on around us. And these metaphors that shape our minds and
structure our thoughts were absorbed by us as we learned the basic terms
of our language. How should we be expected to react when something
threatens the destruction of these metaphors and questions the validity
of the cultural assumptions on which these metaphors are based? We all
need to understand that our laughter, derision, and hostility are defense
mechanisms that protect our minds and enable us to block out viewpoints
that are inimical to our culturally-imposed interpretations of reality.
And we need to understand that Feminism in fact is a movement committed
to the destruction of these metaphors. Of course men laugh at Feminism;
what else can they do?

In our encounters with the world, and in our efforts to classify and
assign meanings to those encounters, we use metaphor as an implicit
(but sometimes explicit) structure for these classifications of objects.
The metaphors themselves are based on our hypotheses about the way
things are in the world, and these hypotheses are predications that
express our evaluations and perceptions of the relations between and
among the objects in our world.

The names that men have given to women who make themselves sexually
available to them reveal the underlying metaphors by which men conceive
of their relationships with women, and through which women learn to
perceive and define themselves. The metaphors that underlie the
terms for sexually promiscuous women define and perpetuate the ambivalent
sex-role stereotypes that a male-dominated culture sets forth for women.
On the one hand, women who "put out" for men are described as hags,
slop jars, and pisspallets; but women who don't put out are damned as
frigid, cold, or maladjusted. All of these terms assume, of course, that
a woman's only means of identification lies in her relationship to a man
(or men). My analysis of 220 such terms for women reveals that the only
way a woman can define her sexuality with the names provided by our
culture is demeaning, shameful, and/or oppressively non-existent, should
she choose to reject the terms that men associate with her sexuality.

The terms for prostitutes provide us with a paradigm of the way both
men and women see each other as things to be used. Prostitution, as an
occupation, is an act of exploitation. But what the prostitute exploits
is not men, but herself as representative of all women, and men's

expectations of women, and the fantasies of women projected by their
expectations. The prostitute capitalizes on the culturally favored stereotypes of women, like passivity, instability, materiality, shrewishness,
and pliancy, and the male attitudes that create these stereotypes. The
prostitute thus validates the fantasy caricatures of women, and her
financial success depends upon her ability to fulfill the male expectations embodied in these stereotypes. Some, of course, specialize.

In our culture, we are taught to be ashamed of our sexuality, to avoid
reference to the sex act, to the sexual organs, in fact, to ignore the
fact that we have bodies. However, up to the present time, women, more
than men, have been intimidated into embarrassment about their sexuality.
Men, in their own private conclaves, the locker rooms of the world, have
been encouraged to boast about their uses of women. In fact, one of the
primary criteria for "manliness" is successful exploitation of women's
bodies. The term that denotes masculinity as a morality is _machismo_,
and its emphasis is on animal sexuality. The adjective _macho_ was
originally used only to refer to male animals, emphasizing their maleness
It is especially used to refer to the male animal's "super-sexuality,"
particularly with reference to over-sized genitals, and/or to the male
animal's brutal, bestial traits (i.e., how wild a horse or bull is).
Recently, the term _macho_ has been transferred to human males with the
same meanings. One lexicographer notes that this usage is popular among
boys as a highly complimentary attributive.[4] _Macho_ is a qualitative
feature attributed to males; _machismo_ is the possessed attribute.

Apparently, the pressure to live within the "masculine" moral structure
accounts for Sagarin's observations on the relationship between the use
of taboo words and masculinity.

> The adolescent, growing in his awareness of sexuality, is
> constantly developing and creating the language of pro-
> hibited terminology. His vocabulary, although satisfactorily
> expressive, is unceasingly expanding. The abundance of neo-
> logisms imparts a feeling, to the youthful males who create
> and perpetuate them, of ribaldry, vitality, and strength of
> a masculine character.[5]

So it is through a "screen of language," the language of exploitation,
that men establish and maintain their masculinity.

A few pages later, in his discussion of the words for breasts, Sagarin
himself feels called upon to comment upon the conflicting emotions that
men express about their relationships with women.

> The abundance of words for breasts, of which the above is
> but a minute sampling, is an index of the intense interest
> in the anatomy of the female on the part of the most imag-
> inative and creative of the slang-using groups, and of the
> need for masculine identification with peer groups among
> those who display toward the breast the ambivalence of
> shame and want, fear and desire, guilt and lust.[6]

Of course, women are expected to be flattered by all of this "intense
interest."

While it is not only women who experience societal pressure in
assuming their sexual identity, it is men as well, I'm concerned here
with the problems of women. Terms like _screw_, _rip off_, _nail_, _shove it
to her_, and _get into someone_ clearly define the role of the woman as
a passive object on whom the male acts out violent, sadistic fantasies.
With an arsenal of terms like that for the so-called "act of love," it's

no wonder that women think twice about indulging themselves. The close relationship between language and culture is perhaps clearest in the area of taboo words in the lexicon, particularly those terms that deal specifically with sexual activities and organs. One radical women's group has put the problem in the following way:

But why is it that women have related to and through men? By virtue of having been brought up in a male society, we have internalized the male culture's definition of ourselves. That definition views us as relative beings who exist not for ourselves, but for the servicing, maintenance and comfort of men. That definition consigns us to sexual and family functions, and excludes us from defining and shaping the terms of our lives.[7]

I have already cited Sagarin's comments on the male point of view inherent in the use of slang for sexual activities, and you may have noticed the terms "imaginative" and "creative" in his discussion. But perhaps the best example of the totally male orientation of such terms and their use is the following quotation from Eric Partridge, cited by Fryer.

Over 1,200 English synonyms for this word [fuck] have been recorded; their 'vivid expressiveness' and 'vigorous ingenuity' ...'bear witness to the fertility of English and to the enthusiastic English participation in the universal fascination of the creative act.'[8]

One wonders about the source of this "universal fascination," but, as we have seen, it is the male portion of the population that is the most active in coining and perpetuating new terms, especially those terms that project their fantasies as realities. It is, of course, the prostitute who, by selling herself as a commodity, makes it possible for men to continue to believe in women who exist only to serve their needs. That is the function of the prostitute in our culture, and that is the reason men permit prostitution to continue. The prostitute personifies for the male the dual aspects of the female that he seems to cherish: he can look down on the prostitute as being inferior to him in social status; at the same time she creates for him a fantasy world in which woman harkens to his every beck and call. On the one hand, women are not supposed to like sex, especially if they are pure and virtuous; on the other, I have heard men say that "All women are whores at heart." These are the definitions of women to which women's liberation is objecting, and these definitions are not made up.

As a prime example of this kind of thinking in our culture, consider a verb I have already mentioned, <u>screw</u>. There is no favorable context in which this verb can occur. Edward Sagarin has made some interesting observations that illustrate clearly how men and women have created a double bind situation in their relations with each other.

Sex is something, of course, that a nice girl is not supposed to like, but submits to with reluctance because the male has the devil in his flesh. By appropriating the verb <u>screw</u> for sexual description, a society perpetuates this concept, and at the same time permits the conquering warrior male to retain an image of himself as having forced himself upon the reluctant female. The language is a reflection of a society that abhors sex while idolizing the male who obtains it and denouncing the female who offers it.[9]

Sagarin goes on to comment on the additional slang uses of <u>screw</u>, none of which are favorable in their connotations.

But a person gets screwed when he gets the short end of the
stick, when someone betrays him. One says that he worked
very hard when his employer needed him, only to be fired in
the slow season: his boss screwed him, or he got a screwing.
Or the same thing would be said of a girl, and it is difficult to imagine any ambiguity.[10]

I am certain that we are all aware of other instances of the use of this
verb, so I won't provide additional examples here. However, I think it
is obvious from these examples that any way you care to look at it,
especially if you're a female, "getting screwed" is not something to enjo

The names that we call prostitutes fully represent the variety of roles
assigned to woman-as-sex-object, and make explicit the metaphorical content of female stereotypes in our society. The entire semantic set
exemplifies the "screen of language" through which men "see" women and,
consequently, the view of themselves that women are taught. A woman
learns to define herself as a piece of ass, bitch, pussy, or gash.
Since women are taught to please men in our culture, it is no wonder that
women go out of their way to "fit into" the semantic categories that
our culture provides.

The semantic features that define the categories represented by the
terms for prostitutes are listed below; those features that inhere in
the reference of the terms are denotative, and the emotional associations
that surround the terms are connotative.[11]

SEMANTIC FEATURES OF SEXUAL TERMS APPLIED TO WOMEN

A. DENOTATIVE: CONNOTATIVE:
    1. COST: FREE(F),   1. NEGATIVE(NEG)
              CHEAP(C),
              EXPENSIVE(E)
    2. METHOD OF PAYMENT: 2. NEUTRAL(NEU)
              DIRECT(D) or
              INDIRECT(I)
    3. TYPE OF ACTIVITY: 3. POSITIVE(POS)
              LITTLE OR MUCH
       --whether the man expects the woman to be passive or an active
         participant --($\pm$A)

B. DYSPHEMISTIC (DYS) or EUPHEMISTIC (EU):
    Whether the term exposes male disdain for the sexuality of women
    or conceals his disdain.

C. METONYMIC (P/W): Whether the term refers to women through referenc
    to a specific portion of their bodies.

D. METAPHORIC (MET): Whether the term refers to women thoough compari
    son to another object or animal.

The denotative terms include Cost, Method of Payment, and Type of Activity. Cost is divided into three parameters, Free (F), Cheap (C), and
Expensive (E), with two overlapping categories, Free/Cheap (F/C) and
Cheap/Expensive (C/E). Method of Payment contains two parameters, Direct
(D) and Indirect (I), and a third possibility is a combination of these
two, D/I, which specifies a term that can be used whether the payment
is Direct or Indirect. Direct payment is the actual exchange of cash;
indirect payment may be something like dinner and a show, or a night on
the town. Either way, the man feels that he is spending money with one

Julia P. Stanley

purpose in mind. I remember one quotation that may explain this point of
view better than I can. A disc jockey in Athens, Georgia had just
finished playing the song, "Treat Her Like A Lady." The idea behind
"treating her like a lady," as it's stated in the song, is that "she'll
be good to you." When the record was over, the disc jockey said, "Yeah,
treat her like a lady, and maybe she'll give you a money-back guarantee."
At any rate, this overlap between the two features also explains why
there are no terms with the single feature Free, and the combination of
Free/Cheap as a possibility. The last feature, Type of Activity, with
the sub-classes Little or Much (+A), isolates the man's expectations of
the woman's sexual role, whether or not she's to be an active participant.
For most of these terms this feature is irrelevant, so they aren't marked
for it.
   The connotative features, listed to the right of the denotative, include
three possibilities: Negative (NEG), Positive (POS), and Neutral (NEU).
Only one term showed overlap, ballbuster, and it's marked NEG/POS. The
term is used with negative connotations when it refers to an aggressive
woman or someone who is a sexual "tease." Ballbuster has positive connotations when it refers to a woman who is very active sexually. Most of
the terms carry only negative connotations. Only four terms have
neutral connotations, lady of the night, entertainer, concubine, and
mistress, and only one term carries positive connotations, courtesan.
Of these terms, four occur with the feature C/E or E, and are in the
range of Extended Contact. The connotative features were the most
problematic, for an obvious reason: most of the men expressed ambivalence
about their feelings for several terms, e.g., piece, ass, and prostitute.
In addition, no single man knew all of the terms, and one can't react
to an unknown term. In such cases, I used consensus reactions to mark
the terms. Initially, I thought that "negativity" would be an inherent,
denotative feature, since prostitution is condemned by our society, but
the ambiguity of reference and the problem of intent negated such an
easy solution.
   In addition to the 13 features I've just discussed, each term was also
marked to indicate whether it is a dysphemism (DYS) or a euphemism (EU),
and if the term is a figure of speech, it is marked as either metonymic
(P/W) or metaphoric (MET). Although it is possible for a term to be
both metonymic and metaphoric, e.g., cockeye, which I've marked at MET,
and brown-eye, which I've marked as P/W, I didn't allow for this kind of
overlap in my analysis of the terms.
   As it is, if we were to set up a parametric grid, we would find that
there are 2,160 possible interactions of parameters, but only 44 of
these possibilities are realized in the semantic set. Of these 44
semantic categories, only ten occur in the Extended Contact range. The
other 34 are in the Contact Irrelevant or Brief Contact ranges. In the
appendix to this paper you fill find a list of the 220 terms, broken
down into Dysphemistic and Euphemistic, then listed alphabetically,
with their semantic features, under these two categories.
   My sources were varied, and there will probably be many terms with
which many are unfamiliar. Aside from dictionaries like the OED,
Partridge's Dictionary of Slang and Unconventional English, Wentworth
and Flexner's Dictionary of American Slang, I have also drawn from
books like Down in the Holler, a book on Ozark slang, from The Sot-
Weed Factor by John Barth,[12] and I have used information provided by
friends, colleagues, and students. Omitted from this list are some

309

Julia P. Stanley

terms that are limited in their use to literature, like bona roba,
demimondaine, callat, callet, giglot, blowen, and fricatrice. I have
also excluded strictly literary coinages like no better than she should
be. In general, I included terms that I found in two or more sources
because the lexicography in this area is uneven, often apparently
whimsical. For this reason, you will find split-tail in the list, which
is used in The Sot-Weed Factor and cited in Down in the Holler. However,
to give you some idea of the difficulty with these terms, Randolph and
Wilson provide the following definition of split-tail.

Similar to feisty is the noun split-tail, a disrespectful
name for an active young woman. A split-tail is not
necessarily a woman of bad morals, but rather one who is
too lively, perhaps inclined to some sort of indiscretion.[13]

It is hard to tell where one should draw the line, but I have tried to
make the list representative and diverse. Sweat-hog has been used in
south Georgia, split-tail is Ozark slang; flap is archaic, but low-rent
is current slang. I should also point out that this is by no means an
exhaustive list and does not include bob-tail, gill-flirt (or jill-
flirt), spoffskins, blister, and many others. I stopped when I had
collected 220 terms because I'd reached the point of diminishing returns.
I think any additional terms would fit into one of the categories that
came out of the terms I analyzed. In fact, this semantic set is probably
one that's infinitely expanding; although some terms may become archaic,
new terms are always being added, probably faster than lexicographers
can record them. The very size of the set and the impossibility of
collecting ALL the terms for prostitute is a comment on our culture.
As linguists, we assume that the existence of a new lexical item indicates a cultural need for a term that expresses a new concept. Isn't
it strange that the set of terms that refer to prostitutes is one that's
constantly expanding? If there is a cultural need, surely it is that
only of men, defining and asserting their "masculinity" through their
use of women's bodies.

I did collect a relatively small number of terms for promiscuous men,
but the two sets cannot really be compared.

TERMS FOR MEN WHO CHASE WOMEN

animal	hooko
ass man	letch
Casanova	male hustler
cockhound	male prostitute
cocksman	male whore
cunnyhunter	snowman
DOM (dirty old man)	sport
Don Juan	stud
gigolo	Svengali
good ole boy	whorehopper
hanger-on	whoremonger

First of all, there's no linguistic reason why the set is so small. As
I've indicated though, most of these words refer to the sexuality of men
in terms of the degree of their success in pursuing women. Three of the
terms, male hustler, male prostitute, and male whore, are actually terms
that refer to women that are marked with the feature [+male]. Second,
only gigolo and perhaps stud, carry the same denotative features as the
larger set for women. Stud, however, has only positive connotations when
it's used, and gigolo carries negative connotations only insofar as it

310

refers to a man demeaning himself by accepting money from a woman. A
gigolo gives up his "right" to dominate a woman because the acceptance
of money represents dependence and passivity in the relationship, and
paying money represents choice and power over the other person. The
gigolo thus violates the prerogatives assigned to men by surrendering
his power. The term carries positive connotations when it refers to the
same violation of sex-role stereotypes, but also draws attention to the
fact that it's a woman paying for sex instead of a man, and the users
find the role-switch humorous. Third, words like animal, beast, and
brute, which do refer to male sexuality, and which are used pejoratively
by women, refer specifically to those personality traits encouraged
by reverence of machismo but not especially sought by women in sexual
relationships. Fourth, the remainder of the terms are all used with
positive connotations and a "boys-will-be-boys" intonation. If a man is
a cockhound, one shrugs one's shoulders; if a woman is a slut, the moral
fiber of women is in danger.

There are two semantic features for which the terms in the appendix
aren't specifically marked in the lexicon; one of the features, Length
of Contact, is used as a major feature for describing the semantic
field, and it ranges from the point at which actual sexual contact with
the woman is irrelevant to the use of a term, to Extended and Extensive
Contact. The other feature is (+FEMALE); all of the terms carry this as
an unmarked feature. If a term is (-Female), that is, if it refers to
a man, then the feature must be marked, and it surfaces in such cases,
e.g., male prostitute, male hustler, male whore.

In setting up the semantic field that follows, I began by centering the
group of terms that included the largest number, so that in the Contact
Irrelevant area you'll find broad and lightheels, both carrying the same
features, differing only in that broad is dysphemistic and lightheels
is euphemistic. After each term, in parentheses, is the number of
terms represented by the category. For example, the category (F/C,
D/I; NEG) includes broad, floozy, hag, hussy, loose woman, low-rent,
pick-up, put out, slut, sor-whore, tramp, wanton, and whore. The
related euphemisms include lightheels, roundheels, and shortheels.
The rest of the categories arranged around these core terms differ in
the addition and/or loss of features, which I've marked beside the lines
drawn between categories. At the outer reaches of the field you'll
find the terms marked either (P/W) or (MET). The terms represented by
bitch, marked (F/C, D/I; NEG; MET), include bird, dog, mattress,
nut-cracker, quail, and sow; the terms represented by cunt, marked (F/C,
D/I; NEG; P/W), include fleshpot, gash, piece, and tail. All of these
are terms that men apply to any woman, and they occur in expressions
like "She's a dizzy cunt," "Wow! what a nice piece!," and "What a
ballbuster she is!"

On page 313, you'll find the range marked as Cheap, with brief sexual
contact necessary for the application of the term. At the center,
you'll find hooker, marked (C, D; NEG), by far the largest single category with 73 members, and the related euphemism, painted lady. The
terms in this category refer specifically to the act of selling oneself
as an object, and the Cost may range anywhere from a quarter, as in
two-bit whore, up to $20.00. Other terms in this category include
harlot, hustler, peddlesnatch, and slattern. This is not only the
largest range within the terms for prostitute, but there are some
interesting things going on semantically. The terms are the most

Julia P. Stanley

A VISUAL REPRESENTATION OF THE SEMANTIC FIELD RELATIONSHIPS AMONG THE SEXUAL TERMS APPLIED TO WOMEN

ACTUAL CONTACT IRRELEVANT

FREE/CHEAP: TERMS THAT CAN BE APPLIED TO ANY WOMAN, WITH SEXUAL MEANING, WHETHER OR NOT THE MALE HAS HAD SEXUAL CONTACT.

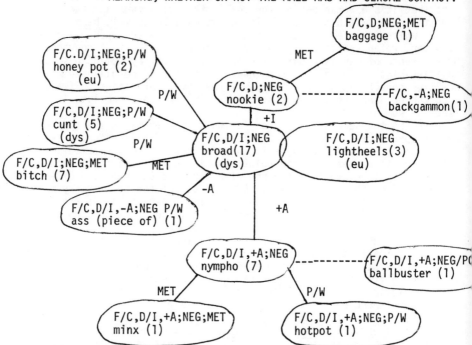

FREE (F)
By definition, sex is never free; the features DIRECT/INDIRECT take care of that possibility. For the male, it comes down to a question of WHAT will be paid to the women in exchange for sex, and HOW MUCH. For this reason, there are no terms for women with the feature [F].

Julia P. Stanley

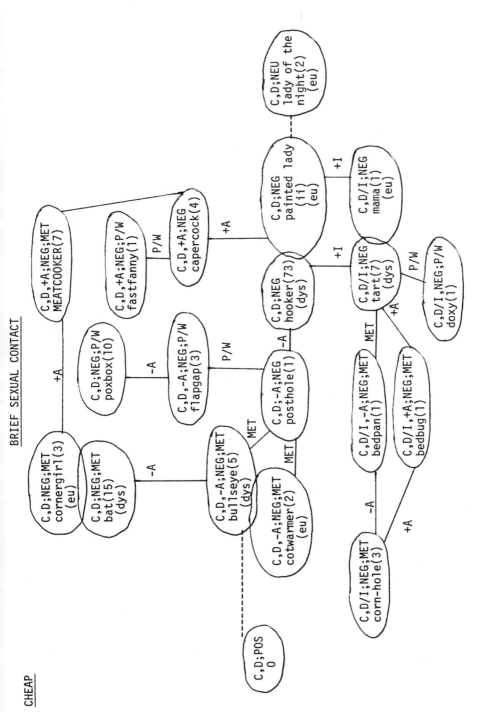

BRIEF SEXUAL CONTACT

CHEAP

313

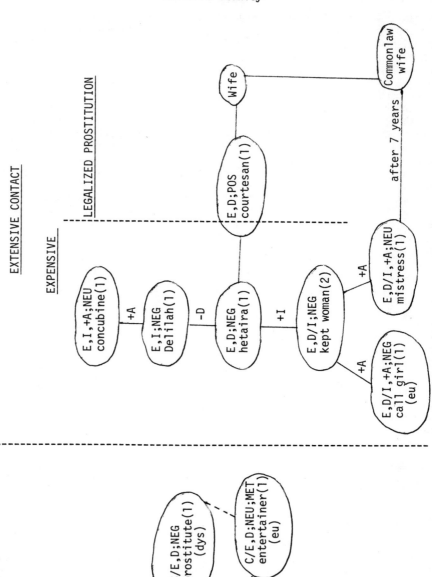

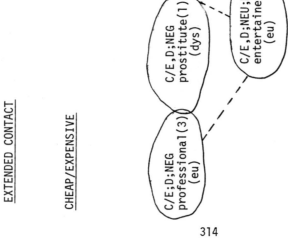

314

Julia P. Stanley

semantically consistent and unambiguous; in order for most of the terms
to apply, they must be Cheap and involve Direct Payment of cash. There
is also what I call a neutralization of features at several points in the
diagram, where the features (+A) and (-A) are lost, and the lines converge
on metaphorical categories that share features with other categories,
except for (+A) or (-A). At the bottom, left-hand side of p. 313 , you'll
find bedpan and bedbug, which differ only in the feature + or -A. Both
of these categories converge at corn-hole, in which the activity of the
woman is irrelevant. The same thing happens with flapgap and fastfanny,
which converge in poxbox, and with meatcooker and bullseye/cotwarmer,
which meet at the category represented by cornergirl and bat. One other
comment: you'll note that there are no terms in the category (C,D;POS).
    Page 314 contains the two smallest sets of terms, C/E, with extended
contact, and E, with extensive contact. Prostitute and professional are
probably the core terms of the entire semantic field, so that the field
is heavily loaded toward the range covered by F/C and C. Only 13 terms
are covered by the categories on this page. Once you get over into the
Expensive range, you find the terms that are marked as NEU or POS, and
the term marked as (POS), courtesan, falls under legalized, state-
sanctioned sexual use, along with marriage. With the categories occupied
by courtesan, common-law wife, and wife we arrive at the point at which
the state and the church institutionalize the use of women. The state of
marriage, signified by the application of the term wife, is one in which
the man pays and pays, sometimes for life, for his use, and exclusive
property rights, of one woman. What we can see in this diagram is a
movement from general terms, applicable to any woman in the world, to
the specific term wife. The more time and money that a man is willing to
invest in a woman, the more he legitimizes her existence in our society.
But it all comes down to the same thing.
    More specifically, an examination of the metaphorical terms for pro-
stitute reveals the object classes to which women who relate sexually to
men are compared. The classes themselves reflect the traditional views
of "woman's place," from bedpan and slopjar, woman as receptacle for the
excretions of men, to narycherry and woman of ill-repute, the woman who
has not "lived up" to the chaste, Madonna stereotype. In a list of
classes of objects, none of which I can sincerely call "unobjectionable,"
the least objectionable class contains only three lexical items: entertainer, full-oᴸtricks, and cornergirl. I say "the least objectionable"
because the terms in this class at least compare the prostitute to other
persons. Thus, she "entertains" in the sense that she "amuses" men;
she is a "girl" who stands on the corner; she is "full of tricks" insofar
as she "performs" for men.
    The next largest class of objects contains the names that compare women
to animals: minx, bird, bitch, dog, quail, sow, fuckin' fillies, canvasback (?), bat, biddy, crane, nannygoat, nightbird, bedbug, pig, and
sweathog. We can see in these terms the underlying conceptual categories
into which men place women: They're something to be hunted and killed,
a quail or a canvasback; they should be subordinated and domesticated,
as a horse, a sow, a dog; they should always be like "a bitch in heat,"
receptive to men; they're things to fear, like bats; and they're vicious,
like the minx.
    But whatever else women should be, they are classified as the exclusive
property of men, and they're to function only as the objects of men's
desires and sexuality. The third class of metaphors, in which women are

Julia P. Stanley

compared to inanimate objects, breaks down into two sub-classes. The
first labels women as passive objects on or through which men "relieve"
themselves. In this class we find the terms mattress, baggage, pisspall
cotwarmer, warming pan, mattressback, quarterpiece, saltflitch, slopjar,
bedpan, and corn-hole. All of these terms define women as objects upon
which men play out their sexual dramas. But the second class of inanimate metaphors makes the role of women even more explicit: we are
specifically "holes" into which a long object is inserted--nothing more.
This is, of course, the basic metaphor that governs our lives and define
the nature of our existence; it is the metaphor upon which our culture
is founded: women have holes, men have external appendages that were
made to fill those holes, and that's the reason that we have holes. It'
all so beautifully simple, and the sub-class includes nutcracker, meatcooker, meat grinder, organgrinder, sausage-grinder, smokehouse, bullseye, cockeye, furrowbutt, goldmine, honey pot, chamberpot, nightbag,
pipecleaner, ragbag, rawhide, ringer. We exist only as holes for men,
as fields to be plowed, as "pots" full of good things for men. And the
semantics of this sub-class of metaphors perhaps explains the neutralization of the features (+A) and (-A) that I mentioned earlier in the
CHEAP/BRIEF CONTACT area of the semantic field. Such features are irrelevant in terms that define women as passive, inanimate objects; no acti
is expected, required, or desired.

To complete the picture of "woman as sex object" in our culture, let
me, in closing, make one or two additional observations. Only a woman
can "go astray"; only a woman can be "loose." But only a man can be
a "cuckold"; there is no term for a woman in a similar situation. But a
woman can be called a cocktease and a pricktease if she doesn't "put out
When a woman calls a man a prick, even though it is a metonymic pejorative, it does not refer to his sexuality, but to his personality, and it
is related semantically to terms like nurd, creep, and queer. Women
insult men by reference to unpleasantness in their personalities, but
men insult women by reference to their availability for sexual use. If
you want to compliment a man, you can say "He has balls," but we cannot
say of a woman "She has labia" or "She has ova."

What I have described is a semantic set and its features that provide
paradigm of the definition of women in our culture, a culture that defin
the "nature" of woman on the basis of untested assumptions, embodies
these assumptions in its metaphors, and uses these metaphors to create
the stereotypes of women with which we have to live.

APPENDIX

The list of terms provided below makes an initial division of the term
into Dysphemistic and Euphemistic. In the spaces that follow each term,
Denotative features are given first, and then the Connotative features a
given. Following these primary features will be (P/W) or (MET) if
either of these classifications apply.

Dysphemistic Terms

arsebender [F/C, D/I, +A;NEG]
arsievarsie [F/C, D/I, +A; NEG]

flapgap [C, D, -A; NEG; P/W]
fleecer [C, D; NEG]

316

ass (piece of) [F/C, I, -A; NEG; P/W]
backbender [F/C, D/I, +A; NEG]
backgammon [F/C, D/I, -A; NEG]
backscratcher [F/C, D/I, +A; NEG]
baggage [F/C, D; NEG; MET]
ballbuster [F/C, D/I, +A; NEG/POS]
bat [C, D; NEG; MET]
bawd [F/C, D/I, +A; NEG]
bedbug [C, D/I, +A; NEG; MET]
bedpan [C, D/I, -A; NEG; MET]
bellylass [F/C, D; NEG]
biddy [C, D; NEG; MET]
bimbo [C, D/I; NEG]
bird [F/C, D/I; NEG; MET]
bitch [F/C, D/I; NEG; MET]
breechdropper [F/C, D/I, +A; NEG]
broad [F/C, D/I; NEG]
brown Bess [C, D; NEG]
brown-eye [C, D; NEG; P/W]
bullseye [C, D, -A; NEG; MET]
bumbessie [C, D; NEG]
bumpbacon [C, D ; NEG]
bunter [C, D; NEG]
canvasback [C, D, -A; NEG]
capercock [C, D, +A; NEG]
chamberpot [C, D, +A; NEG]
Charlotte Harlot [C, D; NEG]
chippie [C, D; NEG]
chubcheeker [C, D; NEG]
claptrap [C, D; NEG]
cockatrice [C, D; NEG]
cockeye [C, D, -A; NEG; MET]
cocktail [C, D; NEG]
codhopper [C, D; NEG]
codwinker [C, D; NEG]
concubine [E, I, +A; NEG]
   (more servitude involved)
conycatcher [C, D; NEG]
corn-hole [C, D; NEG]
courtesan [E, D; POS]
coxswain [C, D; NEG]
crane [C, D; NEG; MET]
craterbutt [C, D; NEG]
cunt [F/C, D/I; NEG; P/W]
Delilah [E, I; NEG]
dell [C, D; NEG]
diddler [C, D; NEG]
doe [F/C, D/I; NEG; MET]
donah [F/C, D/I; NEG]
drab [C, D; NEG]
doxy [C, D/I; NEG; P/W]
fastfanny [C, D, +A; NEG; P/W]
fatback [C, D; NEG]
flap [C, D, -A; NEG; P/W]

fleshpot [F/C, D/I; NEG]
floozy [F/C, D/I; NEG]
fluter [C, D; NEG]
frisker [C, D, +A; NEG]
fuckin' fillies [C, D, +A; NEG; MET]
full-o'-tricks [C, D, +A; NEG: MET]
furrowbutt [C, D, -A; NEG; MET]
gadder [C, D; NEG]
galleywench [C, D/I; NEG]
gamester [C, D; NEG]
game woman [F/C, D/I; NEG]
gash [F/C, D/I; NEG; P/W]
gipsy [C, D; NEG]
gullybum [C, D; NEG; P/W]
gutterflopper [C, D; NEG]
hack [C, D; NEG]
hag [F/C, D/I; NEG]
hamhocker [C, D; NEG]
hardtonguer [C, D; NEG]
harlot [C, D; NEG]
harridan [C, D; NEG]
hedgewhore [C, D; NEG]
hetaira [E, D; NEG]
hipflipper [C, D, +A; NEG]
hooker [C, D; NEG]
hotpot [F/C, D/I, +A; NEG; P/W]
hoyden [C, D; NEG]
hussy [F/C, D/I; NEG]
hustler [C, D; NEG]
Jezebel [C, D/I; NEG]
lay [C, D/I; NEG]
leasepiece [C, D; NEG]
leg-over [C, D; NEG]
loose woman [F/C, D/I; NEG]
lowgap [C, D; NEG; P/W]
low-rent [F/C, D/I; NEG]
Magdalene [C, D; NEG]
mattress[F/C, D/I; NEG; MET]
mattressback [C, D; NEG; MET]
meatcooker [C, D, +A; NEG; MET]
meatgrinder [C, D, +A; NEG; MET]
meat vender [C, D; NEG]
minx [F/C, D/I, +A; NEG; MET]
mistress [E, D/I, +A; NEU]
moll [C, D/I; NEG]
nannygoat [C, D; NEG; MET]
narycherry [C, D; NEG]
nellie [C, D; NEG]
nightbag [C, D; NEG; MET]
nightbird [C, D; NEG; MET
nobjobber [C, D; NEG]
nookie [F/C, D; NEG]

nutcracker [F/C; D/I; NEG; MET]
nympho [F/C, D/I, +A; NEG]
organgrinder [C, D, +A; NEG; MET]
paramour [E, D/I; NEG]
peddlesnatch [C, D; NEG]
pick up [F/C, D/I; NEG]
piece [F/C, D/I; NEG; P/W]
pig [C, D/I; NEG; MET]
pigpoke [C, D; NEG]
pillowgut [C, D; NEG]
pinkpot [C, D; NEG; P/W]
pink toes [C, D; NEG; P/W]
pipecleaner [C, D; NEG; MET]
pisspallet [C, D, -A; NEG; MET]
pole climber [C, D, +A; NEG]
poontang [C, D; NEG]
posthole [C, D, -A; NEG]
potlicker [C, D; NEG]
poxbox [C, D; NEG; P/W]
prick pocket [C, D, -A; NEG; P/W]
priest -layer [C, D; NEG]
prossie [C, D; NEG]
prostitute [C/E, D; NEG]
puddletrotter [C, D; NEG]
put out [F/C, D/I; NEG]
puta [C, D; NEG]
quail [F/C, D/I; NEG; MET]
quarter-piece [C, D; NEG; MET]
queen [C, D; NEG]
ragbag [C, D; NEG; MET]
rawhide [C, D; NEG; MET]
ringer [C, D; NEG; MET]
romp [C, D; NEG]
rum-and-rut [C, D/I; NEG]
rumper [C, D; NEG]
rutter [C, D; NEG]
sally-dally [C, D; NEG]
saltflitch [C, D; NEG; MET]

sausage-grinder [C, D, +A; NEG; MET]
scabber [C, D; NEG]
scrubber [C, D; NEG]
scuffer [C, D; NEG]
sink-o-perdition [C, D; NEG; MET]
slattern [C, D; NEG]
slopjar [C, D; NEG; MET]
slut [F/C, D/I; NEG]
smokehouse [C, D, +A; NEG; MET]
sor-whore [F/C, D/I; NEG]
sow [F/C, D/I; NEG; MET]
split-tail [F/C, D/I; NEG]
spreadeagle [C, D; NEG]
springherder [C, D; NEG]
strawgirl [F/C, D/I; NEG]
strumpet [C, D; NEG]
strumpthumper [C, D; NEG]
sweathog [C, D/I; NEG; MET]
swill trough [C, D; NEG]
tail [F/C, D/I; NEG; P/W]
tart [C, D/I; NEG]
termagant [C, D; NEG]
Tess Tuppence [C, D; NEG]
tollhole [C, D; NEG; P/W]
tramp [F/C, D/I; NEG]
trapan [C, D; NEG]
trick [C, D; NEG]
trollop [C, D/I; NEG]
trotter [C, D; NEG]
trull [C, D; NEG]
tumbler [C, D; NEG]
tup-me-upright [C, D; NEG]
two-bit whore [C, D; NEG]
ventrenter [C, D; NEG; P/W]
wanton [F/C, D/I; NEG]
wench [C, D; NEG]
whore [F/C, D/I; NEG]

Euphemistic Terms

call girl [E, D/I, +A; NEG]
cornergirl [C, D; NEG; MET]
cotwarmer [C, D, -A; NEG; MET]
entertainer [C/E, D; NEU; MET]
fille de joie [C, D; NEG]
giftbox [F/C, D/I; NEG; P/W]
goldmine [C, D; NEG; MET]
honey pot [F/C, D/I; NEG; P/W]
hotel Matron [C, D; NEG]
joygirl [C, D;
lady of the night [C, D; NEU]
lamp-post Lorelei [C, D; NEG]
light heels [F/C, D/I; NEG]
lovely lady [C, D/I; NEG]
mama [C, D/I; NEG]

painted lady [C, D; NEG]
pretty little flowers [C, D; MET]
pro-girl [C/E, D; NEG]
professional [C/E, D; NEG]
roundheels [F/C, D/I; NEG]
scarlet woman [C, D; NEG]
shortheels [F/C, D/I; NEG]
social girl [C/E, D; NEG]
sweet cream lady [C, D; NEG]
warming-pan [C, D, -A; NEG; M
windowgirl [C, D; NEG]
woman of ill-repute [C, D; NE
woman of pleasure [C, D; NEG
working girl [C, D; NEG]

Julia P. Stanley

NOTES

*The earlier SAMLA version of this paper was called "The Semantic Features of the Machismo Ethic in English." Read at the SAMLA linguistics section, Jacksonville, Florida, November 1972.

[1]Germaine Greer, The Female Eunuch (New York: Bantam, 1971), p. 278.

[2]Ruth Herschberger, Adam's Rib (New York: Harper & Row, 1970), pp. 11-12.

[3]Ibid., p. 25.

[4]Maria Moliner, Diccionario de uso espanol, vol. 2 (Madrid: Editorial Gredas, s.a., 1967).

[5]Edward Sagarin, The Anatomy of Dirty Words (Secaucus, N.J.: Lyle Stuart, 1962), p. 122.

[6]Ibid., p. 125.

[7]Woman-Identified Woman (New York: Gay Flames, 1972), p. 3.

[8]Peter Fryer, Mrs. Grundy: Studies in English Prudery (London: Dennis Dobson, 1963), p. 75.

[9]Sagarin, Anatomy, p. 129.

[10]Ibid., p. 134.

[11]Gerald Chambers and Donald L. Smith were very helpful in sorting through and interpreting their own usage of the terms, and that of other men. In all, 17 men, ranging in age from 20-42, were asked to react to each of the 220 terms with respect to cost, method of payment, connotations, etc. Because no one knew all of the terms, I have had to rely on the men's ability to categorize their usage, interpolating from related terms that they did know.

[12]I queried John Barth, trying to find out exactly how many of the terms he had made up on the long exchange between the two prostitutes [Sot-Weed Factor (New York: Grosset and Dunlap, 1966), pp. 466-72]. In his letter of September, 1972, he told me that he could no longer remember which he had made up and which he had heard over the years. Even if he made up as many as 20 of the terms used in the exchange, that would still leave 200 terms, plus all of the ones that I found after I'd reached my cut-off point in compiling the list. I don't think there can be any question regarding the extraordinarily large number of terms referring to the sexual activity of women. In addition, if I could ascertain the terms that Barth had created, they would follow the semantic patterns described in this article.

[13]Vance Randolph and George P. Wilson, Down in the Holler: A Gallery of Ozark Folk Speech (Norman, Okla.: University of Oklahoma Press, 1953), p. 107.

SOURCES CONSULTED

Bart, Pauline B. "Social Structure and Vocabularies of Discomfort: What Happened to Female Hysteria," Journal of Health and Social Behavior, 9 (1968): 188-93.

Firestone, Shulamith. The Dialectic of Sex (New York: Bantam, 1971).

Conrad-Rice, Joy Belle. "Religion, Language, Psychology--Women Left Out." KNOW, Inc. reprint, n.d.

Densmore, Dana. "Speech is the Form of Thought." KNOW, Inc. reprint, 1970.

Eble, Connie. "How the Speech of Some is More Equal Than Others." Paper delivered to SECOL VIII, 1972. (Mimeographed.)

_____. "If Ladies Weren't Present, I'd Tell You What I Really Think." Paper delivered at SAMLA, 1972. (Mimeographed.)

Faust, Jean. "Words That Oppress." Women Speaking. KNOW, Inc. reprint 1970.

Gary, Sandra. "What Are We Talking About?" MS (1972): 72-73; 99.

Goldin, Hyman E., et al., eds. Dictionary of American Underworld Lingo (New York: Citadel, 1962).

Greenwald, Harold. The Elegant Prostitute (New York: Walker & Co., 1970

_____, and Aron Krich. The Prostitute in Literature (New York: Ballantine, 1960).

Hollander, Xaviera. The Happy Hooker (New York: Dell, 1972).

Key, Mary Ritchie. "Linguistic Behavior of Male and Female," Linguistic 88 (1972): 15-31.

Kramer, Cheris. "Women's Speech: A Separate But Unequal Language." 197 (Mimeographed.)

Lakoff, Robin. "Language and Woman's Place," Language in Society, 2 (19 45-80.

Landy, Eugene. The Underground Dictionary (New York: Simon & Schuster, 1971).

Malkiel, Yakov. "A Typological Classification of Dictionaries on the Basis of Distinctive Features," in Problems in Lexicography, ed. Fred W. Householder and Sol Saporta (Bloomington: University of Indiana Press, 1967), pp. 3-24.

Markun, Leo. Mrs. Grundy: A History of Four Centuries of Morals Intende to Illuminate Present Problems in Great Britain and the United States (New York: D. Appleton & Co., 1930).

Merriam, Eve. "Sex and Semantics," in Liberation Now! eds. Deborah Babcox and Madeline Belkin (New York: Dell, 1971), pp. 231-38.

Miller, Casey, and Kate Swift. "Is Language Sexist?" Cosmopolitan (1972

Partridge, Eric. A Dictionary of Slang and Unconventional English (New York: Macmillan, 1961).

Julia P. Stanley

Robinson, Frank, and Nat Lehrman, eds. <u>Sex American Style</u> (Chicago: Playboy, 1971).

Strainchamps, Ethel. "Our Sexist Language," in <u>Woman in Sexist Society</u>, eds. Vivian Gornick and Barbara K. Moran (New York: Basic Books, 1971), pp. 347-61.

Ware, J. Redding. <u>Passing English of the Victorian Era</u> (New York: E.P. Dutton, n.d.).

Wentworth, Harold, and Stuart Berg Flexner, eds. <u>Dictionary of American Slang</u> (New York: Thomas Y. Crowell, 1931).

Weseen, Maurice H. <u>A Dictionary of American Slang</u> (New York: Thomas Y. Crowell, 1960).